"FILM EUROPE"
AND
"FILM AMERICA"

"Film Europe" and "Film America" is the history of two ideas. One is the idea of a pan-European form of cultural production which engaged with ideas of internationalism. The other is a much more practical form of trade collaboration in recognition of the need to compete with the Americans from the strength of a comparable home market. At times these two ideas intertwined, and at other times they were clearly opposed to each other. Inevitably, the American film industry sought to counter such developments by consolidating its hold on the European market. The tension between Film Europe and Film America was compounded by the conversion to sound and the erection of language barriers restricting the patterns of cultural exchange so typical of the silent period.

Exeter Studies in Film History
General Editors: Richard Maltby and Duncan Petrie

Exeter Studies in Film History is devoted to publishing the best new scholarship on the cultural, technical and aesthetic history of cinema. The aims of the series are to reconsider established orthodoxies and to revise our understanding of cinema's past by shedding light on neglected areas in film history.

Published in association with the Bill Douglas Centre for the History of Cinema and Popular Culture, the series will include monographs and essay collections, translations of major works written in other languages, and reprinted editions of important texts in cinema history. The series editors are Richard Maltby, Associate Professor of Screen Studies, Flinders University, Australia, and Duncan Petrie, Director of the Bill Douglas Centre for the History of Cinema and Popular Culture, University of Exeter.

"FILM EUROPE" AND "FILM AMERICA"

Cinema, Commerce and Cultural Exchange
1920–1939

Edited by Andrew Higson
and Richard Maltby

UNIVERSITY
of
EXETER
PRESS

To Billie, Luisa and Ben

First published in 1999 by
University of Exeter Press
Reed Hall, Streatham Drive
Exeter, Devon EX4 4QR
UK
www.ex.ac.uk/uep/

British Library Cataloguing in Publication Data
A catalogue record of this book is available from the British Library

Paperback ISBN 0 85989 546 7
Hardback ISBN 0 85989 545 9

Typeset in Caslon by Kestrel Data, Exeter

Printed and bound in Great Britain by
Short Run Press Ltd, Exeter

Contents

Acknowledgements   vii

Notes on Contributors   ix

1. "Film Europe" and "Film America": An Introduction
   Andrew Higson and Richard Maltby   1

2. "Temporary American Citizens": Cultural Anxieties and
   Industrial Strategies in the Americanisation of
   European Cinema
   Richard Maltby and Ruth Vasey   32

3. The Rise and Fall of Film Europe
   Kristin Thompson   56

4. The Cinema and the League of Nations
   Richard Maltby   82

5. Cultural Policy and Industrial Practice: Film Europe
   and the International Film Congresses of the 1920s
   Andrew Higson   117

6. Options for American Foreign Distribution: United Artists
   in Europe, 1919–1930
   Mike Walsh   132

7. Germany and Film Europe
   Thomas J. Saunders   157

8. Hollywood's "Foreign War": The Effect of National
   Commercial Policy on the Emergence of the American
   Film Hegemony in France, 1920–1929
   Jens Ulff-Møller   181

9. Hollywood Babel: The Coming of Sound and the
   Multiple-Language Version
   Ginette Vincendeau   207

10. Hollywood's Hegemonic Strategies: Overcoming French
    Nationalism with the Advent of Sound
    Martine Danan   225

11. Made in Germany: Multiple-Language Versions and
    the Early German Sound Cinema
    Joseph Garncarz   249

12. Polyglot Films for an International Market: E.A. Dupont,
    the British Film Industry, and the Idea of a European
    Cinema, 1926–1930
    Andrew Higson   274

13. Negotiating Exoticism: Hollywood, Film Europe and the
    Cultural Reception of Anna May Wong
    Tim Bergfelder   302

Documents
   List of Documents   325
   Group 1: German Conceptions of "Film Europe"   327
   Group 2: Kontingents, Quotas and the American
      Response   346
   Group 3: European Access to the American Market and
      the International Film: J.D. Williams and Erich Pommer   386

Index   397

Acknowledgements

This book grew, in part, out of our recognition that our separate research concerns with the American and British film industries in the interwar period shared a common ground. It also developed out of our sense of an unrecognised historical continuity between contemporary arguments over cultural imperialism and freedom of commercial expression and the debates that took place in the period of our own research. As we listened to the rhetoric of mutual recrimination that took root in European-American cinematic relations during and after the 1993 General Agreement on Tariffs and Trade, we were struck both by how often that rhetoric reiterated the debates of an earlier period, and also by how seldom that earlier history was referred to. Rather than simply using the occasion to observe, once again, the veracity of Marx's aphorism about history repeating itself, we felt that there was a purpose in bringing together an international group of scholars to re-examine the phenomenon of "Film Europe," and the complex set of commercial and cultural relationships that it contained. To our authors from Denmark, France, Germany, the UK, Australia, Canada and the USA, we wish to record both our gratitude and our thanks for their tolerance of this book's long journey to fruition.

Many other people have contributed to the production of this book. Brenda Ferris, Brenda Benthien, Tom Saunders and Uwe Brunssen translated material from German to English. Richard Abel, Thomas Elsaesser, Steve Neale, Tom Ryall and Bill Urrichio all encouraged this project at key moments in its development. The Cinegraph team in Hamburg encouraged Andrew to research Film Europe, the Film Studies sector at the University of East Anglia provided him with a friendly and supportive environment in which to work, the secretarial staff of the School of English and American Studies processed much of the paperwork, and the University awarded him a Research Promotion Grant and a sabbatical to complete the project. Colleagues at Sheffield Hallam University helped Richard begin work on the project; colleagues at Flinders University helped him finish it. Our book found the ideal home in the University of Exeter Press series on film history, and staff at the Press have continued to nurture our offspring even as it grew to twice its original size; we thank Simon Baker, Genevieve Davey, Anna Henderson, Jane Raistrick, Rosemary Rooke and Richard Willis.

Our respective partners, Val and Ruth, have borne the usual academic absenteeism that these projects entail with more tolerance and good humour than we deserve. Billie and Luisa Higson would long ago have reached much higher levels of expertise on their computer games had their father not monopolised the computer; still, they're much better practised musicians as a result. Ben Maltby learned his alphabet in the time it took his father to write his chapter, and is still recycling earlier drafts of the Introduction as drawing paper.

We also thank the following for permission to publish material that first appeared elsewhere:

Cinegraph, Edition Text + Kritik and Cassell, who published earlier versions of some of the material in Andrew Higson's two essays, in "Film-Europa: Dupont und die britische Filmindustrie," in Jurgen Bretschneider, ed., *Ewald André Dupont: Autor und Regisseur* (Munich: Edition Text + Kritik, 1992), pp. 89–100; "Film-Europa: Kulturpolitik und industrielle Praxis," in Sibylle M. Sturm and Arthur Wohlgemuth, eds, *Hallo? Berlin? Ici Paris!: Deutsch-französische Filmbeziehungen, 1918–1939* (Munich: Edition Text + Kritik, 1996), pp. 63–76; and " 'A film League of Nations': Gainsborough, Gaumont-British and 'Film Europe,' " in Pam Cook, ed., *Gainsborough Pictures* (London: Cassell, 1997), pp. 60–79.

The Amsterdam Amerika Institut and VU University Press, who published an earlier version of Richard Maltby and Ruth Vasey's essay under the title "The International Language Problem: European Reactions to Hollywood's Conversion to Sound," in David W. Ellwood and Rob Kroes, eds, *Hollywood in Europe: Experiences of a Cultural Hegemony* (Amsterdam: VU University Press, 1994), pp. 68–94.

The History and Film Association of Australia, who published an earlier version of Kristin Thompson's essay under the title "The End of the 'Film Europe' Movement," in Tom O'Regan and Brian Shoesmith, eds, *History on/and/in Film* (Perth: History and Film Association of Australia (WA), 1987), pp. 45–55.

Kristin Thompson, for permission to re-print material, including the table in Document 8, which first appeared in Kristin Thompson, *Exporting Entertainment: America in the World Film Market 1907–1934* (London: British Film Institute, 1985), pp. 211–12.

Screen, for permission to re-print Ginette Vincendeau's "Hollywood Babel," which first appeared in *Screen*, vol. 29, no. 2, Spring 1988, pp. 24–39.

The editor and publishers have made every effort to trace original copyright holders of material used in this book in order to obtain their permission. We would like to take this opportunity of making acknowledgement to any copyright holder that we may have failed to contact.

Andrew Higson, Norwich, UK
Richard Maltby, Adelaide, Australia

Notes on Contributors

Tim Bergefelder is Lecturer in the School of Modern Languages, and Convenor of the Film Studies MA programme at the University of Southampton. He has published on international transactions in European cinema in Germany and Britain, in Andrew Higson, ed., *Dissolving Views: Key Writings on British Cinema* (London: Cassell, 1996) and Pam Cook, ed., *Gainsborough Pictures* (London: Cassell, 1997).

Martine Danan has written on issues of film, language and identity for *Film History, Journal of Popular Film and Television, Contemporary French Civilization, French Review, Nottingham French Studies* and a number of edited books. She is currently completing a book on Hollywood and French cinema.

Joseph Garncarz is Privatdozent in Film Studies at the University of Cologne in Germany. His dissertation on film versions was published as *Filmfassungen* (Frankfurt: Peter Lang, 1992); his post-doctoral thesis on popular films in Germany is to be published as *Populäres Kino in Deutschland. Internationalisierung einer Filmkultur (1925–1990)*. He has written numerous articles on film history for German, English and American journals and books.

Andrew Higson is Senior Lecturer in Film Studies in the School of English and American Studies at the University of East Anglia, Norwich, UK. He is the author of *Waving the Flag: Constructing a National Cinema in Britain* (Oxford: Oxford University Press, 1995), and the editor of *Dissolving Views: Key Writings on British Cinema* (London: Cassell, 1996). He has also written numerous articles and chapters on British cinema, the heritage film, and the concept of national cinema.

Richard Maltby is Associate Professor of Screen Studies and Head of the School of Arts at the Flinders University of South Australia. He is the author of *Harmless Entertainment: Hollywood and the Ideology of Consensus* (Metuchen: Scarecrow, 1983) and *Hollywood Cinema: An Introduction* (Oxford: Blackwell, 1995), as well as numerous articles on American cinema. He is one of the Series Editors for Exeter Studies in Film History.

Thomas J. Saunders is Associate Professor in the Department of History at the University of Victoria in British Columbia, Canada. He is the author of *Hollywood in Berlin: American Cinema and Weimar Germany* (Berkeley: University of California Press, 1994), and articles on cinema, war and national identity.

Kristin Thompson has a Ph.D. in cinema studies from the University of Wisconsin-Madison, where she is an Honorary Fellow. Her latest book, *Storytelling in the New Hollywood*, is forthcoming from Harvard University Press.

Jens Ulff-Møller is Research Professor in the Department of Film & Media Studies at the University of Copenhagen, Denmark. He has recently completed a Ph.D. in the Department of History at Brandeis University on American film trade diplomacy in relation to France, Germany and Scandinavia in the inter-war period.

Ruth Vasey is Lecturer in Screen Studies at the Flinders University of South Australia. Her book, *The World According to Hollywood, 1918–1939* (Exeter: University of Exeter Press, 1997), won the Kraszna-Krausz Moving Image Book Award in 1997.

Ginette Vincendeau is Professor of Film Studies at the University of Warwick. She writes on French cinema, in particular popular stars and genres. Among her recent publications are *Jean Gabin: Anatomie d'un mythe* (Paris: Nathan, 1993), *The Companion to French Cinema* (London: Cassell/British Film Institute, 1996), and *Pépé le Moko* (London: British Film Institute, 1998).

Michael Walsh is Lecturer in Screen Studies at the Flinders University of South Australia. He has contributed to several anthologies, including *Post-Theory: Reconstructing Film Studies* (Madison: University of Wisconsin Press, 1996), and his articles have appeared in a number of journals, including *The Velvet Light Trap* and *Film History*.

1

"Film Europe" and "Film America"
An Introduction

Andrew Higson and Richard Maltby

In a ridiculously short timespan, hardly one decade, Film Europe
has become a colony of Film America.

German trade paper, 1926[1]

Film Europe is nothing more than a security pact, a sort of film
Locarno against America, which will not grant reciprocity. The
more quickly and securely Film Europe is realised, the more quickly
and surely Film America will come to terms with Film Europe.
Here lies the deeper meaning of European film union and the
current intense concentration of European film forces.

Erich Morawsky, Director of the German company Terra, 1928[2]

One of the Bureau's most valuable contacts is the Motion Picture
Producers and Distributors of America, Inc., of which Mr. Will H.
Hays is President. We are particularly anxious that our services to
this industry should be effective and that we should make a special
point of keeping it posted on all developments affecting it throughout the world. . . . The motion picture producers are vitally
concerned with every phase of the local motion picture situation,
such, for example, as the following: New laws or restrictions, actual
or threatened; the activities of local producers; censorship regulations, particularly changes; combinations or re-alignments of film
distributors or theatre owners; new theatre construction or consolidations; changes in the attitude of the public or the exhibitors
toward American and foreign productions; any action threatened,
either governmental or public, which would prove inimical to
American pictures.

Warren L. Hoagland, US government official, Bureau of
Foreign and Domestic Commerce, 1924[3]

There can be no illusion about one point. America, for the time being, can [not] be conquered as a market . . . The very best European film will be met on the other side by a phalanx of most efficient business undertakings, which—perhaps rightly—claims the American Monroe declaration for films: film America to the film Americans.

A. Rosenthal, editor of a German trade paper, writing in a British publication, 1927[4]

It can generally be said that with the exception of the United States, no nation in the world is able to cover its negative costs in its own country. Once and for all, this characterises the weakness of the European film producing nations by contrast with America—so long as they march separately. Everything depends on prominent European industrial heads acknowledging that their primary weakness lies in their fragmentation . . . In our opinion, the new guiding principle for European film politics must be: band together, to even out the financial weaknesses of individual markets through competition. . . . Our motto must be: create the European film, conquer the market, secure the market share—no more profit-making at any price.

German trade paper, 1924[5]

The terms "Film Europe" and "Film America" are no longer in the cinephile's dictionary of current usage, but what they signify is as familiar now as it was in the 1920s, when they formed part of the motion picture industry's lexicon. "Film America" has become "Hollywood," the metonym for the well-organised and substantially capitalised American film industry, with its international market hegemony. In the 1920s, the term "Film Europe" was used, particularly in the German film trade press, to describe the ideal of a vibrant pan-European cinema industry, making international co-productions for a massively enhanced "domestic" market, and thereby in a position to challenge American distributors for control of that market—an industry fit for what some politicians envisaged as a United States of Europe.

This ideal of pan-European co-operation always existed more as a set of principles than concrete practices, but some of the leading film companies in Germany, France, Italy, Britain and elsewhere did adopt loosely related industrial policies which were designed to be of mutual benefit. These developments need to be seen in the context of the aftermath of the 1914–18 war in Europe, when the leading politicians of the moment set about establishing a league of co-operating and peacefully co-existing nations, and economists such as John Maynard Keynes argued that a permanent peace could only be assured through the creation of an integrated, regional European economy. The tensions of both ancient and immediate history, however, remained legion among European nations. Although the United States dissociated itself from the Covenant of the League of Nations and pursued a policy of "independent internationalism" throughout the 1920s, it remained vitally interested in the stability and well-being of the European economy, since it constituted one of the country's major export markets.[6] In this respect, the export policies and practices of the American film industry are typical of American business and industrial activity in Europe during a decade of unparalleled American economic expansion, in which the United States "flooded the world with products, branch plants, and investment capital," and American radio and cable companies, wire services and airlines constructed the foundations of the American communications empire.[7] As the response of European film industrialists, "Film Europe" is equally typical of what historian Carl Pegg calls "the European idea" that emerged in the 1920s.[8]

At one level, Film Europe meant the development of international co-productions, the use of international production teams and casts for otherwise nationally based productions and the exploitation of international settings, themes and storylines in such films. At another level, it meant reciprocal distribution agreements between renters in different nation-states, and other efforts to rationalise distribution on a pan-European basis, in order to secure long-term collective market share by establishing all Europe as their domestic market. It even involved attempts to create exhibition syndicates which paid no heed to national borders, and it is certainly no coincidence that in this same period in the 1920s, one after another, European governments adopted quota, tariff and *kontingent* laws restricting the import of films, laws that were explicitly or implicitly aimed at American films.

While all these and more are clear signs of pan-European activity in the film industry, their long term success was dependent on centrally co-ordinated planning. Competition with the American majors called for a solidly capitalised and stable transnational cartel, on a much more ambitious scale than most of the Film Europe deals envisaged. To succeed against Film America, Film Europe needed a trade association as well resourced as the Motion Picture Producers and Distributors of America Inc. (MPPDA), which co-ordinated many of the Hollywood

majors' export policies and practices, working in close partnership with
the US State Department and negotiating directly with European
governments. Had Film Europe been as well organised, things might
have been different. Various attempts were made to establish some sort
of basis for such co-ordination; among the most notable was a series of
European film congresses, bringing together representatives from all
sectors of the industry and from a wide range of European countries.
But despite the best efforts of the trade and, for a time, of the League
of Nations, Film Europe never acquired the "highly organised, well-
financed, fighting machine" that might have allowed it to assume the
elaborate and ideal form in which the idea was advanced in the German
trade press.[9] Instead, a much more limited, contingent and fragile
co-operation developed between major film entrepreneurs in different
nation-states. Rarely were trade agreements more than bi-national;
collectively, most European film-producing and consuming nations were
involved, but not in a centrally co-ordinated way.

The European idea in cinema thus never produced the coherent
framework envisaged in the more ambitious proposals to be found in
the German trade press. It was a much more fragmented, piecemeal
series of enterprises, with the strongest companies following conventional capitalist logic in their efforts to improve their profit margins
by gaining a greater and more secure control of the most accessible and
profitable markets. Reciprocal distribution arrangements were developed
by individual companies in an effort to secure their own market-share,
and there is little evidence of oligopolistic tendencies in the deals they
actually struck. Not until 1935 was an international trade organisation,
the International Film Chamber, brought into being; created by Nazi
Propaganda Minister Joseph Goebbels as an instrument of German
aggrandisement, it was boycotted from its inception by the British as
well as the Americans.[10]

This book explores the relationship between Film Europe and Film
America in the 1920s and 1930s. It looks at Hollywood's export policies
and practices, at the terms in which they were discussed by leading
industrialists, politicians and reformers of the period, and at the attempts
to create a pan-national cinema in Europe. It recognises cinema as both
a commercial and a cultural institution, and uses a multinational
perspective to examine some of the key points of resistance and some
of the more fruitful exchanges between Hollywood and Europe in this
period. Kristin Thompson provides an overview of the developments,
especially in France, Germany and Russia, and offers an account of both

the emergence of pan-European alliances, and their demise in the early 1930s. Thomas Saunders looks in detail at events and leading players in Germany, probably the most important of the European film industries of the 1920s. He carefully charts the German involvement in pan-European activity designed to ward off further American penetration, but he also makes it clear that the German film industry was unwilling to adopt an entirely anti-American face. Joseph Garncarz also looks at the German context, but focuses more on the film market, audiences and the relative box-office success of American and German films. While he also examines Franco-German film relations, the French predicament is the subject of a more extended consideration in Jens Ulff-Møller's essay. France was one of the more unstable of the large European markets of the period, which accounts for the frequently volatile relations between Hollywood and the French film industry which Ulff-Møller discusses.

One of the best-documented indicators of the emergence of Film Europe and its tense relationship with Film America is the mobility of personnel in the period, both within Europe and between Europe and Hollywood. Will Hays, President of the MPPDA, interpreted Film America's cultural imperialism as a benign process of "drawing into the American art industry the talent of other nations in order to make it more truly universal," but the contributions to this book emphasise the extent to which the Atlantic crossing saw a two-way traffic.[11] Tim Bergfelder and Andrew Higson each take a key figure of the period and use that figure to raise cultural as well as economic questions pertaining to the trade across borders set in motion by the Film Europe developments. Higson uses the case of the German director E.A. Dupont, who moved first to Hollywood, and then to Britain, where he was employed to make international films, all of them Anglo-German co-productions in one sense or another. Bergfelder's case study deals with the Chinese-American star Anna May Wong, who came to Europe to work in both German and British films, including one with Dupont.

In his other contribution to the book, Higson charts the history of the various pan-European film trade congresses of the period; in particular, he explores the tensions between cultural interests, promoted by the League of Nations, who organised the important 1926 congress, and the economic interests of most of the industry representatives at the congresses. Richard Maltby looks more closely at the League of Nations and its interest and involvement in the regulation of international cinema. Focusing initially on the views of film industry reformer

William Marston Seabury, who sought to erect some form of cultural resistance to what many perceived as the Americanisation of world cinema, he demonstrates how key figures working under the umbrella of the League in effect collaborated with the MPPDA to ensure a much more acquiescent role for the League. In a separate essay, Maltby and his co-author Ruth Vasey examine the prevailing debates about the cultural role of cinema, and especially the anxiety that Hollywood's hegemony created in bourgeois circles in Europe. In their treatment of cultural identity and the problem of Americanisation, they focus on the question of language, which became a crucial issue with the conversion to sound.

The transition from "silent" cinema to a cinema of synchronised sound provides perhaps the most fascinating episode in this struggle for international market control: the attempts to overcome the language barrier that the talking cinema had apparently erected in front of the international film and international distribution. By exploring these problems of language, cultural specificity and sound reproduction in some detail, this book provides another perspective on the tensions but also the mutual fascination between Europe and America, between the Old World and the New, between tradition and modernity. Ginette Vincendeau, in a now classic paper reprinted here, charts the history of one particular response to the new problem of how to adapt dialogue to different language markets: the multiple-language film, which involved the simultaneous production of films in several different language versions. While establishing the main industrial developments, she also asks important questions about the status of different language versions of a 'single' film, especially in so far as they relate to national cultural identities. Martine Danan extends Vincendeau's investigations by focusing on the situation in France, and particularly on the efforts of the American majors to maintain their hold over the market with the introduction of talkies. French audiences insisted that the new sound films be sensitive to their own culture, a fact which Hollywood took some time to come to terms with, eventually settling on dubbing films into French when suitable technology became available. Joseph Garncarz also deals with the problem of translation, of adapting a film to different language markets, this time focusing on the German situation. He argues that for all its difficulties, the multiple-language film was a successful response to the question of how to adapt a film to a European market marked by considerable cultural differences. In his essay on Dupont, Andrew Higson also deals with aspects of the history and implications of multiple-language versions and dubbing in the early sound period, as do Tim Bergfelder and Mike Walsh in their essays.

Several contributors focus on the export policies and practices of leading American film companies, and the various stances adopted by Hollywood by way of response to the sometimes disconcerting developments in Europe and in order to consolidate their hold over the vital European market. Jens Ulff-Møller looks at the way the American majors handled the French situation. Mike Walsh makes the important point that not all American companies pursued the same polices or necessarily had identical interests. He focuses on the policies and practices of just one company, United Artists, and its efforts to establish a presence in the European market. Concentrating on the immediate post-First World War period and the years of the conversion to sound, he is able to demonstrate that American market control was never complete and often in doubt because of local factors. He also shows that different companies operated different strategies to secure their market share. Indeed, while the general assumption was that the majors would fight tooth and nail to ensure they maintained their stake in export markets, for smaller companies it was sometimes a viable and rational option simply to withdraw from a particular market. It is important to bear in mind that the major American companies did not necessarily or consistently act as a cartel. In each market, they were in direct competition with each other as well as with domestic producers, and they seldom placed their common diplomatic interests above their short-term economic advantage. Although the MPPDA was the industry's principal negotiating agent with foreign governments, it had no power to coerce its members, and could not always persuade them that their hegemony was, on occasion, best maintained through concession.[12]

"Undeclared War": American Expansionism and the European Idea

Film America and film Europe dominate the world market with 95.6 percent of the total production and 91 percent of the world cinema net. . . . About 90 percent of the world feature film requirements are covered by America, despite the fact that its domestic production only amounts to 53.7 percent, or about one-half of the total world production. . . . Film Europe, as a whole, should be able . . . to compete with America as an equal . . . But the situation in Europe is such that most of the leading European film industries only supply an extremely low percentage of world film requirements . . . The necessity for the European producer to find a larger and more secure market for his output (the domestic market being insufficient to absorb it) is expressed in the general concentration of film Europe's powers (a task so difficult to bring about) which has been felt with such an intensity during the past year. Its practical results are the so-called joint productions, the number of which is gradually increasing. The development of a sane reciprocity in the international film exchange is expressed in a compulsory form by the various regulations affecting imports and exports.

George R. Canty, US Trade Commissioner for the Motion Picture Industry, 1929[13]

The relationship between Film Europe and Film America has been understood by some as an "undeclared war" between rival production industries, in which the economies of scale provided by American mass production have repeatedly overwhelmed but never completely destroyed attempts at resistance and self-determination.[14] The rhetoric of conflict surfaced as early as 1921, when the German political weekly *Die Weltbühne* proclaimed that although German-American peace had been declared, "the German-American film war has begun."[15] Military metaphors pervaded the European trade papers' discussion of relations with the American industry, and have shaped the discourse of European-American relations ever since.[16] This view of Film America's exchanges with Europe is almost exactly reflected in the production history of *Ben Hur*. When the Goldwyn Company acquired the screen rights to General Lew Wallace's immensely successful novel, company head Frank Godsol chose to produce what he planned as "the most magnificent motion picture ever made" in Italy, the nation that had been pre-eminent in the production of costume epics before the First World War. *Ben Hur*'s scale, however, exceeded all previous such projects. Its producers reconstructed the Circus Maximus, the Forum, and the Palatine in Rome, and built a recreation of Jerusalem's Joppa Gate three times the size of the original. The hugely extravagant production began in late 1923, tying up studio facilities in Rome and preventing the completion of several Italian films as the project met long and enormously costly delays, often resulting from conflicts between the American production staff and their Italian workforce.[17]

In 1924 Marcus Loew bought the Goldwyn, Metro and Mayer production companies, merging them into MGM. The new company's production heads Louis B. Mayer and Irving Thalberg replaced *Ben*

Hur's producer, director and star, and discarded all the existing footage, which was marred by ill-fitting costumes and a "silly and typical European" acting style.[18] After the production company had been in Rome for fourteen months at a cost of $2,800,000, it was ordered back to Los Angeles, where Thalberg built a bigger and better Circus Maximus on the corner of Venice and La Cienaga Boulevards. *Ben Hur*'s Italian footage eventually provided no more than a quarter of the picture's running time, but its production caused massive collateral damage to the Italian industry. The volume of domestic production plummeted, and after *Ben Hur* no American production replaced it. Rather than produce abroad, Film America increasingly pursued the far cheaper and more predictable option of importing European talent. For Mayer, the only positive outcome of his five-month trip to Europe in 1924 to bring *Ben Hur* home was that, on a side-visit to Berlin, he signed Swedish director Mauritz Stiller to an MGM contract. At Stiller's insistence, Mayer also signed up his protégée, Greta Garbo.

On its release, *Ben Hur* was a phenomenal financial success, not least in Europe.[19] As Kristin Thompson and Ruth Vasey have argued, Hollywood's foreign market was of crucial financial importance to the American film industry, bringing it approximately 35 per cent of its total income in the late 1920s and 1930s.[20] Europe accounted for approximately 60 per cent of the market outside the USA and Canada: Britain made up 30 per cent, France 8 per cent, Germany 5 per cent, Central Europe 4 per cent, Italy and Scandinavia 3.5 per cent each, and Holland 1 per cent.[21] By the early 1920s, Hollywood movies occupied the overwhelming majority of screen time in all of these markets except Germany, causing commentators to declare repeatedly that the United States was colonising Europe through the cinema.[22] In a typical expression of this concern, London's *Morning Post* warned that "The film is to America what the flag was once to Britain. By its means Uncle Sam may hope some day, if he be not checked in time, to Americanize the world."[23]

Several of the essays in this book, however, question whether American cinematic hegemony was as monolithic as it was frequently represented. Joseph Garncarz suggests that in Germany at least, Hollywood's popularity and profitability in fact derived from a relatively small number of extremely successful pictures, such as *Ben Hur*, and that German audiences preferred German films and German stars. At least one American—significantly an individual unconnected with the major companies—shared this viewpoint. W.W. Hodkinson, the distribution entrepreneur who had founded Paramount only to lose it to Adolph Zukor, visited Europe in the winter of 1926–7. He returned with a firm view of how the European market, which he thought was ten years behind America, could be profitably developed. In contrast to many American analysts, Hodkinson recognised the appeal of local product. A mediocre German picture, he argued, "pleases better a German audience and produces a greater cash return in Germany than a considerably better produced American picture of similar type." He thought the future lay in each country producing "more and more of its own pictures for its own consumption, to the gradual exclusion of the smaller pictures imported from other countries."[24]

Ironically, a version of the policy Hodkinson advocated was in effect pursued by the major American companies through their European subsidiaries investing in local production. These productions, known in Britain as "quota quickies," were in large part brought about by the Americans' need to meet the requirements of the quota and *kontingent* legislation passed to curb their domination of the European markets. These local alternatives to Hollywood may have been, in Jean-Pierre Jeancolas's term, "inexportable"—low-grade productions, many of them dependent on the cultish popularity of local cultural heroes, and destined to be seen only by audiences in their country of origin—but their profits supported the American hegemony in international film finance and distribution.[25]

Hodkinson argued that the American hegemony was maintained more by the distribution strategies of block-booking than by the universal popularity of their mass cultural artefacts. At times, these strategies seem to have been carried to extremes in order to exclude local competition. Jens Ulff-Møller, for instance, quotes a French complaint in 1929 that the American majors rented films at any price, not even covering the wear on their prints, simply to use up the screen time of French cinemas in the smaller towns and rural areas. This complaint suggests that audiences in the larger cities might have had the opportunity to see French domestic productions, but that many smaller cinemas rarely showed them.[26] Such arguments remain, however, to be substantiated by more empirical research of the kind initiated by Garncarz in his contribution to this volume.[27]

Perhaps the most acute contemporary analyst of the American majors' strategy was Hodkinson's occasional business partner, William Marston Seabury. According to Seabury, the leading Hollywood companies were energetically spreading their system of control to Europe by acquiring or building first-run theatres in principal cities: Canada had been "thoroughly contaminated" by 1926, and "England and the continent of Europe have already been infected" by their policy of "world expansion through the acquisition of theatres wherever necessary or by the execution of contracts which assured the exhibition of quantities of American pictures in entertainment theatres on terms favourable to American producers."[28] But like the architects of Film Europe, or that other tireless American entrepreneur J.D. Williams, who tried to create a "film conversation between nations instead of the present Hollywood monologue" by distributing European films in the US, would-be film industry reformers like Hodkinson and Seabury were swimming against a larger economic tide, of American economic foreign policy in general.[29]

While the United States limited its political involvement in European affairs, most obviously by its refusal to join the League of Nations, its economic engagements in Europe were, as historian Frank Costigliola has argued, both broad and deep. From the end of the war until the onset of the Depression, successive American administrations pursued a consistent strategy which sought to rebuild the economies of Europe in order to secure political stability and to develop them as fields for American investment and markets for American goods. Architects of American economic strategy during the 1920s such as Herbert Hoover and Owen D. Young argued that in a world economy open to the trade and investment of all nations, the prosperity of Europe was a matter "of daily importance to every worker or farmer in our country and the whole world."[30]

Managed by an informal alliance of businessmen, central bankers and government officials, and pursued in the main by unofficial economic diplomacy, the policy aimed to bring about an economic order in which American business could strengthen its pre-eminent position in what Young, head of the Radio Corporation of America, described as the "economic integration of the world."[31] That integration was, however, to take place on American terms. Indeed, the ideology of "liberal developmentalism" which underlay the United States' global economic expansion presumed that other nations could and should replicate the American pattern of development, without acknowledging that this also required them to relinquish a conception of nationhood that presumed sovereignty over culture.[32] Film America was a powerful agent of this ideology, not only as a sales apparatus for American goods, but also as an instrument of Americanisation. As Victoria de Grazia has argued,

Film America epitomised "the enduring capacity of the American 'empire without frontiers' to discover, process, and redistribute techniques, styles, and tastes of global provenance."[33] To the extent that cinema audiences in Europe did become "temporary American citizens" for the duration of a movie, they occupied a position from which they could view their own culture, and even the concept of a "national" culture, as alien.[34]

To its proponents, America's expansion was inherently benign, since it was based "not on military force or government design but on the wonders of its private industry, the skill of its experts, the goodness of its philanthropists." But, as Emily Rosenberg argues, entrapped in "misapplied notions of nineteenth-century liberalism and myths of America's exceptional mission, . . . [the] apologists for an American imperium only obscured understanding of the process by which Americans expanded their influence."[35] The principal tenets of this ideology—private enterprise, open access for trade and investment, and the free flow in information and culture—were selectively applied to the benefit of American business, a fact most clearly revealed by American policy on tariffs. The Fordney–McCumber Act of 1922 encouraged the import of raw materials at the same time that it created high tariff barriers to protect American manufacturing industries from domestic competition. The rest of the world was thus encouraged to become "hewers of wood and drawers of water for the American industrial machine."[36] In this economic world order, European prosperity was to be maintained principally by marketing their colonial products and selling bonds and real estate to United States investors. American goods, American business techniques, American tourists and expatriates, and American culture permeated Europe in the 1920s, in search of "new frontiers of profit, adventure, and creativity."[37]

The "American invasion of Europe" was above all an economic invasion fuelled by the United States' position as a creditor nation and by its massive trade surpluses, which averaged $732 million per annum between 1921 and 1929.[38] The 1924 Dawes Plan, which revised war reparations payments and engineered the stabilisation of the German economy, marked the culmination of American policy, easing political conflicts by treating them as economic problems and encouraging the major European nations to advance toward a post-war political peace represented by the Locarno Pact of 1925. It also stimulated a huge influx of American capital into Europe, and particularly into Germany: in the period after 1924, American investment supplied more than three-quarters of the capital borrowed by German public credit institutions and local governments, and more than half the amount loaned to German corporations; by 1928, Americans had invested well over $1 billion in Germany.[39]

These figures provide a context from which to view the economic and investment strategies of the major American motion picture companies, which were in keeping with the general pattern of American business involvement in Europe in the 1920s. The Parufamet deal of late 1925, by which Paramount and Loew's Inc. loaned Ufa $4 million and obtained privileged access to the German market, including half the playing slots in Ufa's theatres, resembled policies pursued by such major American manufacturers as Ford, General Motors and Westinghouse. General Electric (GE) purchased large minority shareholdings in European electrical goods manufacturers, with whom they also secured patents agreements. By 1930, GE's international investments totalled over $110 million, giving it control or influence over almost every major electrical manufacturer in the world.[40] The major film companies' control over the German market was exercised largely through investment in German companies, as the most effective way to secure exhibition sites for American products in Germany and also indirectly in France. By 1927, 75 per cent of German film production was financed by American money.[41]

As F. Scott Fitzgerald observed in a letter to Edmund Wilson, "Culture follows money."[42] Hollywood's acquisition of European talent in order to appropriate the attractions of Europe and sell them back to Europeans was a cultural version of the US economic policy of allowing non-competitive raw materials to be freely imported, but putting up a large tariff wall against competitive manufactured goods. In communications as in trade, American policy-makers denounced state-supported monopolies which inhibited American economic expansion, but they understood the American domination of an economic field to be a demonstration of the triumph of freedom and private enterprise, and did not worry about monopolisation.[43] What many Europeans saw as their cultural colonisation came in the wake of American commercial investment, but the trade in cultural commodities—and the effects that could be attributed to that trade—were almost always in the same direction and were far more visible than the flow of stocks and loans. The most conspicuous items of cultural consumption came from Hollywood; as several of the essays in this collection demonstrate, movies were by far the most frequently cited instance of American cultural influence, whether that influence was welcomed or derogated. Movies also provided the most readily available images of America, it was hardly surprising that European traditionalists should view America, like its films, as "all brilliant energy and no substance."[44] Indeed, the movies often provided the imagery in which "the American conquest of Europe" was recorded. Taking his metaphor from *Ben Hur*, Charles Pomaret, a member of the French Chamber of Deputies, described Europeans as the "galley-slaves" of American finance and culture in 1930.[45] After GE bought his company's stock, a senior official of the German electrical firm AEG commented that "the fear of *Überfremdung* [alienation of control] is preying upon the minds of the people like a nightmare."[46] The form of cultural *Überfremdung* perpetrated by Film America was at the same time both more visible and more amorphous, and thus even more definitely the stuff of nightmare.

The idea of Film Europe as a pan-European production and distribution cartel which might challenge the dominance of Hollywood and keep the nightmares at bay was also in keeping with other European responses to American economic colonisation. As Edward G. Lowry, the MPPDA's European representative, was at pains to explain to the heads of the major companies, no European country had enacted anti-trust legislation comparable to the 1914 Sherman Act, which was the statute most commonly invoked in legal actions against the majors. The industrialists of Europe, asserted Lowry, advocated and engaged in cartelisation and other similar practices which would be deemed in restraint of trade in the United States, and did so with the support of their governments and public opinion.[47] Cartelisation was, indeed, one of the strategies of economic rationalisation advocated by European economists such as Louis Loucheur, the principal architect of the first World Economic Conference held under the auspices of the League of Nations in Geneva in May 1927. Loucheur believed that transnational economic consortia such as the Vereinigte Stahlwerke AG, the Franco-German iron and steel cartel formed in 1926 to control the European export market, could potentially be benevolent entities which might stimulate trade, increase productivity, reduce economic rivalries between nations and reinforce the bases of peace.[48]

Applied to a different cartel, Loucheur's view would have been music to the ears of the MPPDA's members, just as it would have appalled William Seabury. But the steel cartel, described by one German newspaper as "the first step toward Paneuropa," was justified in large part as a defensive measure against American industrial aggrandisement, and objected to by the Americans as an abridgement of free trade.[49] The rhetoric of "the European idea" in the 1920s frequently referred to the United States as a positive model. Advocates of a European customs union, for instance, argued that if Europe could unite to create a common market as large as the American domestic market, it would become as peaceful as Switzerland and as prosperous as the United States.[50] For all its resources of intelligence and experience, they argued, Europe was "inhibited by its division into small competing units from achieving the material prosperity which modern science had brought within the reach of all mankind."[51] In October 1924 the newly elected French Prime Minister Edouard Herriot proposed the creation of "a United States of Europe" as an alternative to the ills brought about by economic nationalism. The idea of a European union, elastic enough to respect the sovereignty of each state, but firm enough to guarantee the benefits of collective solidarity, was put forward throughout the 1920s as either a corollary or an alternative to the League of Nations, but the most concrete proposal for such an entity, made by French Foreign Minister Aristide Briand in 1930, was buried in the resurgence of nationalism that accompanied the Depression.

In the context of the film industry, the one really powerful European multinational cartel that did emerge was the Tobis-Klangfilm-Kuechenmeister group, which was formed in response to the evident opportunities offered by the development of a new market as the European film industry converted to sound.[52] The key to market control was thought by many to lie in the ownership of patents on sound recording and reproduction equipment, and the cartel eventually controlled hundreds of such patents: in effect, as Kristin Thompson argues, "what the patents offered was a way of enforcing systematically the notion of 'Film Europe'."[53] Both Tobis and Klangfilm were created in 1928. Tobis, encouraged by the German government, and backed by Dutch, Swiss and German capital, had the important TriErgon patents as the ace in their pack. Klangfilm was put together by two of the most important German electrical companies, AEG and Siemens and Halske, and a third company, Polyphon, involved in the phonograph industry. Initially competitors, Tobis, Klangfilm and the Dutch holding company Kuechenmeister formed a cartel in March 1929 to consolidate joint control of the European sound-film industry, and to resist the American electrical and film businesses who were energetically moving into the same market. The cartel embraced numerous patents and small companies, as well as interests in radio, phonographs, phonograph disk manufacture and sound films. Klangfilm concentrated on the exhibition end of the business, Siemens on equipment manufacture, and Tobis on distribution rights and production. Tobis rapidly moved into the production of multiple-language films, establishing studios in Germany, France and Britain, the most important of them their showpiece operation in Berlin.

For a time, the Tobis-Klangfilm group was a considerable force in the struggle to control the new European sound-film market. From this position of strength, the group engaged in a patents war with the major American companies, significantly limiting the operations of the latter, and for a while no US films could be shown in Germany. Although the Hollywood majors responded by boycotting the market, Tobis-Klangfilm was powerful enough to break the boycott. As Thompson points out, "the period of the introduction of sound abroad, from 1929 to about 1932, was the last time when there was widespread hope of breaking the USA's hold on foreign markets."[54] The combination of patents ownership and the difficulties posed by language differences suggested that the American movie hegemony might at last be challenged. Matters were more or less resolved at the Paris Sound Picture Conference of 1930, chaired by Will Hays, when a new international cartel arrangement was agreed, according to which the world sound-film market was to be carved up between the major American and European interests. Most of mainland Europe would be the exclusive territory of Tobis-Klangfilm (Western Electric had already made significant inroads into the British market). Much of the rest of the world was left to RCA and Western Electric, with some territories open to both groups. With further agreements in 1932 and 1935, the international cartel continued to operate until the outbreak of the Second World War.

The Problem of European Culture

> Perceptive people know that the increasingly sharp struggle emerging against America's policy of conquest is not only an economic battle; it is first and foremost a cultural struggle which the old world must wage against the eroding influence of American film and which, if current indicators can be trusted, will shortly be waged in unison.
>
> German trade paper, 1926[55]

The history of Film Europe is simultaneously one of economic strategy and cultural practice. On the one hand, there was the very pragmatic form of trade collaboration outlined above and developed in recognition of the need to compete with the American film industry from the strength of a comparable home market. On the other hand, Film Europe was a cultural project which engaged with the prevailing ideas of internationalism. At times the two ideas intertwined, at times they were clearly in opposition. As a cultural practice, Film Europe deserves closer examination, touching as it does on issues of local and national identities, internationalism and the idea of a shared European culture and a distinctive European cinema. The various economic strategies which comprised Film Europe were generally justified in ideological terms which voiced concerns about American cultural imperialism. European commentators bemoaned what they saw as the erosion of the local culture by the forces of Hollywood. At the European film congress of 1929, Leon Brezillon, the President of the French exhibitors' association, declared that the purpose of the congress should be to consider how the European film industries could best organise themselves to defend "our intellectual patrimony, achieved during two thousand years of civilisation" from "passing into other hands, afterwards to be rented back to us by authors of a culture much different to our own."[56]

The substance of the local culture was sometimes envisioned in national terms and sometimes in pan-national terms. Thus the leader of the German trade delegation to the same congress expressed concern about Hollywood's threat to what he called "the artistic force of the authors, actors and producers of old Europe, the centre of the world's culture."[57] Faced with the challenge of Hollywood's new imperialism, the old imperial Europe was forced to turn inward, to construct a new common culture, a shared sense of identity and belonging. This dream of a common European culture held in place by a vibrant local cinema was (and remains) inevitably reductionist, however, a fact rendered only too obvious by the introduction of synchronised dialogue to the film medium. At the very least, even if we put aside questions of ethnicity, local traditions, and the differences between elite and popular culture, "official" and "unofficial" culture, Europe is still made up of a series of sometimes overlapping, sometimes distinct, and sometimes downright antagonistic language communities. Even the geographical space of Europe is less than securely fixed, the centre and the periphery changing from one account or campaign to the next. From this point of view, the shifting, co-operative alliance of mutually interacting forces that was

Film Europe in the 1920s is the ideal model for understanding the nature of both "national" cinema and "European" cinema. To section either off as distinctive and unified is to ignore the fluid, contingent and hybrid quality of any cultural formation or practice. The inter-state coalition, on the other hand, recognises that the borders between nations and cultures are permeable, and that indigenous traditions are often a combination of quite exotic forces.

While the spectre of cultural authenticity was invariably invoked by those promoting the wares of Film Europe, the success of its films surely depended on their ability to embrace hybridity in a meaningful way, or at least to mobilise popular stereotypes successfully. In the language of successful producers of international films like Ufa's Erich Pommer, the local had to be transformed into the universally intelligible.[58] At the level of production, this meant the erosion of local forms of cultural expression, since the international co-production could not afford to be inexportable. It would, however, be wrong to assign an essential quality to the category of the "universally intelligible," for at the level of reception the local might well re-emerge, since a film will be taken up quite differently in different reception contexts. The successful international film is thus precisely one whose hybridity renders it open enough for it to be taken up and interpreted in different ways by different culturally specific reception communities.

In any case, the production and distribution practices of the main Film Europe players were never "pure." If Hollywood could be accused of "Americanising" European culture, so the international co-productions of Film Europe could be accused of "Europeanising" certain sectors of British, French or German cinema. The grand narrative of an "official" European culture thus to an extent overwhelms the particular narratives and iconographies of local and regional culture. Furthermore, while Film Europe was intended as a means of mutually strengthening European companies in order to challenge the dominance of American distributors, some of these same European companies were simultaneously aiming their films at the American market. Success in this market required some form of co-operation with American companies. If there was a Europeanisation of cinema designed to challenge American cultural expansionism, there was also then a much more extensive cultural and industrial internationalisation which involved colluding with and borrowing from Hollywood—what Pommer called the "interchange of ideas and methods in production between Europe and America."[59]

The Americans, however, pursued their own forms of exclusionary parochialism over access to their domestic market. While consistently denying the validity of the cultural arguments that Europeans used to defend their protectionist measures, they readily employed their own version of such arguments in explaining why the American domestic market remained effectively closed to foreign films. In March 1928 the head of the MPPDA's Foreign Office, Col. Frederick L. Herron, informed the State Department that the French would probably defend their imposition of a quota system by claiming that the American industry had restricted the distribution of foreign pictures. This was, he commented, "not so, never has been so, and never will be so. Foreign pictures have had just as much chance for distribution here as domestic pictures have." The problem, according to Herron, was in the standard of the European product. As an example, he cited a film he identified as *The Passions of Jeanne d'Arc* [sic], declaring that "the title alone would cause every censor board in the country to prohibit the showing of the picture." The picture itself, he asserted, "does not measure up at all to our standards of what the public demands," but its French producer was bound to insist, against all reason, "that our producers have all gotten together to keep him from getting distribution here."[60] According to Herron's argument, American "standards" embraced both production values and morality, and were determined by American public demand, which brooked little interest in experimentation or unfamiliarity.

Herron was, indeed, correct in his assertion that there were no formal barriers to the distribution of foreign pictures in the US, but the American oligopoly had constructed powerful and effective barriers to entry. Whereas the "standard" American product, the medium-budget star vehicle, entered foreign distribution as a matter of course, European producers were afforded no opportunity to sell their equivalent output—in Ufa's terminology, *Mittelfilme*—in the American market. Only the most prestigious European products such as Ufa's *Monumentalfilme* of the mid-1920s crossed the Atlantic, and the producers of these films all too often found themselves caught in a matrix of cultural and economic contradictions. Only high-budget films—*Großfilme*—could attract international distribution, but no company could produce them in sufficient quantity to provide a regular supply to American exhibitors. In a lesson that American distributors taught European producers over and over again, the commercial success of an individual film did not establish a secure route into the American market for its successors. In 1925, for example, despite the recent success of *Die Niebelungen*, Erich

Pommer had to pay for a New York press screening of *Der letzte Mann* after it had been turned down, sight unseen, by the major distributors.[61] Film America retained its grip on both its domestic market and each of the foreign markets through its consistent supply of "standard" products, which occupied screen time and provided the stable platform on which the spectacular profits of American *Monumentalfilme* like *Ben-Hur* could be built. By contrast, European *Großfilme* were denied that stable base in the international market, and as a result, despite these films' economic dependence on exports and despite individual successes at the American box-office, the strategy underlying their production failed repeatedly. On average, between 1924 and 1930 no more than one in six of Ufa's *Großfilme* made international profits.[62]

As Ufa's studio policy indicates, the idea of a single, coherent European cinema does not do justice to the facts. Viewed in terms of reception as well as production, European film culture is perhaps best understood as a series of distinctive but overlapping strands. One strand is the Americanised metropolitan popular culture, confidently modernist, knowingly part of the emergent consumer culture and designed to travel. Another is the parochial or provincial non-metropolitan culture which embraces local or national, rather than international, popular traditions, and which is often inexportable (although film production companies addressing this sector may ironically be supported by Hollywood majors). A third strand to European film culture draws on the high culture of "old Europe," and embraces much of what we now understand as art cinema and heritage cinema; again, this is metropolitan-based and designed to travel.

To some extent, each strand involves different types of films, produced and distributed according to different industrial strategies, and addressed to audiences who might be defined by class, age, geography or language. The strands are not, however, mutually exclusive: audiences could choose between them, but they could also consume and enjoy all of them at different times, and the international co-productions of Film Europe drew heterogeneously on all of these strands. Even so, there remained a broad distinction between metropolitan and provincial cultures, which existed in all European countries and also in the United States. The modernist American mass culture of Hollywood's prestige productions may have attracted the urban middle and working classes, particularly the young, with what Lawrence Napper has called its "culture of aspiration."[63] These audiences may well have shared German writer Hans Joachim's perception of the United States as "a good idea

. . . the land of the future," where technology seemed to be "at the service of human life. Our interest in elevators, radio towers, and jazz was expressive of the wish to beat the sword into a ploughshare . . . to convert the flame thrower into a vacuum cleaner."[64]

Provincial cultures, however, were grounded in more local cultural forms, and were therefore, according to the definitions of the period, less "sophisticated." Napper argues that in Britain in the 1930s, older working-class audiences felt "ill at ease" with American films, preferring the slower, dialogue-based narratives and theatrical performance styles of the "quota quickies." He cites critic Richard Carr's deprecating description of such audiences as too conservative to accept change, "too old or too tired to go further than just around the corner to the pictures, or . . . too dazed and bewildered by the luxury of the 'super' and the speed and complexities of the modern film." Napper himself, however, argues that the films such audiences viewed can be understood as both a "culture of affirmation," addressing their audiences with a greater intimacy than Film America could achieve, and also as "narratives of resistance" to American commercial culture, exactly in accordance with the intent of the quota legislation that had brought them into existence: "Unable, because of their minuscule budgets, to construct worlds of glamorous fantasy or protagonists defined by conspicuous consumption, they relied on portraying the spartan world of the British defined by class."[65]

Comparable audiences elsewhere in Europe saw equally "inexportable" films circulating exclusively in domestic distribution. It is worth remembering, however, that much of Hollywood's own low-budget output could be described in similar terms: the rural comedies of Slim Summerville and Zasu Pitts, for instance, were as "inexportable" as those of Will Hay or Harry Baur—which is not, of course, to say that this product was never exported or adapted for a foreign market. Small, late-run cinemas might indeed alternate low-budget American product with their domestic equivalents in a blend of anti-metropolitan culture that must have seemed both depressed and incoherent to a more "sophisticated" visitor like Richard Carr.

To some extent, the "international" European film found itself more directly in competition with Hollywood than the more lowly local product, in that it either presented and sold itself on the strength of an alternative metropolitan modernism, delivered in terms comparable to those of Hollywood's consumptionist excesses, or else it offered a form of heritage cinema, exploiting Brézillon's "intellectual patrimony, achieved during two thousand years of civilisation." It would, however, be a mistake to presume that audiences or cinemas were unified into the consistent and mutually opposed groupings suggested by the anxiously anti-American bourgeois defenders of a narrowly national cultural patrimony. For audiences, Hollywood and local film production were not necessarily in direct competition with each other: American stars offered the glamour of "Hollywood" and "Americanism." Local stars, on the other hand, offered either a more domestic version of glamour—that is, a model of how to adapt American modernism to the national environment—or else an alternative, more firmly based in national popular cultural traditions. As the pages of European fan magazines repeatedly demonstrated, it was perfectly possible for audiences to consume and enjoy all three of these options, choosing preferences without having to make exclusive choices between them.

History Lessons

> If the indicated compromise is reached between French and American motion picture producers, to forestall the quota arrangement proposed by the Herriot Commission, it is possible that the citizens of this country may begin to appreciate what is animating Europe in its determination that American films shall not dominate its theatres. For on the basis of that compromise Hollywood, in order to obtain more representation in European theatres, will be obliged to distribute more German, French and British pictures. And then shall we hear the cry from patriotic societies . . . that European propaganda is seeping into the pure spring of our national life? If we do, and it is probable, we may have more sympathy for the same cry that is now filling Europe, where films portraying American life have been the chief entertainment of the foreign audiences. . . . [European producers] have been held out so far on the ground, and a generally true one, that American audiences do not especially favor foreign films. They feel they have not been given a fair trial, and they now propose by the use of certain clubs familiar to all nations engaged in international tariff matters, to force that trial.
>
> "Our Films Against the World," editorial in the
> New York Times, 1927[66]

The Film Europe developments in the 1920s and 1930s constitute an important phase in the history of the cinema, but they are by no means unique. In 1908–9, an earlier attempt to establish a pan-European film industrial bloc was initiated. Until 1908, European film manufacturers had regarded the US market as one of their most lucrative outlets. In 1908 Edison set up a licensing company designed to control the US market, partly by restricting foreign imports to the US market; by the end of the year, this had developed into the Motion Picture Patents Company (MPPC).[67] This was a serious blow to European manufacturers, who attempted to form their own trust through a series of meetings, the most important of which was the European Convention of Film-makers and Publishers, held in Paris in February 1909. These meetings were twofold in intention: the signatories wanted both to retain a foothold in the US market and to initiate control of the European market. As with the MPPC, it was thus initially the manufacturers who sought to exercise market control and rationalise the European film industry. As with the later Film Europe developments, the participants looked inwards at their own markets but also westwards at the US market.[68]

There are also clear parallels to be drawn between Film Europe and events and activities in the 1980s and 1990s: the terms of the debate about Film Europe and Film America remain current, and there are important lessons to be learnt from the history of this relationship. Many of the political and military struggles waged in Europe in recent years have taken the form of efforts to maintain, or more usually to re-draw, the boundaries which contain local, national and transnational public spheres. The media industries play a vital role in defining those public spheres, in setting the agenda for public debate within and between those spheres, and for imagining those spheres as inhabited by more or less coherent, cohesive and knowable communities. One of the functions of the media industries, then, is to articulate, to stabilise, and of course to sell certain cultural identities, while at the same time marginalising others. In this context, the idea and the hesitant but increasingly institutionalised practices of a pan-European film and television industry are of great interest, not least for the ways in which they map out a European moving image culture while mapping onto existing local, national and transnational cultures.

The GATT (General Agreement on Tariffs and Trade) negotiations of 1993 were only one of the sharpest of many recent reminders of the challenge which the aggressive exportation of American cultural commodities poses for diverse European cultures and media businesses and for any pan-European culture or industry. As Geoffrey Nowell-Smith has pointed out, although cinema may itself no longer be the economic force it was in the 1930s, it remains the central component of America's efforts to maintain its dominance of the world's media markets, as part of a larger design to sustain the American hegemony in high technology goods from bio-technology to software to culture.[69] In 1993 the US was again at loggerheads with European audio-visual industries, arguing for an end to all EC subsidies and quotas, while French officials argued for economic protection of the audio-visual industries on cultural grounds.[70] Developments such as these, but also the renewal of interest in pan-European co-productions, brings to the fore once again all the questions of cultural identity, exchange and collaboration which arose in the 1920s and 1930s. Significantly, in both periods the costume drama has played a key role in exploiting great moments in European heritage culture. *Casanova* (1926), *Napoléon vu par Abel Gance* (1927), *Der Kongreß tanzt* (1931) and *The Private Life of Henry VIII* (1933) were all costume films made with significant international input, whether by multinational companies, or as co-productions, or in multiple- language versions, or with multinational production teams. More recent variants of the same strategies include *Orlando* (1992), *Belle Epoque* (1992), *Howards End* (1992) and *La Reine Margot* (1994).

In many ways, recent history has re-played events of the 1920s and 1930s, but the earlier events have until recently been largely forgotten. Much of the credit for bringing this important moment in film history back to our attention must go to Kristin Thompson, who began to chart what she calls the Film Europe movement in her invaluable book *Exporting Entertainment*.[71] In Europe, the German *Cinegraph* group have done much to unearth the forgotten history of pan-European developments in the 1920s and 1930s in a series of conferences and publications.[72] More generally, the growth of interest in national cinemas and the increasing commitment to archive-based film and cultural history have ensured that the standard histories of the period have been superseded.

An important aspect of this book is its multinational perspective. One of the most pressing problems with so much film history is that, by design or by default, it very often deals with specific national developments and movements, and is unable to situate those developments in a broader international context. The contributions to this book together challenge those studies which look at national cinema in splendid isolation. They also challenge those studies which focus solely on national production, and fail to take into account the range of films exhibited in a particular country and watched by "national" audiences. This book aims to acknowledge and take stock of the international dimension: indeed, that is its *raison d'être*. Our contributors are also at pains to adopt a holistic approach, in which film history is seen as an aspect of cultural, political and business history, and in which markets, distribution, exhibition and reception are as important as production, in which policy is as revealing as practice, and in which the mapping of contemporary cultural and critical debate takes its place alongside studies of trade flow. Inevitably, even here, there remains a tendency toward a national approach: Thomas Saunders concentrates almost exclusively on Germany while Andrew Higson writes from the perspective of British cinema. But when these different pieces are brought together, it is clear that studies of specific national contexts reveal a recurrent pattern, which is not always obvious until they are compared.

At the same time, because our contributors see things from a variety of often competing geographical, linguistic and methodological perspectives, we do not always agree. Saunders and Higson have different views of the efficacy of the congresses and the various European trade agreements of the period. Joseph Garncarz's account of the degree of penetration of American films within the German market is at odds with those of Kristin Thompson and Richard Maltby. Should box-office success and audience interest be indicated by the overall number of tickets sold in a particular market, or solely by first-run sales? Are opinion polls any more or less reliable than so-called "hard statistics"? We would maintain that these are important methodological questions to ask, and that our differences deserve to be aired rather than repressed. We have also provided a selection of primary documents at the end of the book, which may help readers come to their own conclusions. The history of the relationship between Film Europe and Film America is not clear-cut, and the lessons that we can draw from it are undoubtedly salutary, but they are not always straightforward.

Notes

1. Helmuth Ortmann, "Film-Europe II," *Reichsfilmblatt*, no. 17, 24 April 1926; reproduced here as Document 5.
2. Morawsky was explaining that Film Europe was not anti-American but a counterweight to America: "Film-Europa—das gemeinsame Ziel," *Film Kurier*, 31 July 1928. Our thanks to Thomas Saunders for providing this reference.

3. Warren L. Hoagland, Chief of the Specialities Division, Bureau of Foreign and Domestic Commerce to all US commercial attachés and trade commissioners abroad, 24 November, 1924. Quoted in Ian Jarvie, *Hollywood's Overseas Campaign: The North Atlantic Movie Trade, 1920–1950* (Cambridge: Cambridge University Press, 1992), pp. 308–9.

4. A. Rosenthal, "Reciprocity: A Problem for Germany and Britain," *Kinematograph Weekly*, 21 July 1927, p. 29.

5. "European Monroe Doctrine," *Lichtbildbühne*, no. 23, 1 March 1924; reproduced here as Document 1.

6. Joan Hoff Wilson, *Ideology and Economics: US Relations with the Soviet Union, 1918–1933* (1974), quoted in Emily S. Rosenberg, *Spreading the American Dream: American Economic and Cultural Expansion, 1890–1945* (New York: Hill and Wang, 1982), p. 115.

7. Rosenberg, *Spreading the American Dream*, pp. 87–107, 122.

8. Carl H. Pegg, *Evolution of the European Idea, 1914–1932* (Chapel Hill: University of North Carolina Press, 1983).

9. Lars Moen, "The International Congress: A Constructive Help—or a Futility?," *Kinematograph Weekly*, vol. 148, no. 1156, 13 June 1929, p. 25; reproduced here as Document 13.

10. Victoria de Grazia, "European Cinema and the Idea of Europe, 1925–1995," in Geoffrey Nowell-Smith, ed., *Hollywood and Europe: Economics, Culture, National Identity 1945–1995* (London: British Film Institute, 1998), pp. 23–4; Victoria de Grazia, "Mass Culture and Sovereignty: The American Challenge to European Cinema, 1920–1960," *Journal of Modern History*, vol. 61, March 1989, pp. 79–81.

11. Will H. Hays, *The Memoirs of Will H. Hays* (Garden City, NJ: Doubleday, 1955), p. 509. For other accounts, see Jörg Schöning, ed., *London Calling: Deutsche im britischen Film der dreissiger Jahre* (Munich: Edition Text + Kritik, 1993); Graham Petrie, *Hollywood Destinies: European Directors in America, 1922–1931* (London Routledge and Kegan Paul, 1985); John Baxter, *The Hollywood Exiles* (London: Macdonald and Jane's. 1976); Thomas Elsaesser, "Pathos and Leave-Taking: The German Emigrés in Paris during the 1930s," *Sight and Sound*, vol. 53, no. 4, Autumn 1984, pp. 278–83; Jan-Christopher Horak, "German Exile Cinema, 1933–1950," *Film History* vol. 8, no. 4, 1996, pp. 373–89.

12. Ian Jarvie notes several instances in which State and Commerce Department officials expressed exasperation at the MPPDA's limited ability to persuade its member companies to "pull together." Neither these exchanges, nor the apparent personal tensions between some Commerce Department officials and MPPDA personnel, however, should obscure the scale and scope of US government assistance to the industry throughout the period. Jarvie, *Hollywood's Overseas Campaign*, 315–19.

13. George R. Canty, "German Estimates of World Film Production," *Commerce Reports*, 13 May 1929, p. 426.
14. David Puttnam with Neil Watson, *The Undeclared War: The Struggle for Control of the World's Film Industry* (New York: Harper Collins, 1997).
15. Hans Siemsen, "Deutsch-amerikanischer Filmkrieg," *Die Weltbuühne*, 1 September 1921, quoted in Ursula Hardt, *From Caligari to California: Erich Pommer's Life in the International Film Wars* (Providence, LI: Berghahn Books, 1996), p. 37.
16. For recent examples, see French press discussions of the 1993 GATT agreement, cited in Jean-Pierre Jeancolas, "From the Blum-Byrnes Agreement to the GATT Affair," in Nowell-Smith, ed., *Hollywood and Europe*, p. 55.
17. The most detailed account of the production of *Ben Hur* is in Kevin Brownlow, *The Parade's Gone By . . .* (London: Secker & Warburg, 1968), pp. 441–74. See also Roland Flamini, *Thalberg: The Last Tycoon and the World of MGM* (New York: Crown, 1994), pp. 61–77; Bosley Crowther, *The Lion's Share: The Story of an Entertainment Empire* (New York: Dutton, 1957), pp. 91–100.
18. Irving Thalberg to Fred Niblo, 24 September 1924, quoted in Flamini, *Thalberg*, p. 61.
19. Its world gross of $9 million was not, however, sufficient to defray its eventual production budget of $4 million. Adding to the irony, the picture apparently had only limited circulation in Italy, since Mussolini, allegedly outraged that the Roman, Messala (Francis X. Bushman), was cast as the villain, not the hero, banned its exhibition. Brownlow, *The Parade's Gone By . . .* , p. 470.
20. Kristin Thompson, *Exporting Entertainment: America in the World Film Market, 1907–1934* (London: British Film Institute, 1985); Ruth Vasey, *The World According to Hollywood, 1918–1939* (Exeter: University of Exeter Press, 1997).
21. Estimations of the gross revenue returned by the foreign market between the wars vary from 25 to 50 per cent, with most analysts, including the United States Department of Commerce, settling on an average of 35 per cent; see, for example, C.J. North and Nathan D. Golden, "The European Film Market–Then and Now," *Society of Motion Picture Engineers Journal*, vol. 18, 1932, p. 442; Nathan D. Golden, "Brief History and Statistics of the American Motion Picture Industry," *Motion Pictures Abroad*, 14 August 1936, p. 2; Nathan D. Golden, "Brief History and Statistics of the American Motion Picture Industry," *Motion Pictures Abroad*, 1 August 1937, p. 2; and Nathan D. Golden, "American Movies Still Conquering Obstacles Abroad, Says Nathan D. Golden," *World Wide Motion Picture Developments*, 28 October 1938, p. 1.

22. According to William Victor Strauss, in 1928 the market share of American films in Britain was 81 per cent, in France 63 per cent, in Germany 47 per cent; "Foreign Distribution of American Motion Pictures," *Harvard Business Review*, April 1930, p. 311. See also the figures cited in Edward G. Lowry, "Certain Factors and Considerations Affecting the European Market," Internal MPPDA Memorandum, 25 October 1928, Motion Picture Association of America Archive, New York (hereafter MPA) no. 198, 1928 foreign relations file; reproduced here as Document 10.

23. Quoted in Edward G. Lowry, "Trade Follows the Film," *Saturday Evening Post*, 7 November 1925, pp. 12–13. Emily Rosenberg cites an unidentified French critic as accusing Will Hays of assuming that "the only way to assure peace is to Americanize the thoughts, the language, and the souls of foreigners." Rosenberg, *Spreading the American Dream*, p. 101.

24. Hodkinson, "Foreword," (n.d. [1927]), pp. 1–8. W.W. Hodkinson papers, Box 13, Department of Special Collections, University of California, Los Angeles. *Variety* reported the US commercial attacheé as confirming that "German citizens demand a goodly percentage of German films, even if of poor quality, mixed with the best of the American." "German 2 for 1 Plan Continued," *Variety*, 20 July 1927, quoted in Hardt, *From Caligari to California*, p. 104.

25. Jean-Pierre Jeancolas, "The Inexportable: The Case of French Cinema and Radio in the 1950s," in Richard Dyer and Ginette Vincendeau, eds, *Popular European Cinema* (London: Routledge, 1992), pp. 141–8; Jarvie, *Hollywood's Overseas Campaign*, p. 138.

26. Note sur l'action en France de Certains Films Americains, 17 June 1929, US Embassy, France. See pp. 168–9, and note 28, p. 183 of this volume.

27. It is likely that research among exhibition sources will continue to involve the careful interpretation of incomplete statistical data, which may not be entirely reliable. Measurements of popularity, derived for instance from polls in fan magazines, are not directly comparable with statistics about the share of screen time. Both may be skewed by factors to which it is difficult to attribute a clear value.

28. William Marston Seabury, *The Public and the Motion Picture Industry* (New York: Macmillan, 1926), pp. 29–30, 216.

29. J.D. Williams, speech at the annual conference of the National Board of Review, 26 January 1929, MPA Reel 8, 1928 World Wide Films file; reproduced here as Document 15.

30. Herbert Hoover to Benjamin Strong, 30 August 1921, quoted in Frank Costigliola, *Awkward Dominion: American Political, Economic, and Cultural Relations with Europe, 1919–1933* (Ithaca, NY: Cornell University Press, 1984), p. 60.

31. Owen D. Young, speech, July 1930, quoted in Costigliola, *Awkward*

Dominion, p. 140. See also Michael J. Hogan, *Informal Entente: The Private Structure of Cooperation in Anglo-American Economic Diplomacy, 1918–1928* (Columbia MO: University of Missouri Press, 1977).

32. Rosenberg, *Spreading the American Dream*, p. 7.
33. De Grazia, "Mass Culture and Sovereignty," p. 60.
34. A.G. Atkinson, *Daily Express*, quoted in *J. Walter Thompson Co. Newsletter*, no. 183, 1 July 1927," p. 320; quoted in de Grazia, "Mass Culture and Sovereignty," p. 53. See also the essay by Richard Maltby and Ruth Vasey in this volume.
35. Rosenberg, *Spreading the American Dream*, p. 229.
36. Costigliola, *Awkward Dominion*, p. 143.
37. Ibid. pp. 66, 111. For other parallel instances, see Lowry, "Certain Factors and Considerations."
38. Charles Beard, "The American Invasion of Europe," *Harper's Magazine*, no. 158, March 1929, pp. 470–9.
39. Costigliola, *Awkward Dominion*, pp. 124, 206.
40. Ibid. p. 153; Rosenberg, *Spreading the American Dream*, pp. 124–5.
41. Richard Abel, *French Cinema: The First Wave 1915–1929* (Princeton: Princeton University Press, 1984), p. 30.
42. F. Scott Fitzgerald to Edmund Wilson, May 1921, in *The Letters of F. Scott Fitzgerald*, ed. Andrew Turnbull (New York, 1963), p. 326.
43. Rosenberg, *Spreading the American Dream*, p. 89.
44. Modris Eksteins, *Rites of Spring: The Great War and the Birth of the Modern Age* (London: Bantam Press, 1989), p. 270.
45. Charles Pomaret, *L'Amerique à la conquête de l'Europe* (Paris, 1931), p. 190, quoted in Costigliola, *Awkward Dominion*, p. 177.
46. Felxi Deutsch to Owen Young, 20 September 1929, quoted in Costigliola, *Awkward Dominion*, p. 155.
47. Lowry, "Certain Factors and Considerations."
48. Pegg, *Evolution*, p. 59.
49. *Neue Freie Presse*, 1 October 1926, quoted in Pegg, *Evolution*, p. 69.
50. Pegg, *Evolution*, p. 63.
51. F.P. Walters, *A History of the League of Nations* (Oxford: Oxford University Press, 1952, 1969), p. 427.
52. Thompson, *Exporting Entertainment*, pp. 148–58; Karel Dibbets, "L'Europe, Le Son, La Tobis," *Le Passage du Muet au Parlant Mondial de la Production Cinématographique (1925–1935)* (Toulouse; Cinémathèque de Toulouse/Editions Milan, 1988), pp. 38–41; Bruno Kieswetter, "The European Sound Picture Industry," *Electronics*, September 1930, pp. 282–84; Douglas Gomery, "Economic Struggle and Hollywood Imperialism: Europe Converts to Sound," *Yale French Studies*, no. 60, 1980, pp. 80–93; and Gomery, "Tri-Ergon, Tobis Klangfilm, and the Coming of Sound," *Cinema Journal*, vol. 16, 1976, pp. 51–61.

53. Thompson, *Exporting Entertainment*, p. 148.

54. Ibid. p. 148.

55. Felix Henselheit, "A European Front," *Reichsfilmblatt*, no. 10, 6 March 1926; reproduced here as Document 4.

56. Quoted in *Kinematograph Weekly*, 13 June 1929, p. 34. For more details on the 1929 congress, see Andrew Higson's "Cultural Policy and Industrial Practice" in this volume.

57. Herr Scheer, quoted in *Kinematograph Weekly*, 13 June 1929, p. 34.

58. See Erich Pommer, "The International Picture: A Lesson in Simplicity," *Kinematograph Weekly*, 8 November 1928; reproduced here as Document 16.

59. Erich Pommer, "Hands across the Sea in Movie Development," New York *Times*, 16 January 1927, quoted in Hardt, *From Caligari to California*, p. 107.

60. Herron to Arthur N. Young, Economic Advisor, Department of State, 7 March 1928, National Archives, Washington D.C., microfilm 560, roll 46, frames 1080–1.

61. Hardt, *From Caligari to California*, p. 79.

62. Ibid. p. 77, citing figures from Karl Klär, *Film zwischen Wunsch und Wirklichkeit* (Wiesbaden: Verlagsgesellschaft Feldt & Co., 1957), p. 109.

63. Lawrence Napper, "A Despicable Tradition: Quota Quickies in the 1930s," in Robert Murphy, ed., *The British Cinema Book* (London: British Film Institute, 1997), p. 46.

64. Hans Joachim, "Romance aus Amerika," *Neue Rundschau*, vol. 41, part 2, 1930, p. 398.

65. Richard Carr, "Cinemas and Cemeteries," *World Film News*, May 1937, p. 18, quoted in Napper, "A Despicable Tradition," p. 43; see also p. 46.

68. *New York Times*, 28 December 1927, quoted in William Marston Seabury, *Motion Picture Problems: The Cinema and the League of Nations* (New York: Avondale Press, 1929), pp. 57–8.

67. For a discussion of the impact of this development on European production companies' access to the American market, see Richard Abel, "The Perils of Pathé, or the Americanization of Early American Cinema," in Leo Charney and Vanessa R. Schwartz, eds, *Cinema and the Invention of Modern Life* (Herkeley: University of California Press, 1995), pp. 183–223.

68. *The Bioscope*, 14 January 1909, p. 9; 18 February 1909, pp. 3, 5–7; 4 March 1909, pp. 3, 7; 11 March 1909, p. 3; 25 March 1909, p. 7; 1 April 1909, p. 5; *Kinematograph and Lantern Weekly*, 28 January 1909, p. 993; 4 February 1909, p. 1029; 11 February 1909, pp. 1909, 1961; 18 February 1909, p. 1113; 4 March 1909, pp. 1171, 1177; 22 April 1909, p. 1645. See also Thompson, *Exporting Entertainment*, pp. 10–27; Rachael Low, *The History of the British Film, 1906–1914* (London: George Allen and Unwin, 1949), pp. 74–80; and Michael Chanan, *The Dream That Kicks:*

The Prehistory and Early Years of Cinema in Britain (London: Routledge, Kegan and Paul, 1980), pp. 238–43.

69. Geoffrey Nowell-Smith, "Introduction," *Hollywood and Europe*, p. 1.

70. Toby Miller, "The Crime of Monsieur Lang: GATT, the Screen and the New International Division of Cultural Labour," in Albert Moran, ed., *Film Policy: International, National and Regional Perspectives* (London and New York: Routledge, 1996), pp. 72–84; John Hill, "Introduction," in John Hill, Martin McLoone and Paul Hainsworth, eds, *Border Crossing: Film in Ireland, Britain and Europe* (Belfast: Institute of Irish Studies/British Film Institute, 1994), pp. 1–7; and Jeancolas, "From the Blum-Byrnes Agreement to the GATT Affair."

71. Some of the material on Film Europe in *Exporting Entertainment* is reproduced here as part of Thompson's essay, which also draws extensively on her "The End of the 'Film Europe' Movement," in Tom O'Regan and Brian Shoesmith, eds, *History on/and/in Film* (Perth: History and Film Association of Australia (WA), 1987), pp. 45–56; see also Thompson, "National or International Films? The European Debate During the 1920s," *Film History*, vol. 8, 1996, pp. 281–96. For another relatively recent pioneering account of Film Europe, see Janet Staiger and Douglas Gomery, "The History of World Cinema: Models for Economic Analysis," *Film Reader*, no. 4, 1979, pp. 35–44.

72. Conferences include the 4th, 5th and 8th Internationaler Filmhistorischer Kongress, Hamburg, 1991, 1992 and 1995; publications include Jurgen Bretschneider, eds, *Ewald Andre Dupont: Autor und Regisseur* (Munich: Edition Text + Kritik, 1992); Schöning, ed., *London Calling*; Sibylle M. Sturm and Arthur Wohlgemuth, eds, *Hallo? Berlin? Ici Paris!: Deutsch-französische Filmbeziehungen, 1918–1939* (Munich: Edition Text + Kritik, Munich, 1996).

2

"Temporary American Citizens"
Cultural Anxieties and Industrial Strategies in the Americanisation of European Cinema

Richard Maltby and Ruth Vasey

> The film has often been called "an international language." Even though the coming of the sound film may have weakened the force of this statement, the film still remains an international problem.[1]

If the film was ever to speak in "an international language" after the First World War, the industrialists of American cinema were determined that it would speak in the equivalent of American English. From 1916 onwards, the American film business was internationalised far more extensively than any other national cinema, so that by 1932, when the British report on *The Film in National Life* declared the film to be "an international problem," it hardly needed to identify the problem as being Hollywood's pervasive Americanisation of other national cinemas and the national cultures in which they were rooted. The essays in this volume variously describe the efforts that the American film industry made to maintain its hegemony in the 1920s and 1930s, and the attempts by European film industries to challenge that hegemony. This struggle between Film America and Film Europe was primarily an industrial contest, but it was paralleled by another set of concerns which were much more ideological in complexion. Bourgeois commentators frequently worried over the displacement of indigenous cultural, and especially national, identities, and these concerns were at times mobilised by European film spokesmen in their efforts to promote resistive economic strategies or by politicians defending trade restrictions. This chapter explores the terms of these debates, especially where they touch on questions of morality and cultural identity, in order to provide a context in which to place the struggle between Film Europe and Film America. In the latter part of the essay, we shall focus particularly on the conversion to sound, so that our discussion can also serve as an introduction to the other contributions to this book which explore in more detail the specific problems that synchronised dialogue and the spoken language posed for the international exchange of films.

The coming of sound sharpened the issues of cultural identity raised by the international trade in moving pictures, and led producers, audiences and governments alike to reassess their relation to the medium and to the fact of American dominance. During the 1920s, quota legislation and international co-productions had raised questions about what constituted the product of a national culture, but the introduction of sound made these questions much more pressing. The addition of sound to the movies was a cause of cultural anxiety everywhere, including in the United States, where the question of the regulation of the industry was under active debate for most of the 1930s. To American anxieties about whether Hollywood conformed to what one of the Payne Fund Studies called "Standards of Morality," Europeans added a concern over the appropriateness of American standards of cultural conformity. In a directly material sense sound standardised the movies, making them less malleable and restricting their cultural adaptability.[2] Hollywood's American identity became audible, and when its fans imitated its speech patterns, so did its effect. Sound forced Hollywood to confront the cultural and linguistic diversity of its international audience; to those members of European cultural elites already alienated from cinema by its mechanical mode of reproduction, sound comprised an additional *Verfremdungseffekt*.

The "Americanisation of the world," however, was an intricately bilateral process. Legislative definitions of the "national" were vulnerable to commercial manoeuvre: the British Cinematograph Act of 1927, for instance, determined whether a movie counted as "British" not on the basis of cultural considerations, but on the proportion of labour costs paid to British nationals. Equally, commercial manoeuvres that sought to evade a movie's national identity did not always produce the intended effect, as the history of both European international co-productions and Hollywood's investment in multiple-language versions reveal. Perhaps most importantly of all, Hollywood did not appear to its audiences as a national cinema. Summarising arguments made by producers B.P. Schulberg and Joseph Schenck in the mid-1920s, Nataša Ďurovičová

33

argues that they presented Americanness not as a specific national phenomenon but "as the very signifier of universal human evolution, subsuming under it all the local currencies of cultural exchange, a limitless melting pot of mores, nations and classes."[3] The America of the movies presented itself less as a geographical territory than an imaginative one, which deliberately made itself available for assimilation in a variety of cultural contexts. Hollywood's geographical location has always been elusive: the America of American movies was as imaginary to the residents of Des Moines or Atlanta as it was to the citizens of Brussels or Budapest.[4]

In 1935 an Englishman, Major Rawdon Hoare, cousin to the Secretary of State for India, published a book called *This Our Country*. In it he recounted an incident at a filling station on the outskirts of London, where he was served petrol by an attendant who affected an American accent. The Major, his powers of perception sharpened by his cultural conservatism, deduced that:

> The powerful influence of the cinema had changed this youth from the East End into something that was neither one thing nor the other, into something that had lost the many good qualities of the people belonging to that part of London, and yet had failed dismally to give him the American stamp he so desired. He is only one among millions whose entire lives are being influenced by the American Cinema. What good can all this do to England? Will it create patriotism? Will it create a desire to keep our great Empire together? I doubt it. But quite definitely it is creating a race of youths belonging to all classes whose experience of life is based largely on the harrowing and frequently sordid plots of American films."[5]

Such arguments about the cultural influence of Hollywood were part of a pervasive, pan-European discourse of anti-Americanism among European cultural elites; what André Visson called "the fundamental prejudice of the European intellectual élite toward the American conception of the 'Common Man."[6] Or possibly Common Woman: in a House of Commons debate on film industry legislation in 1927, one Conservative Member of Parliament quoted a *Daily Express* article claiming that British viewers "talk America, think America, and dream America. We have several million people, mostly women, who, to all intent and purpose are temporary American citizens." Commentaries such as these were an intellectually pale but vituperative reflection of what Patrick Brantlinger has identified as the "negative classicism" of conservative cultural theorists who

> tend to see mass culture as mechanical rather than organic, secular rather than sacred, commercial rather than free or unconditioned, plebeian or bourgeois and vulgar rather than aristocratic and "noble"; based on self-interest rather than on high ideals, or appealing to the worst instincts in people rather than the best, cheap and shoddy rather than enduring, imitative rather than original and urban, bureaucratic and centralized rather than close to nature, communal and individualized.[7]

According to its detractors, mass culture also possessed two other properties: it was seen as feminine and, in a narrowly nationalistic sense, as "American."[8] As the British report on *The Film in National Life* remarked in 1932, "It is easy to stigmatize Hollywood, to say 'American' films—with an inflection which implies that all such films are shoddy or morally corrupt." The report assumed that what it understood by "national life" was already established and known; it saw the task of the National Film Institute it proposed as being to heal "the breach between national culture and film activity."[9]

As elsewhere in Europe, what was promoted as the "culture of the country" was in fact the particular property of the middle classes in Britain. The report described "the cinema public" as a pyramid. At its base, making up "nine-tenths of its volume" was "the general public." At its apex were members of film societies. But it was most concerned to appeal to a third group, which it identified as the "stratum of educated opinion (largely in the provinces) which will see good films if good films are brought to it, but which will not seek them out." Persuading this critical bourgeois audience that "the film is a serious form of art, worthy of respectful consideration," would heal the breach between national culture and film activity.[10] Quite typically, *The Film in National Life* understood the idea of a national cinema exclusively in terms of production, looking forward "to the time when the film industry in Great Britain has gathered power and is producing films which are an unequivocal expression of British life and thought, deriving character and inspiration from our national inheritance, and have an honoured international currency."[11] But as Andrew Higson has pointed out, if the parameters of a national cinema were to be drawn at the site of consumption rather than the site of production, questions of national and cultural identity would become considerably more complex.[12]

The success of the American product generated conflict between the sectors of other national film industries, since producers and exhibitors had markedly different interests. European exhibitors were almost invariably opposed to any restrictions on American imports, since they were their most consistently successful product. According to Col. Edward G. Lowry, reporting on the European situation in 1928,

> the only people who are satisfied with . . . the predominance of our pictures . . . are the exhibitors and the great mass of people who attend motion picture performances. The exhibitors do not want to be restricted in showing American pictures because their customers like them. Their customers like them because they are better than any other pictures they can see.[13]

Producers, on the other hand, were in direct competition with Holly-wood for access to those exhibition sites in their home market as well as elsewhere. Noting that it was "local domestic producers" who were "behind the agitation for contingents, quotas and other restrictive measures," Lowry expressed their case succinctly:

> We (in Austria or France or Germany or England, as the case may be) cannot make pictures on equal terms with the Americans. Because of their great supply of capital and great resources accumulated during the war while we were fighting for our lives, they dominate our country. They can make and do make many more pictures than all of us together. They recover the negative cost and a profit from their rich and huge home market. They can sell their pictures to us at any price because it is all or nearly all pure profit. If measures are not taken for our protection in our own country, soon you will see nothing but American pictures. . . . We have a right to make our own national pictures but we can't have them unless this powerful foreigner is held in check. . . . If we are to see our own national life in pictures, the American imports must be held down.[14]

However, European governments pursuing policies protecting domestic production industries through the imposition of quotas on American imports found themselves lining up against the economically dominant exhibition sector of their domestic industry. Given the popularity and market dominance of the American product and the general disdain in which cinema was held by cultural elites, only arguments which emphasised the damage done to the country's social and moral fabric by Hollywood were likely to convince governments to take action.

The threat that American mass culture posed to European cultural nationalisms was insidious. Underlying concerns about the mechanical in mass culture were broader political issues, resulting from shifts in cultural authority attendant on the development of consumerism. Cultural elites worried less about the movies themselves than about what was happening to the culturally subject classes as a result of their seeing movies. In particular they worried about what Paul Swann has called "their supposed homogenizing effect," by which "external differences in dress, speech and demeanor, which had previously been clear demarcators of class and background" became increasingly ambiguous.[15] Hollywood, identified as the key industry of mass culture, was scapegoated in a process of displacement of responsibility for social change. Even the American argument that film was an industrial commodity rather than a cultural form seemed to provide evidence of a debased American sensibility. Bourgeois defenders of the status quo such as Major Hoare constructed the consumers of American culture as being simpler than they were, not only in the sense of being comparatively intellectually retarded, but also as monolithic in their adoption of American culture. In the process, the rejection of cinema as a cultural form denied European cultural elites a hegemonic role in the formation of popular culture, and inadvertently encouraged the more thorough Americanisation of European mass culture.[16]

Although cultural arguments were undoubtedly based on sincerely held anti-American prejudices, at the level of legislation governing Hollywood's access to European national markets they functioned rather as a rhetorical justification for policies of economic protectionism. Given the minor role that film production played in a national economy, a special case had to be made for its receiving preferential treatment by emphasising Hollywood's pervasive cultural influence. Arguments about the cultural importance of film were used to justify quotas in policy statements, which therefore expressed a mixture of commercial and cultural motives. In 1932, for example, the French Under-Secretary at the Beaux-Arts told representatives of the French film industry that:

> a collection of enterprises such as the cinema, that is at every moment in contact with the economic, intellectual, moral and aesthetic interests of an entire Democratic Nation, cannot live apart

from the Government just as the Government cannot live apart from you. . . . [The talking film] must be turned to profit . . . [It is therefore necessary] to organize production in France, for . . . only a film made in France can be representative of French culture. . . . It is your duty . . . to collaborate with the French Government in such a manner that the French Cinema Industry may be directed towards the highest and noblest aims and that productions of France may hold their premier place in all the world.[17]

But in practice, as Margaret Dickinson and Sarah Street have argued in relation to Britain, "little account was taken of the claim that film was an 'educational and cultural medium.'"[18] The British government accepted the truth of one of Will Hays's many dictums, that trade no longer followed the flag, but instead "trade follows the film," and justified their protectionist policy on those grounds. A broad consensus of European industrialists, represented by the industrial and banking consortium supporting Ufa in Germany or in Britain by the Federation of British Industries (FBI), developed an interest in questions of cinema because of the threat posed to their own commercial interests by Hollywood's allegedly pervasive power to advertise goods.

Hardly surprisingly, the American motion picture industry invariably denied the validity of culturally based arguments. In 1927 the American commercial attaché at Berlin told representatives of the major companies that a principal source of opposition to American movies in Germany was "the professional newspaper critics, who represent a press which is also engaged in the motion picture business and desires to free itself from competition." Fortunately, "this opposition may be discounted because the general public fails either to read or to observe the advice of the critics."[19] Major F.L. Herron, head of the MPPDA's Foreign Department, insisted that:

the cultural argument is merely another alibi. Conceding their idea that films do have a cultural effect on the community, every one of those countries that are now passing laws against us has national censorship boards. Every motion picture that goes into that country from a foreign country must pass that board before it can be released. If there is anything harmful from a cultural standpoint in such films, there is the place that they can be stopped.[20]

Herron's argument sought to separate cultural and economic questions, and in the process to deny the importance of cultural issues, by suggesting that it was all a matter of detail. Despite the public support the industry received from successive US administrations, however, some State Department officials privately acknowledged the validity of the European cultural argument.

The United States had first achieved its domination of the world's movie screens during the First World War, when its European rivals were largely debilitated. It had consolidated its hold during the 1920s with aggressive marketing procedures. In 1922 the major vertically integrated companies formed a trade association, the Motion Picture Producers and Distributors of America Inc. (MPPDA), to advance their mutual, non-competitive interests, and appointed Postmaster-General Will H. Hays as its President. As Jens Ulff-Møller details in his essay in this volume, many aspects of foreign trade fell under this category, and the MPPDA was extremely effective in soliciting State Department support, in part because of the movies' widely recognized role in increasing the demand for American consumer goods abroad. When bartering for State Department co-operation in the late 1920s, the MPPDA repeatedly cited the Commerce Department's undemonstrable statistic that every foot of film exported from the United States brought back a dollar's worth of trade.[21]

Beyond these contingent commercial factors, however, the problem that American motion pictures presented to European governments and producers was their apparently universal appeal. Why was Hollywood's output so popular? Certainly it was more highly capitalised than any other motion picture industry, and audiences, then as now, were encouraged by the American industry's publicity machine to associate lavish production values with a superior product. For a German or French exhibitor, Hollywood's economic miracle was that it spent much more on the movies it made than domestic producers could, and sold them much more cheaply. In that fact alone, Hollywood projected an image of American material abundance that was of considerable importance to its appeal.

In the 1920s, Hollywood promoted the idea that the movies constituted an "international language" that could communicate ideas and values across national and linguistic boundaries.[22] Silent movies were peculiarly well-suited to consumption in a wide range of different cultural contexts, but this was probably due less to their capacity to impart a single universal message than to the fact that they were amenable to wide range of different interpretations. As "texts," silent movies were inherently unstable: titled in different

39

languages, projected at varying speeds, tinted or toned differently, and presented with a wide variety of different musical accompaniments. In the early 1920s, European release prints were often prepared from different negatives from those used for American domestic prints, because the quality of negative duplication was poor. Many pictures were shot by two adjacent cameras, but on occasions when this did not happen, the European version would be cut together from second takes or alternative set-ups, on occasion producing variations deserving the equivalent of a *Variorum Commentary*.[23] More generally, it was the nature of the medium that metaphor and allusion should predominate. Intertitles could be used to "fix" the meaning of a scene, but the titles themselves could remain vague and euphemistic, and audiences formed a construction of the narrative mainly from visual cues.

At the same time, silent movies were also easily modified, and could therefore be adapted to a wide variety of cultural contexts. National or regional censorship, which affected virtually all of Hollywood products sent abroad, often resulted in the excision or rearrangement of scenes; but there were several other grounds for modification of the basic product. Distributors and exhibitors both commonly edited prints to shorten a programme or "improve" the action. In Switzerland, for example, exhibitors cut all the movies they received so that two features could be packed into a two-hour programme, causing the US Department of Commerce to complain that "whole slices are taken out which are of the utmost importance to a clear understanding of the picture."[24] By 1927 intertitles, which constituted the principal site of international adaptability, were routinely translated into thirty-six languages. Visuals were subject to excision or rearrangement, but titles could be creatively modified to cater to diverse national and cultural groups.[25] Hollywood characters could speak any language or dialect; indeed, in the case of the Baltic States they spoke three languages at once, since historical and political circumstances required the intertitles to be rendered in German and Russian as well as the local language. Theoretically, at least, the process of translation allowed anything inappropriate or potentially offensive to be changed. Even minor cultural differences could be accommodated, as Sidney Kent, General Manager of Paramount Famous-Lasky, explained in a lecture to Harvard students in 1927: "The titles that are used here cannot be used, for instance, in England. Many expressions that we have here are not understood by the rank and file of the people there, and so the titles are translated into the average language of the country."[26]

Intelligibility was not the only matter at issue. By "naturalising" movies, distributors were encouraging audiences to adopt the imaginative content of the movies as part of their own cultural territory. The Hollywood universe was not a foreign country to its *aficionados*, whatever their nationality. As active interpreters, audiences made sense of Hollywood in their own cultural terms. The movie-going habit was a familiar, domestic ritual around the world, and American movies and their stars were a significant part of everyday experience for millions of non-American people. Foreign audiences constituted a market not only for the movies themselves, but also for fan magazines, which encouraged personal identification with American stars. In an article about the effect of recent communications technologies on cultural identity and "the reconfiguration of Europe," David Morley and Kevin Robins have suggested that "American culture repositions frontiers—social, cultural, psychic, linguistic, geographical. America is now within. America is now part of a European cultural repertoire, part of European identity."[27] For substantial parts of the European population, American popular culture had become part of their cultural identity by the 1920s. In 1926 a State Department official observed that:

> If it were not for the barrier we have established, there is no doubt that the American movies would be bringing us a flood of the immigrants. As it is, in vast instances, the desire to come to this country is thwarted, and the longing to emigrate is changed into a desire to imitate.

As a consequence, he argued, "the peoples of Europe now consider America as the arbiter of manners, fashion, sports customs and standards of living."[28] But it was in their own cultures that these audiences imagined America, imitated Hollywood, and irritated their native bourgeois nationalists. Literal instances of the domestication of Hollywood's influence occurred, for example, when British working-class parents in the 1930s named their children Shirley, Marlene, Norma or Gary.[29]

One of the ironies of American cultural imperialism in the inter-war period was that, just as European elite critics perversely intensified the influence of American culture, so it was in the interests of American producers to encourage the idea that Hollywood belonged to the world, rather than to the United States alone. By obscuring the American origins of the movies in sensitive markets, the producers enabled them to take on some of the cultural colouring of their customer nations, subtly combating any consumer resistance that might have been inspired by overt instances of flag-waving; and indeed the American flag was routinely excised by distributors in several foreign markets. The Famous Players-Lasky version of *Peter Pan* (1924) was filmed in "a score" of versions, with Peter running up a different national flag over Captain Hook's pirate ship each time: as reported by the *Christian Science Monitor*, "the children of one country after another are now taking Peter to their hearts assured by the glimpse of their familiar national banner that the triumphant fairy boy is, as they suspected all the time, their very own."[30] Foreign censors did on occasion collaborate in clouding the origins of American films, changing titles reading "Back to America" to "Back home."[31]

European censors of American movies, however, proved to be far more sensitive in dealing with representations of their own cultures than they were in dealing with American representations of America. French sensitivity over Hollywood's version of the Foreign Legion, for instance, was itself almost legendary.[32] Through the MPPDA, the American industry went to extraordinary lengths to accommodate these quite specific anxieties.[33] Consular and embassy officials, including ambassadors themselves, were regularly called in to discuss nuances of plot or representation in Hollywood operettas or melodramas. In 1928 Major Herron advised Universal to switch the locale of *Grease Paint* from Vienna:

> In Austria we are under a contingent system already. If possible, I would suggest that this locale be switched to Russia where there is not a chance of a protest. I realize, of course, that the Viennese waltz and the atmosphere may make this impossible, but it is better to lean backwards in a proposition of this sort than to go ahead and take a chance on stirring up bad publicity.[34]

If the technical and semantic malleability of the silent medium contributed to the success of American movies abroad, the question then arises as to how Hollywood managed to retain its grip on its overseas markets after the introduction of sound at the end of the 1920s. Even when sound tracks were largely limited to synchronised sound effects and music, the new technology meant that the motion picture medium was much less adaptable to diverse cultural contexts than it had been previously. It was no longer possible to rearrange or excise sequences without ruining entire reels. Recorded music could itself cause problems: Italian and German exhibitors, accustomed to providing their own musical accompaniments, complained that the new sound tracks sounded "too American" for the taste of their customers.[35] When "sound" came to mean "talking," the problem of language specificity and the loss of ambiguity in the treatment of sensitive subjects only compounded the difficulties associated with distributing the new medium abroad. But although American producers admitted that there were some problems to be overcome, most expressed little fear that sound would cause them to lose their grip upon their non-English-speaking markets. To understand their sanguine attitude, it is necessary to take into account several factors affecting the economic performance of the industry outside the United States.

Although the timing of the conversion to sound was largely dictated by factors affecting the domestic market, it also happened at a relatively fortuitous time for the American export trade, and when other European production industries were poorly prepared for the disruptions of such a substantial technical advance. For several years prior to 1929 Hollywood's foreign market had been glutted with pictures, creating a buyer's market, especially in Europe.[36] The introduction of quota legislation in the late 1920s obliged American distributors to be more selective in choosing which Hollywood movies they distributed. In order to meet quota requirements for the distribution of domestically produced pictures, the American companies replaced their own cheaper productions with what were known in Britain as "quota quickies," cheap, locally produced movies made largely as ballast to meet quota requirements.[37] As a result, the prestige and attractiveness of the American product was enhanced. Under these circumstances, the increased visibility of the local product was a mixed blessing.

The arrival of sound raised the stakes involved in the motion picture business at every level. The introduction of the new sound technology reduced the number of films available, increasing the value of each picture to the distributor. The changes to exhibition were even more marked. Silent movies had been shown virtually anywhere there was a flat space, including small back-country halls that masqueraded as cinemas one or two nights a week. These tiny operations in foreign territories were of little or no value to the American producers and distributors, who earned the vast majority of their profits from key cinemas situated in the large cities. In the United States approximately 85 per cent of total revenue was obtained from a third of the theatres, and overseas the differential between first-run and subsequent-run theatres was just as dramatic. For example, in Belgium in 1928 a prestigious American film could be let for 50,000 francs to a large first-run venue, but could only hope to bring in 400 francs in a small subsequent-run theatre several months later. In Romania the disparity was even greater, ranging from 2,000 to 600,000 lei.[38]

The Americans had always seen the large numbers of small and medium-sized cinemas in Europe as a blight upon the territory.[39] In the sound era many of these smaller theatres closed, unable to afford the new technology and unable to obtain silent products. They were replaced by new, larger and more centralised establishments purposely built for sound.[40] Fewer, more carefully selected movies played in more expensive cinemas, with longer runs. In general, the changes wrought by sound seemed to point to bigger and better business for American companies abroad, notwithstanding the specific problems associated with sound technology.

The main factor working against the Americans in Europe in the late 1920s was government legislation specifically designed to restrict the Hollywood product. Quota and contingent legislation was either in place or pending in many European countries, including Germany, Britain, Austria, France and Hungary. However, inasmuch as these laws were intended to limit the volume of American imports, they reinforced the tendency of the sound era toward a more careful selection of products for export, and hastened the elimination of the bottom of the range. Reacting to the British initiative to increase the proportion of domestic product seen on British screens, the US Department of Commerce commented:

> Conservative estimates place the American share of the annual [British] feature import market henceforth at practically 70 per cent. This figure is healthier than previous larger percentages, since increased British and Continental competition, forcing the American contribution down to this figure, has only eliminated the poorer output of the American companies, pictures which in the past have been used principally in so-called block-booking transactions.[41]

A similar pattern prevailed in many of the other quota-regulated countries in Europe. Germany, where contingent legislation genuinely eroded American profits, was the exception rather than the rule, primarily because the German industry had a more fully vertically-integrated structure than that of France or Britain, and a production sector strong enough to supply 50 per cent of its domestic exhibition needs. From the American point of view, the real problem with most quotas was not that they were restrictive but that they were subject to change without notice, which made long-range planning for the foreign field a marketing nightmare.[42]

For a while in 1929 the American companies were hopeful that the development of sound might cause quota legislation to be universally abandoned.[43] They reasoned that if public demand for sound pictures continued, most foreign industries would lack the necessary capital and expertise to be able to fulfil their side of quota agreements.[44] In fact restrictive legislation did continue to survive in various forms. But the conversion to sound did in an important sense thwart plans to restrict the circulation of American product in Europe—not at the national level, but across the continent as a whole. The various pan-national industrial initiatives that constituted the "Film Europe" movement were ambitious even in the silent era, not least because in order to compete with the Americans on their own economic terms the Europeans needed to gain a proportion of the wider global market, as well as achieving dominance in their own territories. As Richard Abel has suggested, in at least one respect the European "international" co-productions promoted through the Film Europe initiatives only confirmed American dominance, since they increasingly imitated Hollywood in their appearance, "reflecting a modern style of life whose characteristics of material well-being and conspicuous consumption were basically American."[45] Nevertheless, as other contributors to this volume testify, by 1928 a number of coalitions for European co-production had been made, treaties forged, and displays of European solidarity achieved. Indeed, a part of this defensive co-operation—the combination and control of sound patents around the Tobis-Klangfilm concern—managed to forestall America's entry into the German sound market for twelve months from mid-1929 to mid-1930; American incursions into the European sound market were also interrupted in several other nations.[46] Ultimately, however, the effect of talking pictures was to splinter any incipient European unity into its component language groups. Any sense of cohesion that had arisen from the shared determination to resist the American industry was undermined by the local cultural imperative of hearing the accents of one's own language. In Italy, for example, the Italian Commission for Censorship suppressed the dialogue of American and other foreign sound films after 1929, arguing that they would encourage Italians to learn languages other than their own. A 1931 decree required all foreign films to be dubbed, and in 1933 a tariff was imposed on films dubbed outside Italy. Similar strictures were temporarily instituted in Portugal and Spain.[47]

The extent to which the possibility of pan-European unity had collapsed by 1930 was revealed by a complaint lodged with the MPPDA by the leaders of the French industry. American distributors had briefly instituted a boycott of French exhibitors to resist contingent proposals there, and the French were demanding that the Americans take similar action against new German legislation.[48] Producers in France and Germany also found themselves increasingly alienated from the highly lucrative British market, leaving that field wide open for the Americans. British manufacturers themselves adopted sound-film production with enthusiasm, but were more interested in the ready-made English-speaking market of the British Empire than in the problematic European arena. They also hoped for new opportunities in the American market, and, with some exceptions, were accordingly encouraged to enter into reciprocal distribution deals across the Atlantic rather than across the English Channel.[49] Several Hollywood companies, including Warner Bros, United Artists, Universal and RKO, organised tie-ups with producers in England or entered into production there themselves, encouraged by the need to secure product to satisfy the British quota.

The problem of talking a different language, however, remained an obstacle to the success of American sound films abroad even as it was an important factor in the failure of the European trading bloc, as several of the contributors to this volume demonstrate. By late 1929, the non-English-speaking world was getting tired of patched-up synchronised versions and unintelligible dialogue.[50] C.J. North, chief of the Commerce Department's Motion Picture Division, informed producers that:

> While talking pictures a year ago had passed beyond the novelty stage, English dialogue pictures were still being shown with a fair degree of success. . . . But this situation has undergone a

revolutionary change. Films in the English language stand little or no chance in most non-English-speaking areas.[51]

Nevertheless, the Department of Commerce was confident that the industry would cope with the situation by a process of "bookkeeping and experiment."[52] There was no question of abandoning a large and lucrative section of the foreign trade. The industry would simply have to adapt to the new conditions through economically rational adjustment of its business and production practices in the form of experiments with dubbing, subtitling and multiple-language versions (MLVs), which are discussed in more detail by several other contributors. During this period of experiment, as Hollywood discovered the relative unpopularity of its MLVs, the American industry seemed, ironically, to be caught in the same set of circumstances that had frustrated its foreign competitors since the First World War. American MLVs always seemed compromised, neither genuinely expressive of a local sentiment nor adequate to the prestige of Hollywood. High capitalisation was impossible for these pictures, since their intended markets were too small to recoup large investments, but less expensive productions lacked the drawing power to justify their relatively modest costs.

Subtitled movies found a satisfactory response in several markets, particularly in Latin America, where they were often preferred to those dubbed, or indeed produced, in standard Castilian Spanish. For similar reasons, audiences in Portugal found the Brazilian Portuguese of the casts employed by American companies to be unendurable, and pleaded for subtitled versions instead.[53] As these instances illustrate, subtitles in some cases could not only solve problems of translation, but also ameliorate some of the problems produced by the cultural specificity that characterised sound production, re-introducing some of the advantages of semantic flexibility provided by silent intertitles. Although audiences could hear the action being played out in a foreign tongue, the meaning of the dialogue was less specifically located through being indicated, in condensed form, in the local language. Specific cultural sensibilities could be accommodated by adjustments and naturalisations in the titles themselves. At the same time, however, the existence of the sound track meant that radical modifications of content were generally implausible at the local level, and responsibility for meeting the wider requirements of the international audience passed back to the point of production. The titling process itself was straightforward and inexpensive: the dialogue was analysed in the New York offices of the major producers and condensed into a key list of English titles, which could be translated into any number of languages during distribution. In Europe, however, the performance of titled prints was patchy, especially in the larger markets where there was more competition from local productions. It was with a view to the European market that the American companies continued to experiment with dubbing.

The original problem with dubbing had been that the existing technology had not been capable of mixing or accurately synchronising sound tracks. By late 1930 the invention of the multiple-track Moviola had overcome these limitations, enabling music and effects to be mixed with separately recorded vocal tracks. Dubbing an individual print was not particularly expensive—United Artists estimated the cost of dubbing a picture into Spanish as $3,500 in 1933—but it depended upon the maintenance or rental of a dubbing plant and associated personnel.[54] This was only economically feasible for the major language groups— Spanish, German and French—and for Italian, which constituted a special case due to the governmental restriction on the use of foreign languages in the cinema. Germany and France introduced regulations requiring that dubbing into their native languages be carried out on their home soil, in an effort to secure at least part of Hollywood's business, and presumably to keep some control over the application of their languages.[55] Even for these markets, by no means all of Hollywood's products were dubbed, since the process was only considered appropriate for action pictures with little dialogue. The reasons for this were not merely technical. As Ginette Vincendeau argues in her essay in this volume, if non-English-speaking audiences eventually accommodated themselves to the dislocation of voice and body, its potential for alienation was nevertheless always present. Hollywood's solution lay in a mode of production characterised by action-oriented aesthetics: it was an influential truism of foreign distribution that movies reliant on dialogue to explain their plot and develop their story, known in the industry as "walk and talk" pictures, fared substantially less well in the non-English-speaking market than did action pictures.[56] Hollywood's preference for a cinema of action was at least in part the result of its obligations to its foreign market.

Dubbed versions were culturally and semantically more inflexible than subtitled ones, but they, too, allowed latitude for adaptation during the movie's progress from studio to audience. Small-scale causes of offence could be eliminated in the process of translation, and in Europe the use of a population's first language often helped to localise the action and obscure the foreign origins of the product. Audiences could continue to consume a product that was delicately poised between the "authentic" world of Hollywood, with its international connotations of glamour and fantasy, and a more domestic and personal realm consonant with the culture and experience of the spectator. Although dubbing and subtitles were only partial solutions to the alienating effects of foreign voices, these adaptations of dialogue continued to present the Hollywood original as international, and the negotiated version, which in one way or another divided sound and image tracks, as a local variant. The bifurcation of sound and image localised the act of consumption, not Hollywood's act of production.

Ironically, then, by the early 1930s the necessity of preparing different versions for different language groups actually worked in favour of Hollywood's global trade rather than against it: firstly by undermining the cohesion of Film Europe, and secondly by restoring some of the flexibility of form and meaning that had facilitated the acceptance of the silents around the world. For the rest of the decade Hollywood's biggest production problem arising from the introduction of sound was probably associated with its English-speaking territory. This collective market, mainly comprising the British Empire and accounting for more than 50 per cent of foreign income, had to be serviced with the American domestic product, preferably with a minimum of cultural intervention. This posed so many difficulties that the MPPDA mooted the possibility of making special British versions of "all pictures that would normally be construed as being contrary to their policies . . . in order take advantage of the profits to be made there"; and indeed, the same mixing technology that had facilitated dubbing made possible the "reconstruction" of sound movies for non-American English-language markets.[57] However, this expensive option was only tenable as a last resort; and the English-speaking market, more than any other, had to be taken into consideration during the routine scripting and production of Hollywood's movies.

Such accommodation of details, however, could not satisfy Major Hoare's more general cultural anxiety over the influence of American movies, manners and language. Nothing could. He probably said more than he knew when he suggested that the danger was of Hollywood "creating a race of youths belonging to all classes." Much of the hegemonic anxiety about the influence of American culture lay in its particular appeal to working-class audiences, but the elite critiques of mass culture as American in conception and feminine and working-class in consumption succeeded only in confirming that part of its appeal lay in its ideologically disruptive presumptions of democracy. The movies offered European working-class audiences an escape into an imagined Utopian society called "Hollywood," in which the inflexibility of class distinction either did not exist or was not recognisably coded. The use of American idioms and semiotic systems in general offered European audiences the imaginary possibility of an evasion of class distinction, rather than a repudiation of it. Although the barrier of language operated to some extent as a site of resistance, Hollywood's Utopianism was also intensified by the distance of foreign audiences from the specific forms of American social coding inscribed within Hollywood movies. Thus James Cagney's accent lost its specific class coding and became generalised as "American," not to be distinguished from, say, William Powell's. By contrast, for every European cinema, the coming of sound brought accents into play as unavoidable signifiers of social class. British working-class audiences notoriously objected to British films as being, as *World Film News* called them, "frenziedly upper class":[58]

> The expectation that audiences would prefer to hear British rather than American voices was rudely disappointed as working-class audiences, particularly in Scotland and the North, showed their hostility to and derision for the accents and mannerisms of the London stage. Ironically, they found more to identify with and relate to in the films of what was seen in the 1930s as an alien culture.[59]

Hollywood's Utopianism was part of what made it complexly part of European cultures and separate from them, a familiar foreign country in the environs of European imaginations. Insidiously, then, "American" culture—at least as represented by Hollywood, American popular music and American-styled consumer goods—became "naturalised" within the host cultures. Few French people wanted to be Germans, few Italians wanted to be British, but almost everybody wanted to be Gary Cooper, or James Cagney, and Greta Garbo and Marlene Dietrich showed that you could be, and be so despite your nationality and even your accent. If Hollywood was a foreign country it was also the imaginative home of everybody to whom it appealed. And if that appeal was concentrated, as it was, among women and the working class, then that represented a further threat to bourgeois nationalism. Hence the hysterical tone in Hoare's anxiety of youth seduced away into an alien culture of sameness.

Philip Schlesinger has argued that national or ethnic identity is as much about exclusion as about inclusion, and that "the critical factor for defining the ethnic group therefore becomes the social *boundary* which defines the group with respect to other groups . . . not the cultural reality within those borders."[60] Seen in these terms, identity is "a system of relations and representations" with difference and distinction at the heart of the issue. As James Donald has suggested: "Manifest in racism, its violent misogyny, and its phobias about alien culture, alien ideologies and 'enemies within' is the terror that without the known boundaries, everything will collapse into undifferentiated, miasmic chaos; that identity will disintegrate."[61] Bourgeois cultural nationalism defined mass culture as American in order to define itself against other national cultures. In their assertion of the idea of boundaries, these nationalisms required an Other against which to define themselves. "American culture" served that purpose for different European elites during the 1920s and 1930s as at other times. But the tensions between European nations in the 1930s inhibited the development of any coherent strategy for resisting "the American invasion." If the emerging European cultural nationalisms of the period were defined in significant part in conscious opposition to "American culture," they were also defined separately from each other, and their nationalistic antagonisms were in the event directed more toward each other than to the American model used as counter-definition.

Notes

1. *The Film in National Life: Being the Report of an Enquiry Conducted by the Commission on Educational and Cultural Films in the Service which the Cinematograph May Render to Education and Social Progress* (London: Allen and Unwin, 1932), p. 26.
2. Alan Williams, "Historical and Theoretical Issues in the Coming of Recorded Sound to the Cinema," in Rick Altman, ed., *Sound Theory, Sound Practice* (New York: Routledge, 1992), pp. 128–9.
3. Nataša Ďurovičová, "Translating America: The Hollywood Multilinguals 1929–1933," in Altman, ed., *Sound Theory*, p. 11.
4. For a more Extended discussion of this topic, see Ruth Vasey, *The World According to Hollywood, 1918–1939* (Exeter: University of Exeter Press, 1997).
5. Major Rawdon Hoare, *This Our Country* (London, 1935), pp. 43–5, quoted in Jeffrey Richards, *The Age of the Dream Palace: Cinema and Society in Britain 1930–1939* (London: Routledge and Kegan Paul, 1984), p. 57.

6. André Visson, *As Others See Us* (Garden City, NJ: Doubleday, 1948), pp. 232–3, quoted in Paul Swann, *The Hollywood Feature Film in Postwar Britain* (London: Croom Helm, 1987), p. 3.

7. Patrick Brantlinger, *Bread and Circuses: Theories of Mass Culture as Social Decay* (Ithaca: Cornell University Press, 1983), p. 185.

8. Andreas Huyssen, "Mass Culture as Woman: Modernism's Other," in *Studies in Entertainment: Critical Approaches to Mass Culture* (Bloomington: Indiana University Press, 1986), pp. 188–207.

9. *The Film in National Life*, pp. 4, 41.

10. *The Film in National Life*, p. 83.

11. *The Film in National Life*, pp. 142–3.

12. Andrew Higson, "The Concept of National Cinema," *Screen*, vol. 30, no. 4, Autumn 1989, p. 36.

13. Col. Edward G. Lowry, "Certain Factors and Considerations Affecting the European Market," internal MPPDA memo, 25 October 1928, Motion Picture Association of America Archive, New York (hereafter MPA), p. 20. Printed as Document 10 in this volume.

14. Ibid., p. 39.

15. Swann, *Hollywood Feature Film*, p. 22.

16. Peter Miles and Malcolm Smith, *Cinema, Literature and Society: Élite and Mass Culture in Interwar Britain* (London: Croom Helm, 1987), p. 165.

17. M. Petsche, quoted in *International Review of Educational Cinematography*, vol. 4, no. 2, February 1932, p. 144.

18. Margaret Dickinson and Sarah Street, *Cinema and State: The Film Industry and the British Government, 1927–84* (London: British Film Institute, 1985), p. 2.

19. Douglas Miller, addressing a meeting of the Studio Relations Committee, 25 November 1927, MPA.

20. Herron to Hays, 13 March 1929, Will H. Hays Papers, Department of Special Collections, Indiana State Library, Indianapolic (hereafter Hays Papers).

21. See, for example, Julius Klein, "What are Motion Pictures Doing for Industry?," Frank A. Tichenor, "Motion Pictures as Trade Getters," and C.J. North, "Our Foreign Trade in Motion Pictures," in *The Motion Picture in its Economic and Social Aspects, Annals of the American Academy of Political and Social Science*, vol. 128, November 1926, pp. 79–93, 100–108. Klein was the Director of the United States Bureau of Foreign and Domestic Commerce, and North was the Chief of the Motion Picture Section of the Department of Commerce, established in 1926 to "keep the Department, and through it the motion picture industry, in the closest touch with foreign market possibilities, and also the activities of our competitors in their endeavors to limit the showing of American films within their borders." *Film Daily Yearbook*, 1926, p. 854.

22. See, for example, Lamar Trotti, "The Motion Picture as a Business," Address Delivered by Carl Milliken, Secretary of the MPPDA, 3 April 1928, MPA. Trotti was the MPPDA's chief publicist.
23. See, for example, Kevin Brownlow's description of the differences between the American and European cuts of *The Four Horsemen of the Apocalypse* in "Burning Memories," *Sight and Sound*, vol. 2, no. 7, 1992 (NS), London Film Festival Supplement, p. 13 See also Stanley Fish, "Interpreting the *Variorum*," *Critical Inquiry*, vol. 2, no. 3, 1976, pp. 465–86.
24. *Trade Information Bulletin*, no. 694, 1930, p. 54. See also Richard Abel, *French Cinema: The First Wave 1915–1929* (Princeton: Princeton University Press, 1984), p. 54.
25. Edwin W. Hullinger, "Free Speech for the Talkies?" pamphlet, n.p.: June 1929, reprinted from *North American Review*.
26. Sidney Kent, "Distributing the Product," in Joseph P. Kennedy, ed., *The Story of the Films* (Chicago: Shaw, 1927), pp. 206, 208.
27. David Morley and Kevin Robins, "Spaces of Identity: Communications Technologies and the Reconfiguration of Europe," *Screen*, vol. 30, no. 4, Autumn 1989, p. 21.
28. James True, *Printer's Ink*, 4 February 1926, quoted in Charles Eckert, "The Carole Lombard in Macy's Window," *Quarterly Review of Film Studies*, vol. 3, Winter 1978, pp. 4–5.
29. Richards, *Age of the Dream Palace*, p. 27.
30. Rufus Steele, "7 News Stories About the Movies" (New York: MPPDA, n.d.), reprinted from the *Christian Science Monitor*, 3 July 1926, p. 10.
31. Authur Kelly, memo to other foreign managers, 20 September 1929, 1929 Censorship—Eliminations—Foreign file, Reel 6, MPA.
32. See, for example, Herron to Joy on *Beau Geste*, 16 May 1928, MPA.
33. See, for instance, the Production Code Administration case file on *Plastered in Paris*, 1928. Jason S. Joy, "Resume of Dinner-Meeting of the Studio Relations Committee," 17 May 1928, MPA.
34. Herron, memo, n.d. (1928), MPA.
35. Guy Croswell Smith to Arthur Kelly, 16 May 1930, O'Brien Legal File, Box 6, Folder 1, United Artists Archive, Wisconsin Center for Theater and Film Research, Madison (hereater UA); "The European Motion-Picture Industry in 1929," *Trade Information Bulletin*, no. 694, p. 26.
36. George R. Canty, "The European Motion-Picture Industry in 1927," *Trade Information Bulletin*, no. 542, 1928, p. 15.
37. Equivalent productions in Germany were known as *Kontingent Filme*; some were never given public exhibition. The Germans abandoned this system in 1928 and substituted a system of import permits.
38. George R. Canty, "The European Motion Picture Industry in 1928," *Trade Information Bulletin*, no. 617, 1929, pp. 34, 58.

39. Britain, where even suburban cinemas were often lavishly proportioned and appointed, was an exception to the general European pattern.
40. "The Motion-Picture Industry in Continental Europe in 1931," *Trade Information Bulletin*, no. 797, p. 4.
41. *Trade Information Bulletin*, no. 617, p. 19.
42. *Trade Information Bulletin*, no. 694, p. 4.
43. *Trade Information Bulletin*, no. 694, p. 7.
44. Harold Smith to MPPDA, 14 February 1930. O'Brien Legal File, Box 97, File 5, UA.
45. Abel, *French Cinema*, p. 38.
46. Douglas Gomery, "Economic Struggle and Hollywood Imperialism: Europe Converts to Sound," *Yale French Studies*, vol. 60, 1980, reprinted in Elizabeth Weis and John Belton, eds., *Film Sound: Theory and Practice* (New York: Columbia University Press, 1985), pp. 28–9.
47. James Hay, *Popular Film Culture in Fascist Italy: The Passing of the Rex* (Bloomington: Indiana University Press, 1987), p. 86.
48. Herron to Hays, 29 July 1930, Hays Papers.
49. See, for example, Andrew Higson's discussion of Dupont's co-productions in this volume.
50. There were even reports of Polish and French audiences rioting at the shoddy adaptation of American films. See Ginette Vincendeau, "Hollywood Babel: The Coming of Sound and The Multiple Language Version," *Screen*, vol. 29, no. 2, Spring 1988, p. 28, reprinted in this volume; see also the essays by Martine Danan, Joseph Garncarz and Mike Walsh in this volume.
51. C.J. North, "Meeting Sound Film Competition Abroad," *Commerce Reports*, 10 November 1930, p. 374.
52. *Trade Information Bulletin*, no. 694, p. 4.
53. *Trade Information Bulletin*, no. 797, 1932, p. 56.
54. G.F. Morgan to Arthur Kelly, 21 July 1933, W. P. Philips file, Box 2, Folder 3, UA.
55. This did not always have the desired effect, since Harold L. Smith observed in 1935 that none of the people directing the dubbing operations in Paris were in fact French. MGM came the nearest, with a woman of Polish origin whom Smith thought to have been naturalised. Smith to Herron, 7 February 1935, W.P. Philips file, Box 2, Folder 3, UA.
56. Sam Morris to Jack Warner, 12 November 1937, JLW Correspondence, Box 59, Folder 8, Warner Bros Archive, Department of Special Collections, University of Southern California.
57. Jason Joy to E.A. Howe, 16 June 1931, *Milly* Case File, Production Code Administration Archive, Academy of Motion Picture Arts and Sciences, Los Angeles.

58. *World Film News*, vol. 2, no. 2 May 1937, p. 13, quoted in Richards, Age of the Dream Palace, p. 32.
59. Robert Murphy, "Coming of Sound to the Cinema in Britain", *Historical Journal of Film, Radio and Television*, vol. 4, no. 2, 1984, p. 158.
60. Philip Schlesinger, "On National Identity: Some Conceptions and Misconceptions Criticised," *Social Science Information*, vol. 26, no. 2, 1987, p. 235.
61. James Donald, "How English Is It? Popular Literature and National Culture," *New Formations* 6 (1988), p. 32.

3

The Rise and Fall of Film Europe

Kristin Thompson

The Film Europe movement of the 1920s was a short-lived phenomenon. Yet in the period between 1924 and 1929, co-operation among the film-producing countries of Europe was beginning to show distinct signs of eroding the seemingly overwhelming superiority enjoyed by American films in continental markets.[1] Moreover, international co-operation of a similar sort practised within Europe in recent decades has been a major factor in keeping film industries there viable. Why, then, did the 1920s movement begin to decline in 1929?

Background: 1918–1923

There was no question of co-operation among film-producing countries in the years immediately after the First World War. The conflict had radically altered the balance of control among these countries. France and Italy, which had been forced to cut back production, were in a severely weakened position. The USA took advantage of the war to move into markets like South America, Australasia and Southeast Asia, depriving the main European producing countries of their biggest source of foreign revenue. As of 1917, the USA had essentially gained control of most world markets outside Central and Eastern Europe, the USSR and the Middle East.[2]

This control was to continue in most areas, but that was not at all apparent to people in the film industry at the war's end. American experts speculated nervously in the trade papers as to how to maintain their lead. For a few years it seemed possible to many that one European country or another might cut that lead significantly. France and Italy were possible competitors, but most observers saw Germany as the main contender. Faced with a nearly decimated film industry after the communist revolution, the USSR was not yet a factor, although other countries eyed it nervously as a vast potential market which might fall under German control.

Ironically, Germany had come out of the war with a greatly strengthened industry. Before the war it had exported a negligible amount of film and had in fact been one of America's best overseas customers. But when the German government banned the importation of all but Danish films in 1916, the domestic industry entered a period of isolation that would last for nearly five years. A major breakthrough came in late 1917 with the creation of the Universum Film-Aktiengesellschaft (Ufa) by the government and large industrial investors. This move marked the entry of big capital into the German film industry, as well as the beginning of vertical integration there. Other large companies were soon formed, though none on the scale of Ufa. The ban on imports continued to the end of 1920, and relatively few foreign films seem to have been smuggled in.[3] Government regulation in support of the German film industry would continue throughout the 1920s, another factor contributing to Germany's advantage over other European producing nations. The German in-dustry was gearing up to compete on the world market well before the war ended, and German firms moved systematically into neutral countries during and just after the war.

Aside from a general fear of such powerful economic competition, other European nations retained considerable anti-German sentiment as a result of the war. With American control an accomplished fact and the constant fear of a German "invasion" motivating many in the British, French and Italian film industries, a highly competitive, uncooperative situation existed in America and Western Europe until about 1922. The French industry was initially adamantly opposed to allowing any German films in at all, and an attempt to import Ernst Lubitsch's *Madame Dubarry* in 1921 had resulted in a ban, due to the perceived anti-French propaganda in the piece. But *The Cabinet of Dr Caligari*, the first German film to play in Paris after the war (opening in February 1922), helped change French opinion; soon a small but steady trickle of German films was coming into France, winning mostly favourable reactions. A slow thaw in relations began, culminating in an almost complete turnaround by 1924, when a spirit of friendly co-operation surfaced among some elements of the European film industry. During this thaw, Western Europe was also beginning to recover from the economic depression of 1921; starting in 1922, most countries made greater progress in rebuilding after the war damage and in moving toward currency stabilisation during the mid-1920s.[4]

By 1924, then, the economic situation in Western Europe was less disorganised than it had been just after the war, and there was perhaps less inclination to cut-throat competition among film-producing nations. Furthermore, it became increasingly clear that no one producing nation could make serious inroads into the American control of world film markets. Britain, France and Italy had made virtually no progress in that direction. (The number of films made annually in Italy actually declined during the 1920s after a brief resurgence immediately after the war.) After the lifting of the import ban in 1921, Germany had managed to hold the largest share of its own domestic market as a result of its quota system and the trade barrier of hyperinflation, but during 1923 and 1924 it lost the latter advantage as the mark was stabilised. The American share of the German market rose sharply, from about one-quarter of the total in 1923 to one-third in 1924; by 1925, American films held 42 per cent of the German market, surpassing the domestic product for the first time in a decade. In 1926 that lead widened, with American films at about 45 per cent, to Germany's 36 per cent. These were the years of the German film industry's post-stabilisation crisis; although it remained the strongest in Europe, it faced obstacles comparable to the industries of other countries. The advantages of economic co-operation against the common American enemy were becoming increasingly apparent.

The Spread of Film Europe: 1924–1929

European film experts were well aware of the reasons enabling the USA to maintain its widespread control. America was by far the largest single film market in the world. In the early 1920s it had around 18,000 theatres. Its nearest competitor, Britain, had around 4,000, Germany about 3,700, and France only about 2,500.[5] Moreover, American theatres were on average larger than elsewhere; they operated more days of the week, and their patrons were more regular film-goers. Thus the American firms could afford to spend a great deal more per film, with a guaranteed return from the large domestic market and predictable revenues from abroad. Indeed, as early as 1917, most American producers began calculating negative cost on the basis of estimated world, rather than domestic, revenues. The result was a considerable jump in production values just in time to counter possible post-war competition.[6] American films were not only more lavish than those of other nations' producers, but the American exporters could afford to sell these big films relatively cheaply abroad. Other countries' producers, given a limited domestic market and fewer export opportunities, had to keep budgets low and rentals high in order to ensure even a small profit.

In the early 1920s, however, members of the European film industry began to realise that by combining their individual domestic markets into one large unit, with films circulating freely and regularly across borders through reciprocal distribution agreements, they would stand a chance of competing with America. With a larger guaranteed export market, budgets for individual films could also be raised, and those films could be sold at prices to compete with those charged by American firms.[7] Such films still might not be able to enter the largely closed American market easily, but they could contend on more equal terms with the Hollywood product in such important markets as South America and Australasia. The creation of a larger base for production was the main goal of the Film Europe idea.

During the same period, the idea of pan-European co-operation was gaining much currency in other fields. It had been voiced by left-leaning politicians and writers since the war's end, but during 1922 and 1923 the "European idea" was becoming more widespread and plausible, and the concepts of widespread European political and economic co-operation were widely debated in the popular as well as the specialised press. The French occupation of the Ruhr made some sort of peaceful solution more vital. In August 1923, Gustav Stresemann's election as Germany's Chancellor made the concept of Franco-German collaboration more viable; late that same year he spoke in favour of the idea. With the election in May 1924 of the Edouard Herriot government in France, the idea seemed even more workable, as Herriot had long been an advocate of European economic co-operation. In October of that year he spoke at the Sorbonne in favour of a "United States of Europe." By then, capitalists in various fields had come to realise that the huge American market gave the USA a trading advantage abroad in many areas. European business had lost its central position in the world during the war, and it had become apparent that it would not regain it using current strategies. Business leaders in France, Germany, Belgium, Luxembourg and elsewhere were beginning to make an increasing number of bilateral or mutually beneficial contracts.[8]

The film industry followed this trend in 1924, with an early attempt at reciprocal distribution agreements between European countries, with the intention of building a larger market. During the summer of that year, Ufa signed a mutual distribution agreement with the Etablisse-ments Aubert, one of the major French distributors. There had been many distribution contracts signed between companies of different countries during the years after the war, but most such contracts simply appointed one firm as the foreign distribution agent for another, usually stronger one. The mutual distribution pact was different in that it signalled a willingness to open markets for a two-way exchange. Moreover, this arrangement was explicitly presented to the public as an attempt to create a European market. French reporters repeatedly interviewed the initiator of the pact, Erich Pommer. As head of Ufa, the single strongest film firm in Europe, Pommer was seen as a potential leader in a new pan-European industry. He summed up the new approach which many industry members hoped would guide the European film in the future:

> I think, said Mr. Pommer, that European producers must at last think of establishing a certain co-operation among themselves. It is imperative to create a system of regular trade which will enable the producers to amortise their films rapidly. It is necessary to create "European films," which will no longer be French, British, Italian, or German films; entirely "continental" films, expanding out into all Europe and amortising their enormous costs, can be produced easily.[9]

Similar opinions were expressed repeatedly in the trade and popular press of Europe for the rest of the silent period.[10]

The idea of Film Europe took some time to bear fruit. It came into being shortly before the German industry entered its post-stabilisation crisis. In the autumn of 1924, shortly after the Ufa–Aubert deal, the Wengeroff and Stinnes interest in Germany formed Westi, a production and distribution company with subsidiaries in the major producing countries. Wengeroff intended to sponsor production in all these countries, then to circulate the results throughout Europe. In December, Westi and Pathé formed Pathé-Westi, a mutual production and distribution firm. Again, the move attracted great attention and was seen as a big step forward in the creation of a European film to compete successfully in world markets. A major expansion programme went on in early 1925. But the project's scope went beyond what the current German situation could support; Westi went out of business less than a year later, in July 1925.[11] Apart from the Westi project, there was no successful follow-up to the hopeful beginning made by Pommer and Aubert during 1924 and 1925 (though Ufa and Aubert exchanged German and French films on a regular basis). When Ufa was in financial difficulty in 1925, it turned for a loan, not to its fellow firms within in the European film industry, but to rival American companies. The result was the famous Parufamet agreement, in which Paramount and MGM provided a loan to Ufa of $4 million for ten years. The two American companies were to release ten Ufa films annually in the United States, while the three firms set up a joint company for distribution in Germany: Parufamet, which would distribute twenty Paramount and twenty MGM films annually, as well as an unspecified number of Ufa films. The distribution in Germany, rather than the loan, was the main point for the Americans: Parufamet was a means of gaining import certificates and a secure place in the German market, and they continued to release through this company in Germany into the early 1930s. The loan allowed Ufa to survive the crucial period of indebtedness during Germany's stabilisation crisis.[12]

Once the German post-stabilisation crisis ended in 1926 and 1927, however, the film industry there resumed its role of leading the continent in the serious business of co-operation. As other European countries stabilised their currencies and passed beyond the main period of post-war reconstruction, they too entered the boom years preceding the Depression. Over these years, production companies continued to sign agencies in other European countries. Companies in one country invested in similar companies abroad. One of the most notable of these came when Ufa and Svenska formed a jointly controlled distribution firm, involving French investment, in Paris in mid-1926; its name reflected the sentiments of the period—L'Alliance Cinématographique Européene (ACE). The company announced plans to produce in all three countries, but its main purpose was actually to serve as an outlet for Ufa films in France, and it functioned very efficiently as such for the next few years. Ufa continued to set the pattern, signing a reciprocal distribution agreement with Gaumont-British in December 1927; this was hailed in Britain as the first such major signing for a British firm.

Despite the groundbreaking success of the 1924 Ufa–Aubert mutual distribution pact and later the ACE initiative, France had to be content to play second fiddle to Germany in the Film Europe effort. Hollywood had become the single largest source of films in the French market during the war, and there was no import ban or government regulation during the post-war years to help French film-making to recover its leading position in its own market. While Germany managed to carve out a toehold in several important regions, including South America, France continued to have very limited export possibilities. A trickle of German films even went into the lucrative American market, while French films were largely locked out except for the art-cinema circuit. (In 1925, for example, the prestigious Raymond Bernard film, *Les Miracle des Loups* [1924], was given a five-week run at the Criterion Theatre in New York, specially rented for the purpose of finding an American distributor. Despite favourable reviews no one picked up the film.[13])

The Soviet Union's film industry played no part in the early years of the Film Europe movement. Export was minimal during the period when the government was trying to encourage the rebuilding of the industry after the devastating effects of the Bolshevik Revolution. It was not until the phenomenal success of *Battleship Potemkin* in 1926 that Soviet films gained any prominence in Europe. Over the next few years, however, the USSR did benefit by participating indirectly in Film Europe. In October 1926, a joint Russian–German production and distribution company was formed, called Derufa (DEutscheRUssischa FilmAllianz; the name was later changed to Derussa). The investors were Sovkino and Phoenix Films and they planned to co-produce in Germany and distribute a regular programme of both German and Soviet films. Derussa went bankrupt in the autumn of 1929, after having imported a number of important Soviet films, including Room's *Death Bay*, Barnet's *Girl With a Hat Box*, Pudovkin's *The End of St Petersburg* and Eisenstein's *Old and New*.

The year 1928 was probably the most intense period for international reciprocal agreements. In March, another larger German company, Terra, signed a distribution pact with the French company Cinéromans; in April, British International Pictures did the same with Pathé; in June, Ufa and the state-run film agency LUCE, of Italy, signed to distribute each other's films. Other agreements between smaller companies occurred throughout this period. The net result was a noticeable increase in the circulation of films within Europe. Ludwig Klitzsch, the new director of Ufa, commented at the time of the LUCE deal:

> A European film cartel is actually established now. The German–Italian agreement was only an incidental step in a whole series of general European agreements. A number of leading film enterprises

in important European film countries have joined to form a solid front against America in order to be able to negotiate on terms of equality with the greatest film factor in the world.[14]

In general, the Film Europe movement can be said to have shown distinct signs of achieving its aims on a modest scale. From 1926 until the decade's end, a few countries actually managed to chip away at the American hegemony and to increase the circulation of European films. They did this primarily through distribution contracts and quota laws. As a result of such co-operative measures, the American share in Germany fell from about 45 per cent in 1926 to 32 per cent by 1930, while the German share rose from 40 per cent to 50 per cent in that same period. As Table 3.1 indicates, a similar pattern occurred in Britain and France, with a drop in the American share after 1926, when the European economy had recovered enough to make production more feasible. Germany's share climbed steadily in both the French and British markets, paralleling the rise in contracts between countries for distribution. In Britain, sound caused a drop in foreign-language films; but by dint of making French-language versions, Germany built up its share of the French market again in 1932.[15] Germany's relatively strong production and its quota laws enabled it to regain the largest portion of its domestic market by 1927.

Britain, starting from a very low state of production, with American films dominating its market to a considerable extent in 1926, also managed to improve steadily. The effects of the 1927 quota are obvious in the rising British share of the market. Partly because of the Film Europe co-operation of the period, the quota had a restraining effect on American imports, while German imports continued to rise until sound came in. In the long run France benefited less from Film Europe than its two main partners, Germany or Britain, simply as a result of having too weak an industry to hold up its end.

The Decline of Film Europe: The Depression and Sound

Given that the efforts of the Film Europe participants seem to have seen a relatively hopeful beginning in the 1920s, why did the notion die out in the 1930s? We can attribute the decline, which occurred fairly quickly, to a combination of important historical changes, both in the film industry and in the larger political and economic spheres. Chief among the causes were the Depression, the introduction of sound,

Table 3.1. Source of feature films in circulation in Germany, France and Britain, 1926–1932 (based on numbers of feature films censored in each country)

Year	No. of films from USA	% of total	No. of films from Germay	% of total	No. of films from France	% of total	No. of films from Britain	% of total	Total no. of films
a) Germany									
1926	229	44.5	202	39.2	22	4.3	2	0.4	515
1927	192	36.9	241	46.3	27	5.2	2	0.4	521
1928	205	39.4	221	42.5	24	4.6	15	2.9	520
1929	142	33.3	192	45.1	16	3.8	17	4.0	426
1930	97	31.8	151	49.5	13	4.3	9	3.0	305
1931	80	28.0	148	51.7	32	11.2	3	1.0	286
b) France									
1924	589	85.0	20	2.9	68	9.8	–	–	693
1925	577	82.0	29	4.1	73	10.4	7	1.0	704
1926	444	78.6	33	5.8	55	9.7	2	0.4	565
1927	368	63.3	91	15.7	74	12.7	8	1.4	581
1928	313	53.7	122	20.9	94	16.1	23	3.9	583
1929	211	48.2	130	29.7	52	11.9	24	5.5	438
1930	237	49.6	111	23.2	94	19.7	16	3.3	478
1931	220	48.5	60	13.2	139	30.7	8	1.8	453
1932	208	43.4	99	20.7	140	29.2	7	1.5	479
c) Britain									
1926	620	83.6	43	5.8	24	3.2	36	4.9	742
1927	723	81.1	71	8.0	34	3.8	40	4.5	892
1928	558	71.7	93	12.0	24	3.1	95	12.2	778
1929	495	74.7	60	9.0	16	2.4	87	13.1	663
1930	519	69.5	49	6.6	22	2.9	142	19.0	747
1931	470	72.6	16	2.5	10	1.5	139	21.5	647
1932	449	70.0	18	2.8	7	1.1	153	23.9	641

consolidation within individual national industries, and political up-heavals in Europe and the USSR.

The Depression caused general political and economic policies in many countries to follow a similar path of change. Individual nations tended to draw back from international co-operation, erecting trade barriers in an attempt to improve domestic economies internally rather than through systematic international dealings. The amount of government regulation of commerce increased during the 1930s. National industries tried to raise exports and lower imports, frequently without regard to co-ordinating efforts with other countries. In the film industry, this trend was exacerbated by the fact that the first commercially viable sound systems happened to be introduced in Europe just at the time when the effects of the Depression were spreading. While sound had been innovated in the USA between 1926 and 1928, it did not reach Europe until 1929, and then only on an occasional, initiatory basis. The process of widespread conversion of studios and theatres went on during the early 1930s.

Sound offered several encouragements to increased competition within Europe. Most obviously, it introduced language barriers among countries. Previously films could circulate throughout Europe and the rest of the world with the simple substitution of different intertitles, but now the export-import process among countries without shared languages became more challenging. At first, dubbing was too technically crude to be feasible. Subtitles were not popular initially, and it was not clear that they would prove an acceptable solution. Initially, it was widely believed that Europe would break up into small clusters of countries with shared languages, protected by the language barrier from a large influx of imported films. Sound was thus at first seen as a way of wrenching domestic markets back from American domination. Some industry officials and commentators seem to have hoped that American films would be confined to Great Britain, the Commonwealth and other English-speaking areas. If this had indeed happened, it would have meant that European producers could amortise their films more easily within their domestic markets and the few other countries with the same language. They would have a more limited market but one involving far less competition.

This idea had some currency in France. The editor of *La Cinémathographie française* wrote in 1930 that sound would be good for the French industry: "Numerous are the territories where the French language is spoken and employed, or where it is utilized as the preferred second language." He listed Belgium, Switzerland, North Africa, Egypt and the Near East as such markets. He also pointed out that ticket prices in France had risen with the introduction of sound: "The coming of the 'talkies' is all for the good of the French industry, for now film production can be covered, with considerable profit, within the country itself; in addition to which there is a certain sure [sic] foreign market. Competition from outside is no longer to be feared."[16] This writer was overly optimistic. By 1931, subtitles and dubbing had been improved and began to emerge as the standard ways of dealing with language barriers. American films continued to be a major force on the French market, making up about 43 per cent of the market in 1932, and remaining around that share until about 1935.

By then, it was apparent that the French-language market was not large enough to permit competition on equal terms with English-language production. A 1935 report by a French government official pointed out that about 75 million people around the world spoke French and that there were about 5,000 cinemas catering to them. But English-language films had a world-wide audience of about 225 million, or three times as many; these people had access to 30,000 cinemas, or six times as many. The report concluded: "To protect the French production against foreign production is not only to defend it, but even and above all to place it once more in a position which would permit it to attack, with equal chances, its international competition, at first on its own market, later on foreign markets."[17] It was the same call that had been issued over and over since the late war period (and still is heard in the 1990s): win back the French market, then move into export. The report also called for the poorly organised French film industry to be re-structured.

The huge English-language market mentioned in this report had also caused the British industry to shift its tactics. British firms had had strong links with German and other continental firms in the late 1920s, participating in both co-productions and mutual distribution pacts. Yet they had been largely unsuccessful in sending films into the American market. With the coming of sound, some in the British industry apparently experienced renewed hope. There was a widespread assumption that with great actors speaking the King's English in adaptations of famous literature or in costume pictures based on British history, British films would appeal to American audiences. The tremendous success of *The Private Life of Henry VIII* in 1933 seemed to confirm this assumption. There was a great deal of financial speculation in film production over the next few years, ending in a disastrous decline in production in 1937. Indeed, by the late 1930s American firms had a stronger grip than ever on the British market.[18] The British production sector's gamble on English-language films as its hope for prosperity turned it away from European co-operation during the 1930s and toward the USA. There were many foreign film-makers working for British firms in the 1930s, but they no longer came to participate in

British–German co-productions; these were refugees from Germany and various Eastern European countries.

Sound had another major effect on the European film industry, which exacerbated the effects of the Depression. In every country, the high cost of wiring theatres and studios came in the period 1930–35, during the depths of the Depression. In particular there were many small, locally owned cinemas that had no choice but to pay for the installation of equipment or go under.

Changes within National Industries

The USSR

At the same time that the Depression and the conversion to sound were occurring, other significant changes were taking place within the film industries of various European countries. In general, within major producing nations, there was some attempt at consolidation of the structure of the industry. I will concentrate here on the situations in the USSR, Germany and France. Each country experienced a move toward monopolistic or oligopolistic structures of some sort. In the USSR and Germany, these consolidations were linked to political shifts toward totalitarian regimes, and these political pressures ensured the success of the changes. In France, the attempted restructuring of the industry failed because of the continuing weakness of the film industry.

In the USSR the film industry made a late start after the First World War. The government nationalised the industry in 1919, but relatively few films were made in the next few years. Shortages of raw stock, equipment, personnel and capital plagued production companies for the next few years. Indeed, shortages of basic equipment continued into the 1930s and would influence the whole import-export question and the shape of the first Five-Year Plan as it related to cinema.

Co-operation from abroad was vital to the establishment of the Soviet film industry. In 1922 the Treaty of Rapallo opened the first official trade relations between the USSR and a Western country, Germany. German firms would provide the main source for production equipment imported into the Soviet Union, as well as acting as a distribution conduit through which Soviet film exports subsequently flowed out to other countries.[19] In particular, throughout the 1920s the German Communist group, the Internationale Arbeitershilfe (IAH, the Workers' International Relief) formed a link between the Soviet film industry and much of the rest of the world. This group was responsible for financing a significant portion of the Soviet film industry during the 1922–3 period, supplying credit and German-made production equipment. In 1924 the IAH also set up Prometheus, a German–Soviet distribution firm based in Berlin. Prometheus became one of the main importers of Soviet films into Germany, one of Russia's most lucrative foreign markets, and also distributed them to many other countries. The IAH also established one of the most important Soviet production companies, Mezhrabpom. Mezhrabpom kept up its close link with Prometheus in Germany and was highly successful in producing films for export.[20]

The USSR was certainly never a major participant in the Film Europe movement. The government would hardly have been interested in helping set up a healthy capitalist film industry in a European context. The IAH, however, was interested in using the films it produced in the USSR to promote an international workers' cinema.[21] By their early and continuing links with the German film industry, Soviet producers and distributors indirectly benefited from the Film Europe movement. By the late 1920s, Soviet films had gained a wide reputation abroad, in part because of the kind of international film circulation fostered by Film Europe through, for example, artistically oriented film expositions and conferences. During the early 1920s, such exhibitions had been organised within single countries and focused on the national cinema of the organising body. In the spring of 1928, however, the first internationally focused exhibition, the "Internationale Tentoonstellung op Filmgebied," was held in The Hague. This also happened to be the first foreign exhibition in which the Soviet film industry participated, through screenings of several Soviet Montage films and a display by the All-Union Society for Cultural Relations with Foreign Countries (VOKS). A similar Soviet presence was provided in mid-1929 at the "Film und Foto" exhibition in Stuttgart, organised by the Deutsche Werkbund. These events, which occurred in part because of the growing Film Europe movement, helped give Soviet films a higher profile.[22] Soviet films would become regular attractions at international gatherings of this sort, including the film festivals founded in Venice and elsewhere in the 1930s.

From the early 1920s, however, the Soviet film industry was moving in two contradictory directions. On the one hand, its need for import and export led to increasing participation in the European film industry. On the other, the government was moving toward greater self-sufficiency and isolation from the outside world, and ultimately it would largely choke off the film industry's connections to the European film circulation.

In general, the Soviet government gradually moved toward consolidating its entire film industry into a monopoly, though its progress in this direction was slow and fitful and ultimately did not succeed until several years after the Film Europe movement was moribund. In late 1922, the government tried to create a state monopoly by creating a firm called Goskino. This company is generally held to have been a failure; it never managed to concentrate distribution and import-export functions or to eliminate the private firms that had sprung up under the New Economic Policy. Its general programme included the exportation of films, because foreign currency was still needed to build up the physical assets of the film industry. Foreign films also had to be imported, because Goskino needed to distribute them in order to make money to expand the Soviet film industry. By 1924, Soviet film production was showing signs of health, and another attempt was made to create a state monopoly through the formation of Sovkino. Rather than subsidise industry extensively, the government demanded that the film industry pay for itself. Moreover, the film industry was supposed to expand rapidly and possibly even one day to become a major source of general revenue for the government.

Ironically, Sovkino began operating at the beginning of 1925, the same year in which Stalin's policy of "Socialism in one country" was first put forth publicly. His goal was eventual self-sufficiency, but like many other Soviet industries of the time, the film industry was largely dependent on export and import. Indeed, in the mid-1920s, the Soviet cinema was just gaining its first success in the West. In 1926 the release of Eisenstein's *Battleship Potemkin* in Berlin brought the new Soviet Montage movement dramatically to European and American attention. Late that same year, the distribution company Amkino was formed in New York, acting as the outlet for most Soviet films entering the American market during the 1920s and 1930s.

Sovkino's policies were, however, already under attack within the USSR, and the attacks intensified as the decade progressed.[23] Many viewed both the import and export of films as dangerous to the Soviet film industry. Western films brought undesirable ideological views to workers and peasants, presenting bourgeois ideals and Hollywood's images of the luxuries of consumer society. Perhaps more surprisingly, however, film exports were seen as ideologically suspect.[24] Officials had no particular wish to spread communist ideas through cinematic propaganda, despite what censors and critics in the West seem to have suspected, given the widespread editing and outright banning of Soviet films abroad. The Soviet government and film industry had other, simpler intentions in sending films abroad: to generate an inflow of foreign currency. As far as ideology was concerned, exportation was widely viewed as creating a more decadent Soviet cinema. Sovkino was repeatedly accused of ignoring ideological correctness in its attempt to appeal to foreign audiences. Sovkino films were consistently compared with foreign films and found to be too similar. They were not considered entirely fit for domestic audiences.

Thus Sovkino was caught in a bind. It had to import and export in order to pay for the build-up of the Soviet industry, but it was attacked by government officials and the press for doing so. This kind of criticism continued in spite of the apparent success of Sovkino. During the 1927–8 season, Soviet films for the first time generated more revenue on the domestic market than imported films.[25]

The first Soviet Five-Year Plan was announced in December 1927, and applied to the film industry in March 1928. As in other industries, it called for the elimination of imports and for self-sufficiency in production; exports were to be used to finance the continued build-up of the cinema in the USSR. In effect, this meant that the whole notion of co-operation with European film-producing nations was now against official policy. Soviet film did not achieve the goals of the Five-Year Plan on schedule: while exports continued with some success during the late 1920s and early 1930s, imports also continued into the mid-1930s.

The Five-Year Plan in film took some time to achieve its goals primarily because the industry was wholly dependent on foreign raw stock and equipment at the time the plan started. In order to make the Soviet cinema self-sufficient in these areas, manufacturing had to be built up from scratch. One part of the plan was to avoid the importation of the new sound-film technology pioneered primarily in the USA and Germany. Through government control, the introduction of sound was largely delayed in the USSR until technically successful systems could be invented and innovated domestically. Production of sound films began in 1930, but a lack of funds and a far-flung system of locally owned rural cinema installations caused a slow conversion to sound exhibition. The Soviet industry was still making silent films into the mid-1930s, and the silent period persisted there longer than in any other major producing country except Japan. During the early 1930s, however, the goal of self-sufficiency was achieved. Similarly, the

Five-Year Plan demanded that all raw film stock for the domestic industry be produced in Soviet plants. It took several years to build the promised factories, but they opened in late 1931. During 1932 there occurred a complete switchover from 100 per cent imported to 100 per cent domestic raw stock.[26] Hence the Soviets did succeed in providing the material base which had originally delayed the recovery of the entire film industry.

In 1930, the film industry was again restructured in a way which changed its operations. The foreign dealings of all industries in the USSR came under more centralised control through the formation of a series of import-export combines; the cinema combine was Intorgkino, formed in April. Then, during May and June, Sovkino was replaced by Soyuzkino, a company controlling the domestic market. It formed a more complete monopoly than had Sovkino and was vertically integrated to control all segments of the industry. Together Intorgkino and Soyuzkino changed the earlier policies of Sovkino. Officials at Sovkino had persisted in their orientation toward import despite the Five-Year Plan. Now imports fell more rapidly. According to American customs figures for shipments of film into and out of the USA, 1932 marked the first year when the Soviets achieved a trade surplus with the USA.[27] By 1937, virtually no imports were going into the USSR. Indeed, in that year a major American trade publication, the *Film Daily Year Book*, gave up covering the USSR in its annual survey of foreign markets; there was simply no hope for American firms dealing with the USSR.

In 1935 the last separate production company within the USSR, Mezhrabpom, was dissolved into Soyuzkino. Mezhrabpom, as we have seen, originated through investments and loans from the German communist group, the IAH, in the mid-1920s. By 1933, the remnant of the IAH had fled the Nazi regime, re-establishing itself in Paris. The Comintern dissolved it in 1935, precipitating the disappearance of Mezhrabpom as a separate entity in the USSR.[28] Thus the last vestige of Soviet co-operation with European film interests in the 1920s was eliminated, and a totally monopolistic, nationalistic organisation was achieved within the film industry.

Germany
The situation in Germany presents some parallels to that of the USSR, in the sense that the Nazi government eventually nationalised the film industry and capped the process of cartelisation by forming one large monopolistic company in 1942. The circumstances that led to that

culmination were, however, vastly different. Germany had been the leader and the stabilising force in the Film Europe movement, and the country that had benefited most from the movement's achievements. Yet this success made it all the easier for Germany to turn away from co-operative policies and attempt to dominate its neighbours' markets once the adverse effects of the Depression became apparent.

Germany was among the countries hardest hit by the economic crisis, and it has been argued that some effects of the slump surfaced there even earlier than in the USA.[29] The German film industry suffered through deepening crisis between 1929 and 1932. The introduction of sound meant that costs were rising, and the major producers were competing fiercely among themselves. There was no structure comparable to the relatively peaceful oligopoly within the Hollywood film industry; that oligopoly had established itself in the 1910s and 1920s, functioning without cut-throat competition. By contrast, in Germany large firms frequently absorbed smaller ones or drove them out of business. While there were eighty-three film production companies in existence in 1929, the number had fallen to forty-nine by 1934. Moreover, many of the smaller companies became contractually linked to the three largest German firms during that period. One of the most powerful firms was Tobis-Klangfilm, which had arisen only with the introduction of sound in 1929. During the early 1930s it expanded its influence both horizontally and vertically. Of the forty-nine firms mentioned as existing in 1934, twenty-four had links to Tobis. Nazi policy consistently favoured the trend toward concentration in the film industry.

During the 1930s, the Nazis fostered a course of consolidation, first toward oligopoly and later toward monopoly. The few biggest companies, primarily Ufa and Tobis-Klangfilm, continued to expand, and the many small companies that had typically existed alongside them were gradually eliminated. The nationalisation process began in 1936 with the formation of a government-sponsored company to buy up the existing film companies, and culminated in 1942 with the formation of the state monopoly, Ufa-Film, or Ufi.[30]

Determining the reasons for Germany's withdrawal from its leading role in the Film Europe movement depends on an examination of Nazi policies concerning import and export. Even before nationalisation began, government regulation and policy were influential in these areas. For example, in 1933 the government changed the existing system for awarding certificates to films being shown domestically. Previously such certificates had been used simply to indicate the artistic quality of a film so that it could qualify for tax breaks. Now all films had to have a certificate to be exhibited at all. Some of the categories added over the years were "Politically especially valuable," "Valuable for youth," and "Artistically valuable." This last description was reserved for prestigious films, many earmarked primarily for export.[31] For the most part, however, the Nazis favoured strongly nationalistic films. This attitude went against the Film Europe spirit of the 1920s, when it was widely assumed that films should appeal to an international audience. For example, on 23 March 1933 Goebbels addressed the film producers' organisation for the first time, informing them of new policies and claiming that: "I gain the impression that all present are honestly willing to co-operate. The film can only be re-established on a healthy basis if German nationality is remembered in the industry, and German nature is portrayed by it."[32] This could be interpreted as an anti-Jewish statement, but it also suggests a more general desire to avoid films calculated to appeal to any non-German groups. Similarly, when the new head of the German theatre-owners' association gave an address shortly thereafter, he expressed similar sentiments. David Hull describes his speech:

> He warned the audience that the "Friedrichstrasse crowd" (a reference to the Berlin street where Jewish producers had their offices) was through for good. Germany did not want to cut herself off from the rest of the world, he said, but German films must be made by Germans who understand the spirit of the German people. All non-Germans in distribution must go.[33]

Again, Hull takes this reference to the "Friedrichstrasse crowd" as directed only against Jewish producers. It is worth noting, however, that the Friedrichstrasse was also the location of many of the foreign companies' import and export offices. Quite early on, then, nationalism became the explicit policy of the Nazi government, and this discouraged any sort of co-operation with other countries in regard to the circulation of films.

Exportation, however, was still necessary to various German industries. In general, Germany had only a very small stock of gold and foreign currencies, but the country was still dependent on imports of certain raw materials. Hence it needed to keep exporting goods in order to be able to pay for these imports. When the Depression hit Germany, bank runs and unemployment alarmed foreign lenders and investors, and many withdrew their money from the country in mid-1931. Exports of manufactured goods were central to the Nazi policy of recovery and expansion, and despite lowered film imports, the German industry tried to maintain exports at as high a level as possible. David Welch argues that this was one reason for the delay in nationalising the film industry until the second half of the 1930s, since such a move would have scared away foreign buyers of German films.[34]

Nevertheless, film exports did fall. In 1929 approximately one-third of the cost of an average feature film was paid by export revenues. By the 1934–5 season, these revenues paid only 8 per cent of the industry's income, and they had fallen to 7 per cent by 1938–9.[35] Despite attempts at appeasement abroad, there was much resentment of the Nazi regime. Exhibitors in many countries would not want to risk offending their patrons. For example, when Hitler became Chancellor in 1933, all German films playing in New York theatres were immediately withdrawn—with the significant exception of *Mädchen in Uniform*, which was publicised as an anti-Prussian film and therefore inimical to the new regime.[36] There were also many Jews and others in film industries abroad who despised the Nazi regime and refused to deal in German films.

Customs figures on American imports and exports give an indication of the fortunes of German films abroad. German exports to the American market reached their peak between 1930 and 1932, and then declined. Similarly, American exports to Germany peaked for the entire inter-war period in 1929 and 1930, then fell fairly regularly; there was a considerable drop from 1933 to 1934. As Ufa had its own branch office in New York City during this period, the USA seems a good market by which to judge the general decline of German films on world markets.[37] Government protectionism and support did aid the domestic German film industry until the country began definitively to lose the war. Certainly the long-range Nazi policy was to take over foreign markets through conquest rather than co-operation. Territorial invasions during 1930 and 1940 created an expanded film market with no competition. Welch states that by the end of 1939, German distributors had a monopoly within an area containing about 8,300 theatres, well over double the number of theatres in Germany itself.[38]

Ultimately the effects of the Depression in Germany and the changed policies under the Nazi regime were almost certainly the most significant factors in the decline of the Film Europe movement. The withdrawal of the USSR from extensive participation in the European market would not have made an significant difference by itself, but Germany had been the leader of the movement from the start. It had probably the only film industry capable of fostering a co-operative policy into the sound era, but at that crucial point the German industry moved in an entirely different direction. ·

France

The third producing country, France, also showed signs of attempting to develop a film industry organised around larger companies. In this case the outcome was quite different from the state monopolies that developed in Germany and the USSR. Since the First World War, France's film industry had adhered to the general pattern of business in that country, which lagged behind the more developed industrial countries. While the USA, Britain, Germany and Japan modernised technology and developed large, vertically integrated corporations, France clung to an ideal of small, privately owned businesses. Such companies often lacked the means to modernise and were too small to benefit from economies of scale. Many were family firms and had a small, regular market. Such a situation did not foster competition, and the firms had little reason to innovate. Despite the growth of some large industries during the 1920s, the pattern of small companies lingered into the 1930s.[39]

The film industry was no exception. After the war, there were few companies that were vertically integrated. The relatively large companies had only small theatre chains and were reluctant to undertake production, preferring to distribute independently produced films. This meant that small production companies had to take most of the financial risks. Throughout the 1920s and 1930s, the bulk of the French production sector was made up of dozens of small firms that produced only two or three films before going under. Such firms were constantly entering and leaving the market-place. Moreover, there was little organisation of any type within the industry. Since the vast majority of theatres and distribution companies were individually owned, their interests were often opposed to those of the producers. The French film industry was not particularly successful at controlling its own market, and it also did badly in foreign markets. The number of French films released in Britain and Germany rose only slightly in the late 1920s, and very few French companies succeeded in having their films released in the USA. As a result, producers had a difficult time amortising their films.

Sound did bring a small boost in 1930 and 1931, at least domestically and in the German market. This boost was aided by the fact that the Depression hit France somewhat later than other countries. Moreover, many in France actually believed that the system of small businesses would protect it from the effects of the economic crisis altogether. Such confidence, combined with hopes for high profits from sound films, led to a higher rate of investment in the French film industry. During 1929 big film companies formed or expanded through mergers. Tobis-Klangfilm, for instance, formed a major production subsidiary in France, which soon became one of the most successful exporters of French product, including René Clair's first four sound films. 1929 also saw the formation of Gaumont-Franco-Film-Aubert, a merger of three companies, including Aubert, the French half of the 1924 German–French mutual distribution pact with Ufa. When, in the same year, the largest French firm, Pathé, became Pathé-Natan through a similar merger, the French industry seemed to be moving along a path similar to those of the American firms when they formed the Hollywood oligopoly a decade earlier.[40]

As a result of this investment and growth, production rose significantly over the next few years. However, these big companies and other relatively large ones failed to form a successful oligopoly. Instead, they practised cut-throat competition in an attempt to monopolise the industry. A government report in 1936 concluded that the French industry structure of the early 1930s had been weakened by the great contrast between these big, vertically integrated firms and the many small, independent producers: "The large companies committed the error, in the early years of sound, of wanting to enlarge themselves in order to monopolize the French market."[41]

The competition was simply too intense; it caused a great number of failures among both types of companies in the mid-1930s. The crisis peaked in 1934, when Gaumont-Franco-Film-Aubert almost went bankrupt, and was saved only by a government loan. In the second half of the decade, production was almost entirely given over to a host of tiny independent companies, as the industry reverted to a nearly total lack of vertical integration. As a result, investment and credit remained low, since many companies inevitably failed.[42]

These problems meant that French film was still weak abroad. It fared better in its domestic market, aided by a series of government trade barriers introduced from 1933 on. Up to that point, the French government had offered little protection against imported films. It had set up a weak quota in the late 1920s, allowing seven foreign films to be imported for every one French one released domestically. Even this quota could not be rigidly enforced, since French production was not usually high enough to meet the theatres' demand. In 1933, however, a quota of dubbed features was set for the next year's import, and the required number was raised in each subsequent year. This quota involved the first attempt to set a definite number to imported films, instead of the earlier ratio of imported films to domestic ones. The *Film Daily Year Book*'s coverage of France suggests that this new regulation was the first actually to hinder American firms releasing in France. Over the next few years the French share of its domestic market slowly grew, while the American and German portions declined. After 1935, the German share fell considerably. French films continued to be more popular than American imports in the domestic market. At mid-decade they reached 50 per cent of the French market for the first time since the war. Moreover, after a long decline in box-office receipts induced by the Depression, French revenues finally began to rise in 1937, and the crisis eased slightly.[43]

All this suggests that France was more successful on its own than it had been as part of the Film Europe movement, although the change was slow and unspectacular, and French film-makers and commentators still considered the industry to be in crisis in the late 1930s. During the 1920s, co-operation with other countries had benefited them rather than the weaker French industry. In the first half of the 1930s, German films in particular continued to be important in the French market, and French companies were remarkably willing to continue their co-operation.[44] Germany maintained a policy of making French-language versions of its films long after other countries had stopped doing so. France continued to enter into co-productions with German firms and sent its best personnel regularly to work in Germany.[45] Thus the remnants of the Film Europe policy apparently continued to benefit German firms more than French ones.

Conclusions

The decline of the Film Europe movement paralleled that of the general European idea and the effort to create a federation of European states. After much discussion during the 1920s, this effort came to a head at the Tenth Session of the League of Nations Assembly in September 1929 in Geneva. There Aristide Briand, France's Foreign Minister and one of the central supporters of the European idea, proposed a European federation; he was backed by Stresemann and Herriot. There was much debate over the next few years, but it soon became clear that the project was doomed. The rising right-wing parties in Germany condemned the move as an "enslavement" of their nation. Stresemann's death on 7 March 1929 and Briand's on 7 March 1932 were severe blows. By the autumn of 1931, the European idea was waning quickly, and it was soon largely eclipsed. It never died out completely, however, and after the Second World War it helped form the basis for the formations of the Council of Europe, the Common Market and the developing European Union.

The Film Europe movement, though short-lived, had some significant effects. For one thing, it made many film-makers known outside their own countries who might otherwise have remained primarily national figures. One result of this was probably to pave the way for the assimilation of European émigrés into the Hollywood industry during the 1930s and 1940s. In addition, the circulation of films provided many influences that enhanced styles of film-making throughout the world. (Teinosuke Kinugasa's *Page of Madness* [1926] and Carl Dreyer's *La Passion de Jeanne d'Arc* [1928] are only two of the more obvious early examples.) Ultimately Film Europe contributed institutions which have been far more thoroughly developed in the subsequent decades. Today international film festivals, co-productions, and multinational casts and crews are common strategies. All of them either originated during the 1920s or at least received their first widespread and systematic use then.

Notes

An earlier version of this essay was presented under the title of "The End of the 'Film Europe' Movement" at the Third History and Film Conference, held in Perth, Australia, by the History and Film Association of Australia in 1985; it was subsequently published in *History on/and/in Film*, Tom O'Regan and Brian Shoesmith, eds, *History on/and/in Film* (Perth: History and Film Association of Australia (WA), 1987), pp. 45–55. The essay also incorporates some material originally published in *Exporting Entertainment America in the World Film Market, 1907–1934* (London: British Film Institute, 1985).

1. For figures on the decline in American control, see my *Exporting Entertainment: America in the World Film Market, 1907–1934* (London: British Film Institute, 1985), pp. 124–8, or Kristin Thompson and David Bordwell, *Film History: An Introduction* (New York: McGraw-Hill, 1994), p. 186.

2. For an account of the American move to domination in world film markets and the European response, see *Exporting Entertainment*, chs 3 and 4.

3. Some films did make their way into Germany via the nearby neutral countries; a salesman for one major export company described having seen American films regularly in Berlin theatres during 1919. Some German companies were reported to have block-booked their product into theatres for 1920 and 1921, in order to prevent American films from flooding in. *Moving Picture World*, 8 May 1920, p. 811; 20 September 1919, p. 1824.

4. Derek H. Aldcroft, *From Versailles to Wall Street 1919–1929* (Berkeley: University of California Press, 1981), pp. 125–49.

5. "Die Kinotheater der Erde," *Lichtbilbühne*, vol. 14, No. 4, 22 January 1921, p. 27.

6. A. George Smith, "English, French and Italian Films Will Reduce American Exportation," *Moving Picture World*, vol. 43, no. 9, 28 February 1920, p. 1423.

7. For one of many statements on this point, see W. Wengeroff, "Es darf nicht gezogt werden!," *Lichtbildbühne*, vol. 17, no. 86, 26 July 1924, p. 14.

8. For a general history of this trend, see Carl H. Pegg, *Evolution of the European Idea, 1914–1932* (Chapel Hill: University of North Carolina Press, 1983).

9. C. de Danilowicz, "Chez Erich Pommer," *Cinémagazine*, vol. 4, no. 27, 4 July 1924, p. 11.

10. For a discussion of the debate over what the nature of "continental" or "international" films should be, see my "National or International Films? The European Debate During the 1920s," *Film History*, vol. 8, no. 3, Autumn 1996, pp. 281–96.

11. For a more detailed discussion of Westi, see Thomas Saunders's essay in this volume.

12. For a more detailed discussion of Parufamet, see Thompson, *Exporting Entertainment*, pp. 107–1.

13. C.S. Sewell, " 'The Miracle of the Wolves,' " *Moving Picture World*, vol. 73, no. 1, 7 March 1925, pp. 39–40; advertisement for *The Miracle of the Wolves, Moving Picture World*, vol. 73, no. 6, 11 April 1925, p. 526.

14. *New York Times*, 22 June 1928, p. 5.

15. For further discussion of this development, see Joseph Garncarz's essay in this volume.

16. P.A. Harlé, "1930—France—1931," *Film Daily Yearbook*, 1931, p. 572.

17. Quoted in Francis Courtade, *Les Maledictions du cinéma français* (Paris: Éditions Alain Moreau, 1978), p. 117.

18. For accounts of this period in Britain, see Robert Murphy's "A Rival to Hollywood? The British Film Industry in the Thirties," *Screen*, vol. 24, nos 4/5, July/October 1983, pp. 96–106; and Rachel Low, *Film Making in 1930s Britain* (London: Allen and Unwin, 1985).

19. On the Soviet Union's film trade with Germany during the 1920s, see my "Government Policies and Practical Necessities in the Soviet Cinema of the 1920s," in Anna Lawton, ed., *The Red Screen: Politics, Society, Art in the Soviet Cinema* (London: Routledge, 1992), pp. 24, 28–38, and "Eisenstein's Early Films Abroad," in Ian Christie and Richard Taylor, eds, *Eisenstein Rediscovered* (London: Routledge, 1993), pp. 55–9.

20. For accounts of the IAH's film work, see Vance Kepley, Jr, "The Workers' International Relief and the Cinema of the Left 1921–1935," *Cinema Journal*, vol. 23, no. 1, Fall 1983, pp. 7–23, and Denise Hartsough, "Soviet Film Distribution and Exhibition in Germany, 1921–1933," *Historical Journal of Film, Radio and Television*, vol. 5, no. 2, 1986, pp. 131–48.

21. Willi Munzenberg, *Solidarität: Zehn Jahre Internationale Arbeitershilfe, 1921–1931* (Berlin: Newer Deutscher Verlag, 1931), p. 515.

22. On these and other exhibitions and conferences with Soviet participation, see my "Early Film Exhibitions and the 1920s European Avant-Garde Cinema," in Thomas W. Gaehtgens, ed., *Künstlerischer Austausch/Artistic Exchange: Akten des XXVIII. Internationalen Kongresses für Kunstgeschichte Berlin, 15–20. Juli 1992* (Berlin: Akademie Verlag, 1994), pp. 147–50.

23. Denise Youngblood, *Soviet Cinema in the Silent Era, 1918–1935* (Ann Arbor: UMI Research Press, 1985), p. 112.

24. Richard Taylor, *The Politics of the Soviet Cinema 1917–1929* (Cambridge: Cambridge University Press, 1979), p. 96; Youngblood, *Soviet Cinema in the Silent Era*, p. 112.

25. Taylor, *The Politics of the Soviet Cinema*, p. 65.

26. B. Kotiev, "L'organisation cinematographique en U.R.S.S.," in A. Aroseff, ed., *Le Cinema en U.R.S.S.* (Moscow, 1936), p. 215.

27. Based on annual figures from the *Foreign Commerce and Navigation of the United States* (Washington, DC: Government Printing Office), for the late 1920s and early 1930s.

28. Kepley, "The Workers' International Relief," p. 19.

29. Charles P. Kindleberger, *The World in Depression 1929–1939* (Berkeley: University of California Press, 1973), pp. 116–17; R.J. Overy, *The Nazi Economic Recovery 1932–1938* (London: Macmillan, 1982), p. 18.

30. David Welsh, *Propaganda and the German Cinema 1933–1945* (Oxford: Oxford University Press, 1983), p. 36.

31. Ibid., pp. 20–1.

32. Quoted in David Stewart Hull, *Film in the Third Reich* (Berkeley: University of California Press, 1969), pp. 18–19.
33. Ibid., p. 23.
34. Welsh, *Propaganda and the German Cinema*, p. 30.
35. Ibid., p. 31.
36. "German Films Get a Setback in City," *New York Times*, 9 May 1933, p. 20.
37. *Foreign Commerce and Navigation of the United States* (Washington: Government Printing Office, for years cited).
38. Welch, *Propaganda and the German Cinema*, p. 35.
39. Nathanael Green, *From Versailles to Vichy: The Third French Republic 1919–1940* (Arlington Heights, IL: AHM Publishing, 1970), pp. 5–12.
40. Georges Sadoul, *French Film* (London: Falcon, 1953), p. 56; Richard Abel, *French Cinema: The First Wave 1915–1929* (Princeton: Princeton University Press, 1984), pp. 62–3.
41. Quoted in Paul Leglise, *Histoire de la politique du cinéma français: Le cinéma et la III Republique* (Paris: Librairie Générale de la droit et de juriprudence, 1970), p. 123.
42. Ibid., pp. 107 and 123; Raymonde Borde, "The Golden Age: French Cinema in the 1930s," in Mary Lea Bandy, ed., *Rediscovering French Film* (New York: Museum of Modern Art, 1983), pp. 67–9.
43. Thompson, *Exporting Entertainment*, pp. 119–21, 211–12; *Film Daily Yearbook* (coverage of France, 1929–38); P.A. Harle, "France During 1937," *Film Daily Yearbook*, 1938, p. 1147.
44. On German-French Film relations in this period, see several of the essays in Sibylle M. Sturm and Arthur Wohlgemuth, eds, *Hallo Berlin? Ici Paris! Deutsch-französische Filmbeziehungen 1918–1939* (Munich: Edition Text + Kritik, 1996).
45. Courtade, *Les Maledictions du cinéma*, p. 107.

4

The Cinema and the League of Nations

Richard Maltby

> When monopolists cross frontiers and are no longer subject to the
> control of individual states, they must either become the rulers of
> the world or be controlled by some international agency.
>
> Dr Moritz J. Bonn, German economist,
> *New York Times*, 9 August 1926[1]

By the mid-1920s, cinema was recognised as both a commodity of
national and international trade and as a form of communication, and
as such both liable to regulation and at least potentially a form of art.
Governments had to consider whether to treat motion pictures as
intellectual goods, cultural products or purely commercial commodities.
The question was also discussed in different chambers of the League of
Nations, the organisation for international co-operation established
after the First World War by the Allied powers in the Treaty of
Versailles. Both within those chambers and outside them, some parties
argued that the League should involve itself extensively in the motion
picture's international affairs. Other parties, most prominent among
them the United States government and the Motion Picture Producers
and Distributors of America, Inc. (MPPDA), sought to minimise and
compartmentalise the League's role. In many respects, the debates and
discussions over cinema mirrored the history of the United States'
relationship with the League and reflected in small scale the League's
larger achievements, limitations and failures. This essay seeks to describe
the League's involvement with the international film trade, the film
organisation it established, and the various opportunities and unfulfilled
hopes occasioned by its engagement with questions of cinema.

    Delegates attending the 1926 International Motion Picture Congress
called by the League's Committee on Intellectual Co-operation

(discussed in more detail in Andrew Higson's essay in this volume) were circulated with a book called *The Public and the Motion Picture Industry*, which appropriated Dr Bonn's comments on the formation of a Franco-German iron and steel cartel to describe the American dominance of the international motion picture industry. The book's author, New York lawyer William Marston Seabury, argued bluntly that "the British and European motion picture problem is primarily, America."[2] The motion picture had attained an "immense and virtually unchecked, uncontrolled and unregulated" power to "influence the masses of the world for good or evil," but the existing industrial and commercial regime was failing to discharge the responsibilities attendant on such power. Like the problems of world disarmament and the economic reconstruction of Europe, the motion picture problem required an international solution: only an international movement to establish the legal status of the motion picture "as a new public utility" could compel the industry "to consecrate its service to the cultivation and preservation of the world's peace and the moral, intellectual and cultural development of all people."[3]

These pious conclusions were based on a detailed knowledge and extensive experience of the American film industry. Seabury had been General Counsel to the industry's first two trade associations, but though he had participated in the founding of the MPPDA in 1922, his opposition to the industry's new economic structures of oligopoly and vertical integration made him an increasingly outspoken critic of what MPPDA President Will Hays called the "organised industry." By the late 1920s, when Seabury was engaged in a variety of projects to distribute European films in the US and to facilitate American financing of European production, his attitude combined a proprietorial sense of dispossession, a Progressive stance of principled moral superiority over the cartel of trustifiers and Midwest political fixers who were now in charge, and an element of genteel anti-Semitism that pervaded the Protestant elite's dealings with the industry.[4] Seabury's comprehension of the interrelationship between questions of trade, culture and public welfare gave his analysis a broader and clearer perspective than was exhibited either by other American critics or by the policies of any European government. Like the broadcast reformers of the late 1920s and early 1930s, his critique of the improprieties of a capitalist media system in a democratic society anticipated much later criticism of the structure of the American media; like their critique, too, it proved too radical to have any substantial medium- or long-term effect on the development of that system.[5] Among the congeries of Protestant American reform groups calling for federal regulation of the movies, his views were often echoed, although the echoes usually lost the clarity and coherence of Seabury's own formulation. He was substantially responsible for the creation, in March 1927, of the Motion Picture Research Council, but he rapidly lost control of the organisation to Dr William H. Short, who was more concerned to develop a programme of scientific studies on the effects of motion pictures than to pursue Seabury's objective of "the practical curtailment and control of the existing international monopoly, the prevention of its continued expansion and the production and exhibition throughout the world of new and better pictures."[6] Believing that "it is more important to study the causes of existing conditions which involve the economic and commercial phases of the subject, than it is to examine further into the effects of motion pictures," Seabury saw little value in Short's research programme, which in due course became the Payne Fund Studies, and he abandoned any association with the project in December 1928.[7]

Seabury was not without either influence or access to political power. His elder brother Samuel, a lawyer, judge and politician, achieved national fame in 1932, when his investigation into political corruption in New York brought about the removal of Mayor Jimmy Walker from office, and made him briefly a candidate for the Democratic presidential nomination.[8] William Seabury shared his brother's intellectual and ideological heritage, in which the influence of the Social Gospel joined with Henry George's radical economics in a hostility to the private ownership of public utilities that was often denounced as "socialistic" by more conservative politicians and businessmen. Samuel Seabury's political reputation was built on his advocacy of the operation of such natural monopolies as railroads, the telegraph, urban transport and power supply by government rather than by private capital. This, he argued, was not socialism, but a necessary protection of the individual rights of each citizen. Throughout his political life he argued for "the exercise of social power not merely in relation to territorial or governmental units, but to the industrial functions . . . upon the proper discharge of which the prosperity and happiness of our whole people depend."[9] His brother similarly argued that the motion picture's universally acknowledged capacity for good or evil influence endowed it with a public interest which materially affected its status, placing it in the same category as power, water and transportation companies, "the primary and paramount duty" of which was the provision of public service.[10] The recognition of the industry as a public utility would, he argued, have two effects: one would provide the service at a reasonable price, subjecting profit to government regulation; the other would improve "the moral, educational and cultural quality of the pictures produced and exhibited."[11]

Seabury's perception of the motion picture as a public utility was not in itself far-fetched. Indeed, in 1927 the Treasurer of the MPPDA, J. Homer Platten, published an article entitled "Motion Pictures: A New Public Utility?" in the *Banker's Magazine*.[12] The concept of a public utility was an early twentieth-century American invention: as historian Morton Keller has observed, the term had no place in European law, and as late as 1904 it had no judicial definition. The application of new transportation and communication technologies to the provision of essential public services repeatedly challenged prevailing legal categories and raised new policy issues about the appropriate extent and instruments of government regulation.[13]

The late 1920s witnessed an extended debate over the legal status of radio, the movies' closest rival for the mass circulation of public entertainment, in which it was frequently suggested that radio should be identified as a public utility. Using a phrase borrowed from public utilities law, the Federal Radio Commission was charged with allocating licences according to the "public interest, convenience, or necessity" on its establishment in 1927, but it was not then a settled legal question that the designation of the frequency band as a public resource would be the legal basis that differentiated radio and cinema for regulatory purposes. The parallel Seabury drew between radio and cinema occupied perfectly tenable intellectual ground in the late 1920s, but the extent of his economic radicalism may be indicated by the fact that his argument relied on the proposition that the motion picture theatres of the world should be understood as "the market which belongs in common to all producers of pictures," and therefore a resource comparable to the frequency band.[14] To an even greater extent than those Americans arguing for broadcast reform, Seabury was questioning a fundamental tenet of the capitalist political economy.

In the book he circulated to the delegates at the Paris Congress in 1926, Seabury argued that the solution to the problems of sustaining a production industry in Britain, France or elsewhere in Europe lay not at home but in access to the American market. Several European states were by this stage either enforcing or considering some sort of trade barrier to American film imports. Seabury, however, deplored contingent and quota systems as ineffective, since they forced exhibitors to show inferior and unprofitable domestic pictures and encouraged American producers to evade quota restrictions and buy a portion of the domestic market by producing pictures in the countries concerned:

> The effect of this is to create more pictures which are inevitably American wherever they are made, pictures produced at lower cost than that at which similar pictures can be produced in America, yet pictures for which the world market is open because they are made by American producers who control the American market.[15]

As a remedy he proposed that each of the major European countries prepare a body of legislation designed to disable the market advantages achieved by the American companies' vertical integration: prohibitions on the unification of production, distribution and exhibition, the ownership of theatres by foreign nationals, block- and blind-booking, and laws designed to tax the large American companies on their gross rental income thereby preventing them passing the tax burden on to either exhibitors or the public.[16] He viewed the 1926 Paris Congress as an opportunity to establish an informal union of European nations adopting "a law, substantially uniform in principle . . . for enactment unless specified results to the nationals of the several nations acting in unison were obtainable."[17]

Seabury did not intend that this draconian legislation be passed, but rather that the threat of its passage be used to force the American companies to negotiate. His scheme envisaged the creation of three blocks of interest in the world trade in cinema—the US, Britain and the Empire, and continental Europe—which would negotiate with each other for equitable shares of the international market. He recognised that the British and European industries were not sufficiently powerful to construct counter-hegemonic blocks without legislative support. Even so, he felt the desired result could best be achieved through the negotiation of an agreement "which would compel American nationals to afford world distribution and exhibition for an agreed quantity of European pictures during a period of years, in consideration of the abandonment or modification of drastic policies of domestic legislation."

Europeans, he acknowledged, did not want to reach world markets through American agencies, nor did the American companies wish to act as agents for the international distribution of European pictures.

"But Europeans want to reach world markets now controlled by American nationals and American nationals want to retain all of the market that Europe and other nations will permit them to retain." If the European countries resuscitated their domestic markets through legislation punitive to the Americans, they would still remain excluded from the American market, "the most lucrative market in the world, without which no producers can compete successfully with American producers who enjoy that market." His alternative of an agreement to apportion world trade "on a basis of justice to Europe fortified and backed by Europe's power to enforce its just demands" was better for all parties, as well as being "wiser and more in keeping with a real and not pretended international amity."[18] In the name of international peace, Seabury sought a rational system of trade, in which each nation secured "the representation upon the screens of the world which the merit of the productions of the nationals of each justifies."[19]

I

Although Seabury envisaged a significant role for the League of Nations in creating a permanent organisation to deal with questions of cinema, his proposals ran counter to one of the League's primary economic policies, the reduction of barriers to free trade. The League's two permanent "technical" committees on economic and financial matters carried out investigations into tariffs, exchange controls and commercial policy, developing a body of doctrine which one historian of the League has called "a compendium of financial orthodoxy."[20] The high point of its expression came during the first World Economic Conference in May 1927, which concluded that the general level of prosperity and trade was far below the world's productive capacity, and that the primary remedy was to clear away the mass of obstacles to international trade, above all by reversing the general tendency of post-war governments to increase tariffs.[21]

Among the steps taken to put these principles into effect was a Conference on Import and Export Prohibitions, held in October and November 1927, which drew up a convention to abolish trade restrictions. Although US industries remained protected behind the high tariff walls erected by the 1922 Fordney–McCumber Act, an "open door" trade policy was obviously conducive to American economic penetration of European markets. The motion picture industry saw the possibilities of immediate advantage through the abolition of quota and contingent laws, which appeared to the US government to be in violation of the convention's prohibition on internal regulations intended to function as "a means of disguised prohibition or arbitrary restriction."[22] As Hugh Wilson, the American delegate at the second conference on the convention in July 1928, argued, if the convention only governed "the mere crossing of frontiers for articles of trade," but left nations free to prevent the distribution of those articles within their frontiers, this would mean that American manufacturers could export "typewriters, motor cars or any other form of our products freely to the world," but that importing countries could use internal regulations to control which cars and typewriters could be sold within their frontiers. Such a "legalistic interpretation" of the convention would "make it not worth the paper it is written on."[23]

At the first conference on the convention, the Americans' understanding appeared to be widely shared: the German government, for example, recognised that ratifying the convention would involve abandoning the contingent legislation it used to limit American film imports. The French decree of February 1928, establishing the Cinema Commission (discussed in Jens Ulff-Møller's essay in this volume) appeared to have been carefully constructed so as to avoid being in technical breach of the convention while at the same time, at least from the American perspective, violating the spirit of the agreement.[24] The French government raised the issue of their film restrictions as a matter to be discussed at the second conference on the convention, and the MPPDA feared that other European countries would "fall into line" with the French position, "and the whole question will be thrown wide open . . . in spite of our effort to keep it out of the treaty." Although Hays's negotiations with the French in April produced a modification of the decree's terms, "so that it would be physically possible for us to carry on our business," the MPPDA continued to agitate against this "vicious piece of legislation," since it set a dangerous precedent for other European countries as well as for other commodities.[25] Frederick Herron, head of the MPPDA's Foreign Department, believed that if the decree was not overturned, "Italy, Austria, Czecho-Slovakia, Spain and Germany and probably others will immediately follow in the same tracks," and there would be "less possibility of the repeal of restrictive measures in force elsewhere," including Britain.[26]

When the subject came up for discussion at the second conference on the convention in July, the French delegate, Daniel Serruys, maintained that this protectionism was not "of an economic character";

the "moral inheritance" of his country was at stake, he declared, and the decree's restrictions were thus "a means of spiritual defence" designed to protect the "manners, morals and traditions" of the French people."[27] The Americans regarded this argument as merely "camouflage," since national censors had the power to eliminate any material they thought might undermine national morality or customs.[28] Quotas were designed to protect their national film industries as well as their culture, and thus the control was fundamentally commercial, not cultural, in purpose:

> There is little question that existing film regulations have been brought about and to a large extent dictated by the film industries of the countries concerned. The fact that European governments would undoubtedly consent to remove all forms of control except normal censorship if they were permitted to do so by the film industries of their respective countries is a forceful commentary on their argument that these controls are indispensable to the protection of national culture.[29]

American indignation was increased by their knowledge that in 1926, during his term as Chairman of the League Economic Committee, Serruys had denounced film contingents as "one of the bad habits of Europe," and expressed the hope that the Prohibitions Convention would, when ratified, "put an end to these exemptions of films."[30] Indeed, Embassy officials in Paris understood that Serruys had pointed out the discrepancies between the decree and the convention during its drafting.[31]

In the event, the conference concluded that its terms of reference did not permit it to make a decision in the matter. The German, Austrian, Italian and Indian delegates, however, expressed their broad agreement with the French position, and Wilson reported the sense of the conference as being "that nations have a right to maintain some form of protection for their culture and traditions."[32] The American commercial attaché in Berlin, F.W. Allport, realistically assessed "the ready support of other European countries" for the French position as having "negatived any hopes" that the convention would bring about the end of film import controls.[33] In the longer term, the convention was a casualty of the increasing reluctance of national governments to abandon the immediate political benefits of protectionism when faced with the pressures of the Depression: it was ratified by only seventeen states, one short of the minimum number required to bring it into full operation.[34]

The MPPDA's argument insisted that cultural protectionism should not trespass on the liberty of international commerce; it also sought to keep moral and economic issues physically separated in different pieces of legislation and in different parts of any organisation with which it had to deal, including the League of Nations. Prior to the 1926 Paris Congress, the MPPDA had argued that, since the congress was organised by the League's Committee on Intellectual Co-operation, it should properly restrict its discussions to intellectual and artistic issues, leaving commercial questions to the Economic Committee and welfare topics to the Child Welfare Committee.[35] Wilson's attack on the French decree, particularly his comparison between the distribution of films and typewriters, depended on such a separation: as he put it, "eliminate the question of public order and public morals and the cases are not only analogous but identical."[36] William Seabury's position was almost diametrically opposite. It was the essence of his argument that welfare and intellectual issues "are inseparably linked and interwoven with the economic and commercial questions involved, including questions of interest to the International Labor Office and to the Committee on Transit and Communications." The international problems presented by the cinema could not, he maintained, be dealt with piecemeal, but could only be adequately addressed by a new organisation, placed under the League's direction.[37]

Movies were both commercial commodities and cultural goods, and their two forms were intertwined, as Seabury articulated perhaps more clearly than any other contemporary commentator. They were, of course, not uniquely both. The same argument could be, and was, made over American automobiles and, indeed, typewriters.[38] But the movies were the most conspicuous commodity form of the American economic and cultural penetration of Europe: agencies of modernism, declaring modernity to be American property, and them- selves purveyed as a form of international capitalism. As Seabury understood, this model was fundamentally opposed to the concept of a local public utility which he sought to internationalise through the League of Nations.

II

The history of the League of Nations is most commonly written as an account of the failure of collective security to prevent international conflict. Two achievements must, however, be set against the League's inability to persuade its member nations to "sacrifice their *amour-propre* for the sake of the peace of the world." First, there is the work of its social and economic organisations such as the International Labour Organisation and the Health Organisation; and secondly, the record of the period between the stabilisation of European currencies in 1924 and the onset of the Depression, during which Geneva was the centre of international relations, providing what historian Paul Weindling has called "a sort of interwar magic Mountain—where diplomats and welfare experts interacted."[39] If in retrospect the political agreements formulated under the "spirit of Geneva" from the Locarno Treaty to the Kellogg–Briand Pact appear hollow and self-contradictory, they were viewed far more optimistically at the time. In this short period of economic expansion and international political stability, most of the League's organisations also began to function effectively.

In 1918 Jan Smuts had argued that the League should become "a great organ of the ordinary peaceful life of civilization . . . It is not sufficient for the League merely to be a sort of *deus ex machina*, called in in very grave emergencies when the spectre of war appears; if it is to last, it must be much more. It must be part and parcel of the common international life of states, it must be an ever visible, living, working organ of the policy of civilization."[40] This was a supremely "functionalist" idea: that international political integration could develop most effectively through relatively contained forms of co-operation in specific areas of policy, such as economic welfare, health and education. The League's functionalism was developed through its permanent organisations, which extended the bureaucracy of government into the international sphere, co-ordinating the work of the many international social, humanitarian, scientific and technical organisations which had come into being in the early twentieth century. It was in these areas of its activity that the League's achievements were most substantial and enduring, providing models for the organisations of the United Nations that would continue their work. As US Secretary of State Cordell Hull declared in 1939, through its social and economic institutions the League was "responsible for the development of mutual exchange and discussion of ideas and methods to a greater extent and in more fields of humanitarian and scientific endeavour than any other organization in history."[41]

To optimists in the late 1920s, the League was becoming "a point of convergence between Knowledge and Power," foreshadowing a new co-operative international system in which public and private agencies worked together to a common goal and power politics played no part:

> The doctors, the bankers, the child welfare experts and the "intellectual co-operators" were all of them concerned with finding the best solution for their own particular problem along the lines of their expertise. They were fellow professionals, animated by a common spirit. . . . Little by little, so it began to be believed, the morass of "high politics" would dry up along its edges, as one issue after another was drained off to Geneva. Thus eventually there would be a world-wide co-operative system held together by a network of contacts between government departments (other than Foreign Offices), professional organizations and individual experts.[42]

It was these aspirations of the League that Seabury addressed in his grand plan for equalizing the balance of power in the international motion picture business.

As well as through its economic conferences, the League's concern with cinema surfaced in three of its permanent committees. The Advisory Committee on the Traffic in Women and Children and the Child Welfare Committee concerned themselves, *inter alia*, with the social impact of the cinema within a general approach which approved the regulation of morality by the state.[43] In 1926 the Child Welfare Committee published a report which reproduced the arguments of the American industry's sternest critics:

> The life of the child today is being invaded by the cinema and unfortunately by a cinema almost entirely unadapted to its needs. . . . The film, which might interest and captivate children and the general public in so many different ways, has violently abused its power of pushing sensation to the point of exasperation through the medium of the picture and of thus giving rise to criminal suggestions even under the cloak of morality.[44]

The committee then passed several resolutions on the cinema. Among the encouragements to the international exchange of educational films and the passage of "the necessary measures of hygiene and security" in cinema buildings, it recommended that "in each State, offices for control or preliminary censorship should be established, whose decisions would be enforced by fixed penalties, with a view to preventing the exhibition of demoralising films; the views of educationalists and parents should, as far as possible, be represented in these offices." It also recommended that an international understanding should be entered into by the various national offices with a view to communicating to each other the decisions adopted and the penalties imposed in their respective countries. It was proposed that such understanding should eventually be extended by means of international agreements "to prevent the circulation and use of demoralising films."[45]

In 1928, the committee published a second report on "the Cinematograph Question", which catalogued the detrimental effects the screen could have on children, from ocular tension to sleep disturbance to an excessive appeal to the "lowest instincts and least noble passions" of young viewers. The influence of the cinema on child criminality, it concluded, could "hardly be doubted": "the child acts under the influence of a film and reproduces mechanically, so to speak, the example given on the screen."[46]

The League's Committee on Intellectual Co-operation, established in 1922 with the objective of strengthening the League's influence for peace through the work of teachers, artists, scientists and authors, also commissioned a report on the "Relation of the Cinematograph to Intellectual Life" from Julien Luchaire, Inspector General of Public Education in France and the newly appointed Director of the committee's International Institute in Paris. Luchaire's report acknowledged cinema as "a powerful medium for the diffusion of moral, social and even political ideas or modes of thought," arguing "the mere possibility that the cinema might become a great new *universal art* should earn it the attention of all who have the intellectual future of humanity at heart." In his analysis, the technological fact of its silence meant that "differences of language, which form a barrier between men, do not exist for the cinema," while the commercial fact of its international distribution obliged producers "to compose their works in a form that will enable them to be understood and appreciated by spectators of the most varied races and countries. The consequence is that the national character of films is reduced to almost nothing, or is confined to the picturesque element." Luchaire suggested that the committee give support to the suggestion emanating from the International Congress of Cinematograph Managers held in Paris in October 1923 for the creation of "a permanent international organisation . . . to study all questions of interest in connection with the cinematograph industry," including issues of intellectual property rights, taxation and censorship. Luchaire's proposal of an international congress of "promoters, producers, authors, artists, critics and directors" held "at the Committee's invitation and under its auspices," resulted in the Paris Congress of 1926.[47]

In preparing for the congress, Seabury had hoped that it would be composed primarily of statesmen, government representatives, educators and disinterested men of public affairs, "competent to discuss the problems affecting the intellectual and artistic as well as the economic and commercial phases of the subject." Instead, it was chiefly attended by "industrialists who cared little or nothing for its intellectual aspects." Although the majority of its resolutions bore the "imprint of the intellectuals who were directing the work of the Congress," their achievements were fatally compromised by the group of industrialists charged with studying "the organisation and function of an International Bureau of the motion-picture connected with the League of Nations." This group insisted that the purposes of such an organisation should include "protecting in general the interests of the cinema industry." This phrasing placed the proposed organisation outside the sphere of the League's approval and thus, at least from Seabury's perspective, "spelled the apparent and temporary failure of the Congress," a failure engineered, he felt, by the MPPDA's "secret trade diplomacy," despite their official absence from the congress.[48]

Regardless of this outcome, Seabury believed that the congress had provided the intellectual justification for the creation of "a permanent and truly representative committee of the League of Nations" to consider all aspects of cinema.[49] The entity he envisaged would not include any representative of the cinema trade of any nation; its work would in part be modelled on that of the League's Opium Committee, which had established an international board of control to regulate the importation, sale and preparation of opium. Like the Committee on Intellectual Co-operation, the cinema committee would develop national committees in member countries to oversee the inspection and certification of films, in accordance with a statute to be enacted by each member state "prohibiting in simple terms the production, distribution and exhibition of pictures which are injurious to the public in any respect." As well as collecting and supplying information "on all phases of the subject from all part of the world," the League's committee would circulate the decisions of each national censorship board, along with "advanced information from the country of origin of all pictures . . . about to be offered for importation." It would also determine whether trade practices such as block-booking were unfair methods of competition and recommend their prohibition.

Beyond even this, Seabury proposed that each state's declaration of the motion picture as a public utility would achieve an economic reconstruction of the world's film industries. In countries not opposed to complete governmental control, he proposed that "complete power to deal with the whole subject" be vested in a single administrative official, preferably the Minister of Education. This power might extend to the operation of distribution as a state monopoly. In countries opposed to such state control, he suggested "a re-establishment of fair competition in every branch of the trade" by legislation. Either course of action would force the major American distributors to negotiate agreements by which "the existing monopolization of the screens of the world" would be substantially reduced, and "the cinema production industries of the producing nations of the world revived and restored to a profitable condition. Thus a reapportionment of the world's trade in this pursuit becomes not only possible but inevitable." Moreover, "pictures which are better in the moral, educational and cultural sense than those now prevalent will surely result and the production industries of the world will prosper once more."[50] In Seabury's grandiose vision, the egalitarian economic spirit of Henry George met the spirit of Geneva to universal benefit. But like so many of the League's own projects, it could not overcome the traditional pursuit of national interest, augmented by the machinations of the Americans. In May 1927, when the Second International Cinema Congress was postponed for a year, the Committee on Intellectual Co-operation representative resigned from its organising committee, and the League took up an Italian proposal in the effort to create a permanent organisation to consider the question of cinema. The body it did create was a pale substitute for the entity Seabury had envisaged. In the pursuit of Italian self-interest, it effectively contained the League's engagement with cinema.

III

Formed in the image of the Institute for Intellectual Co-operation, the International Educational Cinematographic Institute (IECI) was the brainchild of journalist Luciano de Feo and Baron Giacomo Paolucci di Calbodi, who had together persuaded Mussolini in 1925 to establish LUCE (L'Unione Cinematografica Educativa—the Union of Educational Cinematography) as a para-state agency to produce documentaries and newsreels "for the purposes of beneficence and national patriotic propaganda."[51] The Italian state expressed a much greater concern with instructional, factual and propaganda films than with its feature industry, and LUCE was the principal embodiment of Mussolini's belief that the cinema was "l'arma più forte" (the strongest weapon) in his campaigns of propaganda.[52] The Italian proposal to establish an Institute under the auspices of the League referred to LUCE as a precedent in the experimental use of "moving pictures for the intellectual development of the nation," and on its establishment de Feo and Paolucci di Calbodi relinquished their positions as director and Vice-President of LUCE to become Director and Vice-Secretary of the IECI.[53] The IECI was thus one of several initiatives by the Fascist state (the founding of the Mostra cinematografica di Venezia in 1932 was another) to draw attention to its own contribution to international cinema.[54]

Crucial to its success, the Italian proposal included an offer of funds for the establishment and maintenance of the Institute, making it possible "for all nations to participate, under conditions of perfect equality and without having any pecuniary burden on them or on the budget of the League of Nations."[55] This offer of funding eliminated a putative rival bid for a similar organisation to be based in Paris under the direct auspices of the International Institute of Intellectual Co-operation.[56] The League Council accepted the Italian offer on 28 September 1927, and draft statutes for the Institute were drawn up in Rome in February 1928.

Initially, the functions of the IECI were imprecisely defined. The original proposal suggested that it would be "a center of information for different problems of the cinema, giving the best opportunity for a mutual interchange and diffusion of every kind of film: scholastic, hygienic, historical, archaeological, artistic, and, in a general way, educational."[57] According to a report received by the MPPDA, Mussolini saw cinema as a new instrument "to transform conditions of intellectual and material life of humanity," and envisaged the Institute spreading cinema through the world's rural areas.[58] Other reports in late 1927 suggested that it would produce educational, scientific, and possibly propaganda films, for world-wide distribution as League of Nations productions made in Italy, and provoked fears that Italy would use the Institute as an agency of propaganda for Fascism.[59] More promisingly, the proposal had declared that the Institute would benefit not only governments but also "public and private institutions and commercial enterprises, which will be able to find in it a powerful help in their business."[60]

The Institute's draft statute described its object as being "to encourage the production, distribution and exchange between the various countries of educational films concerning instruction, art, industry, agriculture, commerce, health, social education, etc., by any means which the Governing Body may consider necessary."[61] It would also have a technical section and an information section with a film library. Its international governing body included representatives from the Committee on Intellectual Co-operation and the Child Welfare Committee. The Italian government guaranteed annual funding to the Institute of 600,000 lire, and provided additional funds for its establishment.[62] Approved by the League Council in August 1928, the Institute was formally opened by King Victor Emmanuel of Italy on 5 November 1928.

In April 1929, de Feo spoke to the Child Welfare Committee about the Institute's proposed investigations of "the great problem of the social character of the cinematograph." Paraphrasing much of the committee's 1928 report, he spoke in disapproving tones of Hollywood stars as "false prophets of the screen," and argued for a censorship administered by "psychologists, educationalists and pediatrists." The Institute would, he said, collect "everything that has been written on the subject all over the world," and examine:

> the nature of cinema as related to the social life of today; the influence of the cinema on the spiritual and mental state of children and young people; precocious criminality and morbid exaltation; the development of abnormal nervous and psychic powers; the development of sensual tendencies; the influence of the cinema on the mentality of country folk and uneducated persons in general; the influence of the cinema on the formation of a civic, political, religious and national consciousness; the influence of the cinema on the formation of manners, habits, standards of living, extravagance, luxury, character, etc. . . . Our Institute desires . . . to attack all these problems systematically, with the help of qualified experts; . . . to carry out enquiries throughout the world, even in the remotest countries; to make a world investigation into the exact views held by all the principal students, psychologists, philosophers,

teachers, criminologists, sociologists, etc. . . . We hope thus to secure . . . an effective system of cooperation with the great cinema industry in researches designed to bring about a constant improvement in the type of film produced.[63]

With such an agenda, shared with the Child Welfare Committee, Seabury and American reform groups such as the Federal Motion Picture Commission, the Institute represented a significant potential threat to American commercial interests. It might, for instance, have played a significant role in the international legitimisation and dissemination of the Payne Fund research and other social critiques of the American industry. But de Feo's rhetoric was much more voluble than his actions, in large part because the MPPDA had taken early action to defuse the Institute's dangerous potential and attach de Feo to its own public relations campaign. During his official visit to the US to study the film situation in the winter of 1928–9, de Feo was given "every aid and help" by the MPPDA's staff, who showed him the Eastman and Harvard educational film projects, and took him to Washington, where "a number of days were spent . . . going through different government departments interested in motion pictures." In New York he visited several of the major companies to "get in touch with the type of work the members of the Association were carrying on."[64]

Following this visit, Carl Milliken, the MPPDA's Secretary, was appointed to the Institute's governing body, and George Canty, the Department of Commerce's Trade Commissioner for Motion Pictures in Europe, became a member of its Executive Committee "at the suggestion of the Sir Eric Drummond, the League's Secretary General." Milliken's appointment effectively gave the American industry a veto power over the IECI's activities, rendering it useless in the eyes of American reformers, since he could block "any serious investigation" by the Institute's conferences or publications of what they saw as "the business of the American producers of motion picture filth."[65] In 1938 Alfred Zimmern cited Milliken's appointment as an example of the League's unfortunate expediency in allowing special interests to be represented on its advisory committees, since this all too easily provided dangerous opportunities for corruption.[66]

Like most of its public relations activities, the MPPDA's involvement with both the League and the IECI was essentially defensive: to ensure that the objectives of the organisations concerned remained compatible with those of the companies the MPPDA represented. In July 1929

Frederick Herron reported that "de Feo has already done a number of very wonderful things for the American industry," using his influence with Mussolini to "head off" a quota law.[67] In addition, Herron reported, "it was through his influence, largely, that Dr. Short's vicious report [*A Generation of Motion Pictures: A Review of Social Values in Recreational Films*] was subdued in Geneva and referred to the Institute in Rome, where it is now buried." "I am," reported Herron, "feeding him all material possible and aiding him in every way that I can."[68]

In December 1929, de Feo again demonstrated his co-operative attitude at a conference held in Paris to draft a convention for exempting "films of an educational character" from import duties. This convention was an outgrowth from the two earlier conferences on the abolition of import and export restrictions. While the Americans wanted all restrictions on film imports removed, the danger of the educational film convention was that European producers might succeed in including "entertainment films with pedagogic elements," within the convention, and then create "a super censor board to choose the type of entertainment films the cinemas should show and silently condemn those not chosen." At the conference, the MPPDA's Parisian representative Harold L. Smith had to insist that the convention contain a narrow definition of what qualified as an educational film, at the same time as arguing that "all our entertainment films are educational" in order to avoid the convention implying that only educational films made a contribution "to physical, intellectual and moral progress and the mutual understanding of the peoples." With de Feo's assistance, Smith succeeded. He reported to Herron:

> The Conference got through all right . . . de Feo was fine. He is even accused of favoring Americans and he told them frankly he favors collaborating with us. The trip was worth while and I believe that further talks with the people there will make them realize that collaboration with us is absolutely necessary.[69]

In practice, De Feo sought to limit the role of the Institute to that of "an information, enquiry and co-ordination centre; that and no more." Invited by the Committee on Intellectual Co-operation to extend the Institute's research into "questions connected with broadcasting in the service of educational cinematography, to television and to the recording of speech and sounds," he responded that broadcasting "is not our business . . . questions related to television . . . do not fall within our province." In the same statement he observed that "theatrical and commercial cinematography . . . also lies outside our specific duties."[70] As a further qualification, he suggested that, in studying the question of the cinema's influence, "the Institute has seen fit to leave the theoretical aspects of the question to its collaborators and to contributors to its Review, its own work consisting in the collection of observations from those concerned, those, namely, who make up the vast body of active and passive screen spectators."[71]

IV

Under de Feo's editorship, the Institute's publication, the *International Review of Educational Cinematography*, declared its neutrality on all issues of importance in florid terms. In January 1930 the *Review* initiated an enquiry into "the most crucial of all the questions connected with the cinematograph . . . whether the cinema is a blessing or a curse; whether or not it may exercise on the exquisitely delicate and personal sensibility of the child an influence that goes beyond those normal reflexes of sensation and emotivity that are harmless to the unfledged spirit."[72] It distributed more than 200,000 copies of a questionnaire addressed to schoolchildren, and supplemented this with others aimed at teachers and psychologists, prepared by Professor Maurice Rouvroy of Brussels University and designed to survey existing research into the effects of cinema on "the minds and lives of children."[73] In the early responses to this survey there was widespread agreement that the cinema's influence was deleterious, but de Feo carefully positioned the *Review* as a forum for debate and discussion, while veering toward the conclusion that the cinema was not "the prime offender that its detractors would have it to be."[74] In March 1930 he published an essay by Dr Albert Hellwig, Chief Justice of the Provincial Tribunal of Potsdam, arguing that "though there may be a certain connection between criminal propensities and the film, especially as regards child crime . . . I am . . . convinced that the influence of the film in this domain has been greatly exaggerated."[75]

The *Review* published a regular digest of research and actively encouraged debate: "all information, news, and matters of real documentary value that may assist in the enquiry and afford the material for future study are welcome."[76] This included the material that Herron was "feeding" the Institute from the MPPDA, which it reported with the same reverence afforded the eminent European academics: in its first issue the *Review* published an essay by Carl Milliken on "Crime and the Cinema in the United States"; in March 1930 it asserted authoritatively that Hollywood "has directed its production along lines more consonant with social and humane necessities . . . There is an ever increasing slump in films dealing with crime and sexual themes."[77] In January 1931 de Feo described the Production Code as "probably much more effective than any of the many official censorship systems of other countries," and reproduced Milliken's claim that increasing attendance figures were "a consequence of a higher moral and artistic standard of film production."[78] In August 1932 the *Review* published an article by Herron in defence of block-booking. Although de Feo declared the Institute's neutrality by announcing that the *Review* would also publish "polemical articles disagreeing either wholly or in part with Mr. Herron's ideas," it did not, in fact, do so.[79] In March 1935 the *Review* published an article in favour of the American system of film regulation, arguing for an emphasis to be placed on parental responsibility, and suggesting that state censorship was "gratuitous."[80] Two months later, another article commented favourably on Hollywood's response to the Legion of Decency campaign.[81]

American research hostile to the industry was on occasion derided in the *Review*. In what may be a misreported reference to Charles C. Peters' Payne Fund Study into *Motion Pictures and Standards of Morality*, the *Review* observed that "not all enquiries . . . are distinguished by rigorous scientific methods":

> A questionnaire has, for instance, been circulated in the schools of Norwalk, USA, with the object of eliciting to what extent the film influences the outlook on life of children aged between ten and fourteen years. This questionnaire, which comprised some hundred questions, roused the indignation of the parents, who protested against their children answering such enquiries as the following: "Do you think it right for a young man to throw over his sweetheart merely because she allows another man to kiss her?"[82]

In August 1933 the *Review* reported that Dr Short's paper describing the Payne Fund Studies to the Society of Motion Picture Engineers had been criticised as unscientific by Dr Alfred N. Goldsmith of the American Association for the Advancement of Science.[83] Apart from an occasional mention of some of its statistical research into children's preferences for different types of movies, the *Review* seems, remarkably, to have ignored the Payne Fund Studies—an absence that suggests the extent of the MPPDA's influence.[84] It did publish material from European researchers that was similar in both opinion and technique to the Payne Fund work: an article describing research undertaken in France by Marianna Hoffman included quotations from girls in reformatory schools almost identical in tone and content to those in Herbert Blumer's investigations into the effects of movies on "sexual delinquents":

> It was the cinema that corrupted me. I loved to see fine clothes and beautiful actors and actresses, but what I enjoyed most of all were fine ladies and gentlemen amusing themselves amid luxurious surroundings with champagne and music. I used to go over and over again to see films of that kind. I longed unspeakably to enjoy such pleasures myself and I sought ways of gratifying my desire. That's how I found my way to the reformatory.
> . . . What I enjoyed most were the scenes in which the actors and actresses kissed. After every love film I used to walk about until I found some man with whom I could act the film I had been watching.[85]

The MPPDA could not regulate European opinion, but it kept as tight a rein as it could on the opinions expressed by Americans at the Institute's conferences and in its publications. For example, in October 1931 the Institute hosted a Cinema Congress organised by the Cinema Commission of the International Council of Women. Dr Elsa Matz, a member of the Reichstag, spoke in favour of a proposal to establish "an international agreement to harmonise the principles and the methods of censure." Acknowledging that while such a proposal would encounter "extraordinary difficulties," she asserted that existing German legislation was in harmony with the proposals to regulate both film content and industry trade practices contained in the Hudson Bill sponsored by anti-industry reform groups in the US. Such views were outside the MPPDA's control, but they were much more alarmed by American newspaper coverage of the speech by the chief American delegate, Mrs Ambrose (Frances White) Diehl, Chairman of the Motion Picture Committee of the National Council of Women, and wife of the President of Carnegie Steel. Herron reported to Hays that Mrs Diehl had been quoted by the *New York Times* as having declared, "I do not believe . . . that the mothers of civilized countries will stand for the trash which most motion picture producers are now giving us."

Exasperated, he suggested that "we be a little more careful of the type of individuals that we pick out" in future.

> Mrs. Diehl has done as bad a job in Rome as it is possible for any one to have pulled off . . . I went to great lengths in writing to de Feo at the Institute, Mitchel at the Embassy and Curioni, Metro's representative in Rome, asking them to go the limit for Mrs. Diehl; saying she was reliable, etc. This statement of hers is not only a direct insult to them, but to our Foreign Departments here. . . . The next time, perhaps, it would be better to send Mrs. Gilman [Catherine Cooke (Robbins) Gilman, Chairman of the Parent–Teachers' Association National Committee on Motion Pictures and one of the MPPDA's most trenchant American opponents] on these tramping tours. At least we will know what she is going to say.

Herron also complained that Reginald Wright Kaufman, ostensibly in Rome as the European representative of *Motion Picture Monthly*, but also retained by the MPPDA to manage its press relations at the conference, had failed to secure the co-operation of the American press.[86] Kaufman, apparently oblivious to the American press coverage of the event, reported a quite different version of events to Hays, in which "thanks to Mrs. Diehl and her collaborators" and "the goodwill of Mr. de Feo (organizer) and Mrs. Dreyfuss-Barney (Chairman)," the hostile tone taken by most delegates at the opening of the conference "was decidedly softened" by its end. De Feo, he reported, had also helped to restrict Mrs Gilman's protests by threatening to eject her if she protested against Milliken's membership of the Institute's governing body.[87]

As printed in the *Review* and the *Motion Picture Herald*, Diehl's speech was a model of reasonableness, balancing the "screen's affirmative services" against its "harmful tendencies," and suggesting that motion pictures in general (rather than just in Hollywood) should preserve a respect for religion and the home, and represent women "with true proportionate stress on the great urges that motivate her life" rather than "solely in the role of sex protagonist."[88] However, both the Associated Press and United Press reports suggested that her speech was critical of American movies, provoking editorial commentary hostile to the industry and a small rash of headlines such as "Woman Urges Movie Reform" and "Calls Movie Censorship Complete Failure".[89]

Recording the conference's resolutions to prohibit block-booking and draw up an international convention on censorship, the *Christian Century* triumphantly reported that "Mr. Milliken and the Hays organization . . . slipped a cog in their smooth-running machine."[90] The event indicated the extent to which such conferences could be flashpoints for the expression—and more importantly the reporting—of unfavourable opinion, and the scale of the MPPDA's surveillance.

V

In commenting on the resolutions of the International Council of Women's Congress, de Feo remarked that that the IECI "cannot for the moment give its opinion" on the relative merits of official censorship or self-regulation: "a real solution must necessarily be the outcome of a long and profound discussion of the whole matter, a discussion to which this review opens its pages and which alone can bring about an international discussion of the problem."[91] He also promised "a very detailed work," which would compare the "different systems of censure" in use in sixty-two countries and draw conclusions as to "the best methods to be employed" on an international basis. Like other of the Institute's large-scale projects, including the two-volume *Enciclopedia del cinema* edited by Rudolf Arnheim, it was never completed. The Institute's policy of studied neutrality may have been a matter of political expediency in Mussolini's Italy, but it was also well suited to American interests, since it effectively neutralised the Institute as a source of criticism. While the Institute was not simply a mouthpiece for the Fascist state, its fortunes were, nevertheless, dependent on the usefulness of an international cinematic profile to the Italian government, as well as on the continued vitality of the League itself. By 1932 the economic crisis, the Manchurian crisis and the rising tide of nationalism had begun to undermine belief in the institutions of international co-operation, and the Institute's gradual decline reflected that of the "spirit of Geneva."

Until 1933 the *Review* published essays by Italian writers out of sympathy with state policy, but its contents increasingly suggested that the Institute was coming under the sway of the Fascist regime.[92] In November 1933 an article by Alberto Consiglio on "The Social Function of the Cinema" argued that it was "the duty of the modern state to influence the character of cinematographic production directly and to impose certain limitations within which the views of life must be kept. There must not be a conflict with the views of the state."[93] The modern Fascist artist must show man as the triumph of work and virtue. In April 1934 an article on "The State and the Scholastic Cinema" celebrated LUCE as instrument of the corporate state.[94] Most explicitly, Luigi Freddi, head of the Direzione Generale per la Cinematografia per la Disciplina e la Tutela della Produzione (General Office for the Discipline and Guidance of Film Production) in the Ministry of Popular Culture, published an article in September 1935 justifying the subordination of artistic energy to the requirements of the state, and expounding his programme for the revival of the Italian film industry as an instrument of the regime.[95] A month after its publication, Mussolini invaded Abyssinia and the League instituted economic sanctions against Italy. Not surprisingly, Italian state interest in supporting League organisations withered rapidly. Although the Institute did not actually close until Italy withdrew from the League in December 1937, *Intercine* (as the *Review* had been renamed in January 1935) ceased publication in December 1935, and the Institute's last two years were a period of parochial inactivity.

The Institute's last major conference, on educational aspects of the motion picture, was held in April 1934, and attended by 700 delegates from forty-five countries. The official US delegates included both Milliken and Dr W.W. Charters, the Director of the Bureau of Education Research at Ohio State University and the Research Director of the Payne Fund Studies. Despite Charters's position as Vice-President of the congress, it did not greatly occupy itself with social questions, restricting its resolutions to issues dealing strictly with educational cinema, narrowly defined.[96] After the Institute's closure, the Advisory Committee on Social Questions, the successor body to the Child Welfare Committee, published a report on *The Recreational Cinema and the Young* in 1938. This was the culmination of four years' enquiry, and relied extensively on the Payne Fund Studies as authoritative sources of information and opinion. By this stage, however, the studies' authors had distanced themselves from the didactic interpretations imposed on their material by Short. In its conclusion the report quoted Edgar Dale, author of two of the studies, as pointing out that "there may be a tendency to over-emphasise the importance of the influence of the cinema on the mental and moral make-up of young people." The authors also incorporated the studies into a conclusion which suggested that "it is just as unwise to exaggerate the place of the cinema in the leisure of the young as to regard it as an unmitigated evil from which they must be protected at all costs." In so doing, the committee expressed a viewpoint entirely acceptable to the MPPDA, and indicated that as a political issue, the effects of movies on the world's young was, at least temporarily, contained.[97] In its final years, the *Review* could say what it liked about Hollywood, since its merely aesthetic opinions were of no commercial consequence, and could safely be disregarded: thus, in a January 1935 review of *Our Daily Bread* Arnheim declaimed:

> The cinema has become a hotbed of lies: they say they are showing us human beings, and give us instead the product of a jelly factory, sickening in its relentless sweetness . . . they filter the irritating poisons from crime, want, and cruelty . . . all they draw from actuality are attractions for the box office. . . . Has the cinema not turned into a house of ill-repute? It is immoral, in a totally different sense than what is meant by boycott-happy housewives who think ignoring problems is moral. It is immoral because base speculation is called love, and because life-promoting desires have been turned into meaningless, purposeless additions to pleasure and titillation.[98]

VI

This essay has traced the involvement of the League of Nations in the Americanisation of world cinema from a dream of cultural resistance to an engineered acquiescence. Much like the larger history of the League, this has been a story of grandiose visions, unfulfilled promise, and projects left uncompleted. When the IECI closed, its encyclopaedia covering "the historical, artistic, social, technical, educational and juridical aspects of the motion picture," on which Arnheim had worked for four years with "experts all over the world," was in page proof.[99] Only a handful of its entries have subsequently emerged into print.[100] The *Review*, which never quite became a successful international journal of research into the sociology and psychology of cinema, met a fate comparable to the multiple-language film versions with which it was contemporaneous, condemned to obscurity not only by its present scarcity but also by the arcane nature of its content. It is seldom that even the most dedicated scholar can unearth even a footnote to its output. But among the articles on censorship in Lithuania, authors' rights in Iraq, the cinematographic education of the rural masses and the possible uses of the cinema in the domain of medical jurisprudence, the *Review* also published a sustained lament for the passing of silent cinema.[101] Rudolf Arnheim provided an account of "the decay of the art of expression in film" brought about by the incompatible marriage of sound and film, and the violent "mechanisation and commercialisation of human creativity" in Hollywood.[102] A sequence of articles mourned the lost internationalism of silent cinema's "illustrated Esperanto." For these writers, the "precious universality" of late silent cinema was replaced by talk, by the misunderstandings too often produced by translation, and by the re-assertions of national distinctions and national boundaries.[103] It is, perhaps, not too far-fetched to find in these arguments an elegiac lament for the spirit of Geneva itself.

Much like the spirit of Geneva, the projects of Film Europe were creatures of that fleeting period of economic prosperity and political stability in the late 1920s, destined not to survive the resurgence of nationalism brought about by the Depression. The insubstantial pageant of William Marston Seabury's schemes had faded even earlier, out-manoeuvred by the monopolists, by Italian national ambition, and even by Dr Short. His only reward was to be nominated "Officier d'Academie" by the French government "in recognition of his writings on international motion picture problems" in June 1929.[104] Seabury's analysis of the international power of American media corporations, and of their effect on a world trade in culture, however, remains as persuasive, and indeed as relevant, as it was when it was written; his remedy, by which governments and exhibitors together used their buying power to force entry into the parochial American market, remains as convincing and as impractical now as it was then. The League, perhaps, was never more than a figurative site around which alternative cinematic orders were sketched: the American industrialists never needed to take it seriously, except as a public relations issue. The last word in this tale of inconclusion should be Seabury's, describing his plans come to nothing at the 1926 congress, but also anticipating the history of the cinema and the League over the next ten years:

> The lesson which this international event, of such great possibilities, teaches is the lesson which the trade in America has consistently taught for many years. The industry's only interest in discussions of ways and means of improving the service of the trade to the public, is to vitiate the discussions and by skilful publicity and by other effective means to prevent the accomplishment of any substantial results.[105]

Notes

1. Quoted in William Marston Seabury, *The Public and the Motion Picture Industry* (New York: Macmillan, 1926), p. 179.
2. Ibid., p. 206.
3. Ibid., pp. vii, ix–x.
4. In a memorandum entitled "The Kind of Men Who Control the Motion Picture Industry," Seabury commented that "it is as unthinkable that America shall continue to entrust the amusements of her children to alien and uneducated men as it would be to turn over her schools, her pulpits, or her press to such men," Quoted in Garth S. Jowett, Ian C. Jarvie and Kathryn H. Fuller, *Children and the Movies: Media Influence and the Payne Fund Controversy* (Cambridge: Cambridge University Press, 1996), p. 352, n. 55.
5. For a discussion of the broadcasting reform movement, see Robert W. McChesney, *Telecommunications, Mass Media, and Democracy: The Battle for the Control of US Broadcasting* (New York: Oxford University Press, 1993).
6. Seabury, memorandum, 5 September 1927, quoted in Jowett, Jarvie and Fuller, *Children and the Movies*, p. 36.
7. Seabury to Short, 13 December 1927, quoted in Jowett, Jarvie and Fuller, *Children and the Movies*, p. 41. In his account of the Motion Picture Research Council, Garth Jowett notes that after Short's death in 1935, the MPRC "devoted itself almost entirely to combating the motion picture industry through the support of legislation aimed at curbing and controlling industry practices." Jowett regards this as ironic, "because this is exactly what Seabury had hoped for when he first envisaged what was to become the MPRC." Jowett, Jarvie and Fuller, *Children and the Movies*, p. 55.
8. Herbert Mitgang, *The Man Who Rode the Tiger: The Life and Times of Judge Samuel Seabury* (Philadelphia: Lippincott, 1963), p. 329.
9. Quoted in ibid., pp. 75–6, 326.
10. Seabury, *The Public*, p. 166.
11. Ibid., p. 168.
12. J. Homer Platten, "Motion Pictures: A New Public Utility?," *Banker's Magazine*, 1927, pp. 453–8, 486–92. The article, which was in all probability actually written by the MPPDA's chief publicist, Lamar Trotti, was typical of the association's publicity, recounting the industry's progress toward an ever-greater degree of financial stability and extolling the virtues of the MPPDA as its "responsible headquarters." Beyond citing the number of shares in motion picture securities in the hands of the public, and referring to it as a "public servant," Platten

offered no argument in favour of his claim that the industry was a new public utility.

13. Morton Keller, *Regulating a New Economy: Public Policy and Economic Change in America, 1900–1933* (Cambridge, MA: Harvard University Press, 1990), pp. 56, 62.

14. Seabury, *The Public*, p. 228.

15. Ibid., pp. 212–14.

16. In Britain, he also advocated the formation of an exhibitors' co-operative society as a means of stimulating British production. Such an organisation could, in imitation of the original First National Exhibitors Circuit of America, contract with British producers for a number of films, and then negotiate reciprocal access to the American market for those productions, as part of the terms by which they rented films from the American majors. Seabury, *The Public*, pp. 220, 230–5.

17. Seabury, *The Public*, p. 260.

18. Ibid., pp. 267–8. "This suggestion was nothing more than the application of an old and well established principle in the structure of national tariffs so frequently utilized by America in the past and so well described by the distinguished French member of the Economic Committee of the League of Nations, M.D. Serruys . . . whereby nations formulate proposed tariffs as a basis for discussion, negotiation and compromise with those adversely affected by them." William Marston Seabury, *Motion Picture Problems: The Cinema and the League of Nations* (New York: Avondale Press, 1929), p. 134.

19. Seabury, *The Public*, pp. 273–4.

20. Alfred Zimmern, *The Leage of Nations and the Rule of Law, 1918–1935* (2nd edn, London: Macmillan, 1939), p. 322.

21. F.P. Walters, *A History of the League of Nations* (Oxford: Oxford University Press, 1952, 1969), p. 425; David Armstrong, *The Rise of the International Organisation: A Short History* (London: Macmillan, 1982), p. 42.

22. "Hays and Wilson Confer on Films," *New York Times*, 28 April 1928.

23. "Speech made by US Ambassador Hugh Wilson, to the Geneva Conference for the Abolition of Import and Export Prohibitions and Restrictions, July 7th, 1928," Motion Picture Association of America Archives, New York (hereafter MPA), Reel 7, 1929 foreign relations file, pp. 8–9. For further exposition of the US government position, see "Certain Factors and Conditions Affecting the European Market," and State Department Note, 19 April 1929, reproduced in the Documents Section; and Ruth Vasey, *The World According to Hollywood, 1918–1939* (Exeter: University of Exeter Press, 1997), pp. 45–6.

24. Harold L. Smith, memo, 27 February 1928, National Archives,

Washington D.C. (hereafter NARA), microfilm 560, role 46, frame 988. I am grateful to Jens Ulff-Møller for showing me this and other NARA documents relating to the Geneva conferences and the French decree.

25. Herron to Arthur N. Young, Economic Advisor, Department of State, 7 March 1928, NARA microfilm 560, roll 46, frame 1081.

26. Herron to J. Theodore Marriner, Chief, Division of Western European Affairs, Department of State, 12 June 1928; Herron to Saul E. Rogers, 2 June 1928, MPA, Reel 5, 1928 foreign relations file.

27. League of Nations, Second Conference for the Abolition of Import and Export Prohibitions and Restrictions, Addendum to Minutes of the Ninth Meeting, p. 22 (CIAP/2nd Conf./PV9 Addendum), attached to Edward G. Lowry to Hays, 24 July 1928, MPA, Reel 5, 1928 foreign relations file; Hugh Wilson to Secretary of State, 7 July 1928, NARA microfilm 560, roll 46, frame 1140.

28. Dr Paul Koretz (Austrian lawyer advising Col. Lowry at Geneva) to Hays, 19 July 1928, MPA, Reel 5, 1928 foreign relations file.

29. F.W. Allport, Commercial Attaché to the American Embassy, Berlin, memo 17 December 1928, US Embassy, France.

30. R. Eldridge, International Chamber of Commerce, Paris, to George A. Gordon, American Embassy, Paris, 21 June 1929, US Embassy, France. Serruys was "a key figure in the French Ministry of Commerce, and an ardent champion of Franco- German economic collaboration." At a press conference in May 1927, he had declared that "Europe is nothing more than a single economic unit in the world . . . what is now urgently needed is collective action by the governments for the demobilisation of customs." Carl H. Pegg, *Evolution of the European Idea, 1914–1932* (Chapel Hill: University of North Carolina Press, 1983), pp. 83, 87.

31. Harold L. Smith, "Developments in Motion Picture Contingent Agitation in France Meeting of the Cinema Commission on January 11, 1928," 16 January 1928, NARA microfilm 560, roll 46, frame 934.

32. Wilson to Secretary of State, 7 July 1928, NARA microfilm 560, roll 46, frame 1140. Seabury's eloquent defence of the French position in *Motion Picture Problems*, pp. 138–42.

33. Allport, memo, 17 December 1928.

34. Walters, *History of the League of Nations*, p. 428.

35. Declaring the timing of the Congress "inappropriate," the MPPDA also declined to attend. *New York Times*, 1 July 1926. See also Andrew Higson's essay on the congress in this volume.

36. "Speech made by US Ambassador Hugh Wilson, 7 July 1928," pp. 7–8.

37. Seabury, *Motion Picture Problems*, pp. 176–81.

38. "Typewriters have pioneered the way for a whole battalion of office equipment devices which have converted many people to doing business

according to American methods," *National Geographic Magazine*, 1928, quoted in Frank Costigliola, *Awkward Dominion: American Political, Economic and Cultural Relations with Europe, 1919–1933* (Ithaca, NY: Cornell University Press, 1984), p. 140.

39. Aristide Briand, French Foreign Minister and the European statesman most associated with "the spirit of Geneva," on the occasion of Germany's entry to the Council of the League of Nations, 8 September 1927; Paul Weindling, Introduction: "Constructing International Health between the Wars," in Paul Weindling, ed., *International Health Organizations and Movements, 1918–1939* (Cambridge: Cambridge University Press, 1995), p. 8.

40. Quoted in Armstrong, *Rise of the International Organisation*, p. 11.

41. Quoted Walters, *History of the League of Nations*, p. 176.

42. Zimmern, *The League of Nations*, p. 326.

43. The Child Welfare Committee's agenda was in large part an amalgamation of the preoccupations of its members, and to an even greater extent than was true of economic matters, their proposals met with resistance from governments wary of an erosion of national sovereignty: British Foreign Secretary Austen Chamberlain told the Council in 1926 that "child welfare is not primarily a matter for international action and . . . the purposes which the League can serve in this direction are limited." There was, he argued, "a danger for the League in thus invading the purely national sphere of its Member States lest these states should be indisposed by the interference and the real purpose of the League should be obscured." Carol Miller, "The Social Section and Advisory Committee on Social Questions of the League of Nations," in Weindling, ed., *International Health Organizations*, p. 161.

44. Dr F. Humbert, *Effects of the Cinematograph on the Mental and Moral Well-Being of Children: Report by the Secretariat submitted to the Child Welfare Committee of the League of Nations, March 27, 1926*. Reprinted in Seabury, *Motion Picture Problems*, Appendix 2, p. 341.

45. League of Nations, Advisory Commission for the Protection and Welfare of Children and Young People, Child Welfare Committee, Fourth Session, 19 March 1928, *Report on the Work of the Child Welfare Committee on the Cinematograph Question*, presented by M.F. Martin, Rapporteur (Geneva: C.P.E. 149), p. 13.

46. *Report on the Cinematograph Question*, pp. 6–8.

47. Julien Luchaire, *Relations of the Cinematograph to Intellectual Life: Memorandum submitted to the International Committee for Intellectual Co-operations, on 28 July 1924*. Reprinted in Seabury, *Motion Picture Problems*, pp. 237–8, 256–62. See also Andrew Higson's essay in this volume.

48. First Resolution of the Eighth Commission of the International Motion

Picture Congress, quoted in Seabury, *Motion Picture Problems*, p. 379; the Fourth Commission had proposed a more appropriate resolution, which had the support of both Seabury and the Committee on Intellectual Co-operation: "That a permanent and autonomous committee should be set up, entrusted with investigation from the international point of view both of the international status of cinematographic art and industry and of the moral as well as material rights of those intersted in the industry." Seabury, *Motion Picture Problems*, pp. 152, 154–8.

49. Seabury, *Motion Picture Problems*, p. 159.

50. Ibid., pp. 216–21.

51. Quoted in Elaine Mancini, *Struggles of the Italian Film Industry during Fascism, 1930–1935* (Ann Arbor, MI: UMI Research Press, 1985), p. 122. The Institute had five official languages, and even within its own publications there is some variation in the English translation of its title. In the latter stages of its existence, it was frequently referred to as the International Institute for Educational Cinematography, but for the sake of consistency I shall refer to it throughout by the name given to it in the English versions of its founding documents.

52. Ibid., pp. 29, 121.

53. Ibid., pp. 122–3.

54. James Hay, *Popular Film Culture in Fascist Italy: The Passing of the Rex* (Bloomington: Indiana University Press, 1987), p. 16. Mussolini had previously established an International Institute for the Unification of Private Law, along similar lines to the IECI and with a comparable relationship to the League. Zimmern, *The League of Nations*, p. 323.

55. *League of Nations Journal of the 8th Ordinary Session of the Assembly, Geneva*, 7 September 1927, p. 24. See also League of Nations, Fifty-first Session of the Council, 30 August 1928, C.5/1st Session, P.V.1.2235. Document C.383, 1928. Document C. 435, 1928 XII.

56. Harold L. Smith, Memorandum, "Formation of a French Motion Picture Control Commission," 20 February 1928, NARA microfilm 560, roll 46, frame 975.

57. *League of Nations Journal*, 7 September 1927, p. 24.

58. The occasion of these debates was a European conference on the Educational Cinema held at Basle in December 1927. The report, by an unnamed French official, also suggested that the Institute was expected to receive a donation of 50 million francs from Rockefeller. Report, 21 November 1927, MPA, Reel 3, 1927, League of Nations file.

59. Harold L. Smith, Memorandum, 20 February 1928, NARA microfilm 560, roll 46, frame 975.

60. *League of Nations Journal*, 7 September 1927, p. 24.

61. League of Nations, International Educational Cinematographic Institute, Draft Statutes (Geneva: C.63, 1928 XII [C.I.C.I.191]).

62. This was later raised to 800,000 lire, with 90,000 lire in addition for entertainment allowance. The Italian government also "endowed the Institute with magnificent quarters in the Villa Falconieri at Frascati, where the Director's office and the technical services will be installed, and the Villa Torlonia in Rome, for the administrative services. In addition, it has furnished the whole of the indispensable supplies— from a motor-car to typewriters and pencils." League of Nations, International Educational Cinematographic Institute, Report to the Council on the first Session of the Governing Body of the Institute (Geneva: Extract No. 45 from the *Official Journal* (January 1929) [C.573 (revised) 1928.XII]). The Institute was also authorised "to receive further funds for its working and expansion in the form of such cash payments, gifts, bequests, legacies or subsidies as the governing Body may decide to accept." League of Nations, International Educational Cinematographic Institute, Letter from the Italian Prime Minister to the President of the Council of the League of Nations, 7 January 1928 (Geneva: C.12 (1) 1928 XII).

63. League of Nations, Child Welfare Committee, Fifth Session, 12 April 1929, "Communicated by M. de Feo, Director of the International Educational Cinematographic Institute," MPA, Reel 7, 1929 League of Nations file.

64. Frederick Herron to Earl Bright, 22 July 1929, MPA, Reel 7, 1929 League of Nations file.

65. "Women Demand Movie Investigation," *Christian Century*, 9 December 1931, p. 1549.

66. Zimmern, *The League of Nations*, p. 468.

67. As Thomas Saunders notes in his essay in this volume, the Fascist state's practical support of feature production was no more than gestural until the mid-1930s, The quota laws were resisted as strongly by Stephano Pittaluga, the Italian cinema's leading entrepreneur, "in virtual control of whatever was left of the Italian film industry" in the late 1920s, as they were by the American distributors, and they were rendered ineffectual by the precarious condition of the domestic production industry. See Peter Bondanelli, *Italian Cinema From Neorealism to the Present* (New York: Ungar, 1988), p. 12; Pierre Sorlin, *Italian National Cinema 1986–1996* (London: Routledge, 1996), p. 57.

68. Frederick Herron to Earl Bright, 22 July 1929, MPA, Reel 7, 1929 League of Nations file.

69. Harold L. Smith, report, 19 December 1929, MPA, Reel 7, 1929 foreign relations file. The convention, which required that such films be certificated as educational by the IECI, was eventually ratified in 1936.

70. League of Nations, International Committee on Intellectual Co-

operation, Report by the Director of the International Educational Cinematographic institute on Point 6 of the Agenda, 20 July 1929 (Geneva: C.I.C.I./214).

71. "The Cinema and the School," *International Review of Educational Cinematography* (hereafter *IREC*), vol. 3, no. 5, May 1931, pp. 558–9.
72. "The Cinema and Children," *IREC*, vol. 2, no. 1, January 1930, p. 43.
73. "A World Enquiry," *IREC*, vol. 2, no. 3, March 1930, p. 247.
74. "Immorality, Crime, and the Cinema," *IREC*, vol. 2, no. 3, March 1930, p. 327.
75. Albert Hellwig, "The Cinematograph and Crime," *IREC*, vol. 2, no. 3, March 1930, p. 254.
76. "Immorality, Crime, and the Cinema," p. 319.
77. Ibid., p. 323.
78. Guiliano de Feo, "The Cinema as a Social Factor," *IREC*, vol. 3, no. 1, January 1931, pp. 93–5.
79. F.L. Herron, "Block Booking," *IREC*, vol. 4, no. 8, August 1932, p. 597.
80. Guiliano de Feo, "Film Censorship," *Intercine*, vol. 7, no. 3, March 1935, pp. 171–2. The *International Review of Educational Cinematography* changed its title to *Intercine* in January 1935, and published under that name until its closure in December 1935.
81. "American Cinema Reform," *Intercine*, vol. 7, no. 5, May 1935, pp. 262–4.
82. "Social Aspects of the Cinema," *IREC*, vol. 2, no. 4, April 1930, p. 464.
83. Goldsmith was also President of the Society of Motion Picture Engineers. "Pseudo-Scientific Studies of Cinematography," *IREC*, vol. 5, no. 8, August 1933, pp. 557–8.
84. Laura Dreyfuss-Barney, "The Cinema and Education," *IREC*, vol. 6, no. 3, March 1934, pp. 184–8; Laura Dreyfuss-Barney, "Cinema and Protection of Infancy: Summary Report of the Cinema and Broadcasting Commission of the International Women's Council," *IREC*, vol. 6, no. 4, April 1934, pp. 280–4.
85. Marianna Hoffmann, "Children and the Cinema," *IREC*, vol. 2, no. 9, September 1930, pp. 1072–3.
86. Memo, Herron to Hays, 10 October 1931, Will H. Hays Papers, Department of Special Collections, Indiana State Library, Indianapolis (hereafter Hays Papers).
87. Memo, Reginald Wright Kaufman to Hays, 21 October 1931, Hays Papers.
88. Mrs Ambrose A. Diehl, "The Moral Effect of the Cinema on In-dividuals," *IREC*, vol. 3, no. 12, December 1931, pp. 1123–37; "Women Present Plea for Film Progress to League Institute," *Motion Picture Herals*, 17 October 1931, p. 20.

89. Daily Report, K.L. Russell to Hays, 19 October 1931, Hays Papers.
90. "Women Demand Movie Investigation," *Christian Century*, 9 December 1931, p. 1549.
91. *IREC*, vol. 3, no. 10, October 1931, p. 1120.
92. "The Cinema as a Civilizing Art: Symposium among Intellectuals of the New Italy," *IREC*, vol. 5, no. 6, June 1933, pp. 391–411.
93. Alberto Consiglio, "The Social Function of the Cinema," *IREC*, vol. 5, no. 11, November 1933, pp. 706–11.
94. Amedeo Perna, "The State and the Scholastic Cinema," *IREC*, vol. 6, no. 4, April 1934, pp. 220–9.
95. Luigi Freddi, "The Cinema in Italy," *Intercine*, vol. 7, no. 9, September 1935, pp. 58–69. See also Mancini, *Struggles of the Italian Film Industry*, p. 126.
96. Cline M. Koon, "The International Congress of Educational Cinematography," *Education*, vol. 55, no. 2, 1934, pp. 71–5.
97. League of Nations, Advisory Committee on Social Questions, The Recreational Cinema and the Young (Geneva: IV. SOCIAL 1938 IV.13. C.256.M.152.1938.IV), p. 31.
98. Rudolf Arnheim, Review of *Our Daily Bread*, *Intercine*, vol. 7, no. 1, January 1935, pp. 14–18. Reprinted as *"Our Daily Bread"* in Rudolf Arnheim, *Film Essays and Criticism*, trans. Brenda Benthien (Madison: University of Wisconsin Press, 1997), p. 203.
99. Rudolf Arnheim, "A Personal Note," in *Film as Art* (2nd edn, Berkeley: University of California Press, 1968), pp. 5–6.
100. Some of Arnheim's essays for the encyclopaedia can be found in *Film as Art*. More are included in Arnheim, *Film Essays and Criticism*: for a bibliography of Arnheim's writings while at the Institute, see *Film Essays and Criticism*, pp. 242–4.
101. "Cinema Censure in Lithuania," *IREC*, vol. 4, no. 3, March 1932, pp. 214–15; "Authors' Rights in Iraq," *IREC*, vol. 4, no. 10, October 1932, p. 797; Matilda de la Torre, "Cinematographic Education of the Rural Masses," *IREC*, vol. 5, no. 5, May 1933, pp. 321–3; Attilo Ascarelli, "The Cinema and its Possible Applications in the Domain of Medical Jurisprudence," *IREC*, vol. 6, no. 2, February 1934, pp. 92–5.
102. Rudolf Arnheim, "The Film Critic of Tomorrow," *Intercine*, vol. 7, nos 8–9, August–September 1935, p. 90; Arnheim, "Erich von Stroheim," entry for *Enciclopedia del cinema*. Both translations from Arnheim, *Film Essays and Criticism*, pp. 107, 203.
103. G. Moulan, "The Cinema and International Amity," *IREC*, vol. 4, no. 12, December 1932, pp. 907–14. For other examples, see Anto-Giulio Bragaglia, "Cinema and Theatre," *IREC*, vol. 3, no. 1, January 1931, pp. 11–23; Francis Birrell "How Much of a Sound Picture Should Talk?," *IREC*, vol. 5, no. 2, February 1933, pp. 138–41; Tullio Balboni, "Some

Aspects of the Cinema Crisis," *IREC*, vol. 5, no. 11, November 1933, pp. 722–5; Claude Farrere, "Nationalism of the Cinema," *IREC*, vol. 6, no. 8, August 1934, pp. 523–4.
104. New York *Evening Post*, 8 June 1929.
105. Seabury, *Motion Picture Problems*, pp. 160–1.

5

Cultural Policy and Industrial Practice

Film Europe and the International Film Congresses of the 1920s

Andrew Higson

In a key article of 1924, a leading German trade paper suggested that "the new guiding principle for European film politics must be: band together."[1] By 1928, another German trade paper could proclaim "Film Europe—no longer a theory."[2] There had been much talk in the European, and especially the German, trade press over the intervening years of the need to establish a pan-European cinema as the only coherent means of challenging the international supremacy of the Hollywood machine. By 1928 these discussions had come to a head, and it did indeed seem for a year or so that Film Europe could be more than a theory. Since 1924, several of the strongest European film companies had established trading agreements and co-production arrangements with each other across national boundaries. Around 1928, there was a flurry of such activity—although it was still rare outside German trade circles to talk of a coherent and centralised Film Europe project.

The claim that Film Europe was no longer a theory was made in August 1928. The timing was not coincidental. This was the same month in which Berlin hosted the First International Cinema Exhibitors' Conference, intended as a focus for pan-European developments (for although it took for itself the title of an international conference, it was primarily European in focus). The conference was also intended to prepare the ground for and bring into existence a pan-European trade body which might co-ordinate further European co-operation in the film industry and promote the interests of the film trade collectively.

This was not in fact the first such conference. An earlier international conference of cinema exhibitors had been held in Paris in 1923, and in 1926 another international film conference was held in Paris, organised under the auspices of the League of Nations. The Berlin conference of 1928 was the first of several to be organised by exhibitors: Paris hosted a further meeting in 1929, and Brussels another in 1930. During the same period, there were also a number of international film exhibitions, more concerned with film as an art-form, as well as various more general economic conventions organised by the League of Nations.[3] These various congresses, conventions and exhibitions form an important backdrop to the efforts to establish a pan-European film industry in the 1920s; at the time, they provided a space in which the cultural policies and industrial practices of Film Europe could be debated. My focus in the pages that follow will be the efforts by the European film industries to co-ordinate activities through the various film congresses of the 1920s. In particular, I will address the extent to which policy and practice were often at odds with one another, and argue that the sort of permanent body which might have co-ordinated such efforts never materialised.

What we can see in the various film congresses is a series of efforts by the industry to establish a means of internal self-regulation and organisation, in order to combat the crushing competition from the American film industry and to establish more substantial profit margins for European film companies. While cultural arguments were repeatedly mobilised by industry executives, often quite eloquently, the debates at the film congresses were rather different from those outlined by Richard Maltby in the previous chapter. William Marston Seabury and the various League of Nations cinema officials of the 1920s were more concerned with imposing external regulations upon the world's film industries, especially upon the American film industry. Their motivation was also much more thoroughly cultural than economic, and this tension between the cultural and the economic is one of the most significant features of the debates taking place in the 1920s.

As Kristin Thompson notes elsewhere in this volume, chauvinism, competition and trade restriction prevailed in the European film industry in the immediate post-First World War period, rather than thoughts of co-operation. By the early 1920s, however, various people began to call for a greater degree of co-operation and collaboration between European film industrialists. The 1923 conference was the first concrete pan-European initiative, but simmering antagonisms and the inflation crisis meant that no German representatives were invited, and there was much bad feeling in the trade press between the French hosts and Germany. Even so, the German trade press recognised the importance of international co-ordination for what was pre-eminently an international industry, and looked forward to participating in the next such conference.[4] Three years later, the trade press around the time of the 1926 conference was awash with talk of the need for co-operation between France and Germany, the two acknowledged market leaders.[5] The Paris setting for the 1923 and 1926 conferences was perhaps as much a sign of France's political significance in Europe in these years as it was of the strength of its film industry. The fact that the 1928 conference was held in Berlin was a clear sign of the vitality of the German film industry and of its aspiration to lead a European cinema. And in each case, the host nation made the most of the opportunity to put on a good show and promote the facilities of the domestic film industry.

The 1923 conference in Paris was in many ways typical of these congresses.[6] Most commentators of the time saw it as a major event of potentially enormous significance, despite the fact that the conference's internationalism embraced neither German nor American representation, while its industrial scope was restricted to exhibition interests. The central debate of the conference concerned what one delegate described as their "one common enemy": not American competition, which seems to have remained implicit at the proceedings, but taxation.[7] Plans were made to lobby governments throughout Europe to remove the various taxes imposed on film exhibition. Other conference resolutions concerned the need for standardisation of equipment, the problems of localised and piecemeal censorship and resistance to what exhibitors perceived as unnecessarily long films.

The work of the conference as a whole was justified not in trade terms or on economic grounds, however, but in cultural, political and moral terms. Taxation was improper, it was argued, because cinema was a vital artistic and scientific instrument of modern society, and a vital means of maintaining public morale. Several speeches acknowledged how important it was for the trade to champion cinema as a means of education and so raise the status of the film industry. A further resolution therefore set up a commission whose purpose was to promote educational films.

The conference also resolved to create a permanent consultative and administrative body which might co-ordinate the efforts of the film industry to improve its standing and promote its interests world-wide. It was agreed—controversially for some of the French delegates—that Germany should be invited to become a member of this putative international trade federation. While this was officially to be a federation of exhibitors, it was much discussed at the time as a "Film League of Nations."[8]

This was no doubt an attempt both to uplift the profile of the federation and to link it to production interests. In an editorial under the title "Internationalising the film", one British trade paper wrote of how the conference might "set up a standard of production that should so considerably widen the scope of appeal of each individual film as to bestow upon it an international appeal, which must inevitably result in the broadening of the scope of bigger and better pictures, the adopted slogan of every producer, and creating an opening for every picture, no matter what the nationality of its origin, in the markets of the world."[9] The editorial went on to link economic logic to cultural and political principles, arguing that "the photoplay, speaking in an universal language, is capable of being made the ambassador of nations, to the advancement of trade, commerce and general security, and the welding into one common brotherhood of the peoples of the whole universe."

In the end, the efforts to establish a pan-European trade federation made little headway. Nonetheless, the reference to the League of Nations and the appropriation of its discourse is important, not least because it was this body which sponsored the 1926 conference in Paris.[10] The League spawned various advisory committees, among them the International Committee on Intellectual Co-operation. This committee debated a report on cinema in 1924, in which Julien Luchaire, director of the committee's executive body, the Institute for Intellectual Co-operation, argued that cinema was a vital force in contemporary culture and as such a major means of educating the citizens of the world and promoting ideas of intellectual and international co-operation.[11] His concerns were thus primarily political, cultural and moral, and coincided with the terms in which the 1923 conference had called on governments to abolish taxes on film exhibition.

Luchaire noted that the efforts to establish an international cinema federation had come to little, and proposed that the International Committee on Intellectual Co-operation should take over this initiative. In effect, a putative trade federation was to be transformed into a cultural body. The League of Nations was attempting to impose its moral and political concerns about cinema as a public service on a trade whose prime concern was profit. The stance of the League poses in the sharpest terms this distinction between trade and culture. In reality, of course, the distinction was never that clear, since the film industry, and certainly film-makers, were themselves concerned with cultural questions, and not always as a smokescreen for more thoroughly economic motivations.

The International Committee on Intellectual Co-operation adopted Luchaire's report and proposed that an International Cinema Conference be organised. This eventually became the 1926 Paris Conference, organised by the French National Committee on Intellectual Co-operation and the International Institute, which was based in Paris. The organisers of the conference invited intellectuals and educationalists of all nations, professional moralists and reformers, cultural commentators, politicians—and, of course, representatives of the film trade. Inevitably, the event generated a range of tensions between intellectual and trade concerns. Initially, representatives of the film trade in all countries were reluctant to become involved in what seemed destined to be a purely intellectual event. In the event, trade interests dominated many aspects of the proceedings of the conference. The German film industry, for instance, initially declined all invitations, but then Germany had only very recently joined the League of Nations, which was not anyway noted as a body of great interest to the trade. In the end, the German film industry provided the largest and best-organised delegation at the conference, with some forty or fifty delegates and a clear agenda of trade-related issues. There were also many French film-makers and industrialists at the conference, which eventually attracted 427 delegates from twenty-eight countries, the vast majority of them European.

On the other side of the Atlantic, the American film industry was extremely wary of the conference. The USA had dissociated itself from the League of Nations, and saw this conference very much as a European initiative, and as a potential threat to American film interests. According to one contemporary source, the Hays Office lobbied hard to have the conference abandoned, then tried to have it postponed for a year, arguing that they needed this much time to prepare detailed statistics on the organisation of the world film trade, which only they could provide.[12] When this tactic failed, they resorted to trivialising the conference through the American trade press. One paper, for instance, wrote that:

some twenty nations will gather in Paris to discuss the future of motion pictures. . . . Art, literature, education and internationalism will be discussed. Some eighty papers will be read in many different languages. That's interesting, in view of the fact that there is but one international language—motion pictures. The result of the gathering may or may not be important. The world is a tremendous audience. Like all audiences, big or small, it is fickle. Certain standards of American production have been set. They must be maintained and improved with the march of progress. Perhaps some constructive practical thoughts will come from the Paris gathering; but whatever the outcome, it's a good safe bet that American producers will continue on their merry way of giving the public of America and of the world what it wants.[13]

American officials also tried to ensure that trade concerns were off the agenda of the conference and that it stuck to its professed intellectual and artistic concerns, and the conference was eventually planned on these terms. The official announcement declared: "the congress will be neither industrial nor commercial." At the conference itself, however, this agenda was partly overtaken by trade interests.[14]

The anxiety of the American film industry about this conference can be gauged by the tone of various articles in the American trade press, especially in the pages of *Film Daily*, which predicted the "organisation of an offensive campaign against the American world 'monopoly'", including the implementation in European countries of quota regulations and other restrictions on film imports.[15] Such blatant antagonism towards the American trade is very rarely a feature of the European trade press reporting on the conference, which is probably an indication that much of that press was sympathetic to American interests. *Film Daily* was in no doubt of the real work of the conference, however. A front page article commented that:

camouflaging its motives with an altruistic program of the uplift of motion pictures, the first International M.P. Congress [sic] is seeking to perfect a combination against the American film 'monopoly' . . . Wholesale attack on American producers featured [in] meetings of the eight congressional committees into which the conference has divided itself . . . But beyond the general idea of a rival combination, there was a lack of any definite proposals for circumventing "the movie kings of New York and Hollywood."[16]

Other reports in the European trade press confirm this sense of a cultural and political forum overtaken by trade interests, but they also indicate a lack of concrete developments that might yield tangible results for the European film industry. The discourse of the League of Nations and its International Committee on Intellectual Co-operation was what might be called the official discourse of the conference, the discourse of internationalism and of cinema as an educative and civilising public service. There was, however, also an unofficial trade discourse.

The official discourse had three main effects for the conference. Firstly, it envisaged cinema in cultural terms, a view which many of the film industrialists present at the conference were more than happy to appropriate in order to justify their more commercial desires. Secondly, this discourse ensured that at least part of the work of the conference was given over to consideration of non-fiction films, scientific and educational films, what we would now call documentary films. And thirdly, this discourse produced a series of more or less unenforceable resolutions. There were discussions about the relation between film and the other arts, and resolutions calling for all film-makers and industrialists to avoid the production of films which might incite hatred between peoples, or denigrate other nationalities. Instead, they were encouraged to produce films which promoted international under-standing and co-operation and which operated at a high moral level. Another resolution concerned the desire that all historical films should be accurate in their representations and should develop properly sympathetic portrayals of the nation whose history is being depicted. There was no means of enforcing such resolutions and good intentions, however; no equivalent to the Hays Office of the Motion Picture Producers and Distributors of America Inc. (MPPDA). There were attempts to develop some sort of permanent committee, but as at the 1923 conference, those attempts came to little.

If this was the official discourse of the conference, there is plenty of evidence that *Film Daily* was right to fear the emergence of a much more properly trade-oriented discourse concerned with establishing various forms of pan-European collaboration. There was indeed much resentment in the trade about the intellectual concerns of the conference organisers: "Cinema is an industry and a business and these men seem to have forgotten this."[17] One reporter noted that "in the actual work of the Congress, the *film trade* carried all before it." Most of the committees were made up of representatives of the film business, "so that the Congress, which opened on an 'intellectual pedestal', soon came down to what was practically an *international film trade debate.*"[18]

The trade papers of the period made the most of the conference, producing special editions for circulation at the conference and reporting widely on the discussions. Here one can find many statements along the lines that the conference is best understood as a stimulus to a well-organised, collaborative European cinema alliance, a European bloc which might put up serious opposition to the American film industry. There were plenty of film-makers ready to be quoted about what an important forum this conference was for establishing international understanding, which meant in effect establishing contact with fellow industrialists from other European countries. There was also much in the press about the importance of collaboration between the two strongest producing nations of the period in Europe, France and Germany. It is clear, too, that various film companies took advantage of the conference to trade show the new season's films to a captive audience (though not officially as part of the conference itself).

There was, then, a clear tension between the official League of Nations discourse of the conference and the discourse of business which came to dominate much of the proceedings. But there was some common ground in the anti-American sentiments of both. For the International Committee on Intellectual Co-operation, American cinema was too often morally objectionable, a fact that was compounded by the virtual trade monopoly that the American film industry enjoyed. For the European film-makers and industrialists, American cinema was the economic adversary. But if there was some common ground, it was neither extensive nor very stable, not least because the trade wanted to have its cake and eat it. For Herr Correll of Phoebus Films, "What's most important [about the conference] is the chance to establish contacts with European industry representatives and their desire to create a far-reaching film policy. But, above all, don't form an anti-American policy."[19] If the Film Europe idea was anti-American, it was clear that the European film industry as a whole could not afford to antagonise the American film companies. There was much dismay, and even anger, that the American film industry had failed to send representatives to the conference, even though these were the same delegates who were trying to establish a European film alliance designed to increase their market share at the Americans expense. As one journalist noted, "during the film congress, the Europeans waited for the Americans as if they were waiting for a rich uncle."[20]

Kristin Thompson has suggested that "the congress was one of the most potentially progressive undertakings in the history of the cinema. Had there been any systematic way of carrying through the resolutions, world cinema would have benefited enormously."[21] The potential remained largely unfulfilled. Indeed, it would be difficult to say that this conference, or any of the others, had any really profound impact on the development of European cinema in the period. The resolutions about international understanding would have been almost impossible to enforce. While the conference was a place where contacts could be made and deals no doubt struck—and was seen by its participants as vital in this respect—Film Europe as such was never solidly on the agenda. Indeed, given the official intellectual discourse of the conference, it could not have been. The conference was, however, a forum at which the idea of a pan-European cinema alliance came to take on a more solid and extensive understanding. If it was to be taken further, some sort of permanent commission to co-ordinate the activities and interests of members was required.

As in 1923, a permanent commission was in fact one of the intended outcomes of the conference and a resolution was passed calling such a body into being. The tensions between industrial and cultural concerns made progress very difficult, however. The industrialists and film-makers felt hampered by the "intellectuals" on the commission, while the representatives of the Committee for Intellectual Co-operation felt that the terms of the committee had been dictated too much by the trade (the commission was mandated to protect the interests of the film industry, rather than the interests of mankind, for instance).[22] The most concrete task of the commission was to organise a planned second conference in Berlin in 1927. In May 1927 it was announced that the second conference had been postponed until 1928, and that all the representatives of the International Institute for Intellectual Co-operation had resigned from the commission.[23] This then was the end of the League of Nation's involvement in the conferences, though some elements of its cultural reformist and internationalist discourse lingered on in later conferences.

The conference which eventually took place in Berlin in 1928 was entirely a trade-organised event. It was, indeed, specifically an exhibitors' conference: the First International Cinema Exhibitors' Conference, as it was somewhat misleadingly titled.[24] The various committees were this time much more carefully organised around trade concerns—the problems of the various taxes on cinema exhibition, the difficulties of over-long films and blind-booking, the desire for standardisation of technical equipment, and so on. In effect, little progress had been made since 1923. There were, however, still traces of the League of Nations discourse, with one of the resolutions proclaiming that

> no more films shall be exhibited that defame any nation or may be considered as calculated to wound national susceptibilities. The delegates are aware of the immense possibilities of influencing the masses by means of the film and of the responsibilities resting upon themselves, and have passed this resolution in the interest of the furtherance of international good understanding.[25]

As commentators at the time noted, it was extremely unlikely that any way could be found of enforcing such a policy, but it was typical of one strand of the debates at the conference, as well as of the general sensibility of "fostering . . . international goodwill and understanding."[26]

One of the more concrete proposals discussed at the conference was a plan put forward by the Deutsches Lichtspiel Syndicat to form a European-wide exhibitors' syndicate, or trust, with thousands of cinemas, as a basis from which they might then move into production of films which would have a guaranteed market. This was envisaged along the same lines as First National in America, and was described in one of the British trade papers as "one of the most important steps ever initiated in the history of European films."[27] Inevitably, things were not so straightforward. Producers and distributors were apparently represented on the proposed council of the new organisation. The implication was that this was a production and distribution-led initiative to establish a strong European market within which they could circulate their own wares, a state of affairs which frightened off some of the exhibitors.[28] At the same conference, there were renewed efforts to create a Europe-wide trade association for exhibitors. With these two developments afoot, the American trade press once again expressed great anxiety about what *Variety* saw as the launching of "a formidable opposition to combat American film supremacy."[29]

By the time of the 1929 conference, the problem of sound was taken up on the agenda, mainly in terms of calls for the standardisation of equipment and systems and the standardisation of contracts. The question of import restrictions, tariff barriers and quota systems was also raised. One might expect an exhibitors' conference to have come down strongly against such import restrictions, since for exhibitors films are good not because they are of a particular national origin, but because they are popular with audiences. But in fact the conference resolved that national production was important and that it needed protection, so that some sort of quota system was necessary. How seriously the exhibitors took this resolution is difficult to gauge, for one of the events during the conference was a special screening of MGM's *Broadway Melody*. To some extent, it was the same old problem of passing resolutions which were impossible to enforce, and it is depressing to find that the promised pan-European trade association had still not been properly established, and that there was still no permanent business office capable of following through the resolutions of the various conferences, or of co-ordinating the Film Europe idea.

The keynote speakers at the conference continued to borrow from the League of Nations cultural discourse. Leon Brézillon, President of the French Exhibitors' Association, justified the need to organise the industry across Europe in just these terms: "We must ask ourselves if our intellectual patrimony, achieved during 2000 years of civilisation, is not passing into other hands, afterwards to be rented back to us by authors of a culture much different to our own. We must consider the means of uniting—defending ourselves on our own territory."[30] Another industry spokesman, Charles Delac, claimed that "we are today the trusted librarians of a modern encyclopaedia, and as such the pioneers of a future United States of Europe."[31] The reference to the United States of Europe, which was a concept promoted by the French government from 1924, in the context of general debates about pan-European trade, links developments in the film industry to wider economic trends.[32]

By the 1930 conference, sound had become an even more pressing issue, albeit a mainly hypothetical one for most countries other than Britain. For the Film Europe project, and the idea of the international film, it was crucial, since no adequate means had yet been found of transcending the language boundaries that had been so easily overlooked in the silent era. The key to success for the European film industry here was seen in terms of the development of multiple-language productions, as I and others argue elsewhere in this volume.[33]

Film Europe was hardly a unified project, and to that extent the term is misleading, or at least rhetorical. If it had any real existence, then it is perhaps best understood as a series of overlapping and interrelating, and sometimes contradictory, discourses and practices. The major European film industrialists established various reciprocal distribution and co-production arrangements with each other, across national boundaries, and efforts were made to establish a pan-European cinema chain. Such developments should be seen as part of the general trend in this period away from the open competition of the film industry's pioneer days to the economic concentration and consolidation typical of capitalist development. Pressure was put on governments to introduce quota systems of one sort or another, designed primarily to restrict the entry of American films to European markets. There was little co-ordination between the different countries, however, and in 1927, at the behest of the United States, the League of Nations sponsored an economic convention designed to remove all trade restrictions between member nations. This convention was used by the American film industry to challenge France's right to introduce the film quota system it established in 1928.[34]

Alongside these various economic measures, both hypothetical and real, is the cultural discourse of international co-operation and understanding. It is perhaps this more than anything else which holds the various conferences of the 1920s together, even if only in rhetorical terms. The discussion that took place in and around each conference stressed two things repeatedly. On the one hand, commentator after commentator suggested that it was asking too much for the conferences to achieve anything concrete. On the other hand, the same commentators readily acknowledged the importance of the conferences as a basis for what we would now call networking, for establishing the possibility of collaboration, for exchanging ideas and information, for debating the future of cinema at a cultural level. The irony of this is that the failure to achieve anything as concrete as a permanent trade body meant that the same debates were repeated at every conference, only to evaporate once the conference ended.

Despite the efforts of the delegates at each conference, there was still no pan-European trade association which could co-ordinate these various cultural policies and industrial practices and shape them into a coherent and sustainable strategy for European cinema. Nevertheless, at the 1930 conference it could be claimed that:

> to expect any immediate benefit to accrue from the work of the conference would be beyond the bounds of reason. A considerable advance has, however, been made towards a wider understanding of the collective and individual difficulties of exhibitors in the

fifteen countries which sent delegates (America unfortunately made default).[35]

It was still necessary, in other words, to make contacts and share experiences because there was as yet no equivalent of the MPPDA to do that work routinely, day in, day out. There was still no body to ensure that all the resolutions against chauvinistic films, or, more practically, about the need to standardise projection speeds, poster sizes, sound equipment, employment and insurance contracts, and so on, were actually carried through.

When one reporter claimed, in the previous year, that the 1929 Paris conference "will have served its purpose if it demonstrates to the American industry that there is a definite Pan-European movement with its own aims and interests," the threat seemed a little empty, since that movement was so slow and piecemeal.[36] One of the problems was the diversity of interests which the Film Europe idea had to hold together: cultural policy and industrial practice, the divergent interests of producers, distributors and exhibitors, the need to both work with and struggle against Hollywood.

Underlying the discourse of internationalism which the various conferences inherited from the League of Nations was a resilient concern for national cultures. The conversion to sound and the imposition of national languages on the apparently international language of silent film began to disturb the internationalist discourse. It was further displaced by the emergence of the increasingly aggressive nationalisms of the 1930s. As a result, the idea of a centrally co-ordinated Film Europe project, in so far as it ever existed, more or less petered out. Even if the most powerful companies in each of the European countries continued to promote versions of the international film and the co-production, the idea of a 'Film League of Nations' now seemed overly rhetorical, or even downright unpatriotic.

Notes

This is a revised version of a paper which originally appeared in German, as "Film-Europa: Kulturpolitik und Industrielle Praxis", in Sibylle M. Sturm and Arthur Wohlgemuth, eds, *Hallo? Berlin? Ici Paris!: Deutsch-französische Filmbeziehungen, 1918–1939*, (Munich: Edition Text + Kritik, 1996), pp. 63–76. Parts of the paper were subsequently used in "'A film League of Nations': Gainsborough, Gaumont-British and 'Film Europe'", in Pam Cook, ed., *Gainsborough Pictures*, (London: Cassell, 1997), pp. 60–79. My thanks to both sets of editors and publishers for allowing me to re-use material here. My thanks too to the staff of Cinegraph, and to Lawrence Napper, Uwe Brunssen, Sonia Paternoster and Nick Riddle for help in researching the original paper.

1. "European Monroe Doctrine" *Lichtbildbühne*, no. 23, 1 March 1924 (reproduced here as Document 1).
2. *Film Kurier*, 7 August 1928.
3. See Kristin Thompson, "Early Film Exhibitions and the 1920s Avant-Garde Cinema," in Thomas W. Gaehtgens, ed., *Künstlerischer Austausch/Artistic Exchange: Akten des XXVIII. Internationalen Kongresses für Kunstgeschichte Berlin, 15–20. Juli 1992* (Berlin: Akademie Verlag, 1994), pp. 147–150; and on the League's economic congresses, see Richard Maltby's chapter in this volume.
4. See, for example, *Film Kurier*, 22 October 1923 and 2 November 1923.
5. See, for example, *La Cinématographie française*, 29 September 1926 and 1 October 1926.
6. For contemporary reports of the conference, see issues of *Film Kurier, The Bioscope*, and *Kinematograph Weekly* for September, October and November 1923.
7. Quoted in *The Bioscope*, 1 November 1923, p. 29.
8. See, for example, *The Bioscope*, 1 November 1923.
9. *The Bioscope*, 25 October 1923.
10. For details of the 1926 conference, see William Marston Seabury, *Motion Picture Problems: The Cinema and the League of Nations* (New York: Avondale Press, 1929), also issues of *Film Daily, Film Kurier, La Cinématographie française, The Bioscope* and *Kinematograph Weekly* for September and October 1926; and Kristin Thompson, *Exporting Entertainment: America in the World Film Market, 1907–1934* (London: British Film Institute, 1985), pp. 114–16. See also Richard Maltby's chapter on the League of Nations and the cinema in this volume.
11. See Seabury, *Motion Picture Problems*, pp. 147–8ff., and appendices 1 and 3.
12. Ibid., pp. 148–64.
13. Unidentified American trade paper, quoted in *The Bioscope*, 22 July 1926, p. 21.
14. Details from Seabury, *Motion Picture Problems*, pp. 148–54.
15. *Film Daily*, 27 September 1926.
16. *Film Daily*, 30 September 1926.
17. *La Cinématographie française*, 2 October 1926.
18. Georges Clarrière, *The Bioscope*, 14 October 1926, p. 46 (italics in original). See also Seabury, *Motion Picture Problems*, p. 154: "The congress was chiefly industrial."

19. Quoted in *La Cinématographie française*, 1 October 1926.
20. *Film Kurier*, 5 October 1926.
21. Thompson, *Exporting Entertainment*, p. 115.
22. Seabury, *Motion Picture Problems*, pp. 379 and 156ff.
23. Ibid., pp. 159–60.
24. For details of the 1928 conference see issues of *Variety*, *Film Daily*, *La Cinématographique française*, *Film Kurier*, *The Bioscope*, and *Kinematograph Weekly* for July, August and September 1928; also Andor Krazsna Kransz, "The European Kino-congress," *Close Up*, vol. 3, no. 4, October 1928, pp. 14–22.
25. Quoted in Kraszna Krausz, "The European Kino-congress", pp. 18–19.
26. *The Bioscope*, 29 August 1928, p. 25.
27. *The Bioscope*, 29 August 1928, p. 24.
28. See *Kinematograph Weekly*, 30 August 1928, p. 33, and *Variety*, 22 August 1928, p. 8.
29. *Variety*, 22 August 1928, p. 8.
30. Quoted in *Kinematograph Weekly*, 13 June 1929.
31. Quoted in *Kinematograph Weekly*, 13 June 1929.
32. See Kristin Thompson, "The end of the 'Film Europe' movement," in Tom O'Regan and Brian Shoesmith, eds, *History on/and/in Film* (Perth: Hitory and Film Association of Australia (WA), 1987), p. 47, reproduced in a revised version in this volume as "The Rise and Fall of Film Europe."
33. See also Andrew Higson, "Way West: Deutsche Emigranten und die britische Filmindustrie," in Jörg Schöning, ed., *London Calling: Deutsche im britischen Film der dreissiger Jahre* (Munich: Edition Text + Kritik, 1993), pp. 42–54; see also my essay on E.A. Dupont, and the essays by Joseph Garncarz, Ginette Vincendeau and Martine Danan in this volume.
34. Seabury, *Motion Picture Problems*, pp. 131ff. See also Jens Ulff-Møller's essay in this volume.
35. *Kinematograph Weekly*, 12 June 1930.
36. *Kinematograph Weekly*, 6 June 1929, p. 25.

6

Options for American Foreign Distribution
United Artists in Europe, 1919–1930

Mike Walsh

It is common to conceive of American films flooding into Western Europe in the years following both world wars. Thomas Guback, for example, has described Europe after the First World War as "a vacuum into which American pictures flowed."[1] While such an idea might have a broad force in describing the efforts of the American film industry, it is inadequate and often misleading as a description of the process and the outcome of these efforts. Such overviews typically substitute for detailed studies of the diverse methods of American distribution companies in Europe, the varying degrees of their shorter-term success and, crucially, the modes of their interaction with local film institutions, which are too often reduced to the sameness of doomed resistance. Movements toward an increasingly international organisation of film markets around American production did not progress along the line of an undisturbed teleology. Rather they involved different agents making a variety of decisions between a series of options, with American distributors, in particular, moving back and forth between these options in response to large-scale change within the international industry as well as localised economic and social factors.

To address these issues, I want to focus on two moments of tension in the relation between American distributors and European markets: the expansion of American film exports to Europe in the period immediately following the First World War, and the coming of sound. As a way of focusing more closely on the issues and options for American distribution, I will centre on the activities of one company, United Artists (UA), in its attempts to establish itself in Europe and maintain its presence. Although UA was in some respects unrepresentative of the practices of the Big Five major studios, it still faced many of the same conditions as the majors in foreign distribution. American distributors often adopted similar models for their overseas subsidiaries, and in many instances shared legal representation, accountants, auditors and information concerning their subsidiaries' operations. To a limited extent, they also worked together through the industry bodies they established in foreign countries.[2]

As Kristin Thompson has shown, before the First World War American producers tended to sell their foreign rights either to overseas agents or to US-based exporters such as David P. Howells, who resold the rights in London.[3] In the post-war period, major companies with aspirations for market dominance, such as Fox and Famous Players-Lasky (FPL), sought growth by establishing their own foreign representation as well as through domestic vertical integration. There were, however, several stages to this process and transitions often did not take place without hesitation and reversal. American producers attempting to move into Europe had four options available to them: the two that Thompson outlines, of using foreign agents or establishing their own distribution subsidiaries, and two intermediate positions, involving contracting with franchise agents or joint distribution with other American companies. Smaller companies such as UA moved back and forth between these positions in response to the often adverse conditions they encountered in attempting to access European markets.

Establishment Options

Sales through overseas agents often involved a string of intermediaries, all extracting profit from any deal. In 1918, for example, First National sold all its foreign rights to David P. Howells, who negotiated the French rights with English-based J. Frank Brockliss, who was acting on behalf of the final French distributor, Mundus.[4] This indirection not only diluted profit, but also created a situation thick with conflicting interests. One American sales manager criticised the system for educating "the foreign buyer to play the agent off against the manufacturer, or vice versa."[5] UA's founding producer-stars had declared their initial purpose to be strengthening the structural link between production and exhibition.[6] They were even more concerned to adopt the same policy in international dealings, yet paradoxically UA was slow to undertake its own foreign distribution.[7]

The question of whether the company would market its own films internationally was one of the first tests of UA's internal coherence and of its ability to maintain the pre-eminent place that it enjoyed on the basis of its stars' reputations. While FPL, Fox and Universal were expanding by using their larger production slates as the basis for their international distribution networks, promising exhibitors a complete service, UA's chronic shortage of product appeared to militate against direct foreign representation. To grow into an industry leader, UA would have to follow Fox and Zukor and distribute internationally, but to establish an international distribution network was costly, especially when there was little product for it to distribute. The hesitation with regard to foreign distribution was in part a product of the gap between the company's aspirations and its capacity.

UA's solution was to temporise and look at the offers from agents. Throughout 1919 and 1920 a variety of agencies put forward propositions for the rights to UA films. In March 1919 *Variety* noted a particularly strong demand for the overseas rights to Pickford's and Fairbanks's films.[8] UA legal counsel Dennis O'Brien noted that: "There seems to be more activity on the part of the foreign buyers here than on the part of the domestic exhibitors toward the new organisation."[9] One instance was the intense bidding for the Scandinavian rights: UA received offers from Guy Croswell Smith, John Olsen and Company, the Scandinavia-American Trading Company and the Liberty Trading Company. Two factors were important in the negotiations. First, and most obviously, were the financial terms. The bidding escalated rapidly throughout 1920 from a flat $5,000 per film up to 60 per cent of the gross against a minimum guarantee of $12,500 per film.[10]

The other vital factor was the relation of potential agents to the exhibition sector. Potential Scandinavian distributors were at pains to prove that they could place films in the largest circuits of first-run theatres. Close links to exhibitors were, however, a two-edged sword. No matter how generous the terms of the distribution contracts, a vertically-integrated local distributor could skew the rentals by hiving off a larger proportion of the box-office gross to its exhibition arm. UA had found this to be an early problem in its dealings with the Canadian combine, Allen's. This situation led the company to open its own offices in Canada in June 1919, and taught UA's General Manager Hiram Abrams caution in dealing with foreign distributors.[11] While much has been written on the vertical integration of the American film industry, it trailed many other countries in the extent to which individual integrated companies could dominate a market. The international tendency for the consolidation of first-run exhibition into circuits vertically linked to distribution clearly hastened the move of American producers to direct foreign distribution, if only as a defensive measure.

The negotiations over UA's foreign rights point to a larger debate over where UA's profit centres should be located. The use of foreign agents brought in additional revenue without requiring start-up investment costs for the company, which was plagued by cash shortages.[12] Two problems followed, however. The first was that this income was channelled toward producers, with UA receiving only a 5 per cent commission from the producer's share for acting as a sales agent while the foreign distributor retained 30–40 per cent of the rentals as a distribution fee. So long as UA adhered to its initial conception as "a service organisation rather than an investment which would return dividends," its owners may have seen no problem with revenues being channelled directly to production.[13] However, as UA's corporate deficit rose, and also as the production sources for UA expanded away from its initial four owners, the force of this motivation waned.

The second argument against foreign agents was that working through them inevitably produced a smaller financial pie, regardless of the way it was sliced. An agent distributing a range of films could not be expected to give his best efforts to ensuring that those of any single producer would be publicised strongly and booked into the best theatres at prime times. Without local representation it was impossible to make sure that local exhibitors submitted accurate returns. Shipping films to agents also involved a loss of control over prints which could be duped or re-exported once they had been played out in the territory for which the rights were held. One of the major tasks of American distribution representatives in Asia and South America was to guard against piracy, which often involved the re-export of "junk" prints from Europe. A final factor in the decision to establish local subsidiaries was that once everyone else was doing it, UA's hand was forced if it wished to maintain a position as a major. Given that companies such as FPL pursued block-booking policies with even greater ruthlessness once outside the jurisdiction of the Sherman Act, UA needed strong local distribution in the most lucrative overseas markets if it was not to be excluded from scarce first-run theatres.

The returns from UA's films rose immediately with the change from agency contracts to direct representation. UA's continental European subsidiary reported that Mary Pickford films had previously returned no better than 60,000 francs in France but *Through the Back Door* had rentals of almost 150,000 francs.[14] Apart from increasing their producers' shares, UA's distribution business also benefited by taking 30–40 percent of total rentals rather than the 5 per cent commission for the sale of rights. In Belgium, where Fairbanks and Pickford had previously been selling rights for $2,000 per film, direct representation more than tripled rentals, giving UA a distribution fee of $1,800 (30 per cent of rentals of $6,000) as opposed to the $100 commission it would previously have gained from a sale of rights.[15] The crucial task for UA lay in collecting that $1,800 without incurring over $1,700 of additional expenses in the process.

Direct distribution was not, however, the only alternative to foreign agents, and before setting up its own foreign distribution network in Europe, UA first explored an intermediate option. In June 1920 the company concluded a deal giving the British entrepreneur Morris Greenhill the foreign rights to its output. A conjunction of factors (including the economic weakness of Britain relative to the US) was to lead UA to another model of foreign distribution, which funnelled films through British agents—though with the difference that the local agent would now act exclusively in the name of the American company.

The "Logical Bourse"

In March 1919 *Wid's Daily* reported that the "rivalry between American and English dealers is keen and getting more pronounced every day." In September John D. Tippett, an American based in London, had bought out the local distribution outlet for Universal and announced plans to become a major international film broker.[16] Tippett publicised this as a move toward restoring London to its pre-war position as the central exchange for international film rights.[17] He claimed that his buy-out of the Universal franchise was "the first step towards restoring London's prestige as the film centre of the world" and stated in both *Variety* and *Moving Picture World* that "London is the logical bourse of the film industry."[18]

In the British trade papers of the time, the idea of London as the logical centre of international film dealings was a popular sentiment. Sometimes this involved plans that production would move to Britain, but more generally it relied upon the notion of London as the crossroads of world trade.[19] As *The Bioscope* put it: "The marketplace, and not the farm or the factory, is usually considered to be the centre of any particular industry."[20]The ambitions of the British to leadership, if not in film production, then at least in the international film trade, can be seen as an instance of Britain's larger struggle to retain a pre-eminent place in world trade, which the US had gradually usurped, and then dramatically captured during the war.

European financial instability was a major factor in UA's hesitation in setting up its own foreign subsidiaries during 1919 and 1920. This early post-war period was one in which the hegemonic aspirations of American film companies were tempered by adverse export conditions. It seemed to many in the US that the end of the war should have opened the floodgates for film exports, which had fallen by 50 per cent since 1916.[21] In anticipation of the end of the war and the burgeoning of export opportunities, *Moving Picture World* added a monthly International Import and Export Section in October 1918. William Fox sailed to Europe in March 1919 to establish distribution and laboratory facilities in France.[22] Richard Rowland, President of Metro, made a similar trip to Italy in June, and Samuel Goldwyn made the crossing in September.[23] Lewis J. Selznick was quoted as saying that "the re-opening of the European market is the big opportunity we've been awaiting for four years."[24] The rhetoric of world-wide invasion was used openly and unashamedly by the American industry.[25]

This rush to export was seen by many as a factor that would glut the market and depress prices.[26] In April 1919 independent exporter David P. Howells criticised the way in which Goldwyn's films were dumped in France, resulting in a situation where "exhibitors got the pictures at any price at all because the market is surfeited with stuff."[27] Not only were prices lowered by oversupply, but the prevalence of programme booking meant that leading English theatres were commonly booked up to twelve months in advance, and thus new distributors would have a long wait before seeing any returns.[28] The American trade press was increasingly filled with stories of alarm among film exporters. By the end of 1919, *Moving Picture World* had discontinued its Import and Export Section as a regular monthly feature. In March 1920 it carried a special section filled with reports on the problems plaguing exporters. Howells criticised "what appears to be a concerted action by several film exporters to abandon their foreign affiliations." In the same issue, Goldwyn's foreign manager, Arthur Ziehm, acknowledged that American producers would be "obliged to abandon their dream of continuing what has come close to a monopoly of the foreign market."[29]

Added to the problems of oversupply was the depreciation of

European exchange rates. The immediate post-war period saw the rapid decline of most European currencies due to war debts, reparation payments, disrupted production, and decreased trade because of high tariffs. The fall in the British pound, from its pre-war value of $4.86 to $3.38 in 1920, was particularly harmful to American film exporters in their biggest market and in other countries whose currencies were pegged to sterling. Exporters complained that overseas distributors could no longer afford to rent or buy films at US dollar prices, and that British distributors who had contracts written in dollars were facing ruin unless American exporters either varied the terms of the contract or accepted barter arrangements.

The film industry's export problems were part of a "general curtailment of purchases" in Europe in the immediate post-war period noted by the US Department of Commerce. American exports to Europe fell sharply from $5.2 billion in 1919 to $2.1 billion in 1921, part of a drop in total American exports from $8.23 billion in 1920 to $3.76 billion in 1922. Foreign sales dropped from around 14 per cent of total American industrial production in 1919 to around 7 per cent in 1923.[30] In line with the overall decline in American exports of all manufactured goods, the amount of film exported from the US in 1922 had fallen by nearly 25 per cent from the postwar peak of over 175 million feet in 1920.[31]

This short-term economic climate must surely have diminished UA's estimation of foreign returns and made it more amenable to a proposal for all of its foreign rights. In October 1919 Morris Greenhill, Chief Executive of Greenhill and Sons, an English company with interests in Europe and Asia in the manufacture of celluloid and the clothing trade, approached Douglas Fairbanks about UA's foreign rights. Greenhill proposed forming a British company, to be named the United Artists Corporation—the same as the American company—capitalised at £1 million. It was to have the sole rights to UA's films everywhere except the Americas. The producer-artists were to receive 60 per cent of rentals against a minimum guarantee of $225,000 for each of Pickford's and Chaplin's films, while Griffith and Fairbanks had guarantees of $200,000. Greenhill would pay print costs out of his 40 per cent share, while UA was to receive a 2 per cent commission from the producers' share. In order to secure a quick return which could be put back immediately into production, Greenhill was to pay $125,000 in advance on delivery of each negative.[32] When Greenhill later tried to have these advances decreased, he was told that UA saw them as the most important part of the deal and that it had traded down the producers' share of rentals in order to secure these advances.[33]

This makes it clear that lack of cash was one of the major motivations for the company to use an external foreign distributor in preference to its own network. However, Greenhill's proposal to act as UA's franchise distributor offered UA the next best thing to having its own distribution. Greenhill was prepared to set up a single organisation which would handle UA's films exclusively throughout the world. (Although the initial deal excluded South America, Hiram Abrams delayed negotiations for these rights so that Greenhill could bid for them as well.[34]) Greenhill also promised to: "pattern our European activities entirely upon the lines so successfully conducted in America by means of daily exchange of cables with your American office . . . making our European offices to all intents and purposes branch offices of your own organisation and subject to your own ideas."[35] Greenhill continually stressed that executive control would remain with New York, adding that UA would have "practically their own ideas carried out in all markets in a consistent way."[36] If the deal had the disadvantage of giving away foreign distribution, it maintained the coherence of UA as a unified distribution presence, established international distribution under the control of New York, and provided a guaranteed source of liquidity for production.

After signing a three year contract guaranteed by a $100,000 advance in July 1920, Greenhill failed to raise the £1 million necessary to capitalise his company. Given UA's interest in cutting through the proliferation of distribution middlemen, his position was always tenuous. He had been forced to make promises beyond his means in order to stay in the running for foreign rights, and he had also alienated UA by forming a separate company to acquire foreign rights to First National films.[37] He could not have chosen a worse time for this expansion, since it coincided with a severe downturn in the British economy. In January 1920 the London *Daily News* had reported that "(t)here is not a bean in the City for films today" and that "(e)very contract made by Americans who have spent a lot of money to come here and do the business, has vanished under the pressure of the financial situation."[38]

By the end of 1920 the general feeling within UA was that, apart from his now-dubious ability to provide upfront cash, Greenhill brought nothing in terms of expertise that UA could not supply itself. If UA took over foreign distribution, it would earn a share of the 40 per cent distribution fee rather than a mere 2 per cent commission. The three

artists (Pickford, Fairbanks and Griffith, with Chaplin being a significant exception) signed contracts on 15 December, 1920 for UA to
distribute their films internationally. Having had a unified, international
distribution network within its grasp, UA was in no mood to turn to
an outmoded, piecemeal system of territorial agents, most of whose
offers they had so recently disdained. In February 1921 UA formally
began the process of setting up its own foreign subsidiaries with a view
to commencing operations in Britain within two months.[39] Since
Greenhill had registered the name United Artists, the subsidiary was
called Allied Artists.

Greenhill's private assurances of American control raise a parallel with
FPL's operations in Britain during 1919. When FPL moved from a
franchise distribution to direct distribution in 1918, it turned from the
small-scale integration of British capital at the level of distribution
to the re-integration of local capital on a much grander scale. Both
Famous Players-Lasky British Producers and Picture Playhouses
Limited, formed in May and June 1919, had the backing of British coal
and financial interests.[40] The formation of a production arm was
generally welcomed by the British trade press, but the formation
of Picture Playhouses to build a chain of cinemas galvanised the
Cinematograph Exhibitors' Association (CEA) into bitter denunciations
of an American-inspired invasion. The CEA saw it as the beginnings
of an attempt to take over the British exhibition industry, a reaction
which demonstrated the greater financial importance of exhibition
relative to production within the British industry. The resolution
discussed at the most confrontational CEA meeting was not a ban on
American films but a ban on the building of picture houses unless they
were controlled by British subjects.[41] When Thomas Buchanan, the
Vice-President of the Scottish branch of the Exhibitors' Association
said that a "non-British Prime Minister would be less dangerous than
a non-British film-making combine controlling the British cinema
screen," he was not talking about what would be shown on those
screens.[42] The issue was not the national origin of the films but rather
the ownership and control of exhibition.

The Biograph (which led the fight against the CEA) pointed out that
Picture Playhouses was British-owned, but the proponents of a boycott
against FPL responded that control, and not ownership, was the issue.
The proposed structure of UA's Greenhill venture, if it can be cited as
a parallel, bears out the relevance of these claims, and is in line with
political economies of the media which stress the importance of

executive control rather than ownership.[43] The policies of UA and FPL indicate the strategies of indirect expansion pursued by American film companies at a moment when the terms of international trade inhibited direct capital investment. Ownership of capital resources was not immediately necessary for the expansion of the American production industry. Instead, the Americans centralised capital investment at the production phase, concentrating on volume and production values. Their stable supply of expensive films provided the basis for associations with foreign capital which could exploit American production downstream in distribution or exhibition. It made sense to European capital interests to specialise in areas which complemented international inputs. Greenhill and FPL's British associates saw their primary role as being the exploitation of a product which originated upstream in the marketing process. American international distributors took advantage of a capital-intensive production sector, priding themselves on making the most expensive films in the world (as one leading film exporter put it in 1919, "it is pretty generally conceded that Americans excel in the ability to spend money with real abandon"), though this did not initially involve large flows of capital into foreign countries.[44] The American film industry ideally expanded at this time by creating a situation in which local capital could be profitably invested.

The establishment of direct distribution by the American majors was crucial, as it drove a wedge into vertically integrated foreign companies, encouraging them to maximise their investment in exhibition. Post-war European film industries tended to skew toward exhibition, where their best profit potential lay. The Americans were keen to encourage this as they considered Europe "underdeveloped" in terms of theatre-building and cinema-going. The lack of suitable theatres cut into distribution revenues by shortening runs and increasing competition for scarce first-run theatres. Once local companies had centralised their investments in exhibition, they often had common cause with American distributors in arguing against measures by their own governments to restrict the import of foreign films. Government actions were seldom sufficiently finely tuned to shelter the local exhibitors who relied on imports. Entertainment taxes and exhibition quotas impacted directly on exhibitors. Increased customs duties and remittance taxes against American companies were an attractive source of tax revenue, but they inevitably led to the Americans increasing their licensing charges.[45] Import quotas also elicited opposition from exhibitors who wanted American distributors to bring as many popular films as possible into the market-place. A steady flow of imports ensured a regular supply of films. It also helped the bargaining position of exhibitors, since it meant that more films competed for scarce screen time; this brought down rental costs for the exhibitors and improved their bargaining position with distributors.[46]

The 'Independent' Subsidiary: Les Artists Associés

UA was quick to follow the establishment of Allied Artists, its British subsidiary, with a similar operation in continental Europe. Les Artists Associés (LAA) Société Anonyme was established in April 1921 by Guy Croswell Smith, a veteran of the Motion Picture Division of the Creel Committee. Smith's own distribution company, based on the rights to several of Griffith's films, had fallen victim to the slump of 1920 and he had been engaged by UA to open its Paris office. From here Smith set up branches in Marseilles and Lyons, and later in Belgium, Switzerland and Czechoslovakia. By the start of 1924 LAA had thirteen offices in eleven European countries.[47]

LAA was formally an autonomous French company, separate from UA but renting films from that company. This arrangement deferred profit offshore to the parent company. For the French company, the 70 per cent of rentals payable to the producers became a business expense and hence was not taxable. French taxes would only be paid on profits made by the French company from its 30 per cent of rentals. For the fully integrated American majors this was a marvellously flexible arrangement. Their foreign subsidiaries could negotiate a fee for the films which they would pay to their domestic production arm. The fee would be of sufficient size that the French subsidiary would make only a meagre profit and hence there would be little or no tax paid in France.

UA was in a slightly trickier position as its producers were independent of the distribution company and UA was trying to cut back on the terms offered to producers for international distribution, raising its distribution fee from 30 per cent to 50 per cent in some territories. The solution was to institute a commission fee to UA on top of the sum paid to producers, although its purpose was similar to that of the majors in converting potential profit into an untaxed expense against the local company. The fee was supposedly for publicity materials and legal representation in the US. Given the necessary fiction of the autonomy of local subsidiaries, they could not be charged for administrative costs and salaries. (Guy Croswell Smith was paid $75 per week by LAA in Paris, but was also paid $425 per week in New York on the books of the American company.[48]) These commissions represent what economists term *transfer pricing*, where value is added to the product as it is passed from one section of the corporation to another. Generally, commission fees were set at 5 per cent of rentals but this figure was flexible. In countries where the taxation authorities refused to recognise this as a legitimate expense, no franchise fees were levied. In other countries where the local companies were accruing large, taxable profits, the commission fee was set higher, at up to 20 per cent of rentals.

A memo prepared by Price Waterhouse during an audit of UA's German subsidiary in 1926 lists four common features of American distribution subsidiaries, all of which are applicable to an analysis of UA's European operations:

(1) Small capitalisation and large debt due on Current Account to the Parent Organisation.
(2) Substantial losses being shown on the [local] books.
(3) Complete admission on the part of the Film Companies that they are subsidiaries of definite American Film Corporations.
(4) Very small amounts being paid by way of taxes.[49]

Allied Artists had been capitalised at only £7,000.[50] By 1933, LAA still had a book capital of only 50,000 francs, but was carrying a deficit of 1.5 million francs. Given that virtually all of its debt was owed to UA and the producer-owners, there was no chance that it would be forced into bankruptcy. Hence the subsidiaries only increased their capital if governments demanded they do so through linking capitalisation to taxation formulae. Undercapitalisation was a means of generating debt to the parent company, which supported the subsidiary through loans rather than equity investment. When the subsidiary moved into profit, it could then dispose of surplus by remitting it as debt repayments, which were generally not taxable, as opposed to declaring taxable dividends.

The purpose of a local subsidiary was to export profit, not to show profit itself. In the course of the 1926 audit, Price Waterhouse sternly admonished the UA accounting department when LAA declared a profit of $100,958.29, reporting that "it is rather difficult for us to understand what advantage there can be in allowing the French company to make large profits in view of the heavy taxes they are subject to."[51] In 1927 this situation was rectified when LAA showed a profit of only $4,886.79. The American companies wanted their subsidiaries to show a minimal profit so that further government regulation would not be called down on them.[52]

As the Price Waterhouse memo shows, local ownership of the company was an open fiction. LAA had to maintain the legal forms of independence from the American parent, so as not to force the issue with the French government. While UA was officially asserting that LAA was "a regular French company with its own capital and Board of Directors," Arthur Kelly, UA's Vice-President in charge of international distribution, elsewhere noted that "I think it is well known in France, as well as every place in the world, that Les Artists Associés is a branch of the United Artists Corporation."[53]

The Coming of Sound

Between 1925 and 1926 UA's foreign network began to reach a point of early maturity. During this period domestic rentals rose by over 26 per cent but fell by almost 11 per cent as a proportion of UA's world-wide income. Table 6.1 shows that by 1926 UA's world-wide rentals had reached a point where foreign markets accounted for approximately 35 per cent of rentals. While UA's domestic rentals peaked in 1928 and continued in the $10–13 million range as the company completed its transition away from reliance on its initial founders, foreign sources of income, at $6–8 million, kept pace with the domestic market. The British subsidiary, Allied Artists, was the most important of UA's foreign operations, regularly returning rentals equivalent to between 20 and 25 per cent of the American market (10 to 15 per cent of UA's world-wide rentals.) Behind this apparent stability, however, an enormous challenge was looming as it became apparent that synchronous sound films would become the new industry standard. Continental Europe, which had grown to almost 12 per cent of world-wide rentals in 1927, began losing ground with the spread of import restrictions and the introduction of sound.

The problems that sound posed for international film distribution had long been recognised. In 1919 Britain's *Kinematograph Weekly* reported sceptically on the rumoured introduction of sound, repeating what it saw as a time-honoured argument that it would make no sense for the American industry to sacrifice its non-English speaking markets.[55] When sound came, many international observers still held to this belief.

Table 6.1. Regions as a percentage of UA's world-wide rentals, 1922–1932

	1923	1924	1925	1926	1927	1928	1929	1930	1931	1932
North America	75.30	63.88	75.31	64.58	65.46	63.81	64.24	63.61	57.30	53.18
Britain	11.06	16.89	10.23	15.10	9.29	13.43	15.36	17.93	23.76	28.64
Continental Europe	3.50	6.54	5.14	9.16	11.97	10.78	8.20	8.77	7.89	7.56
Asia	1.66	3.82	4.19	3.77	4.15	3.54	3.81	2.16	1.44	2.45
Latin America	2.01	3.83	2.49	4.44	6.32	5.54	5.11	3.79	4.10	3.72
Australia	6.46	5.05	2.65	2.95	2.81	2.90	3.29	3.73	2.71	2.12
Foreign rights									2.80	2.33

Source: compiled from UA Consolidated Balance Sheet[54]

J.C. Barnstyn, through whom UA had dealt in the Netherlands, wrote that: "For non-English speaking countries, such dialogue pictures have absolutely no value."[56] More recently, Ruth Vasey has argued that: "Although there was reason to fear that spoken dialogue would disrupt the American producers' hold upon non-English speaking markets, the enthusiasm with which the new technology was greeted abroad made the industry initially sanguine, if not complacent, about the future."[57] In the long term, sound may have furthered the dominance of American production by causing larger problems for production industries employing languages other than English, thus enhancing the comparative advantage enjoyed by US. In 1930 Universal's export manager wrote that: "Old Man Quality is not going to take a back seat for any new-comer—no matter what language he speaks."[58]

Although this argument is persuasive in general, it can gloss over the specific ways in which sound affected different sectors of the American industry, and it can also obscure the short-term perceptions of participants. After an initial enthusiasm for novel American sound films, sound acted as a stimulus for non-exportable local production emphasising the attraction of hearing one's own language. This resurgence in local production and the problems that the American industry experienced in arriving at internationally acceptable foreign language versions resulted in a contraction in rentals coming from the non-English-speaking markets in continental Europe, Asia and Latin America after 1929. Table 6.1 shows that in 1927 these three areas accounted for over 22 percent of UA's revenues, but that by 1932 they had shrunk to 13 percent, with Britain emerging as the sustaining force behind UA.

As Ginette Vincendeau has pointed out, one of the striking things about this period was the rapidity with which companies altered their plans for dealing with the new situation.[59] It is important to emphasise that the American response was by no means unified in its approach to the changed international mediascape produced by sound. Smaller companies and independents were more pessimistic than the majors about the prospects for dialogue films in foreign markets. While Paramount and MGM experimented with dubbing and multiple-language versions, UA's major strategy was to retract and see how things would work out. This involved contemplating a return to franchised distribution, experiments in joint distribution, and ventures into local production.

UA's foreign distribution network had barely been set in place when it had to adjust to the introduction of sound, and then to the Depression. Several of UA's subsidiaries had accumulated large deficits which the parent felt it could no longer finance in the new economic climate. For some smaller non-English-speaking markets sound appeared to be the final blow. At a board meeting in October 1929, UA President Joseph Schenck argued that:

> in view of the condition in the motion picture industry caused by the introduction of talking films, a majority of the producers of the United Artists Corporation do not intend to make any silent pictures to supply the non-English-speaking countries, and it was therefore deemed necessary and advisable that the best interests of the Corporation be served by disposing of the United Artists Corporation's Far East exchanges.[60]

Faced with what it perceived as the end (at least temporarily) of its business in many parts of the world, UA demonstrated that the options for foreign distribution were still fluid and that returning to a franchise situation was still a viable option.

While the larger American producers searched for an acceptable multiple-language format for sound, for smaller companies an institutional option was to retreat from direct representation. UA explored this option throughout 1929 in continental Europe. Guy Croswell Smith formed a management syndicate and approached UA with a proposition to buy all of UA's exchanges for $100,000 and thereafter to distribute UA films on a 65–35 per cent basis. Smith's proposition amounted to a return to the type of arrangement envisaged with Greenhill. Like Greenhill, Smith had difficulty raising the money but he successfully bargained UA down. UA reasoned that it would have to meet Smith's terms, since it looked to be going out of business in Europe in any case. Arthur Kelly, Vice-President in charge of UA's Foreign Department, wrote that "if we did, by chance, have a few silent pictures to sell" in continental Europe, UA could use its old network.[61] Legal counsel Dennis O'Brien put it even more strongly:

> As Kelly states there is no alternative for operation, there is no decision left but to accept [Smith's offer]. I think the security is meagre and will need competent representatives to enforce— because we are abandoning the territory for fear of losses and all our employees are accepting a losing venture—hence our entire efforts should be directed upon enforcement of contract.[62]

In such terms UA showed itself ready simply to retreat from direct distribution in the non-English-speaking sectors of Europe. In the latter part of 1929 UA began laying off staff at its European exchanges and demanding that branch managers take pay cuts of between 20 and 25 per cent "until such time as we have more pictures to distribute."[63] In October 1930 Kelly was still writing in reference to Europe that "we do not know how long we can stay in business in that territory," and the following month he added that "the motion picture business in foreign territories is in a rather precarious condition and our future in France is uncertain."[64] The same pessimistic assessment was registered within LAA. The resignation letter of its Treasurer in November 1929 cites "the desire to find employment in some industry offering prospects more calculable than those of the distribution in Europe of films produced in America."[65] Even Guy Croswell Smith, while negotiating to buy out UA's European agencies, went heavily into debt to buy a hotel and restaurant in a bid to diversify his business affairs.

The 1929 UA balance sheet shows that the wholly English-speaking segments of the world market (North America, England and Australia) accounted for almost 83 per cent of rentals. Continental Europe represented 8.2 per cent of UA's world-wide rentals, 5.97 per cent of producers' revenues and about 7.25 per cent of UA's total pre-tax profit. Given that the company was moving to give greater weight to its activities in Britain through the distribution of Columbia's films and the incorporation of British production, UA may have been wise to consolidate its position around its major profit centres.

UA's distribution of Columbia's films in key markets, primarily

Britain, bears analysis as another distribution option available to American companies at this time. The spirit of common interest and (sometimes grudging) co-operation established by bodies such as the MPPDA and its foreign counterparts set the context for the major American companies to explore closer associations through joint distribution ventures in some foreign markets. The best known of these was Parufamet in Germany in 1926. This was followed in 1927 by the association of First National, Paramount and MGM to distribute in Eastern Europe as Fanamet. *Film Daily Yearbook* saw Fanamet as part of a larger trend but noted that this co-operative behaviour made sense primarily in small markets: "The group [Fanamet] which stands ready to extend the coordinated selling operation throughout the world will never enter important markets where competitive selling, in the ultimate, means better results for all concerned."[66]

The studio system always entailed a degree of domestic co-operation among the majors, but it was in overseas territories that this co-operation was put to the test. To distribute through another major was generally seen as a unsatisfactory compromise in that it had to be assumed that the other company would give preference to its own pictures when publicising films, constructing programme blocks to protect weaker releases, and negotiating more aggressively with exhibitors. While UA was ceding its autonomy to the larger MGM in Asia, it sought to exploit a weaker partner in Britain, which was emerging as UA's major profit centre.

Columbia was still struggling to establish international distribution at the coming of sound. In 1927 it had arranged British distribution through Film Booking Office, which had a distribution network established by its forerunner Robertson-Cole. In October 1930 UA was approached by Columbia (which shared the Godfrey Building on Seventh Avenue as its New York headquarters) to distribute six features and 104 shorts over the 1930–1 season. The alliance was cemented when UA loaned Columbia $50,000 in January 1931 and a further $150,000 in June against the collateral of Columbia's 1931–2 output.[67] Over the next two years UA began to distribute Columbia in Spain, Brazil, India and Denmark.

The British contract gives an insight into the issues involved in joint distribution. UA charged Columbia its standard foreign distribution fee of 30 per cent (in the other countries it was 40 per cent) and received exclusive British rights to Columbia films for four years. Columbia retained the right to roadshow any of its films, with the proviso that

UA receive 10 per cent of any roadshow grosses. UA guaranteed to release only "a fair percentage" of Columbia's films during the summer months (when film attendance was typically lower) and specified a sum to be spent on the promotion of Columbia's films. Columbia agreed to furnish its share of the quota pictures required by Britain's Cinematograph Films Act, but it was agreed that the budgets of these "quota quickies" should not exceed £6,000. The deal was to be reviewed after ten months with Columbia having the option of immediate termination.[68]

The contract was extended by both parties in 1932 and finally ran until 1933, but the relation between UA and Columbia proved to be an uneasy one because of the restrictions it placed on UA in particular. Columbia had prior foreign rights commitments to some of the product it distributed domestically (notably Disney films), while UA had undertaken to distribute no films other than its own and those of Columbia, along with British quota films. As UA extended its production interests in England this became increasingly restrictive. In July 1932 UA's British subsidiary concluded a deal with Herbert Wilcox's British and Dominions company (B&D) for a package of thirty-six films to be distributed throughout Britain, Australasia and India. This violated the Columbia contract, which specified that UA distribute only a sufficient number of British films to satisfy the Films Act. UA's British representatives saw no problem with this as the original Columbia contract was to expire in August 1932, well before any B&D films would be supplied. Problems arose, however, when New York renewed the Columbia contract with its exclusivity clause intact through to August 1934, without consulting the British subsidiary. The British office insisted that the B&D contract, which called for twelve B&D films to be handled in the upcoming year (four above the requirements of the quota), was "almost fundamental to our continuation." As UA was also negotiating with Alexander Korda at this time, the restrictiveness of the Columbia contract was keenly felt, leading the British office to plead to Dennis O'Brien, "Cannot you and the New York directors get us back our freedom?"[69] New York was reluctant to challenge Columbia on this point, as Columbia had been "more or less adamant" on the exclusivity arrangements during negotiations.[70] The renewed agreement with Columbia was finally terminated in October 1933 as UA pursued its interest in B&D and Korda as a source of films suitable for the domestic market as well as for international distribution.[71]

This episode demonstrates the variance of interests between American companies, as UA moved beyond the standard American policy of viewing British production simply as a means of satisfying quota requirements. As I have already indicated, the system of interrelation between American and British capital prior to this point was primarily a complementary one. Within this system, American companies produced and distributed popular high-budget films, providing a regular source of supply that allowed for the expansion of local exhibition. The spread of quota legislation, allied (in continental Europe) to the demand for films in local languages, dialects and accents, made for short-term imbalances within this system, leading American distribution companies into positions where they were forced to acquire local productions. While UA led the way in its integration of British production, its attempts to incorporate local production in continental Europe were piecemeal and inefficient.

In 1930 Joseph Schenck authorised LAA to borrow 750,000 francs for the production of French talkies. Guy Croswell Smith borrowed twice that amount, apparently without authorisation—once more demonstrating a lack of unity between head office and subsidiary.[72] The demand for French-language films temporarily gave producers the upper hand in negotiations. LAA invested in four films ceding producers 60 to 65 per cent of rentals, although the share of rentals normally remitted to American producers by LAA had dropped to 50 per cent by this time. This production investment also entailed a new risk for LAA: external debt. Before then the company's deficit had been financed by debt to the parent company. Advancing money for production was a departure from UA's domestic policy of arranging a distribution contract which the producer could then use as a means of securing finance elsewhere. UA had hoped that each of the films (*Coeur de Lilas, Casque de Cuir, Un Homme Heureux* and *Nuit au Paradis*) could earn rentals of 4 million francs in France, Belgium and Switzerland. Instead the four films combined earned less than 2.1 million francs, leading to a loss estimated at between 210,000 and 500,000 francs.[73] This was in spite of the fact that the four films far outperformed any of UA's American releases in France through 1933. (The 1933 balance sheet shows the French films as accounting for almost 68 per cent of UA's French business for that year.[74]) Following these initial losses, UA returned to a policy of only considering limited distribution of European films (including those of Harry D'Arrast's Soriano Films and Lianofilm) without any involvement in production funding.[75]

Conclusion

By focusing on two critical moments in the history of American film distribution in Europe—the post-war establishment of direct distribution and the introduction of sound—I hope to have given a sense of the variety of options and the different choices made by participants between these options. Much of the recent interest in foreign distribution deals in large-scale questions about globalisation and transnational capital. We need, however, to contextualise these large-scale concepts within a historical perspective which also registers change from the bottom up. From such a perspective, the actions and motivations of the participants are foregrounded, thereby restoring a greater sense of agency to the diverse interests involved in the process of international film distribution.

In this case, it becomes easier to grasp the complex relationship between American production and European capital, and to see this relationship as one constantly changing in response to local as well as global factors. The international ascendancy of American production throughout much of this period was one that was mutually rewarding for American distributors, who could concentrate their resources on production (as well as other domestic investments), and for European companies, who could centre their resources on the expansion of exhibition. These specialisations allowed for an overall increase in the profitability of the cinema, attracting more consumers who were prepared to pay higher prices. However, this alliance of interests was by no means complete or stable. It was open to the internal problems and priorities of American companies just as it was open to the social and political challenges, which gave rise to political actions such as import restrictions and local production quotas. Finally, it was open to the kind of technological challenges that were represented by the conversion to sound and the introduction of synchronised dialogue.

Notes

1. Thomas Guback, "Hollywood's International Markets," in Tino Balio, ed., *The American Film Industry* revised edition (Madison: University of Wisconsin Press, 1985), p. 465.
2. There is also the more pragmatic factor that United Artists' corporate records constitute one of the best-archived collections available to film researchers. All references to UA corporate documents contained in this

chapter derive from the United Artists Collection, held at the Wisconsin Center for Film and Theatre Research in Madison, Wisconsin.

3. Kristin Thompson, *Exporting Entertainment: America in the World Film Market, 1907–1934* (London: British Film Institute, 1985), pp. 28, 72–4.

4. *Moving Picture World*, 16 November 1918, p. 736. Another instance of this is the sale of the rights to Chaplin's First National films. This involved William Vogel, who held the foreign rights, negotiating with Gillespie Brothers, a European importer, who then sold the films to Salm Ltd for Spain and Portugal (*Moving Picture World*, 22 February 1919, p. 1086).

5. *Moving Picture World*, 21 December 1918, p. 1397.

6. From its very beginning, UA was sold in the trade press as an attempt to limit the influence of distribution companies. In announcing the formation of the company, Mary Pickford was quoted as saying: "Under the new plan, the producers will deal with the exhibitors direct. The middleman, or distributor will be eliminated entirely." A cartoon accompanying the story showed the stars as pioneers setting out to canoe downstream, leaving a Native American guide (labelled "distributor") out of the canoe. *Wid's Daily*, 22 January 1919.

7. *Wid's Daily*, 28 March 1919. UA's reluctance to form an international distribution network has been noted in Gaizka S. de Usabel, *The High Noon of American Films in Latin America* (Ann Arbor: UMI Research Press, 1982), p. 18.

8. *Variety*, 7 March 1919, p. 73.

9. Dennis O'Brien to John Fairbanks, 7 April 1919, United Artists Collection, O'Brien Legal Files (hereafter "O'Brien") 208/1.

10. From UA's point of view percentage contracts were much more attractive than flat rate deals. If the deal involved a flat fee, the price offered was likely to be lower, because the foreign distributors calculated in the extent to which the risk was being transferred to them. The films of UA's Big Four were assumed to be pre-sold successes with very little chance of failure, and thus the distribution company would clearly want arrangements which allowed it to participate heavily in successes. Flat rate deals were generally used for smaller territories where it was expected that returns would be low and that it would not be worth the trouble of chasing a percentage. In UA's case percentage deals also had the advantage that they allowed for a consistency which would allay internal tensions, such as Griffith's fears that favouritism was being shown to Pickford and Fairbanks. Griffith could argue about the fairness of flat sums extracted from exhibitors, which could vary greatly between bookings, but not the fairness of a percentage applied to all three film-makers. Carl K. York to O'Brien, 22 March 1920; Alfred E. Bailey to Hiram Abrams, 28 May 1920, both O'Brien 201/8.

11. O'Brien to Millard Johnson, Australasian Films, 18 June 1920, O'Brien 201/8; *Wid's Daily*, 27 June 1919. (FPL encountered similar problems with

Allen's which it attempted to solve by buying into Allen's theatres. When it failed at this, FLP similarly established their own Canadian distribution and bought into the rival Regal Film Corporation as an alternative. *Wid's Daily*, 3 June 1919; *Variety*, 24 October 1919, p. 66).

12. Tino Balio, *United Artists: The Company Built by the Stars* (Madison: University of Wisconsin Press, 1976), pp. 30–51.

13. Ibid., p. 28.

14. Guy Croswell Smith to M.L. Malevinsky, 1 August 1922, O'Brien 216/13.

15. Croswell Smith to Hiram Abrams, 19 July 1921, O'Brien 216/12.

16. *Wid's Daily*, 29 March 1919 and 5 May 1919.

17. The move of international film sales from London to New York as a consequence of the First World War is one of the central themes of Thompson's *Exporting Entertainment*.

18. *The Bioscope*, vol. 41, no. 657, 15 May 1919, p. 4; *Variety*, 23 May 1919, p. 65; *Moving Picture World*, vol. 40, no. 9, 31 May 1919, p. 1341; see also Thompson, *Exporting Entertainment*, pp. 63–71.

19. Tippett arrived in the US in March 1920 announcing his plans to build a studio there. Whether these plans had any substance, they demonstrate a division between the location of production centres and international distribution centres (*Variety*, 5 March 1920, p. 65).

20. *The Bioscope*, 19 June 1919, p. 6.

21. US Department of Commerce figures show that over the first seven months of 1916, the US exported 114,463,687 feet of exposed film with a value of $4,687,534. For the corresponding period in 1918, exports totalled 50,208,925 feet with a value of $2,689,925 (*Moving Picture World*, vol. 38, no. 2, 12 October 1918, p. 205).

22. *Wid's Daily*, 7 March 1919.

23. *Variety*, 6 June 1919, p. 58, 13 June 1919, p. 54, and 26 September 1919, p. 57.

24. *Wid's Yearbook*, 1919–20, p. 93.

25. The president of NAMPI, William A. Brady, said that "the South American market is now ripe for an American invasion and that an extensive and aggressive campaign on the part of American producers would result shorting in practically monopoly" (*Wid's Daily*, 9 April 1919).

26. *Variety*, 8 November 1918, p. 45.

27. *Wid's Daily*, 30 April 1919.

28. *Variety*, 26 September 1919, p. 64.

29. *Moving Picture World*, 27 March 1920, pp. 2136 and 2154.

30. Frank Costigliola, *Awkward Dominion: American Political, Economic, and Cultural Relations with Europe, 1919–1933* (Ithaca, NJ: Cornell University Press, 1984), pp. 65–7 and p. 103; "Foreign Trade of the United States in the Calendar Year 1926," United States Department of Commerce, Bureau of Foreign and Domestic Commerce, *Trade Information Bulletin*,

no. 460, 1927, pp. 1, 25. The figures on the ratio of foreign sales to production come from Costigliola. The *Trade Information Bulletin* gives a slightly different figure, from 16.4 per cent in 1919 to 8.9 per cent in 1923 (p. 19). Thompson also deals with this period on pp. 102–4.

31. "Home-made Movies Libel Us Abroad," *Current Opinion*, no. 77, July 1924, p. 75; *Trade Information Bulletin*, no. 460, p. 21.
32. "Memorandum of Agreement between Morris Greenhill and United Artists Corporation," 30 July 1020, O'Brien 211/6.
33. O'Brien to FW Guedalla, 16 December 1920, O'Brien 211/4.
34. Abrams to Greenhill, 20 August 1920, O'Brien 211/3. Thompson also makes a point of stressing the pre-war American industry's interest in the convenience of only dealing with a single set of foreign rights (*Exporting Entertainment*), p. 32).
35. Greenhill to Douglas Fairbanks, 22 October 1919, O'Brien 211/3.
36. Greenhill to Robert P. Lewis, the New York manager for Greenhill and Sons, 20 December 1919, O'Brien 211/3.
37. Abrams to O'Brien, 29 September 1920, O'Brien 211/3.
38. London *Daily News*, 20 January 1920.
39. O'Brien to Guedalla, 8 February 1921, O'Brien 211/4; Press release from Hiram Abrams, 19 February 1921, O'Brien 201/8.
40. *Wid's Daily*, 16 May 1919.
41. *Wid's Daily* 17 July 1919. UA had an early taste of this type of reaction a bare month after the announcement of its formation when rumours were reported in Britain that it would build a major chain of theatres. This rumour was enough for *The Bioscope* to run a cartoon of UA members crucifying the British film industry (*The Bioscope*, 20 February 1919, p. 15).
42. *Variety*, 18 July 1919, p. 50.
43. See, for example, Graham Murdock, "Large Corporations and the Control of the Communications Industries," in Michael Gurevich, Tony Bennett, James Curran and Janet Woolacott, eds, *Culture, Society and The Media* (London: Methuen, 1982).
44. *Moving Picture World*, 24 May 1919, p. 1205.
45. This line of argument was used explicitly (and successfully by the Czech Manufacturers' Association in 1935 when the government proposed a 12 per cent tax on all overseas remittances (MPPDA Foreign Department circular, 13 December 1935, O'Brien 60/1).
46. The co-operation between American distributors and local exhibition interests can be most clearly seen in the French film industry of the 1920s and 1930s where struggles to limit the influence of the American film distributors usually lined up the Chambre Syndicale de la Cinématographie Français, which was dominated by smaller producers and headed by Charles Delac, against the Syndicate Français des Directeurs de Theatres

Cinématographiques, headed throughout the 1930s by Raymond Lussiez. Lussiez worked hand in hand with the MPPDA representative Harold L. Smith to co-ordinate French exhibitors and American distributors in their opposition to quota measures. Smith briefed MPPDA members on the way Lussiez had "collaborated with us for years" describing him as "our only friend in whom I have complete confidence" (Harold L. Smith to F.L. Herron, 21 March 1935 and 27 September 1935, O'Brien 59/3). UA's European manager wrote about the efficiency of "reaching the Senators through convincing the exhibitors'" when quota laws were being contemplated in 1928 (Croswell Smith to Kelly, 5 January 1928, O'Brien 58/9). So effective was this pressure that Edouard Herriot, then Minister of Fine Arts, had to resort to decree rather than parliamentary legislation to institute the controversial quota controls which were later overturned by the MPPDA's boycott. A further point of alliance between American distributors and French exhibitors came with the introduction of sound. Both groups opposed attempts by authors' and composers' societies who enforced royalty payments of 3.3 per cent collected from the exhibitors' share of the gross and who then attempted to expand those royalty payments through negotiations over the Berne Convention (Gabriel Hess, MPPDA attorney, to O'Brien, 19 April 1935, O'Brien 59/8).

47. Abrams to O'Brien, 24 January 1924, O'Brien 216/13.
48. Arthur Kelly to Coudert Frères, 16 January 1931, O'Brien 59/1.
49. Price, Waterhouse & Co. memo, 20 August 1928, O'Brien 149//7.
50. O'Brien to Coudert Brothers, 29 April 1921, O'Brien 216/12.
51. Price Waterhouse to Kelly, 20 July 1927, UA Consolidated Balance Sheets, 1/11.
52. UA's Vice-President Arthur Kelly wrote to Smith that "we want each unit to show a suitable profit which would satisfy the tax authorities of each respective country" (Kelly to Smith, 8 February 1929, O'Brien 58/9).
53. T.P. Mulrooney to Paul O'Brien, 24 January 1935, O'Brien 59/3; Kelly to E.C. Raftery, 30 January 1931, O'Brien 59/1.
54. UA Consolidated Balance Sheets and Income Statements, Boxes 1–12.
55. *Kinematograph Weekly*, 6 March 1919, p. 51.
56. *Film Daily Yearbook*, 1929, p. 1001.
57. Ruth Vasey, *The World According to Hollywood, 1918–1939* (Exeter: University of Exeter Press, 1997), p. 86.
58. *Film Daily Yearbook*, 1930, p. 997.
59. Ginette Vincendeau, "Hollywood Babel," *Screen*, vol. 30, no. 1, Spring, 1989, pp. 24–39, reprinted in this volume.
60. UA Corporate Minutes, 18 October 1929, microfilm 6009, UA Collection, Wisconsin Center for Film and Theatre Research.
61. Unsigned memo, 1 August 1929, O'Brien 135/7.

62. Initialled marginalia in Raftery to O'Brien, 19 August 1929, O'Brien 135/7.
63. Croswell Smith to Kelly, 28 November, 1919, O'Brien 58/9.
64. Kelly to O'Brien, 24 October 1930; Kelly to Coudert Frères, 1 November 1930, O'Brien 59/1.
65. Kelly to O'Brien, 13 November 1929, O'Brien 58/9.
66. *Film Daily Yearbook*, 1927, p. 941.
67. Raftery to Benjamin Pepper, undated (August 1931?), O'Brien 151/4.
68. Agreement between Columbia Pictures Distribution Company, United Artists' Corporation and United Artists' Corporation, Limited (U.K.), 12 December 1930, O'Brien 151/3.
69. Guedalla to O'Brien, 7 October 1932, O'Brien 151/4.
70. Raftery to Guedalla, 3 November 1932, O'Brien 151/4.
71. UA released nine B&D films in the US between 1932 and 1935 and thirty films produced by Alexander Korda beginning in 1933.
72. Kelly to O'Brien, 24 October 1930, O'Brien 59/1.
73. M. Le Blanc to William Philips, 5 January 1934; Philips to Le Blanc, 19 January 1934. UA Collection, Philips Files 3/7.
74. Les Artists Associés Balance Sheet, 2 September 1933, Pilips Files 3/6.
75. Agreement with Soriano Films, 23 July 1934; agreement with S.A. Lianofilm, 27 December 1934, Philips Files 3.7.

7

Germany and Film Europe

Thomas J. Saunders

By the mid-1920s national film industries from Britain to Soviet Russia saw the colonisation of Europe by Hollywood as a primary challenge to their commercial and cultural well-being.[1] Co-operative responses to this challenge grew with the recognition that Hollywood's ascendancy was not a temporary side-effect of wartime disruptions but an unshakeable fact of life unless novel strategies were developed to counter it.[2] Both positively and negatively the movement for European film co-operation revolved largely around the axis Hollywood–Berlin, with Hollywood representing the threat and Germany providing the rallying point. Germany, the motion picture as well as the geographical heart of Europe in the 1920s, therefore assumed a critical role in the emergence of Film Europe. Behind the shield of import regulation and an inflated currency, Germany initially fantasised about breaking the American stranglehold. Its mid-decade defeat and disillusionment in the contest against Hollywood, which coincided with its emergence from post-war isolation, laid the foundation for multilateral collaboration linking Western to Central Europe.[3]

Recent research has identified a series of positive developments toward the goal of Film Europe, from international conferences through collaborative production projects to international engagements of prominent directors and actors.[4] Some impressive joint ventures were launched in the second half of the decade. While they all have claims to inclusion in the movement toward a European cinema, and were indeed viewed by contemporaries as steps away from national exclusiveness to co-operation, neither individually nor collectively did they represent fulfilment of the vision. The term Film Europe connoted more than the sum of proliferating agreements to co-finance production or to distribute across national borders. From the German perspective,

Film Europe had, at least for a time, broader and more unitary implications.

As Andrew Higson notes in his essay in this volume, the international film congresses of the 1920s formed one tangible expression of Film Europe and proved of particular symbolic importance for Germany insofar as they marked the transition from isolation to inclusion in the international community.[5] German film representatives did not receive an invitation to a preliminary congress which met in Paris in late 1923. Still excluded from the League of Nations, Germany was also in the final stages of an undeclared war with France in the Ruhr. German opinion both resented the exclusion and dismissed the conference as little more than a social event and a chance for the French to draw attention to their cinema achievements.[6] German delegates did attend the subsequent international film congress in Paris in September 1926, held under the auspices of the League of Nations, to discuss the cultural and educational aspects of the medium. As a demonstration that wartime enmities were shrinking quickly, this congress could be judged a step toward more broadly based co-operation.[7] Practically speaking, however, it remained little more than an opportunity to exchange views, underscored by the requirement that resolutions required unanimous support if they were to be adopted. The fact that the Paris congress had no direct sequel indicates that the set of issues (youth, hygiene, education etc.) it had a mandate to address were not the most pressing concerns of the European film industry. German opinion welcomed reintegration into the international film world, but had few illusions about the limitations of such a forum. A leading trade journal described the conference as a disappointment precisely because it skirted the central issue of the day: Europe's motion picture relationship with the United States.[8]

The Paris congress served as a point of departure for another kind of international conference which brought together national associations of European exhibitors. The first of these met fully two years later in Berlin; a second took place in Paris in the middle of the transition to sound and on the eve of general economic crisis in June 1929. Here economic issues came to the forefront. For instance, a draft federation of European exhibitors emerged and with it agreement in principle by delegations from eleven nations to create a European syndicate of cinema owners.[9] In 1928 some observers therefore celebrated the progress toward Film Europe since the Paris congress of 1926, but progress remained piecemeal and largely bilateral: the multilateral exhibitors' syndicate did not become reality. Moreover, subservience to America persisted. Ludwig Klitzsch, Ufa's chief executive and head of SPIO (Spitzenorganisation der deutschen Filmwirtschaft), the umbrella organisation of the German film industry, captured European ambivalence in a major speech to the conference. In a remarkable piece of diplomatic double-talk, Klitzsch professed to welcome the movement toward greater European film co-operation; but he simultaneously excised its anti-American impulse and heaped flattering words on his American counterpart, Will Hays. His caution *vis-à-vis* Hollywood reflected a broader reserve. Despite initial planning for a European federation of exhibitors, this conference did not mark a milestone on the road to Film Europe.[10]

The international congresses represent what one German commentator described as the Platonic version of Film Europe.[11] It would be misleading to judge them as misguided or stillborn insofar as they failed to create enduring supranational organisations. It is germane to inquire to what extent the ideas they floated found concrete realisation outside the conference circuit. A series of collaborative agreements between private companies of the leading European film countries, chiefly France, Britain, Germany and Italy, and the movement of personnel from one national industry to another, testify to practical co-operation. Yet, whether this co-operation represents a European design rather than simply a web of independent arrangements to exchange motion pictures or create joint productions remains debatable. One must ask if the rhetoric of Film Europe embroidered unexceptional commercial developments.

To answer this question it is necessary to revisit the interrelated complexes of Hollywood and the German film industry. By mid-decade German reactions to American inroads, like reactions in other European countries, involved resentment of economic exploitation, dislike of a motion picture formula widely blamed for alienating movie-goers and fear of cultural domination. Germany's delayed and relatively limited invasion by Hollywood made it at once the model to emulate and the European leader in other markets. German firms had extensive bilateral ties with the American majors but also continued to make a distinctive national product which enjoyed international artistic respect. Under these circumstances German interest in a pan-European project was a prerequisite to concrete progress.

German references to international co-operation date from early in the decade. In 1922 Erich Pommer, then Production Chief with

Decla-Bioscop, and Fritz Lang were invited to Paris to attend a meeting with a handful of counterparts from France, Italy and Britain respectively to discuss reciprocal distribution of each other's motion pictures. German trade reports on this meeting welcomed Germany's reception as an equal among other film nations. This helps explain headlines whose grandiose tones were overblown and misleading.[12] Behind the inflated language also lay the fact that France had recently begun to screen German films again and that French critics responded warmly to a number of these, among them *Der müde Tod, Scherben* and *Der brennende Acker*.[13] German sources admitted that the meeting itself proved more pragmatic than visionary. The only approximation to co-production came in the suggestion that the films for exchange be based on distinct national themes but be made with an eye on the international market, a proposal neither startling nor controversial. More important was the fact that at a parallel press conference Pommer had to face charges that the German quota system was directed particularly against France. French dissatisfaction with the discrepancy between their own willingness to import German pictures and Germany's very restrictive import controls indicates that at a very fundamental level Film Europe was a long way from realisation.[14]

Viewed in the light of later developments, two elements of German perceptions at this time are striking. The first is that for Pommer, and for the German trade press, the defence of Germany's right to regulate the influx of foreign films ran parallel to the open admission that free exchange of motion pictures was normal and natural. Film experts, like economic leaders and policy-makers, assumed that normalcy meant restoration of pre-war conditions: that is, a high degree of integration of the European market. From this perspective the notion of Film Europe represented a resurrection of the past rather than a novel departure. There was, of course, no going back. Germany's film role in Europe had grown substantially since before the war, and Hollywood's new-found hegemony gave unrestricted exchange a different meaning. Yet German conviction that the quota system was a transitional instrument to ease reintegration of the German film industry after the market dislocation caused by the war suggests that on the distribution front Film Europe did not represent a radical break.

The second point which deserves highlighting concerns Hollywood. Germans were certainly aware of the saturation of European markets with American films. One report on the Paris meeting offered excerpts from a half-dozen French papers in which European collaboration as a defence against Hollywood was a prominent theme. Nonetheless, German sources did not express concern about the American threat.[15] (Pommer did, however, defend Germany's quota with reference to French inundation from unnamed foreign sources!) Their indifference not only to the plight of their neighbours but also to the prospect of a similar fate was consistent with general perceptions in the German industry prior to the collapse of the national currency in 1923. Sheltered by the quota and especially by the rapidly falling value of the German mark, German producers and distributors were able to export cheaply. Having not yet experienced American inroads first-hand, they took a more offensive than defensive stance, anticipating continued expansion in international outlets for their product.

Pommer assumed a pioneering role in this expansion, but one must be cautious in equating his objectives, either then or later, with those of the nascent Film Europe movement. His consistent promotion of 'international cinema' entailed collaboration with Hollywood rather than common cause against it. It is no accident that later in the decade he was employed in Hollywood precisely as interest in Film Europe became strong. On his return to Germany he promoted 'international cinema' rather than a cinema born of Europe's cultural or filmic traditions. Had Europe enjoyed reciprocal film exchange with America, as many of its protagonists hoped, the difference between these two visions would have been minimised. Since it did not, Pommer's position must be distinguished from that of those frustrated by Hollywood and interested in Europe for Europeans.[16]

From the German side, preliminary discussion of Film Europe therefore took place in an optimistic environment rather than the beleaguered position of subsequent years. It thus lacked much of the later rhetorical baggage. Exchange between European countries represented a norm to be re-established and an opportunity to be exploited by an industry which had risen from relative impotence before 1914 to become the European leader. This meant that as international relations permitted, formal alliances could be pursued. Once the diplomatic crisis between Germany and France eased after 1923, German companies, Ufa prominent among them, began to widen the net of European links. In spring 1924 Ufa signed a contract with Louis Aubert exchanging distribution rights for France and Belgium with those for Germany and Central Europe. It also arranged with Herbert Wilcox to co-produce *Decameron Nights* with an English–German cast in Decla-Bioscop's Berlin studio. These were forward-looking moves in so far as they left behind the estrangement caused by war. They aimed, however, less to pave a road to Film Europe than to widen distribution markets through conventional bilateral arrangements. Although pursued against the backdrop of Hollywood's omnipresence, they were not presented as challenging it.[17]

In France more than in Germany the breakthrough in post-war film relations exemplified by the Ufa–Aubert alliance acquired pan-European connotations. When Louis Aubert visited Berlin in May 1924 he attributed both immediate and long-term significance to the contract. He emphasised the renewal of pre-war international ties and the fact that in this case reciprocity was established, unlike in the over-whelmingly one-way trade with Hollywood. He also pointed forward to a loose bloc of European producing countries which could share costs and markets, allowing them, like Hollywood, to recover expenses from major projects. Although admitting that this was a distant prospect, he made an open plea for its creation:

> In future I anticipate . . . the 'European cinema' will, alongside preservation and highlighting of the respective national identities, together form a uniform whole which can counter the superior competition of America. We are not opposed to America, but we also want our place in the sun, as we deserve.[18]

The final statement here, a paraphrase of Bernhard von Bülow's famous words regarding Germany's turn-of-the-century imperial ambitions, rings oddly coming from a French visitor, but it exposed the growing frustration with American domination and also clearly aimed to catch German attention.

Sooner than Aubert anticipated, a German firm attempted to realise his vision on a very large scale. In 1924 Westi-Film, a company in the vast industrial empire built by Hugo Stinnes, created the European Film Syndicate, the decade's outstanding, albeit short-lived, venture in pan-European cinema. Founded on the artistic and entrepreneurial vision of an émigré Russian, Vladimir Wengeroff, this scheme pioneered strategies for joint defence against American supremacy. Wengeroff saw in the pooling of European production resources and distribution/exhibition circuits a way by which to create outstanding motion pictures of European flavour to rival the American product.[19] Thanks to the enormous resources and international ambitions of the Stinnes empire, Wengeroff enjoyed the means to realise his scheme. From distribution ties with Hugenberg's Deulig-Film and distribution and exhibition subsidiaries across Europe to production affiliates in France (Ciné-France), Italy and Sweden, Westi-Film created a European network of production and rental companies. The key to the complex remained the Franco-German connection: in late 1924 Westi and Ciné-France allied with the Pathé-Consortium (distribution and theatres) and the production company Société des Cinéromans. This pact projected a dozen features in its first year, half of them by Westi, with cost recovery assured by its far-flung exhibition network.[20]

After creating a considerable stir in international film circles, the European Film Syndicate collapsed just months after its founding when the Stinnes concern went into receivership and was parcelled out to meet the claims of multiple creditors. Deulig and Ufa acquired a number of its assets, in the former case the rights to the handful of feature films that eventually came from Ciné-France and Cinéromans— *Michel Strogoff*, *Les Misérables*, *Casanova* and Abel Gance's monumental *Napoléon*, which was the final and much-delayed stepchild of the venture. Daniel Otto suggests that the ignominious collapse of the syndicate discredited both the concept of a European film consortium in general and German parties to such a scheme in particular.[21] Had the experiment been successful, it would certainly have convinced the sceptical and invited much imitation. There are, however, two caveats to be registered. The first is that the obstacle to comparable endeavours was less the failure of the European Film Syndicate *per se* than the generic challenges of co-ordination and funding which this one case illustrated. Opportunities for such grand ventures hardly obtained, particularly at a time when the German film industry faced very tight credit conditions. The second point is that the vision of Film Europe did not in fact die: experts continued to discuss ways to effect it, and several attempts, admittedly of limited scope, were made utilising the same principles. The Wengeroff project came at the beginning, rather than the end, of broad interest in a union of European film countries to counter American ascendance. Viewed in light of subsequent calls for some form of European film coalition, it had prophetic significance, even if some of its features were judged flawed or premature.

Despite the dramatic collapse of Westi-Film and the European project which it championed, within a year of Louis Aubert's observations German experts began to echo his opinions. By 1925 both the quantity and quality of American motion pictures distributed in Germany sparked a backlash against Hollywood. Although some allowance must be made for a tendency to dramatise critical and popular reaction, there is enough evidence to indicate that the mass of American imports did not find particular favour with German movie audiences. Coincident with this reaction Hollywood began to secure its place on the German market with a series of contracts providing import permits in exchange for loans. Germany remained less beholden to American capital and motion pictures than the other European states, but it no longer enjoyed independence. As German film companies gradually conceded the futility of single-handedly besting Hollywood, the logic and language of Film Europe gained wider resonance. Growing resentment of Hollywood served as grist for the European mill.[22]

The shifting perceptions of German experts can be traced through 1925/6. One year after Louis Aubert's statements in Berlin, *Reichsfilmblatt*, the journal of independent exhibitors, lamented German slowness in recognising that friendliness to America meant subjugation. It argued that whereas other European film industries—Britain and France—were appealing for measures to restrict Hollywood's inroads and bolster domestic production, Germany continued to import American movies, oblivious to the consequences. Ironically, and typically, however, while borrowing its criticism of German practice from a French source, in this case the critic Emil Vuillermoz, it displayed assumptions of German superiority which paralleled those resented in American motion picture moguls. To Vuillermoz's suggestion that large-scale, artistically impressive European productions could shake American dominance—essentially the strategy of Wengeroff—the German journal replied that first Britain and France had to attain the more advanced artistic and economic level of German cinema! "Only when that has happened will we be united and strong as civilised Europeans; only then will we be able to present the phalanx against Hollywood which can force America to at least a partial capitulation."[23] Hand in hand with this expression of national exclusivity went continued insistence that the ultimate objective of European co-operation was penetration of the American market. This objective was a holdover of the early post-war years when a number of German feature films released in the United States appeared to be the advance guard of a German invasion. These earlier ambitions stubbornly resisted surrender to the reality that American distributors accepted European releases only reluctantly and in minimal numbers. Renunciation of this conceit, more than demonstration of equality by France and Britain, would condition German interest in participation in a European motion picture bloc.[24]

For Germany then, as for the other European film countries, the incentive for continental solidarity developed in direct proportion to frustration with American inroads and the recognition that independent efforts to parry Hollywood were futile. A turning point was the agreement of late 1925 between Ufa, Paramount and Metro-Goldwyn (Parufamet) which made Germany's leading company an accomplice in mass import of American motion pictures. Despite promises of the coveted access to the American market, it signified to many observers defeat in the struggle against Hollywood. Even before this partnership, German opinion betrayed growing sobriety, though German ambition to take the lead in Europe remained. Ernst Jäger, editor of *Film-Kurier*, juxtaposed the ongoing colonisation of Europe by Hollywood (particularly Metro-Goldwyn's recent take-over of Gaumont as its French distribution outlet) with the inability of European film nations to organise their defence. Like Britain and France, Germany now found itself 'encircled' by American cinema. Jäger therefore admitted the link between German film fortunes and those of Europe in general. Yet despite this admission, he proposed traditional and national answers to the question of how to break the ring of American encirclement. Not European but *national* cohesion formed the core of Jäger's solution to Germany's ills. He recommended solidarity of the German industry to facilitate maximum motion picture circulation, ongoing quota protection and emphasis on standard-setting, major productions.[25]

Before the year was out *Film-Kurier* began to widen the scope of its solutions. It welcomed French suggestions, prompted by further American inroads, that Germany should become the pivot and model for European resistance to Hollywood.[26] Identifying Germany's fate as inseparable from that of the rest of Europe, it issued a wake-up call to domestic entrepreneurs:

> Are things going so brilliantly for the German industry that it has no need to establish contacts with other countries? Don't we witness the daily spectacle of America gaining ever more ground in Germany? Can one honestly believe that the massive flow of American film industrialists to Berlin has no significance? The German film industry must finally begin to develop a global policy. It must finally stop letting itself be lulled to sleep by the pleasant words of the Americans in Berlin.[27]

Film-Kurier now recommended that the German film industry shift its focus from export to America to collaboration with those European countries that did not erect artificial barriers against exchange of each other's motion pictures. It also presented a loosely defined 'European film alliance' (essentially for distribution rather than production) as the only means to break America's stranglehold. Here it gave prominence to the opinions of the French expert, Henry Lepage, who was calling for a cinematic League of Nations with Franco-German entente as its cornerstone.[28]

Interest in Film Europe as the solution to the *Kulturkampf* created by American influence in Europe created some odd bedfellows. Take, for instance, the position of the independent cinema owners, represented by the National Association of German Exhibitors. In the conviction that American motion pictures were alienating movie-goers and ruining theatres, this group, of decidedly national outlook, began to weigh the attractions of Film Europe.[29] Their publication outlet, *Reichsfilmblatt*, became a determined and clever champion of the European idea. In April 1926 it presented a two-part case for Film Europe which compared the growing, though still small number of European enthusiasts with the believers in German unity scoffed at in the first half of the nineteenth century. This examination entertained no illusions about the current state of Europe, whose institutional and diplomatic expressions, such as the League of Nations and the Treaty of Locarno, were judged to be as rudimentary as its cinematic ones. It also pinpointed Germany's blindspot to Film Europe as its undying vision of conquest in America. Instead of focusing attention on the European film market, which was as large as that of the United States, German film-makers surrendered their creative identities to try to conquer America. In the meantime Hollywood exploited the European market. The German film industry and its European counterparts overlooked indigenous potential, choosing to pay enormous sums to import American pictures instead of investing in quality production at home.[30]

In support of its position, *Reichsfilmblatt* quoted extensively from a leading motion picture executive, David Melamerson, Director of Deulig-Film. This company, a former partner of Westi owned by the nationalist media magnate Alfred Hugenberg, prided itself on independence from Hollywood. Its rationale was a blend of economics and culture. Melamerson maintained that Europe had a distinct filmic identity which it needed to cultivate in opposition to America. While individual nations had created motion pictures with a European complexion, financially no single country could afford to do so consistently. Although Melamerson indicated willingness to accept American funding within a consortium of European companies, the first step was to create European alliances. To this end Deulig teamed with Westi's former affiliates, Ciné-France and Cinéromans, on several co-productions featuring Russian émigrés, distributing *Michel Strogoff* (*Der Kurier des Zaren*) and *Les Misérables*. Melamerson's formulation of company policy, though more projection than reality, proclaimed the merger of German and European objectives:

> From the experience of the last two years Deulig has concluded that with the current oversupply of films and competitive struggle against America only highly select films have prospects of real success. We therefore believed we had to take the path of developing the German motion picture into a co-operative European super film and to establish a distribution link with the few films already produced in Europe . . . which can be set beside the best films of the world.[31]

The gathering momentum in favour of co-operation affected a wide spectrum of German film opinion. It also gave the idea of Film Europe an increasingly proactive cast. Although defensive reactions against Hollywood never disappeared, the case for European film union acquired a broader rationale. Felix Henseleit, a prolific critic and trade expert, articulated this rationale when he admitted that the American challenge provided the spur to European co-operation but that longer traditions gave it substance. History, culture and economics combined to link the peoples of Europe to a degree not experienced between Europe and the United States. In his opinion this predetermined the preference of European audiences for domestically produced film entertainment over the mass of what came from America. Co-production agreements, such as those between Ufa and Aubert, presented one means of exploiting this preference. Equally desirable were associations of theatre owners and distributors which could rationalise their respective branches of the industry to profit from the large European market.[32]

A bolder and more programmatic proposal for Film Europe came from the prominent entrepreneur and publisher, Karl Wolffsohn. In the aftermath of the Paris Film Congress of 1926, Wolffsohn revived a design for syndication of the European film industry which his journal, *Lichtbildbühne*, had first sketched in 1924. Wolffsohn shared the prevailing conviction that Europe's motion picture weakness derived primarily from overestimation of and overdependence on Hollywood. He advocated a planned film economy for Europe in which major pictures would be financed according to a formula based on distribution potential in each country (Britain 22 per cent, Germany 18 per cent, France 16 per cent, Italy 10 per cent, Scandinavia 12 per cent, Austria 12 per cent, with the remaining 10 per cent falling to the country of origins). Wolffsohn's scheme closely resembled that of Wengeroff, even though he faulted the Russians for utopian ambitions to co-ordinate the entire film industries of member nations. He saw groupings of companies across national borders as the pillars of European cinema. These would simultaneously rescue national industries, Germany's chief among them, and create a bloc which the Americans would have to treat as an equal rather than a poor cousin.[33]

Wolffsohn's design, while very much theory, was one which with some variations independently caught the imagination of a number of film entrepreneurs. It provided at least the skeleton for several other attempts to realise a pan-European cinema. Two deserve brief mention. The first came from the Deutsches Lichtbild Syndikat (German Film Syndicate or DLS), an association of exhibitors formed in 1926 to unite independent theatre owners in a production/distribution company which could free them from dependence on Hollywood and its German partners. By 1928 DLS membership embraced roughly 20 per cent of German cinemas, among them the larger and more successful non-chain cinemas in Berlin and the provinces. Its early films proved popular, the first of them spectacularly so, indicating that pooling of capital through exhibition could succeed on a national level. Having attracted attention from theatre owners in other German-speaking countries in Central Europe, it announced the formation of a European Film Syndicate (ELS) at the international conference of exhibitors in Berlin in August 1928. Initial hopes did not, however, result in a functional organisation. ELS enjoyed a brief and shadowy existence until DLS itself encountered increasing financial difficulties, conditioned both by the advent of talking pictures and the onset of the Depression.[34]

The other, likewise abortive, experiment in co-ordination of European interests copied on a rather more limited scale the objectives of Westi. In 1927 a German studio (Filmwerke-Staaken) and Russia's Sovkino formed the Deutsch–Russische Film-Allianz (German–Russian Film Alliance or Derussa) to distribute Soviet films in Germany and other parts of Europe. Provision was also made for a limited number of major co-productions. On paper the alliance constituted a typical bilateral arrangement, with emphasis on bringing Soviet features to Germany. However, the German owner of Filmwerke-Staaken, Georg Sklarz, hoped to capitalise on the current international interest in Soviet films by securing advances on the co-productions from major distributors across Europe. In other words, he aimed to fund Russo-German feature films on a European basis. For the first co-production he acquired guarantees from French, Spanish, English and Italian distributors for sums exceeding the projected budget. Before it could be completed, Derussa, like Westi's European Film Syndicate, collapsed under a massive debt burden from other obligations.[35]

Since the principle behind all these endeavours was difficult to fault, the failure of these omnibus, multilateral schemes did not stop pursuit of narrower arrangements. Sharing of resources and distribution outlets to permit production on a scale impossible in one national context still justified bilateral agreements. In the second half of the decade a number of German companies established ties with European counterparts. Generally these ties were trumpeted by the firms involved and by the trade press as developments *en route* to Film Europe.[36] For instance, the Director of Terra Film, Erich Morawsky, boasted that his firm was the first to translate the idea of international co-operation into reality by complementary agreements with counterparts in Britain, France and Italy. He also prophesied that by this route an authentic, as opposed to theoretical and utopian, Film Europe would emerge in which joint productions would involve contributions from all four nations.[37]

While arrangements of this type contributed to a patchwork Film Europe, they did not necessarily represent equal partnerships. Collaboration could suggest paternalism as well as partnership. In the case of an agreement struck between Ufa and the Italian LUCE, Ufa was able to exploit its superiority much as Hollywood did in agreements with European firms. In Italy, where the film industry had gone through an extended crisis since the war and been overwhelmed by the American product, the incentive to find reinforcement against Hollywood was strong. Some film experts, including those who left the country to find employment elsewhere, heralded the European idea as the answer to national misfortune. For instance, the director Augusto Genina, active in collaborative projects abroad, saw Film Europe as the only means by which to challenge Hollywood.[38] Stefano Pittaluga, the quasi *Duce* of what was left of Italian production and distribution, was even more outspoken. From his perspective atop the industry he argued for high-level consultation among the four main nations of Film Europe to co-ordinate production and film rentals. Each would produce twenty films annually, contributing equal shares to production costs. By commanding distribution outlets in their respective countries these would guarantee the market exploitation required to cover production costs. Unlike the abortive Westi venture, such a consortium would have the requisite international theatre chain at its disposal and would be in the hands of experienced film experts rather than relative newcomers.[39] In all this Pittaluga made two striking assumptions: first, that the leading five to ten film industrialists of Europe could among themselves effect the co-ordination required to make Film Europe a reality; and second, that success was primarily a matter of business expertise. The dramaturgical and cinematic genius required to support production of eighty major European films annually was simply assumed.[40]

As Pittaluga set out to create a web of ties with other European film corporations, including an agreement with Terra Film for co-production of four pictures,[41] the newly founded state cinema firm, LUCE, negotiated a broad arrangement with Ufa. LUCE looked to Europe for help in pursuing its official mandate to revive the moribund Italian cinema. While its pact with Ufa was outwardly similar to the numerous bilateral contracts of the time, and was touted as another step toward Film Europe, it differed in two respects. First, LUCE made its overtures through diplomatic channels. In the spring of 1928, a former Under-Secretary in the Italian Foreign Office, now on the board of LUCE, approached the German ambassador in Rome, Constantin von Neurath, to explore possibilities of collaboration with German film companies as a prelude to a broader European combination. These feelers were communicated to the German film industry by the Foreign Office in Berlin. The second point to note is that the contract prescribed a degree of oversight in Italian production by Ufa which outdid the influence granted Paramount and Metro-Goldwyn in the infamous Parufamet pact of late 1925. Ufa was to provide the personnel and technical expertise for modernisation of the Italian film industry, train Italian film specialists in their respective areas, make available directors and artistic personnel for major LUCE film productions, and distribute these films abroad. In return it would gain access to the Italian market—twenty Ufa features would be distributed by LUCE in 1929/30—and receive a substantial cash advance as payment for its services. This collaborative venture therefore clearly reflected Germany's primacy in European film.[42]

Ufa drew fire for this agreement in the first instance from those who suspected political motives—an alliance between Italian Fascism and Hugenberg's radical nationalism.[43] However, the more substantial charge, especially as information leaked out about state involvement on both sides, was that while Ufa presented the contract as another link in the chain of Film Europe, it in fact constituted a monopoly which would restrict European exchange. Given Italy's quota system and its limited productive capacity, Ufa effectively pre-empted Italian trade with other German and European firms, creating a condominium with Hollywood in Italy. *Lichtbildbühne*, at the time highly critical of Ufa policy in general, claimed that not only German but also British and French trade circles opposed Ufa's privileged position on the Italian market.[44]

The Ufa–LUCE agreement indicates that Film Europe could mask ambitions quite the opposite of those it would normally suggest. The particular tension in this case, inescapable given the uneven status of national film industries, can be noted in one other area germane to European film co-operation. In the second half of the decade the flurry of industrial and journalistic interest in Film Europe went hand in hand with a broad move to defend national markets by legislating film import restrictions. In 1927/8 Britain, France and Italy all introduced measures to this end. While superficially at odds with collaborative objectives, this move largely reflected the same Hollywood–Berlin axis which shaped Film Europe. The primary purpose, of course, was to contain the threat of American control. Although there were few illusions that legal measures could reverse American hegemony, they at least offered a means to prevent total collapse of domestic production and thus secure national cinematic identity. Here the German experience provided a model to emulate: thanks to its quota system Germany retained slightly less than half of its market for domestic production. Elsewhere in Europe the American market share ranged from 70 to 95 per cent.[45] However, since Hollywood captured three-quarters or more of the German quota, the system also tended to work against Germany's neighbours. The introduction of quotas in other European countries could have similar consequences, particularly for Germany, which was the leading exporter next to Hollywood.[46]

Whether and how to regulate imports created sharp controversy, particularly in Britain and France, where distributors and exhibitors had so long been dependent on the American product that they generally opposed legislative interference.[47] For producers the circle to be squared was how to preserve sheltered access to the domestic market while creating opportunities for export. In addition to domestic wrestling in this regard, national industries clashed over the relative balance of bilateral trade. For instance, in 1928 leading figures of the French film industry visited Berlin to discuss what they perceived as blatant inequity in German–French film exchange. While France was a major export market for Germany, the latter's quota continued, as it had earlier in the decade, to limit sharply the number of French films distributed in Germany. The French did not demand strict reciprocity, but they wished for some measure of accommodation. Jean Sapène, publisher and head of Cinéromans, proposed that for every French feature sold to Germany three German pictures could be sent to France. This proposal recognised the uneven status of the two industries as well as Hollywood's corner on German import permits, but still represented improvement of the French position.[48]

Within Germany itself, despite long experience with import regulation, the system came under heavy fire in 1925/6, just as the discussion of Film Europe became animated. The existing quota stipulated that for every domestic picture distributed a permit was granted to import one foreign film. Controversy revolved, as later in Britain, around its tendency to foster production of cheap 'quota' films which discredited the domestic industry and offered little competition to Hollywood even as they earned import permits for American films. Advocates of a stiffening of the quota, from 1:1 to 2:1, maintained that this would preserve enough of the home market to stimulate German production. They also pointed out that in practice the 1:1 quota had always been a misnomer: by calculating the number of domestic productions over more than a year at a time, it allowed the balance to tip in favour of imports. Opponents argued that a 2:1 quota would compel production of twice the number of feature films for essentially the same capital outlay. In other words, quality would plunge even further and with it Germany's international competitiveness. Opponents also saw production of so-called quota films with American funding as preferable to the situation elsewhere in Europe where domestic production bases had been decimated.[49]

At the same time that France, Britain and Italy proposed relatively limited restrictions on foreign films, German trade circles showed some interest in co-ordinating solutions to the import question so as to facilitate European interchange without leaving domestic markets over-exposed to Hollywood. In late 1926 the director Gregor Rabinowitsch, an impassioned opponent of American market domination, appealed for sharpening of the German quota to 2:1. He also called on other European countries, France above all, to face the reality that American and European film interests were in competition rather than co-operation. Without a strong regulatory mechanism American firms would continue to swamp European movie markets and would not be compelled, as in Germany, to invest in national production to earn import permits.[50] The critic Felix Henseleit conceded that a tighter quota could work against European film exchange, but proposed circumventing the restriction with 'most favoured nation' clauses. In his schema European import co-ordination presented the point of departure for more direct collaboration:

> The European quota must be established; for only behind its protection—at the moment other organisational forms are not available—is European film co-operation conceivable. . . . When the responsible parties are at all serious about a European film bloc then it has to be under the flag of a common European quota which is simultaneously defence against America and a broad platform for collaboration.[51]

Such appeals notwithstanding, import regulation remained a national exercise. Neither the French nor the British nor the Italian film industry could supply more than a fraction of domestic requirements. The very modest initial quotas enacted by Britain in 1927 (1:20), Italy in 1927 (1:10) and France in 1928 (1:7) corresponded to the relative impotence of their industries. They also reflected the determined resistance of Hollywood: France met a boycott from American distribution companies over its legislation.[52]

From the German perspective these discrete national approaches threatened to hamper European film exchange. Yet at another level they also favoured Germany. Since co-production and joint ventures provided a means to qualify motion pictures as domestic products in more than one market, Germany's position as the hub of European cinema gave it an advantage. Moreover, since there was no suitable means by which to discriminate against Hollywood without provoking retaliation, minimal quotas paired with collaborative projects satisfied the demand for cultural preservation without blocking inter-European film trade.[53] Rationalised on cultural as well as commercial grounds, the quotas also stood as a defence against pressure from the United States to eliminate all trade restrictions at economic talks in Geneva in 1928.[54] Like bilateral film contracts, quotas did not therefore work uniformly in favour of or against Film Europe. Indeed their timing and extent illustrated the persisting ambivalence in European responses to American cinema.

For Germany, Film Europe, though spurred by the threat of an American take-over, did not ultimately assume an anti-American face. Expressions of indignation at American conceit in flooding European cinemas while resisting all but a token film import from Europe were certainly sincere. They were, however, neither consistent nor consensual. Given the indispensability of the American product for European cinemas, the appeal to European shared interests was generally presented as compatible with, if not outright friendly toward, Hollywood's place in Europe. For companies like Ufa which had partnerships with American firms, friendliness toward Hollywood had very concrete dimensions: they were not prepared to repudiate American liaisons in favour of either a vague European film community or specific, more limited agreements.[55] Moreover, the appeal of a common front against Hollywood never overrode rivalry for partnerships with America. In addition, immense pressure to conciliate Hollywood meant that inter-European trade in motion pictures could not be privileged by quota regulations to the detriment of America. In this respect Film Europe remained fragmented. Common objectives remained subordinate to private ones which were still primarily national in orientation. And just as in the latter-day debate over the degree to which national sovereignty should be surrendered to serve a supranational goal, film concerns weighed the risks of being swallowed by European partners, primarily German firms, no less than by American competitors.

All this being said by way of qualification, one cannot dismiss Film Europe as mere diplomatic camouflage, as has happened with regard to such international agreements of the same period as the Locarno Treaty or the Kellogg–Briand Pact against war. That it was proposed and pursued at all is revealing. In the final years of silent film, European co-operation provided a rallying point for an assortment of otherwise competing interests. Although none of the loftier visions of a film community reached fulfilment—one must treat the rhetoric as a motivational tool more than as a guide to policy—several attempts were made and narrower steps to the goal were taken in a series of co-production and exchange agreements. Behind them lurked American cinema as model as much as threat. Ironically but appropriately, the commercial rationale for Film Europe derived essentially from American success in pairing extensive theatre chains with carefully managed production programmes. Film Europe was in many respects an attempt to counter Hollywood with its own methods.

Although the introduction of talking motion pictures did not terminate European film co-operation, it also did not bring the broad pooling of European production and distribution resources promoted in the last years of silent film. The rationale for co-operation remained strong as major companies turned to multiple-language production to retain markets abroad. Yet the coincidence of economic and political crisis also made national industries increasingly defensive and in Germany revived dreams of leadership of European cinema. Insofar as the introduction of sound acted as a brake on American inroads, there was less incentive for collaboration as opposed to competition. At least as it was conceived in the second half of the 1920s, Film Europe remained short of its goal.

Notes

The research for this chapter was made possible by a grant from the Social Sciences and Humanities Research Council of Canada.

1. On American film export in this period see Kristin Thompson, *Exporting Entertainment: America and the World Film Market, 1907–1934* (London: British Film Institute, 1985) and Ruth Vasey, *The World According to Hollywood, 1918–1939* (Madison: University of Wisconsin Press, 1997).
2. Ian Jarvie, *Hollywood's Overseas Campaign* (Cambridge: Cambridge University Press, 1992), outlines Hollywood's strategy toward Canada and Britain.
3. See Thomas J. Saunders, *Hollywood in Berlin* (Berkeley: University of California Press, 1994).
4. See particularly several volumes from CineGraph: Jörg Schöning, ed., *London Calling: Deutsche im britischen Film der dreißiger Jahre* (Munich: Edition Text + Kritik, 1993); Jörg Schöning, ed., *Fantaisies russes: Russische Filmmacher in Berlin und Paris 1920–1930* (Munich: Edition Text + Kritik, 1995); Sibylle M. Sturm and Arthur Wohlgemuth, eds, *Hallo? Berlin? Ici Paris!: Deutsch-französische Filmbeziehungen, 1918–1939* (Munich: Edition Text + Kritik, 1996); also Andrew Higson, "Film-Europa: Dupont und die britische Filmindustrie," in Jürgen Bretschneider, ed., *Ewald André Dupont: Autor und Regisseur* (Munich: Edition Text + Kritik, 1992), pp. 89–100, an expanded version of which appears in this volume.

5. Details on these are in Andrew Higson, "Film-Europa: Kulturpolitik und industrielle Praxis," in Sturm and Wohlgemuth, eds, *Hallo? Berlin? Ici Paris!*, pp. 63–76; a revised version appears in this volume.

6. See "Der 'Internationale Filmkongreß' in Paris," *Film-Kurier*, 2 November 1923: "One of the most significant and largest film producing countries of the world was denied participation for the usual chauvinistic reasons."

7. Just weeks before the conference convened, and after considerable wrangling in response to German demands, the committee in charge conceded that German should be the third official language of the proceedings. On the problem of hate films (*Hetzfilme*) see Thomas J. Saunders, "German Diplomacy and the War Film in the 1920s," in Karel Dibbets and Bert Hogenkamp, eds, *Film and the First World War* (Amsterdam: Amsterdam University Press, 1995), pp. 213–22.

8. For advance expectation see "Was bringt Paris?," *Film-Kurier*, 4 September 1926; Paul Medina, "Am Vorabend des Pariser Kongresses," *Film-Kurier*, 23 September 1926, which stressed that the conference was of "moral-social" compass to the exclusion of all political issues. "Stimmen zum Kongreß," *Reichsfilmblatt*, 25 September 1926, pp. 13–14, cited several prominent representatives of the German film industry to the effect that Paris would prepare the ground for greater internationality, a statement both innocuous and obligatory. For the post-mortem see "Vernichtende Kritik des 'Matin'," *Film-Kurier*, 6 October 1926.

9. "Die Europäische Föderation," *Lichtbildbühne*, 23 August 1928; "Die internationale Föderation ist gegründet" and "Vor Gründung des europäischen Lichtspielsyndikates," *Film-Kurier*, 23 August 1928. For more on the European Film Syndicate see below.

10. See "Internationale Filmprobleme," *Film-Kurier*, 23 August 1928. Cf. Higson, "Film-Europa," pp. 67–72. For the inflated rhetoric of co-operation see "Kinobesitzer Europas, kommt nach Berlin," *Film-Kurier*, 11 August 1928.

11. See the argument to this effect in "Während Paris gegen Hetzfilme stimmt," *Film-Kurier*, 30 September 1926.

12. "Europäische Film-Entente . . . ?," *Lichtbildbühne*, 1 July 1922, 19–22; "Die internationale Filmkonferenz in Paris," *Film-Kurier*, 12 July 1922.

13. On French reception of these early imports see Jürgen Kasten, "Boche-Filme: Zur Rezeption deutscher Filme in Frankreich 1918–1924," in Sturm and Wohlgemuth, eds, *Hallo? Berlin? Ici Paris!*, pp. 40–4.

14. Although the charge had historical significance, by 1922 the growing tide of American imports in Germany and France's own saturation with the same made it increasingly anachronistic. Quota regulation remained, however, an ongoing issue in Franco-German film exchange. See Jeanpaul Goergen, "Entente und Stabilisierung: Deutsch-französische Filmkontakte 1925–1933," in Sturm and Wohlgemuth, eds, *Hallo? Herlin? Ici Paris!*,

p. 53. Pommer's position on international cinema is outlined in Wolfgang Jacobsen, *Erich Pommer* (Berlin: Argon Verlag, 1989), pp. 43–4.

15. "Europäische Film-Entente . . . ?," *Lichtbildbühne*, 1 July 1922, pp. 19–22.
16. Cf. Pommer's opinions in "Internationalisierung des Films ist nur noch eine Frage der Zeit," *Film-Kurier*, 10 September 1927, and "Der internationale Film," *Film-Kurier*, 28 August 1928.
17. On German ties with the British industry see Andrew Higson, "Way West: Deutsche Emigranten und die britische Filmindustrie," in Schöning, ed., *London Calling*, pp. 42–54; Rachel Low, *The History of the British Film, 1918–1929* (London: George Allen & Unwin Ltd, 1971), pp. 133–4, 166–86. See Richard Abel, *French Cinema: The First Wave, 1915–1929* (Princeton: Princeton University Press, 1984), p. 46, for reference to German attempts to duplicate Hollywood in exploiting the French market.
18. See "Interview mit Louis Aubert," *Film-Kurier*, 24 May 1924. The same issue reported an agreement between *Film-Kurier* and the English trade paper, *Film-Renter*, to publish a joint issue in August 1924.
19. Goergen, "Entente und Stabilisierung," p. 54.
20. On the whole venture see Daniel Otto, " '. . . Die Filmindustrie Europas retten!" ' Wengeroff, Stinnes und das " 'Europäische Filmsyndikat'," in Schöning, ed., *Fantaisies russes*, pp. 59–82.
21. Ibid., pp. 73, 76.
22. See Saunders, *Hollywood in Berlin*, ch. 4. Abel, *French Cinema*, p. 30, argues that the stabilisation of the German currency and Hollywood's investment in the German cinema cut across the Franco-German bridge to European collaboration. Yet as his later comments suggest (pp. 35, 46), had it not been for German dependence on Hollywood, the bridge may have been more of a spearhead for a German invasion.
23. "Eine europäische Filmfront?," *Reichsfilmblatt*, 19 November 1928.
24. Abel, *French Cinema*, pp. 41–2, notes similar French aspirations at the start of the decade.
25. Ejott [Ernst Jäger], "Die Einkreisung Deutschlands," *Film- Kurier*, 9 June 1925.
26. "Unsere Politik—Europäischer Kurs! England–Frankreich–Deutschland gegen Amerikanisierung," *Film- Kurier*, 31 October 1925. It also recognised French concern that German leadership of Film Europe potentially meant Berlin taking the place of Hollywood.
27. "Europas Filme den Europäern!," *Film-Kurier*, 11 November 1925.
28. "Auf zur Europa-Kontingentallianz," *Film-Kurier*, 10 November 1925. Cf. the references, borrowed from Lepage, to a "Locarno scheme of European Film" including Scandinavia, Italy and Austria in "Und England," *Film-Kurier*, 12 November 1925.

29. See in particular the speech of Ludwig Scheer, head of the National Association of German Exhibitors, to the annual convention of 1926: "Die Düsseldorfer Tagung," *Reichsfilmblatt*, 31 July 1926, pp. 3–4.

30. Helmuth Ortmann, "Film-Europa" (I & II), *Reichsfilmblatt*, 17 April 1926, pp. 1–2; 24 April 1926, pp. 2–4 (reproduced here as Document 5). Ortmann rehearsed the cycle of German response to Hollywood: eagerness to acquire American films after 1918, initial enthusiasm when these began to show in the early 1920s, and then the growing tide of dissatisfaction by mid-decade.

31. Felix Henseleit, "Europafront: Randbemerkungen zu einer Rede D. Melamersons Über das neue Deulig-Programm," *Reichsfilmblatt*, 6 March 1926, pp. 3–5 (reproduced here as Document 4). Henseleit's editorial reflection on this formulation included the usual national caveat: "when this goal can be attained without surrender of our national values and distinctiveness it will represent the most that is possible for today and the future."

32. Felix Henseleit, "Film-Europa," *Reichsfilmblatt*, 24 July 1926, pp. 74–5 (reproduced here as Document 6). Cf. the later perspective of Georg Fuchs, "Los von Amerika," *Reichsfilmblatt*, 22 January 1927, p. 14.

33. Kark Wolffsohn, "Europa den Europäern," *Lichtbildbühne*, 16 October 1926, pp. 9–11 (reproduced here as Document 7). Cf. the lead article "Sanierung des Weltmarktes," in *Lichtbildbühne*, 4 August 1928, pp. 7–8.

34. See "Vor Gründung des europäischen Lichtspielsyndikats," *Film-Kurier*, 23 August 1928.

35. Derussa also joined with English and American partners in a massive and short-lived multilateral holding company, International Talking Screen. On Derussa see Thomas J. Saunders, "The German–Russian Film (Mis)Alliance (Derussa): Commerce and Politics in German-Soviet Cinema Ties," *Film History*, vol. 9, 1997, pp. 168–88.

36. See, for instance, "Europäische Produktionsgemeinschaft: Svenska-Hisa-National," *Lichtbildbühne*, 22 June 1927; "Deutsch-französische Gemein-schaftsarbeit," *Reichsfilmblatt*, 3 December 1927, 24; "Das europäische Vertragsnetz," *Lichtbildbühne*, 3 August 1928.

37. Erich Morawsky, "Der Ring ist geschlossen," *Lichtbildbühne*, 18 August 1928, pp. 13–14. Reference to utopian projects was a barb directed at schemes such as that of Wengeroff.

38. Augusto Genina, "Internationale Verständigung," *Der Film*, Christmas 1926, p. 17. Despite recent setbacks, Genina believed conditions remained auspicious for Film Europe.

39. C.C. Schulte, "Schafft einen europäischen Filmkonzern: Gespräch mit Stefano Pittaluga," *Der Film*, 1 May 1927, p. 5. Cf. Schulte's subsequent article: "Der Pan-Europa-Film marschiert," *Der Film*, 3 September 1927, p. 10.

40. The elitist leanings of this solution reveal less sympathy for Fascism than entrepreneurial egotism and frustration with fractured markets. For a German perspective see "Führer gesucht," *Lichtbildbühne*, 7 May 1927, pp. 11–12.

41. "Terra-Pittaluga," *Lichtbildbühne*, 6 August 1928. An interview with Pittaluga the next day presented his far-reaching scheme for Film Europe in some detail: "Film-Italiens Weg," *Lichtbildbühne*, 7 August 1928.

42. Details are in the contract of 9 June 1928 in Politisches Archiv des Auswärtigen Amts, Bonn: Botschaft Rom, Pol. 14, 821a, vol. 1a.

43. For defence against the charge that Ufa favoured Fascism see the following articles from *Film-Kurier*: "Film-Europa," 13 June 1928; "Ufa-Luce. Die verlängerte Europafront," 16 June 1928; "Ufa-Luce-Abkommen ratifiziert," 1 August 1928.

44. Cf. the following from *Lichtbildbühne*: "Planlose Film-Subvention," 1 September 1928, pp. 7–8; "Italien und die Ufa: Ein verstecktes Monopol?," 4 September 1928; "Frankreich gegen Ufa-Luce," 8 September 1928, pp. 7–8. The polemic here betrays itself in the simultaneous dismissal of French objections as sour-grapes.

45. The table in Jarvie, *Hollywood's Overseas Campaign*, p. 315, underrepresents Hollywood's market share in Germany. Cf. Saunders, *Hollywood in Berlin*, p. 54.

46. See "Europas Kontingent-Aufrüstung: Der Ring um Deutschland schließt sich," *Lichtbildbühne*, 6 February 1928. Again this helps explain the attractiveness for Ufa of its deal with LUCE.

47. On the British controversy see Jarvie, *Hollywood's Overseas Campaign*, pp. 103–34; on France see Abel, *French Cinema*, pp. 42–3, 47–8.

48. See "Ultimative Forderungen der Franzosen," *Film-Kurier*, 1 October 1928; "Französisch-deutsche Verhandlungen," *Lichtbildbühne*, 1 October 1928; "Sapène in Berlin," *Lichtbildbühne*, 15 October 1928; "Sapènes große Programmrede," *Lichtbildbühne*, 22 October 1928.

49. Cf. Walter Levy (head of distribution for Phoebus-Film), "Unabhängig von Amerika!," *Film-Kurier*, 18 November 1926. Levy assumed that the Americans would force acceptance of roughly the same number of films, regardless of the quota system: "Die Kontingenteingabe der Fabrikanten," *Reichsfilmblatt*, 11 December 1926. The German quota actually functioned to domesticate as well as to restrain America's film presence.

50. Gregor Rabinowitsch, "Deutsches und europäisches Kontingent: die Rettung Filmeuropas," *Film-Kurier*, 23 October 1926. Rabinowitsch insisted that rather than wait in vain for Hollywood, as at the recent Paris Film Conference, European film concerns should assume responsibility for their own fortunes. Cf. Goergen, "Entente und Stabilisierung," p. 56.

51. Felix Henseleit, "Am Scheidewege," *Reichsfilmblatt*, 30 October 1926, pp. 15–16.

52. See Abel, *French Cinema*, pp. 47–8. German film circles followed these developments very closely: Cf. "Will Hays Sendung," *Lichtbildbühne*, 7 April 1928, pp. 9–10; "Der Pariser Kontingent-Friede," *Film-Kurier*, 7 May 1928.
53. Cf. "Europäische Film-Mißwirtschaft," *Lichtbildbühne*, 7 May 1927, pp. 12–13; "Europäische Film-Entente," *Lichtbildbuühne*, 9 June 1928, p. 10. On the consequences for co-production in Britain see Higson, "Way West," pp. 46–8.
54. These talks were a source of much concern in Germany, where it appeared the government was prepared to sacrifice film protection for the sake of broader interests.
55. See, for instance, "Der Aufbau von Film-Europa richtet sich nicht gegen Amerika," *Film-Kurier*, 19 June 1928.

8

Hollywood's "Foreign War"

The Effect of National Commercial Policy on the Emergence of the American Film Hegemony in France, 1920–1929

Jens Ulff-Møller

Hollywood's international dominance over the moving image was established in the aftermath of the First World War, but the mechanisms that upheld it have been little studied. In contrast to the common assumption that the superior entertainment qualities of American cinema secured its dominant position, this essay will argue that the success of American film exports was largely the result of American business methods and governmental interference. The assistance provided by the United States government to the Motion Picture Producers and Distributors of America Inc. (MPPDA) was a vital advantage in its dealings with foreign governments. Diplomacy and political manoeuvring were crucial to the American film industry's successful maintenance of a 50–80 percent share of the European market throughout the inter-war period.

Hollywood had secured almost full control of the British market during the First World War, but in the 1920s the American industry had important "foreign wars" with France, Germany, Italy and the Scandinavian countries.[1] This essay makes use of the wealth of documents in American governmental archives to examine the conflict with France.[2] American film policy makers considered France to be a strategic market, an inroad to continental Europe and the French colonies. More generally, they believed that the outcome in France could influence the situation of American films in the rest of the world. The American documents provide a deeper insight into French film policy than do French governmental archives, which is in itself evidence of the attitude of successive French administrations.[3] In contrast to the support given the American industry by its government, France, along with several other European governments, failed to give its domestic film industry appropriate protection against Hollywood's incursions.[4] Further, French fiscal policy and legislation on cinema impeded the development of its film industry.

The scale of the American film hegemony can be observed in the statistics of films censored. Available French statistics only cover the period 1924–39, but because trends were similar across most of Europe, it is possible to estimate earlier developments on the basis of more complete Swedish statistics.[5] The United States became the largest supplier of films to Sweden in 1915. American imports peaked at 557 films in 1919, dropped throughout the 1920s to 238 in 1929, and stabilised at a slightly lower level during the 1930s. American films accounted for roughly 70 per cent of films censored in Sweden in the 1920s and 60 per cent in the 1930s. As American film exports increased, the number of European films declined by 50–90 per cent of the 1917 level. American films did not, however, merely supplant European productions: the total number of films available increased by 200–300 per cent.

It is likely that the number of American films entering France also peaked in 1919–20, declining sharply during the second half of the 1920s from 589 in 1924 to 211 in 1929, before stabilising at around 230 films per year throughout the 1930s.[6] The percentage of American films on the French market fell from 85 per cent in 1924 to around 50 per cent in 1929, and that level was maintained throughout the 1930s, largely as a result of a series of agreements between the French government and the MPPDA, beginning in 1929 and discussed in detail below. However, as a way of protecting its domestic industry French film policy was of limited effect: throughout the 1930s, twice as many American as French films were shown in France, while the export of French motion pictures to the US continued to decrease.

The French and American governments organised their film policies quite differently. The MPPDA enjoyed government support at the highest level: the assistance it received from the State Department and the American embassy in Paris had the approval of the presidents of the United States. As Secretary of Commerce in the early 1920s, Herbert Hoover introduced commercial attachés at all American embassies to support exporters and collect information. Motion picture exports received special attention, and this diplomatic effort intensified after 1926, when Congress appropriated special funds to operate a Motion Picture Section in the Department of Commerce to collect and publish information concerning the motion picture situation abroad.[7] In September 1926 this section sent George R. Canty as a special trade commissioner to Paris to study the European motion picture situation at close range.[8] Diplomatic and political information was confidential, and the officers of the MPPDA were the only outsiders to have access to it. In the mid-1920s the MPPDA created its own Foreign Department, headed by Major Fredrick L. Herron, a long-time friend of Will Hays. Herron directed the film policy of the MPPDA towards France through almost daily consultations with the State Department or the American embassy in Paris. In 1928 the MPPDA opened a Paris office headed by Harold L. Smith, a former diplomat at the Paris embassy. Although all the major American film companies operated local offices in Paris, headed by European agents, they were not directly involved in film policy making, which was left to the MPPDA representatives and American diplomats.

While all American agencies were united in promoting American film exports, the French government followed an ambivalent film policy, in large part because of the deep division of interest within its domestic film industry between its producers, numbering perhaps two dozen, and around 3,500–4,000 cinema-owners. The Americans were able to use this division to dismantle measures designed to protect and promote French film production.

At the beginning of the 1920s, French film production was at a nadir. The leading French film production company was the Pathé-Consortium, formed by Pathé's merger with three other companies: Cinéromans, Films de France and the Lutetia cinema circuit. The Consortium owned the largest and best studios in France, producing a dozen films a year. It also operated some twenty cinemas and controlled the bookings of several hundred others. From 1923 its *de facto* Director was Jean Sapène, publicity editor of the right-wing newspaper *Le Matin*, Director of Cinéromans and the *eminence gris* of French cinema in the 1920s. American strategies for undermining measures to protect the French film industry were based on their recognition that Sapène was the most powerful figure in the French film world and, according to Colonel Edward G. Lowry, the MPPDA's European representative, "a person to be reckoned with in everything done in France, both on the political and the business side."[9] Throughout the 1920s Pathé-Consortium remained the largest distributor of French-produced films in France, and thus in practice the strongest single force resisting American hegemony.[10] In 1923 Sapène took Pathé-Consortium into a partnership with Hugo Stinnes and Vladimir Wengeroff's Berlin-based Westi Corporation, to form the largest single enterprise of the Film Europe movement, initiating several of Sapène's largest productions including *Les Miserables* and *Michel Strogoff* as well as Abel Gance's *Napoleon*. Despite his continued involvement in European co-productions, however, Sapène's policy toward the American film industry remained extremely pragmatic and self interested, motivated less by a concern to improve the position of the entire French industry than by the desire to expand the sale of his films. Like several other French producers, he tried on a number of occasions to reach an agreement with American firms for them to finance his production and distribute his films in the US.[11] Sapène also had ambitions to monopolise French film distribution through his control of the patents for safety film stock. Through his political contacts he influenced the government to issue a decree prohibiting the use of inflammable nitrate films.[12] Implementation of the decree was, however, regularly postponed throughout the 1920s, because of the poor quality of safety films.

The second most important company was the Etablissements Louis Aubert, S.A., which comprised a half dozen companies producing six to eight films per year and controlling twenty cinemas. Louis Aubert mainly distributed French and German films, and showed American films in his first-run movie houses. The Gaumont company produced film only on a small scale during the 1920s, when it was mainly the local subsidiary of MGM. When the contract with MGM expired in 1928, the company merged with Franco Film and Aubert to form Gaumont-Franco-Film-Aubert (GFFA), which became one of the two largest producing companies in France. Aubert was the leader of this syndicate, and the Director of the film industry's trade association, the Chambre Syndicale Française de la Cinématographie et des Industries qui s'y Rattachent. At first this organisation represented both producers and exhibitors, and as a result of its divided interests it failed to support any protectionist measures against American imports. In March 1926, however, Sapène became Honorary President of the Chambre Syndicale, and from then on producers dominated the organisation, using it to advocate a contingent policy to reduce the number of American films entering France, despite strong resistance from the cinema owners.

In 1920 there were 2,400 cinemas in France; by 1929 there were 4,200. Of these, around 3,000 were small, provincial cinemas, independently owned and operating only at weekends. Very few of these were housed in purpose-built modern buildings; takings in these theatres accounted for 60–65 per cent of all French receipts.[13] According to American estimates, only 500 French cinemas paid "good" film rentals.[14]

Provincial cinema owners often operated their cinemas as a second occupation, renting film programmes at the lowest rate, which usually meant showing old American movies. As a result, they were opposed to any restrictions on imports, and unwilling to sacrifice themselves to aid French producers, who had never shown any inclination to favour them. Many exhibitors distrusted Sapène for his monpolistic methods in handling the safety film question, and they criticised him for trying to use protective legislation to further entrench himself in all branches of the industry.[15] In reaction to the producers' take-over of the Chambre Syndicale, the owners created their own organisations, of which the most important was La Fédération Générale des Association de Directeurs de Spectacles de Province. Exhibitors argued that while the Chambre Syndicale claimed to promote French film production, it in fact acted in the interest of only a few film producers and to the detriment of cinema owners.

The Ministère de l'Instruction Publique et des Beaux Arts had general jurisdiction over French cinema and tried to mediate between the two sides in matters of film policy. The ministry held this jurisdiction because antiquated and restrictive laws governing temporary public entertainment were applied to film exhibition. Cinemas were not treated as permanent theatres but were defined as temporary, minor amusements, on a par with street fairs, side-shows and travelling circuses, regulated under a decree of 1864. The laws governing cinemas came under the jurisdiction of several ministries and demanded the local licensing of movie houses, the censorship and control of performances by local authorities, as well as payment of amusement taxes to both the state and municipalities. Local authorities had a great deal of power over cinemas: a licence to operate a cinema had to be renewed annually, and could be withdrawn at any time. Although a form of national censorship was introduced under a central commission in 1919, the mayor could prohibit any show he believed might cause public disorders, in accordance with a law of 1790.[16] This potentially arbitrary local control made investing in French cinemas a risky proposition.

The Ministère des Beaux Arts sought to promote French film production by restricting the import of American films, but not so severely as to oust American interests; the French state relied on the income from amusement taxes, which were mainly derived from the showing of American films. By 1930, the tax revenue from cinema exhibition amounted to 300 million francs, three times the value of the annual business conducted by French producing companies in their domestic and foreign markets.[17] Between 1914 and 1941, three different amusement taxes were applied to the French cinema, draining from it the resources necessary for developing both exhibition and production. The oldest amusement tax, the "droit des pauvres," originated in a decree of 1407 and was fixed at 10 per cent of the box-office. During the First World War this was augmented by separate graduated state and municipal taxes, introduced in 1914. In 1929 the *Film Yearbook* commented: "Development of the industry in France is largely retarded by too excessive state, poor and municipal taxes which run all the way from 17 to 40 per cent of the gross receipts in Parisian houses and from 15.10 to 31.25 per cent in all other theaters. This is an important contributing reason to the dearth of theater construction."[18] In 1925 the largest cinema in Paris, the Marivaux, paid 1.5 million francs in amusement taxes on receipts of 6 million francs. Table 8.1 gives the gross receipts and the amount paid in amusement taxes by all Parisian cinemas.[19]

Because the cinema had become an integral part of the French government's fiscal policy, the authorities paid little attention to complaints from the trade, and demands for proper legislation were seen

Table 8.1. The number of Parisian movie houses, their receipts, and taxation

Year	No. of houses	Gross receipts (francs)	Taxes (francs)	Taxes as percentage of receipts
1923	169	85,428746.75		
1924	159	100,606,575	20,479,416	20.6
1925	157	117,443,824	25,121,747	21.4
1926	180	145,994,959	31,975,568	21.9
1927	176	177,655,896		
1928		204,023,570		
1929		230,187,461		
1930	182	308,197,011		
1931	180	364,266,914	81,400,000	22.3

as impertinent. In 1920 the Minister of Finance, Louis Klotz, justified
the continuation of these taxes by saying that "the cinema can bear the
tax more easily than anybody else."[20] A year earlier, industry representatives had warned the government of the commercial and political
dangers that would result from the screen's cultural colonisation
by American films, but such fears were then thought unjustified.[21]
Throughout the 1920s, the excessive tax burden placed on exhibition
provided one of the main explanations for the French industry's inability
to generate sufficient profits from its domestic market to sustain a secure
and stable production industry.[22] Even though the cost of producing
films grew over time, the government was not inclined to lower its taxes.
In 1927 the MPPDA noted that French production had increased from
fifty-five films in 1926 to seventy-four in 1927, but added that "excessive
cinema taxation prevented exhibitors from paying rentals which would
better enable producers to amortize production costs in the French
market."[23] In 1934 industry leaders were still vainly complaining that
the cinema had become the milk cow of the state.[24]

Some film historians have underestimated the economic importance
of exports to the American film industry in the inter-war period,[25]
probably because the MPPDA did not reveal how successful they were
in promoting their films abroad, fearing that foreign governments would
be more likely to introduce sanctions if they did so.[26] According to the
industry's own estimates, it depended on foreign distribution for 35–40
per cent of its total production costs, and often a feature film barely
earned its cost in the US.[27] The American dominance of the European
cinema was largely secured through the exploitation of two trade
practices, dumping and block-booking. In 1919 American film companies dumped large quantities of Hollywood films on the European
market, where they were bought cheaply by local entrepreneurs. French
cinema owners then booked the films in blocks lasting up to a whole
year, which effectively excluded films from other companies from
exhibition for the duration.

Block-booking contracts were already well-known in Europe. The
practice was probably first introduced through the "stable customer
service" of the Danish company Fotorama in 1909, but only American
companies produced films in sufficient quantity to use block-booking
effectively. In order to book lavishly produced epics such as *Ben Hur*,
exhibitors were compelled to book as many as forty other films, some
of them mediocre low-budget productions, in the same block. As French
producers frequently complained, one consequence of block-booking was

that competitors were excluded from many exhibition outlets, particularly in the smaller towns and rural areas.[28] The American embassy recognised the problems created by block-booking—one embassy official described it as a "menace"—but it remained legal in France as late as 1934.[29] In the US, small exhibitors persistently complained about the improprieties of block-booking, while the MPPDA justified it on the grounds that it enabled renters to obtain films at wholesale rates.[30] In Europe, the Americans claimed that their success resulted from the better quality of their films; if only the quality of French films improved, they suggested, they would succeed domestically as well as in exporting to America. According to Will Hays, "a really good motion picture, no matter by whom it might have been made, is bound to have proper distribution and exhibition."[31] Block-booking was, however, especially harmful to the distribution of French films. Ironically, although Abel Gance's *Napoleon* was the single most expensive European co-production, its distribution was handled by MGM after the collapse of the Westi Corporation in 1925: in order to book it, French exhibitors also had to book between ten and fifteen American films. According to one critic, although MGM's international distribution of the film might make it possible for *Napoleon* to recoup its costs or even make profits, "if a French exhibitor wants to show the film in his cinema, he is compelled to contract at the same time for a series of foreign films, whose drawing power is very problematical. The work of Gance is being used to place poor films which will handicap more than ever our own productions."[32]

The French government was slow to realise the scale of American dominance, in part because of a lack of statistical information. Rather than introducing specific measures to restrict film imports from the United States, it used conventional policy devices such as tariffs and import quotas. Prior to 1921, import duties on motion picture films had been negligible, but in October of that year the French cabinet raised the tariff on imported American goods to 20 per cent of their value, in retaliation against the proposals in the Fordney Tariff bill to increase American tariffs on foreign imports.[33] In March 1922 the Inter-Ocean Film Corporation (IOFC), which specialised in distributing American films abroad, complained to the Department of Commerce about the new tariffs, and the MPPDA sent a similar complaint to the State Department, arguing that the French appraising experts were over-estimating the value of the films they examined.[34] The law specified that the value of the films was to be estimated on the basis of how much it would cost to produce the film in France. Not knowing the cost of film production, customs officers called in experts from Pathé and Gaumont. The IOFC maintained that these valuations increased the duty to almost 100 per cent of the royalties it would receive, and thus made it impossible to do business in France.

In practice, the increased tariffs had little effect on the importation of American films, which could jump over any protective tariff wall because their production costs had already been redeemed on the home market, so that their earnings in Europe were exclusively profit.[35] The tariff did, however, have the unintended effect of creating unemployment in the French film industry.[36] American film companies had previously sent negatives to France to make positive prints and texts in different languages, but the tariff increase led them to transfer post-production work to Germany, producing extensive job losses in French laboratories. Because the French duty on positives had only been raised slightly, the completed movies were imported from Germany to France at little extra cost. Another method had to be found to reduce the import of American movies. When German quota legislation proved successful in reducing the import of American films in 1924, other European film industries began to agitate for similar legislation. Sapène had already begun to argue for quota restrictions, but the Chambre Syndicale failed to pass a motion urging the government to require that an export licence for a French film be issued for every import licence granted a foreign film. In December 1924 ambassador Myron Herrick brought representatives of Sapène and other French interests together with officials from Famous Players Lasky for a meeting in which the French requested better treatment of their industry by the Americans.[37] This informal action appeared to be successful in quieting down Sapène's anti-American agitation, but by September 1925, after the collapse of Westi, French producers again resumed their pressure for a quota system.[38] The Paris embassy suggested that: "the best move on the part of the American interests would be to try to placate Sapène by arranging for the exhibition in the United States of more of the films in which he is interested. . . . a little tact on the part of American film interests, involving, perhaps, some small sacrifice in the putting on of French pictures, would close the whole question."[39]

During the summer and fall of 1925 the MPPDA sent Oscar Solbert, a military aide to President Calvin Coolidge, on a mission to Europe.[40] Solbert suggested that the MPPDA organise film exports through a co-operative form of marketing, along the same lines as other large export areas such as steel, copper or textiles. As he explained, the Webb–Pomerene Act of 1918 had exempted export cartels from the Sherman Antitrust Act, which prohibited both foreign and domestic cartels from operating inside the United States. American companies operating under the Webb–Pomerene Act were thus better able to compete with foreign cartels abroad. The export association proposed by Solbert would have representatives at strategic points abroad, gathering information for its members on business conditions and the policies of foreign governments. The association's home office would be in direct and constant communication with all departments of the federal government that might assist the moving picture trade. The strength of such an organisation would lie in its agreements on price fixing, and on its members having similar types of contracts. Another great advantage would result from the membership deciding together on the percentages of total productions to be exported to any country, so that the American companies would not depress prices by competing among themselves in a flooded market. Such an organisation, established on a permanent and well-regulated basis, would increase profits and expand market share; Solbert argued that "such a cooperative association would present a solid front in any country to its government or combined producers or exhibitors."[41] Although the MPPDA did not implement Solbert's report in full, it did, as noted earlier, create a Foreign Department, headed by Fredrick L. Herron, which effectively functioned throughout the inter-war period as a Webb–Pomerene exportation cartel without registering under the Act. Like other cartels, the MPPDA organised a group of competitors under an agreement that covered uniform prices, credits, discounts, regulation of output, and division of markets.[42]

The MPPDA's new foreign office immediately became useful in the fight against French demands for contingent restrictions on the import of American films, in close collaboration with the State Department and the American embassy in Paris. In October 1925 the embassy reported that only two men were in favour of a contingency system: Charles Pathé, who now headed Pathé's raw film production, and Sapène, who had published propagandistic articles in Le Matin, and who was interested in promoting the exhibition of French films in the United States. The embassy was certain that the French government would not introduce import restrictions on its own initiative, because of the effect on exhibitors.[43]

Having found himself in the minority in the Chambre Syndicale,

Sapène created his own organisation, which he launched in November 1925 at a banquet of the cinematographic press, in the presence of the Minister of Fine Arts.[44] The organisation's programme included a proposal to prohibit film imports, except for contingents for certain countries that patronised French films. Import licences would be limited to firms that were members of the Chambre Syndicale, and these firms would be obliged to produce French films.[45] These proposals were developed in an article by Pierre Gilles in *Le Matin*, suggesting that film imports should be limited to two metres for every metre of French film produced.[46] At first, the Chambre Syndicale found this proposal attractive, but it was soon realised that it favoured producers who were also importers, such as Sapène, to the detriment of the others, and nothing came of it, because the other film producers remained suspicious of Sapène's motives.[47]

In January 1926, in response to a letter from Hays, the State Department instructed all its embassies to report on any agitation or governmental activities directed against American films; they were also asked for suggestions about how to overcome the harmful effects of such activities.[48] The commercial attaché in Paris, Chester Lloyd Jones, replied that agitation was carried out in France chiefly by "private interests," and was directed almost entirely at American films. It would probably not be possible to protest against potential legislation on the grounds of direct discrimination, since it would be of a general nature. Because American films dominated the French markets, however, they would be most affected. The attaché doubted that drastic legislation against American films would be introduced, since the prosperity of French distributors and exhibitors depended on a continuous, adequate supply of good films, which French producers were unable to provide. However, a minority of French producers might profit from restrictive measures, and their strength in political manoeuvring might enable them to have legislation passed. The embassy had informed the French authorities that drastic measures against American films might lead to retaliation.[49]

American concerns were provoked by the fear that the impending international film congress in Paris, due to be held in September 1926, might be the occasion for concerted European action against American imports.[50] Had Sapène succeeded in becoming the undisputed leader of the French film industry, he might also have emerged from the Paris conference as the natural leader of a European film community campaign against American films. In February 1926, however, he suddenly reversed his policy: his own film association had proved ineffective in persuading the government to establish a contingent, and he rejoined the Chambre Syndicale as an Honorary President.[51] He also began to distribute films from several American producers, and two of his own films, *Michel Strogoff* and *Les Misérables*, were shown by Universal in the United States with some success. Like the Americans, Sapène took no part in the Paris conference. Herron later explained to the State Department that:

> The main purpose of the conference had been to get publicity for the movement in support of measures directed against American films. This movement had collapsed because arrangements had been made privately for restraining the French press from publishing the material in question. This matter had been attended to through Sapène.[52]

In all probability, Sapène acted from lack of funds, and in order to gain some access to the American market. He also harboured an ambition to elevate his wife, the "café-chanteuse" Claudia Victrix, to Hollywood stardom, in imitation, perhaps, of William Randolph Hearst's promotion of Marion Davies.[53] The Americans, on the other hand, had realised that by purchasing a few of Sapène's films, they could win his support and thereby prevent both European film co-operation and the passage of French quota legislation.[54]

They made the arrangement for strategic reasons rather than strictly commercial ones, and most of the films they bought, including *Surcouf, Titi—King of the Kids, Captain Rascasse, Colette's Tears, Antoinette Sagbrier, Mademoiselle Josette My Wife* and *Belphegor*, were not released in the United States.[55]

For much of 1927 Sapène negotiated with the Americans while continuing to promote a policy of protection for French films. In March of that year, Léon Bailby published three editorials in the film journal *L'Intransigeant*, which reopened the campaign for a contingent. The idea was given further encouragement by the passage through the British Parliament of the Quota Act in April. The American consul Alphonse Gaulin reported that several ministers had taken an interest in the film industry recently, and that their interest might result in higher import duties or a contingent system.[56] In May, however, Sapène decided to delay his campaign for contingent legislation for several months, after a visit from Charles Pettijohn, General Counsel of the MPPDA, who promised to put Sapène's demands to the American industry. Sapène would, apparently, be satisfied if the Americans bought three or four of his films per year for distribution in the United States. The consul thought that if Sapène was pacified, the agitation would stop.[57] Sapène's latest feature film, *Casanova,* was sold to Universal for distribution in America, and the Americans would also take *Princesse Masha,* starring Claudia Victrix.[58]

In June 1927 the Ministère de l'Instruction Publique et des Beaux Arts established a Cinema Commission composed of forty-four members representing different departments of the government, motion picture producers, exhibitors, artists, authors, and practically every branch of the industry.[59] At a meeting on 10 November, the minister Edouard Herriot decided to form three subcommissions, the first to report on film production, the second on the exhibition and distribution of films, and the third on the use of films in education. Herriot explained to the French Senate that he had been shocked to discover the scale of American film imports, when France might produce enough for its own needs: "France would soon be colonized by foreign motion picture interests if we do not do something about it."[60] Charles Burguet, the French author, movie director, and President of the Film Authors' Society, told American consul Harold L. Smith: "Herriot knows very little about motion pictures, and must rely upon the Cinema Commission for guidance."[61]

Sapène had initially been unwilling to collaborate with the Cinema Commission, but in November, after the number of German films imported into France rose sharply, and after the American companies' rejection of *Princess Masha,* he became the chairman of the first subcommittee, and he drew up the contingent project together with Burguet.[62] They proposed that distributors of foreign films would have to export a French film in order to obtain a licence to release a certain number of foreign films, in a ratio of either 7:1 or 10:1. The report of the subcommission of distributors and exhibitors, however, was completely opposed to any contingent measure, and most of the commission, including Herriot, rejected it. On 29 December 1927 a compromise proposal, put forward by Léon Gaumont, was agreed, limiting the releases of foreign films to nine metres for every one metre of French film produced.[63]

Frederick Herron complained to the consul that Sapène's new policy was entirely uncalled for: "We have in the last year taken six French pictures in this market for distribution—two by Universal, two by Metro and two by Paramount. Of these six, four are M. Sapène's own pictures. This goes very plainly to show that no matter what you do for these French motion picture people, they demand something new in addition." Herron insisted that so few French films had been imported because American exhibitors lost money on showing them, and that "our people" would have to "force the French films down the throats of the exhibitors." It was out of the question to buy a certain number of French pictures each year in order to keep off the quota legislation, he argued: "we can no more do this for France than we can for England, Czechoslovakia, Poland, Russia, Italy, Spain or any other country of the world."[64] He did not, of course, mention that France had bought 565 films from the United States in 1926.

On 11 January 1928, the Cinema Commission considered the report of the second subcommission on the problems of the distributors and exhibitors, and also examined the question of which parts of the contingent project could be enacted by decree, rather than requiring the passage of legislation. There was also some discussion of how many permits a producer would obtain for the release of a French film in foreign countries.[65] Although the proposed decree caused a storm of protest in cinematographic circles, on 15 January the Chambre Syndicale resolved to authorise its members in the first subcommission to vote for the contingent decree. With this decision and a promise to the exhibitors that they would have sufficient film for their programmes, the Cinema Commission decided to accept the decree proposed by Herriot, with one dissenting vote. According to Harold L. Smith, "The meeting was not without incident, for Mr. Sapène and one of the representatives of the exhibitors came to blows and the latter was floored."[66]

The decree was issued on 18 February 1928, and went into effect on 1 March. It consisted of three essential parts. Firstly, it assimilated the cinema laws to those of the theatre, reducing arbitrary local control over the licensing of French movie houses, which increased in number and quality in the following years. The Ministère de l'Instruction Publique censored the films, but the local police could still prohibit shows under the laws of 1884 and 1790.[67] Secondly, the decree gave autocratic powers to the new Cinema Control Commission regarding the release and censoring of all films. All films from a company which had produced an "anti-French" film might be barred from French screens. Finally, the decree gave the commission the power to compel foreign film producers to buy French films in order to release their films in France. Herriot had by then abandoned his plan to have the Parliament pass a contingent measure. Instead he gave the Cinema Control Commission arbitrary powers to regulate the release of foreign films in France.

Daniel Serruys, a senior official at the Ministry of Commerce, then also serving as President of the League of Nations Economic Committee, pointed out that the contingent project would violate the Geneva convention of the 1927 International Conference for the Abolition of Import and Export Prohibitions and Restrictions, which was intended to maintain international free trade. France had signed the convention, although the US had not. France had not, however, included films in the list of products which should continue to be restricted. The Cinema Commission had given little thought to the decisions of this conference, believing that the contingent project's restrictions on the release of foreign films in France, rather than on their importation, made it a matter of internal French policy. Britain, Germany and Italy had also signed the conference convention and upheld contingent laws at the same time, and it was unthinkable that France would not be able to introduce similar measures. In addition, since the United States had prohibited the importation of French wines, on the basis of protecting the health of its citizens, the commission thought that France would have the right to limit the number of American films released in order to protect the minds of the youth of the nation. There was, however, some opportunity for argument in the wording of Article 5 of the convention:

> Should the High Contracting Parties, in pursuance of their legislation, subject the importation or exportation of goods to certain regulations in respect of the name, form or place of importation or exportation, or the imposition of marks, or to *other formalities or conditions*, they undertake that such regulations *shall not be made a means of disguised prohibition or arbitrary restriction*.[68]

American Consul A. Gaulin believed that the decree was a clear violation at least of the spirit of the Geneva convention, and his interpretation seemed confirmed by Herriot's declaration that the primary objective of the decree was to limit the release of foreign films in France, to control the release of foreign films treating French subjects, and to compel foreign producers to buy French films.[69]

Will Hays sailed to France on 28 March 1928, after all imported films were held up because the censorship committee had stopped censoring American films on 1 March 1.[70] At the beginning of April the Cinema Commission suspended the operation of the quota system temporarily because the exhibitors complained that they lacked films, and French production was totally inadequate to meet the needs of the domestic market; American films had to be imported whether domestic producers liked it or not. The producers, on the other hand, remained determined to force the sale of their productions on the Americans, while Americans were equally determined not to enter into such a deal.[71] At Easter, Herriot told Hays that he had no desire to drive American films out of France, but neither did he want to let the French industry die unprotected. He asked Hays to submit proposals for a solution.[72] In response, Hays submitted an "ultimatum" on 20 April, 1928, demanding that the requirement for obligatory exportation of French films be repealed, and that an importation quota of seven American films for every film *produced* in France should be introduced. He promised that American movies would not be offensive to the French, and that the American film industry would look with favour on the circulation of French films in the United States. [73]

The US State Department supported Hays's stance. Ambassador Herrick saw the situation as a business fight between the American film industry and the French producers, interested in enacting the decree that created the Cinema Commission and its regulations. American film interests in France supported Hays's course of action, making it clear that if Hays did not obtain an agreement for the suspension of these regulations, they would cease doing business in France.[74] Herrick explained to Herriot that the regulations would force the American motion picture industry to suspend its operations in France.[75]

The other members of the government let Herriot grapple with the difficult situation. At the beginning of May 1928, Sapène, who knew the content of the ultimatum, urged the minister to seek a compromise.[76] Further negotiations with Hays resulted in a modification of the decree on 4 May. Under this new agreement, instead of the American companies having to buy one film for distribution in the United States for every four American films distributed in France, a producer was granted licences to import seven foreign films for every film produced in France. The obligatory purchase of French films for distribution in the United States was repealed. In addition, 60 per cent of the American films shown in France during 1927 could be imported without being subject to contingent restrictions,[77] and the agreement would be negotiated after one year.[78] The quota was so generous that American film imports never reached its ceiling, and this agreement effectively crushed Sapène's attempts to protect the French film industry.

Nevertheless, the MPPDA continued to combat European quotas at the Second Conference for the Abolition of Import and Export Prohibitions and Restrictions in Geneva in the summer of 1928, where the United States and France were again the principal adversaries.[79] The Americans insisted that films were merely a commercial product, whereas the French delegate, Serruys, claimed that film contingents and quotas were legitimate means of cultural protection. The arguments were strikingly similar to those presented at the Uruguay round of the GATT (General Agreement on Tariffs and Trade) negotiations in 1994.

The next confrontation between the United States and France occurred when the quota year ended on 1 March 1929. At a meeting on 27 February 1929 the Chambre Syndicale agreed that because the regulations had failed to protect the French industry, it would be necessary to restrict the import to three American films for every French film produced. Ambassador Herrick thought that the best American tactics would be to refuse to negotiate, since any negotiation would imply an American concession. He thought the French film interests were trying to bluff, and that they would not be able to carry on without American films.[80] The MPPDA followed this policy of confrontation. Claiming that they could not operate profitably under the new conditions, the American companies announced that they were suspending their activities in France on 10 April, confident that after six months' cessation of sales, they would have defeated the quota system completely.[81] Hays believed that a total withdrawal would provoke a public demand for their return, and when that happened they would be able to dictate terms.[82] His opinion was bolstered by a petition signed by nearly 2,000 exhibitors from the provinces, urging the government to abandon quota restrictions.[83] On 26 April 1929, Warner Bros decided to resume sales. This would have given the company an important advantage in the French market. It would also have undermined the MPPDA's strategy, and would doubtless have been followed by other companies, but under strong pressure from Hays, Warners was kept in line.[84]

During the confrontation, the MPPDA promoted a policy that would replace the quota with a high tariff on motion picture imports, claiming that this would promote the exportation of good films. In practice, such a measure would have impeded exports from other European film producers, and from independent American companies.[85] Although the

Under-Secretary of Fine Arts, François-Poncet, was dissatisfied with the quota system and wanted it supplanted by an increased customs duty, he could not disregard Sapène and the Chambre Syndicale.[86] In June 1929, however, Sapène suddenly sold his interests in the Pathé-Consortium to Bernard Natan and withdrew from the film industry. His attempts to elevate Claudia Victrix to stardom in *Princesse Marscha* and *L'Occident* had been a complete failure, and his increasingly personal involvement in Cinéromans' production policy had been no more successful. It was clear that the MPPDA's new strategy would offer no opportunities to enter the American market, and any hope he harboured for controlling distribution through his safety film patents had been destroyed by Kodak's introduction of a cheap acetate film in 1928.

With Sapène's withdrawal from the industry, François-Poncet saw a solution to the dispute with the Americans by agreeing to maintain the status quo. An agreement signed on 19 September 1929 prolonged the Herriot–Hays agreement until 1 October 1930, and until 1 October 1931 if no other arrangement had been reached before 1 May 1930. More amicable relations were immediately re- established between the French and American industries: the French abandoned the plan to institute a quota of 4:1, and the Americans were assured that no new regulations would be adopted without their consent during the period of the accord.[87] The Americans wanted the French to commit themselves to abolish the quota system, but the agreement stated only that a new arrangement should be based on "a method of protection different from the present principle."[88] This recognition of the futility of the quota system did, however, have repercussions for the contingent principle throughout Europe. The State Department considered this accord to be the most important achievement in the fight against European quota and contingent regulations, not just for the American film industry but for all American exporters; the contingent principle was spreading like a disease, and had already been used to limit imports of American cars. If it had been upheld, the quota principle would sooner or later have been applied to other products and on a more extensive scale.

As American Consul Alfred D. Cameron noted, the practical effect of the continuation of the 7:1 quota was the virtual abolition of the quota arrangement as a protection of the French film industry. The number of films that could be imported under the quota was about 1,200 annually, while the maximum requirement of the French market for foreign films was around 800 films.[89] The leaders of the French film industry entered the agreement because they thought that the new conditions brought about by the advent of sound would protect them.

Many factors led to the destruction of the measures to protect French film production. Excessive amusement taxes meant that French films could not recuperate the cost of film production in the domestic market. The French state drained the resources from the film industry, and the antiquated regulation for cinemas impeded the growth of the French exhibition sector. The lack of unity and collaboration between French producers and exhibitors excluded the possibility of establishing a policy to protect French film production; Sapène's attempts to obtain profitable deals for himself from the Americans also precluded broader French and European collaboration.

Furthermore, through the opportunities provided by the Webb–Pomerene Act, the MPPDA was able to break the French measures to protect the national film industry, preventing the French from playing one American company off against another. The MPPDA presented a united front of American distributors and French exhibitors to the French government. Block-booking arrangements further ensured that the American distributors dominated the booking of films to French cinemas. The vigilance of the State Department and the American diplomatic corps was of crucial importance to the success of American motion picture exports.

Notes

1. For a description of the American film industry's foreign relations as a war, see "Hollywood has a Foreign War," headline in *New York Times*, 4 March 1928; *New York Times Encyclopedia of Film, vol. 1 1896–1928* (New York, 1984). See also David Puttnam with Neil Watson, *The Undeclared War: The Struggle for Control of the World's Film Industry* (London: Harper Collins, 1997).

2. In preparing this essay, I have examined documents from the following archives in the National Archives (NARA), Washington D.C.: the American Embassy, France, the Consulate in Paris, the State Department, the Department of Commerce. I have also made use of the private archive of Will H. Hays, President of the MPPDA 1922–45, available in published form as *The Will Hays Papers*, 78 microfilms edited by Douglas Gomery with an introduction, *A Guide to the Microfilm Edition of the Will Hays Papers* (Frederick, MD: University Publications of America, 1986) (hereafter *WHP*).

3. Several ministries had jurisdiction over different aspects of French film policy, but the Ministère de l'Instruction Publique et des Beaux-Arts had overall responsibility. I have examined the archive of this ministry in Les Archives Nationales, Paris. Even though a few scholars have investigated French cinema law, none seem to have studied the disorderly archive of this ministry. See Paul Leglise, *Histoire de la politique du cinéma français*, vols 1 and 2 (Paris: Libraire générale de droit at de jurisprudence, 1970); G. Lyon-Caen and P. Lavigne, *Traité théorique et pratique de droit du cinéma français comparé* (Paris: Librairie Générale de Droit et de Jurisprudence, 1957); Georges Billecocq, *Le régime fiscal de l'industrie cinématographique en France* (Paris: Occitania, 1925).

4. For an account of comparable policies followed by the Danish government, see Jens Ulff-Møller, "Da filmen kom til Danmark: Biografvaesenets udvikling, bevillingssystemet og biograflovgivningen af 1922," in *Sekvens FilmvidenskabeligÅrbog, 1989* (Copenhagen: Institut for Filmvidenskab, Københavns Universitet, 1990).

5. Swedish film censorship began in 1910 and was the oldest in Europe. The statistics are available in Bertil Wredlund and Rolf Lindfors, *Långfilm i Sverige, vol. 1, 1910–1919* (Stockholm: Proprius förlag, 1991), p. 224. Vol. 2: 1920–1929, Vol. 3: 1930–1939; Colin Crisp, *The Classic French Cinema, 1930–1960* (Bloomington: Indiana University Press, 1993), p. 11; Leglise, *Histoire*, vol. 2, p. 214.

6. In 1918, 80 per cent of the new film stock available in France was foreign, mainly American, and in October 1919, 90 per cent of the film titles were foreign. Richard Abel, "Survivre à un 'novel ordre mondial,'" in Jacques Kermabon, ed., *Pathé: Premier Empire du cinéma* (Paris: Centre Pompidou, 1994), p. 163; V. Guillaume Danvers, "Entente industrielle, artistique et commerciale," in *La Cinématographie française*, 14 June 1919, p. 9; Jean Toulet, "Le métrage d'une semaine d'octobre," in *Le Cinéma et l'Écho du cinéma*, 28 December 1919, p. 2.

7. *Film Year Book 1927* (New York: Alicoate, 1927), p. 925.

8. Telegram, American consul to the Secretary of State, 22 September 1926, US Embassy, France.

9. Edward G. Lowry, July 1926, *WHP*, reel 28, frame 93.

10. Richard Abel, *French Cinema: The First Wave, 1915–1929* (Princeton, NJ: Princeton University Press, 1984), pp. 4, 48.

11. Report from Harold Smith (1 May 1928), p. 10, *WHP*, reel 40, frame 765. For other French attempts to break into the American market, see Abel, *French Cinema*, pp. 18, 41–2.

12. Exhibition of inflammable moving picture films was prohibited after 1 January 1925, according to an Ordinance of 10 April 1922 from the Prefect of Police of Paris. The letter has a confidential section: "it is generally understood in Paris moving picture circles that this prohibition is the result

of the efforts of the 'Société Pathé-Cinema' to control the film trade, since it claims to be the only manufacturer of non-inflammable films. This opinion is supported by the reference in the first paragraph of the Ministerial Circular to a circular request made to the Departmental Prefects by the 'Société Pathé-Cinema' that Orders be issued making the use of non-inflammatory films obligatory within a maximum period of two years." 11 May 1922, US Consulate, Paris.

13. Statistics in *La Cinématographie française*, 9 July 1927; 9 December 1933; 20 May 1933. *Film Yearbook 1927*, p. 937.

14. Smith, confidential report to Hays, 1 May 1928, *WHP*, reel 40, frames 755ff.

15. Consul Gaulin to Herron, 3 June 1927, US Consulate, Paris.

16. Gaulin to Herron, 1 February 1928, US Embassy, France.

17. André Chevanne, *L'Industrie du cinéma, le cinéma sonore* (Bordeaux: Delmas, 1933), p. 81; Howard T. Lewis, *The Motion Picture Industry* (New York: Van Nostrand, 1933), pp. 413–14.

18. *Film Yearbook 1929* (New York: Alicoate, 1929), p. 1022.

19. *Film Yearbook 1927*, p. 937; *Film Yearbook 1928* (New York: Alicoate 1928), p. 957; Billecocq, *Le Régime fiscal*, pp. 136–7.

20. "En raison de la vogue dont il jouit, le cinématographe peut plus facilement que tout autre supporter le poids de la taxe," in Billecocq, *Le Régime fiscal*, p. 136.

21. "In 1919, the redoubtable commercial and political danger liable to result from a colonization of our screen was signaled to the French Government by producers, authors, composers and moving picture actors. In 1917, Mr. Klotz, then Minister of Finance, had already received the same complaints. The American film, our sole serious competitor at that time, not having been installed so solidly in our country eight years ago, our fears seemed chimerical." Translation by Gaulin of article in *La Cinématographie française*, 31 Dexember 1927. Appendix to despatch, 9 January 1928, US Embassy, France.

22. "A large French production can not be profitable if limited to the home market," *Film Yearbook 1926* (New York: Alicoate, 1926), p. 394.

23. "Foreign Department, Annual Report 1927–1928" (New York: MPPDA, March 1928), p. 39.

24. Opinion of M. Charles Delac. "Les taxes des spectacles seraient allégées," *Le Courrier cinematographique*, 15 December 1934, p. 6. The Italian film industry suffered under a similar burden: in 1925, 25 per cent of all tax collected by the Italian government was supplied by the cinema. Elaine Mancini, *Struggles of the Italian Film Industry during Fascism, 1930–1935* (Ann Arbor, MI: UMI Research Press, 1985), p. 29.

25. Peter Lev, *The Euro-American Cinema* (Austin: University of Texas

Press, 1993), p. 17; Thomas Guback, *The International Film Industry* (Bloomington: Indiana University Press, 1969; introduction.

26. Kristin Thompson, *Exporting Entertainment: America in the World Film Market, 1907–1934* (London: British Film Institute, 1985), pp. 123–4 and 187. "Hays office Denies 'Lid' is Placed on Foreign Film News," *Moving Picture World*, 11 June 1927, p. 401.

27. Raymond Moley, *The Hays Office* (Iindianapolis: Bobbs-Merrill, 1945) p. 169.

28. "Dans les villes importantes où la clientele est plus difficile, l'exploitation se fait avec les meilleurs films bien que, souvent, et si un film exceptionnel, genre 'BEN-HUR', est possedé par une maison Americaine, celle-ci impose par contrat, et souvent par surprise, l'obligation d'acheter 40 films de sa production, sans les avoir vus, ce qu'on appelle le 'Blind Booking'. Si devant les milles de copies importées, les films produits en France, soutenus par le public qui les préfere, trouvent à s'exploiter dans les villes importantes, il leur est impossible de lutter contre les producteurs Americains dans les villes de petite importance et dans les agglomerations rurales car, la, grace aux prix de location qu'ils pratiquent, et qui ne représentent meme pas l'usure des copies, les maison Americaines pour nous barrer la route, acceptant de louer les programmes à n'importe quel prix! Il y a des cinémas nombreux qui passent 35 à 50 programmes Americains par an contre 8 à 10 Francais. Il y a nombre de petites salles où jamais on ne projette un film Français!" ("In the most important towns where the customers are the most demanding, exploitation often uses better films, and if an American company has an exceptional film like *Ben Hur*, it often imposes the obligation to buy forth other films without having seen them; this is called 'Blind Booking.' If among the thousands of imported films in the big cities, the public can find the French films which they prefer, in the smaller cities and rural areas it is impossible to compete with the Americans, because they rent their films at any price, not even covering the wear on the prints, just to block the way for us! There are many cinemas that show thirty-five to forty American films a year, and only eight or ten French ones. There are many small cinemas that never show a French film.") Note sur l'Action en France de Certains Films Americains, 17 June 1929, US Embassy, France.

29. Memorandum to Mr Reagan, 19 June 1928, US Embassy, France: *Le Courrier cinématographique*, 15 December 1934, p. 6.

30. "Complaint from the Federal Motion Picture Council in America, Inc., to the Federal Trade Commission," *United States Daily*, 8 October 1927, *WHP*, reel 35, frame 901; "Foreign Department, Annual Report 1927–1928," MPPDA, p. 39; Block-booking in Canada, *WHP*, reel 39, frame 907.

31. "The motion picture industry is in splendid condition, with sound business

methods prevailing, complete harmony in the ranks of his [Hays] association, and ever-increasing artistry in the pictures themselves," Will Hays speech at the Inland Press Association Convention, West Baden, Indiana. Press release, 26 May 1925. *WHP*, reel 22, frames 439–40.

32. Translation of article by Antoine, published in *Le Journal*, cited in *Le Courrier cinématographique*, 5 November 1927. Translation by consul A. Gaulin in appendix to letter to Herron, 14 November 1927, US Embassy, France; *Film Yearbook 1927*, p. 937.

33. Séance 20 January. Extract from *Journal Officiel* Paris, 21 January 1923, US Embassy, France.

34. Paul H. Cromelin, Inter-Ocean Film Corporation to Herbert Hoover, Secretary of Department of Commerce, 30 March 1922, and later, Department of Commerce, Index file no. 281, France.

35. "Pour la Cinématographie Francaise. Du Contingentement," *Le Matin*, 27 November 1925, NARA microfilm 560, roll 46, frames 588–93.

36. Mercure Prudhomme, *Semaine Cinématographique*, 7 April 1922, Department of Commerce, Index file no. 281, France.

37. Sheldon Whitehouse, Chargé d'Affaires interim, US Embassy Paris to the Secretary of State, 7 October 1925, NARA microfilm 560, roll 46, frames 490–3.

38. Jack S. Connolly, MPPSA to the Secretary of State, 30 September 1925; Telegram, Secretary of State Kellogg to the Embassy in Paris, 1 October 1925, NARA microfilm 560, roll 46, frame 487.

39. Sheldon Whitehouse to the Secretary of State, 7 October 1925, NARA microfilm 560, roll 46, frames 490–2.

40. *Who Was Who in America*, vol 3, 1960, p. 803; and *New York Times*, 17 April 1958, obituary.

41. "Solbert's report which you asked for F.L.H.," undated report [1925], *WHP*, reel 36, frames 1130–5, reproduced as Document 9 in this volume.

42. William F. Notz and Richard S. Harvey, *American Foreign Trade: As Promoted by the Webb-Pomerene and Edge Acts* (Indianapolis: Bobbs-Merrill, 1921), p. 120.

43. US Embassy Paris to Secretary of State, 7 October 1925 NARA microfilm 560, roll 46, frame 490.

44. Vice Consul Alfred D. Cameron, "Postponement of Decree Prohibiting Inflammable Motion Picture Films," 10 November 1925, US Embassy, France.

45. Cameron, "Motion Picture Situation. Report to State Department," 19 January 1926, NARA microfilm 560, roll 46, frame 500.

46. Pierre Gilles, "Pour la Cinematographie Francaise. Du Contingentement," *Le Matin*, 27 November 1925, NARA microfilm 560, roll 46, frames 588–93.

47. "Protection du Film Français," *Bulletin Officiel de la Chambre Syndicale de*

la Cinématographie et des Industries que s'y Rattachent, Enclosure to despatch, 15 January 1926, US Embassy, France.

48. Leland Harrison, State Department, Unnumbered Instruction to several American Embassies in Europe, 30 January 1926, State Department file 800.4061/34.

49. Memorandum Cheter Lloyd Jones, Commercial Attaché to Mr. Hallett Johnson, First Secretary, "Agitation against American Films in France," 1 March 1926, NARA microfilm 580, roll 36, frames 581–7.

50. William Victor Strauss, "Foreign Distribution of American Motion Pictures," *Harvard Business Review*, vol. 8, 1929, pp. 307–15. See also the essays by Andrew Higson and Richard Maltby in this volume.

51. Comité de Direction de la Chambre Syndicale Française de la Cinématographie, Réunion du vendredi 19 fevrier 1926, US Embassy, France.

52. Conversation: Major Herron. Subject: Motion Picture Situation. Department of State, Office of the Economic Adviser, 13 February 1928, State Department file 800-4061/96.

53. "Sapène, qui rêvait de devenir le W. Randolf Hearst français. Ce *Citizen Kane* au petit pied essaya d'imposer vainement au public sa Suzanne Alexander, l'actrice Claudia Victrix." Georges Sadoul, *Le Cinéma français (1890–1962)* (Paris: Flammarion, 1962), p. 44. The American lawyer Chales Campbell, a friend of Claudia Victrix, informed Hays that she wanted to go to Hollywood for the prestige. Campbell to Hays, 4 May 1928, *WHP*, reel 40, frame 889.

54. "Universal's friendly dealings with Sapene . . . were one of the interesting developments of the year insofar as the American industry and France were concerned 'Les Misérables' and 'Michael Strogoff' were released by Universal in America, the latter opening for an engagement at the Cohan theater, New York city on Dec. 5," *Film Yearbook 1927*, p. 937.

55. Smith, "Motion Picture Notes," 18 February 1927, NARA microfilm 560, roll 46, frame 684.

56. Gaulin to Herron, 6 April 1927, US Consulate, Paris.

57. Gaulin to Herron, 2 May 1927, US Consulate, Paris.

58. Smith, "Exhibitor's Opinionon the Proposed Measures for the Protection of the French Motion Picture Producing Industry," 6 May 1927, p. 5, NARA microfilm 560, roll 46, frame 768.

59. Gaulin to Herron, 21 June 1927, US Consulate, Paris; Smith, 9 January 1928, NARA microfilm 560, roll 46, frames 918–19.

60. The Embassy, France to Herron, 28 November 1927, US Embassy, France.

61. Smith, to Herron, 15 December 1927; 9 January 1928, US Consulate, France.

62. Conversation: Major Herron. Subject: Motion Picture Situation. Department of State, Office of the Economic Adviser, 13 February 1928, State Department file 800.4061/96.

63. Gaulin to Herron, 12 December 1927, 23 December 1927, US Consulate, France; Smith, "Motion Picture Contingent Project Approved by Cinema Commission," 9 January 1928, NARA microfilm 560, roll 46, frame 918.
64. Herron to Gaulin, 23 December 1927, US Consulate, France.
65. Smith, "Developments in Motion Picture Contingent Agitation in France. Meeting of the Cinema Commission on January 11 1928," 16 January 1928, NARA microfilm 560, roll 46, frame 934ff.
66. Smith, "Formation of a French Motion Picture Control Commission," 20 February 1928, NARA microfilm 560, roll 46, frame 969.
67. Marcel Nussy, *Le Cinématographe et la censure* (Montpellier: Imprimerie Emmanuel Montane, 1929), p. 67.
68. Gaulin to Herron, 14 February 1928, US Embassy, France, emphasis in original.
69. *Le Matin*, and in an editorial by Leon Bailby, *L'Intransigeant*, 19 February 1928; Gaulin to Herron, 14 February 1928, US Embassy, France.
70. Department of State, Office of the Economic Advisor, 17 March 1928, NARA microfilm 560, roll 46, frame 1028.
71. *New York Times*, 5 April 1928, NARA microfilm 560, roll 46, frame 1077.
72. Herrick to Secretary of State, 27 April 1928, NARA microfilm 560, roll 46, frames 1068–9.
73. *WHP*, reel 40, frames 454–8.
74. Herrick to Secretary of State, 27 April 1928, NARA microfilm 560, roll 46, frames 1068–70.
75. Herrick to Edouard Herriot and Hays, 1 May 1928, NARA microfilm 560, roll 46, frames 1101 and 1108.
76. Canty to North, 25 April 1925, Department of Commerce.
77. Canty to North, 4 May 1925, Department of Commerce.
78. Canty to North, 25 April 1925, Department of Commerce. The text of the decree is reprinted as Document 11 in this volume.
79. International Convention for the Abolition of Import and Export Prohibitions and Restrictions, *Abolition of Import and Export Prohibitions and Restrictions: Convention and Protocol between the United States and Other Powers* (Washington, DC, 1930). This issue is also discussed in Richard Maltby's article in this volume.
80. Telegram, Herrick to Secretary of State, 1 March 1929.
81. Cameron, "Motion Picture Quota Situation," 13 April 1929, NARA microfilm 560, roll 47, frame 116; MacLean to State Department, 2 May 1929.
82. W.R. Castle, Department of State to Normal Armour, US Embassy, France, 10 June 1929.
83. Cameron, "New Film Quota Agitation," 2 March 1929, NARA microfilm 560, roll 47, frames 32ff. *New York Herald*, 9 March 1929.

84. Memorandum, Department of State, Office of the Economic Adviser, 2 May 1929, NARA microfilm 560, roll 47, frames 166–70.
85. Memorandum, Department of State, Office of the Economic Adviser, 26 April 1929, NARA microfilm 560, roll 47, frame 129.
86. Armour to State Department, 29 May 1928, NARA microfilm 560, roll 47, frame 200.
87. Undated memorandum in the archive of State Department: "History of the French Film Contingent Regulations" (Posted 19 September 1929).
88. "Franco-American Film Accord"; Hays to Stimson, Secretary of State, 19 September 1929, NARA Microfilm 560, roll 47, frame 386.
89. Cameron, "French Motion Picture Quota Virtually Abolished," 8 October 1929, NARA Microfilm 560, roll 47, frame 398.

9

Hollywood Babel
The Coming of Sound and the
Multiple-Language Version

Ginette Vincendeau

In histories of the cinema the question of multiple-language versions (hereafter MLVs) figures generally as a negligible episode worthy of a line or two, at most a paragraph, which goes as follows: with the coming of sound, films are no longer automatically exportable. Hollywood studios find themselves obliged to produce films adapted to national markets (at least the most important ones linguistically and financially, i.e. the Spanish, German, French and Swedish) in order to satisfy the demand for films in European languages as well as to dodge import quotas then imposed by most European countries. One of two strategies is usually adopted: importing directors, scriptwriters and actors from each country to Hollywood (the MGM solution) or setting up production centres in Europe (the Paramount method). Both solutions, against the background of the Depression, prove equally costly and are rapidly dropped in favour of dubbing, or (more rarely) titling, as we know them today.

Apart from the considerable difficulty of access to archival prints, MLVs have remained unexplored for two main reasons. Firstly, in terms of industrial practice, the phenomenon was overshadowed by the sound patents struggle between the USA and Europe for the domination of European markets. Secondly, in terms of an aesthetic history of world cinema, or of the national cinemas concerned, multiple-language films, and particularly those produced by Paramount in Paris, are considered worthless, the universally recognised exceptions (*Marius, The Threepenny Opera*) being attributed entirely to the talent of their (European) *auteur*. Historian Charles Ford's opinion on the subject is typical: "In eighteen hectic months at Joinville Paramount produced only one film that is still remembered (*Marius*)."[1]

My intention is not to attack this interpretation of film history in order to replace it with my own version, although even a quick scan through *Variety* of that period reveals facts and positions much more complex than is usually recognised. There is a mass of archaeological work to be done.[2] Nor is the point to unearth forgotten "masterpieces" (there probably aren't any), though of course our view of the history of that period is precisely coloured by the Ford-type search for "masterpieces". My intention is, rather more modestly, to shift the terms of the debate and concentrate on what is generally regarded as a weakness. MLVs interest me because they failed: aesthetically these films were "terrible", and financially they turned out to be a disaster. They can, however, be of use to the historian because they are located at the point of contact between the aesthetic (this term being used here rather loosely to cover cultural, thematic and generic constructs) and the industrial dimensions of cinema. In this sense they can become precious instruments of knowledge for a crucial period of the history of cinema. Beyond the debate on European resistance *versus* American cultural imperialism, the different solutions applied to linguistic and cultural barriers raise generic, theoretical and ideological questions that are also important for an exploration of the notion, apparently self-evident but rarely challenged, of national cinemas.

I

MLVs were usually films shot *simultaneously* in different languages, in one of several fashions:

- Where a film was shot in two or three languages only, the director was often the same; Pabst shot the German and French versions of *The Threepenny Opera* in Berlin, Lubitsch the French and American versions of *One Hour With You* in Hollywood, Jean de Limur the French and American versions of *The Parisian* in Paris, etc. This formula tended to be used, although not exclusively, in European studios.

- For higher numbers of versions (up to fourteen), particularly at Paramount, each version could have a different director, generally of the nationality corresponding to the language used. *The Lady Lies* (Paramount), for instance, had as many directors as versions (six).

Sometimes the same director shot two or three versions. Charles de Rochefort in his memoirs remembers having shot the Czech and Romanian versions of *Paramount on Parade* (Raymond Chirat's catalogue attributes the Italian version to him too[3]).

• For actors the permutations were as numerous. When polyglot actors were used, the star of the film could remain the same while the rest of the cast (except extras) changed. Claudette Colbert and Maurice Chevalier are the stars of the American and French versions of *The Big Pond;* Brigitte Helm stars in the French and German versions of *Gloria, Gold* and *Die schönen Tage von Aranjuez;* Adolphe Menjou in the French and American versions of *The Parisian,* etc. In other cases, the whole cast was different, the individual combinations on the whole being dictated by the coincidence of linguistic competence and script requirements. In *Baroud* (directed by Rex Ingram), Pierre Batcheff, a Russian émigré living in Paris at the time, plays the part of an Arab in both the French and American versions of the film.

There is a second type of MLV: films made from the same source material, but with a short time gap. This category is more difficult to define and catalogue, as the filmographies available adopt different criteria. Variations can be considerable: E.A. Dupont and Jean Kemm shot the French version of *Atlantic* in January 1930 after Dupont had directed the German and English versions in July 1929 in London. Two years after he had directed *L'Equipage* in Paris, Anatole Litvak remade his own film under the title *The Woman I Love* in Hollywood. Should *Atlantic* be considered a trilingual film and *The Woman I Love* a remake? Herbert Mason shot *First Offence* (also known as *Bad Blood)* in London, based on *Mauvaise Graine* which Billy Wilder had shot in Paris a year before. The country of origin, the studio, the cast and the director were all different. Yet the production of *First Offence* attempted to copy *Mauvaise Graine* to the letter: careful duplication of outdoor locations, meticulous research to retrieve as many as possible of the original costumes; some actors were even imported for character parts (such as Maupi, out of the Pagnol stable, who plays the same part as in *Mauvaise Graine,* speaking execrable English). The two films are remarkably similar, except for the superior quality of the sound in the English version.

The two main categories above still have enough in common to be considered as part of the same phenomenon. In both cases the intention is to adapt the same text for different audiences, within a short period of time. Remakes as we know them now tend to copy an older text, appealing to the cinematic memory of the spectator. While the relationship between the two versions (e.g., of *Scarface, A Star is Born, Breathless*) is diachronic, in MLVs it is synchronic. The distinction is important because one of the main characteristics (and limitations) of the MLV is that only one version is given to a particular audience who in most cases has not (and more importantly must not have) any knowledge of the others.[4]

Finally a third, small category must be mentioned: the polyglot film, in which each actor speaks his or her own language, such as Pabst's *Kamaradschaft* and Duvivier's *Allo Berlin! Ici Paris*. Unlike other attempts like *Camp Volant* (Max Reichmann) or *Les Nuits de Port Said* (Leo Mittler), these two films were very successful, which clearly has to do with the fact that they integrate diegetically the interlingual apparatus which is their industrial *raison d'être*.

II

Seen from Europe, the coming of sound only reinforced American hegemony. Nino Frank, in his essay "Babel-on-Seine" on the Paramount studio in Paris, summarises the situation thus: "One would have thought that the '100% talkies' by establishing cinematic national borders, would demolish the American penetration of our studios. Well, rather the opposite: we are the new Eldorado. The Americans are upon us, loaded with millions of dollars, and they merrily start reorganising French production."[5] On the other side of the Atlantic, however, C.J. North and N.D. Golden of the Department of Commerce saw the situation in a different light: "The demand of people for films in their own language plus the difference in technique between the silent and sound picture is operating to increase competition for American films abroad".[6]

Nino Frank's error was to call Europe the *new* Eldorado. As North and Golden put it, "Europe, . . . after all, remains our principal revenue market"[7] (though the profitability of American films in foreign markets was hotly debated within the studios). By ascribing the reorganisation of the French industry caused by the coming of sound solely to American influence, Frank was also ignoring the "helpful" role played by French personnel such as Bernard Natan (of Pathé-Natan), who was responsible for installing the RCA sound system in most French studios, over and above the interests of European patents.

MLVs, as a film industry phenomenon, are situated along a rather blurred line of division between the two types of discourse mentioned above: that of a European resistance (however ephemeral, disorganised and doomed to failure) to American hegemony, and that of a continued expansion by Hollywood in the face of a sudden increase in foreign competition. For, despite the instant success of *The Jazz Singer* and other early Hollywood sound productions, the news of hostile reactions —sometimes going as far as riots[8]—started flooding in from all over Europe and South America, from audiences outraged at being presented with shoddy adaptations of American films (to which subtitles, music and dubbed passages had been added). At the same time, the popular success of German- and French-speaking films in Berlin and Paris was becoming increasingly evident.

The first MLV was an Anglo-German production: *Atlantic*, shot by E.A. Dupont for British International Pictures in these two languages at Elstree, and released in November 1929 (with a third, French version shot at the beginning of 1930). Then came another Anglo-German film, *The Hate Ship*, also shot at Elstree followed by American MLVs shot in Europe: United Artists produced *Knowing Men* (Anglo-German) and Warner Bros produced *At the Villa Rose* (Anglo-French), both made in London. Meanwhile some American studios briefly produced a few films in foreign languages only, such as *The Royal Box*, shot by Warner Bros entirely in German.[9] The first film with a French version shot in Hollywood was *The Unholy Night*, directed by Jacques Feyder for MGM. These had been preceded by a few shorts in foreign languages produced by various American studios, notably Paramount. Purely European MLVs continued to be produced throughout the 1930s (although their production slowed down after 1933), but the vast majority of MLVs were made under the impulse of Hollywood studios. It is on these that I will concentrate.[10]

On 2 October 1929, *Variety* announced that "while Paramount is in the lead in foreign tongue shorts production, Warner Bros is ahead on features. These two companies, of all in the field, so far as could be ascertained, are the only companies indulging in this foreign stuff". What was first considered an indulgence soon became a necessity. A month later, the same paper declared that, apart from projects by Paramount to shoot *The Big Pond* in French, Radio (RKO) was making its first steps towards the "invasion" of foreign lands (with the dubbing of *Rio Rita* in Spanish and German without, however, any illusions about the efficiency of the dubbing system); MGM was about to make foreign versions of practically all its films (to start with, a German

version of *Sunkissed* directed by Victor Sjöström and a Spanish version
of The Siege of Seville by Ramon Novarro); and Fox had decided not to
waste any time with dubbing but to start straight away with MLVs
produced in Europe.

Although they are generally seen as manifestations of the efficiency
of the Hollywood machine, American-generated MLVs are, under close
inspection, symptomatic rather of a great deal of disorganisation. This
is despite the creation, in February 1930, of a special commission of the
Academy of Motion Picture Arts and Sciences, responsible for consultation between major studios and with the aim of reaching a
standardised means of producing foreign language films.[11] The reason
for the failure to reach such standardisation for many years can be
understood if MLVs are seen as symptoms of one of the basic
characteristics of the film industry (as of all capitalist industries):
the constant tension between the necessity for standardisation to
increase profitability on the one hand, and on the other the need for
differentiation to ensure the renewal of demand. MLVs were, on the
whole, too standardised to satisfy the cultural diversity of their target
audience, but too expensively differentiated to be profitable.

Despite assertions to the contrary, dubbed films did not come after
MLVs but preceded them, their low cost making them desirable despite
the recognised technical deficiencies of the dubbing process. Articles in
Variety over the period 1929–32 reveal an incredible confusion on the
subject. Strategies varied between studios, and changes of policy within
a studio were common. On 9 April 1930, *Variety* indicated that "All
foreign picture managers . . . have reached different conclusions as to
the solution which at the moment is the leading trade question. Most
are in the air and stalling while they wonder if the potentialities of
foreign markets are worth the cost." On 14 January 1931 MGM "is still
uncertain whether dubbing or direct shooting (in a foreign language) is
the best policy".[12] So in spite of the self-satisfied Hollywood discourse
on its superior competence in terms of planning, it was precisely the
lack of long-term strategies which engendered this confusion.

The fiasco of Spanish versions in Latin America offers a good
example. As soon as the question of foreign versions came up in
Hollywood, the Latin American Spanish-language market was clearly
the most attractive, in terms of both audience and number of theatres.
All studios immediately launched into Spanish versions, facilitated by
the presence of Spanish-speaking personnel in Los Angeles. Two years
later, most of that production had to be declared redundant; not only

did many linguistic blunders hinder distribution, but they lacked outlets, as many cinemas in South America had not converted to sound. Hesitation was the order of things, policy within studios changing from day to day, following the success or failure of individual films.

Equally, once the principle of MLVs was accepted, the debate shifted to the location of production. There, too, the standardisation/ differentiation dialectic operated. Policies switched between production in Hollywood, more cost-effective and conducive to standardisation, and production in Europe, economically less favourable, but more apt to adaptation to local needs, thus to product differentiation. In May 1929 Jesse Lasky confirmed Paramount's intention to make films in foreign languages in France, while Warner Bros opened studios in Germany and Britain. In March and April 1930 Paramount and MGM were openly in favour of films made in Europe, to ensure better choice of foreign actors at a lower cost, except for Spanish-language versions. Warners acquired 20 per cent of Tobis-Klangfilm and signed an agreement with the German production company Nero for the production of ten films in June 1930. By September 1931, all the major American studios had established a production presence in Europe, in addition to their distribution presence: Warner Bros, Universal, RKO, Paramount, United Artists and MGM in London; Paramount, United Artists and Fox in Paris; Fox and United Artists in Berlin.

The high water mark for European-made MLVs was reached in July 1930, when *Variety* announced that 75 per cent of all foreign language films would be produced in Europe over the next six months, with all such productions taking place there within a year. A major exception was MGM, since Arthur Loew had declared that foreign-language versions had to be made in Hollywood "in order to combine the genius of Hollywood with the European mentality".[13]

Whatever the location of production, however, multiple-language films meant an enormous increase in costs. In December 1930, for instance, MGM had more than sixty foreign actors, scriptwriters and directors under contract in Hollywood, at a total estimated cost to the studio of $40,000 a week (most of the foreigners were repatriated in February 1931). Productions in Europe, however, were not much more profitable, and both types of solution were thus soon revealed to be equally inadequate. By late 1930 and early 1931, most Hollywood studios concluded that their main error had been importing foreign personnel to Hollywood, while an American official report on foreign trade strongly advised the film industry not to set up productions units in Europe. Their conclusions seem to have been based on the performance of Paramount's Joinville studio, near Paris, which cost $1.5 million in fixed investments and had an annual salary bill of $6 million.[14] Later, Paramount would admit that the Joinville studio only became profitable after two years of operation, by which time it had become a simple dubbing laboratory.

III

The activities of the Paramount Studio in Joinville have attracted enough attention for it to be unnecessary to dwell on the more picturesque details—crews of all nationalities sharing canteen tables, sound stages working twenty-four hours a day, and the like. Observers such as Ilya Ehrenberg and Marcel Pagnol (who satirised it in his 1938 film *Le Schpountz*) have left lively accounts of this particular episode.[15] But the myth which has developed around Joinville needs re-examining on a couple of points. First, it is as well to remember that this ostensibly American production-line method (so apparently incompatible with 'European sensitivity') actually originated in London and Berlin. As *Variety* of 7 May 7 1930 put it, "Elstree, London's Hollywood, started that idea of working different companies day and night, leaving the sets standing". Secondly, though legend has it that Bob Kane and his team at Paramount were blind to the gap between its films and their local reception, constant adjustments were made. The material (often plays) on which the films were based changed from predominantly North American to local texts. In January 1931 Kane also decided to reduce the number of versions to French, German, Spanish and Swedish, in order to "give their production for each one of these countries a more individual treatment, such as is now necessary on account of local improvement in production'.[16] He added that "There's a better chance of bringing up the quality of the Paris made pictures than of lowering the cost of the versions here".[17] These adjustments did not prove sufficient. The Depression, as well as internal difficulties within Paramount (as Dudley Andrew and Douglas Gomery have shown[18]), contributed to the end of the Joinville studio as a production unit in July 1932. In other parts of Europe, as in Hollywood, studios reverted to dubbing, more economical (about one-third of the cost of a MLV) and by now somewhat improved.

Finally, another solution was applied, which consisted in selling the rights to a script as soon as a film had been distributed in a country, a method rightly considered detrimental to European cinema. P.A. Harlé, the editor of the main French trade journal *La Cinématographie française*, warned his readers that: "The sale of the story of a French film can ruin its career abroad. It is a new method. Instead of selling *Pépé le Moko* in America, its subject was sold. Not only will the Gabin film not be shown on the other side of the Atlantic, but even in French-speaking countries, *Algiers*, with Charles Boyer in the Gabin part, will be shown instead of the French original!"[19]

IV

The relevance of MLVs to a history of the cinema goes beyond economic and industrial factors, though. Other variables, notably cultural and technical variables, come into play. The main period of MLVs (1929–32) more or less corresponds to the time lapse necessary for Hollywood to establish the sound cinema and for film-makers to so completely integrate sound with the practice they had acquired for silent cinema that, according to David Bordwell, "By 1933, to make a sound film corresponded exactly to shooting a silent film only with sound."[20] The struggle to improve and impose sound technology was combined with a struggle to improve and impose its *credibility* and, given the primacy of the human body and thus the human voice, that of dialogue.

At the beginning of sound cinema, much attention was paid to the relationship between sound and the "reality" of hearing. Linguistic barriers added another dimension to this problem. At the same time, however, there was also concern with the audibility of dialogue.[21] This tension between the desire for a certain auditory "realism" and the necessity for audible dialogue explains why dubbing was not immediately accepted by either audiences or critics. The coming of sound did not simply cause technological problems, but fundamentally altered the relation of spectator to film.

In 1930 North and Golden, of the American Department of Commerce, asked the following question:

> As the chief objection to [dubbing] as straight dialogue is the fact that it shows actors talking perfectly in a language of which obviously they have no knowledge . . . I wonder if any American producer has ever considered saying quite frankly to his foreign audience by means of an explanatory title, that while the actors do

not speak the language in question, it was considered fair, in the interests of realism, to employ voice doubles.[22]

Dubbing, a process which underlines the separation between body and voice, disconcerted audiences of the late 1920s and early 1930s. Speaking of the dubbing of Anny Ondra by Joan Barry in Hitchcock's *Blackmail, Film Weekly* asked: "What if the voice, tired and resentful of anonymity, clamours for publicity, to be featured as itself . . . like the Siamese twins, Face and Voice are inseparable, the death of one implying the death of both."[23] Dubbing upset the feeling of unity, of plenitude, of the character, and thus the spectator position. Moreover, it produced in the contemporary audience a feeling of being duped. A trade paper announced in June 1930: "Dubbed films are easily recognised as such by audiences who daily get more sophisticated."[24] Dubbing was on the whole accepted only because of its novelty, and even then it was considered that it would "go for a while on the novelty angle" but would soon by found unsatisfactory on account of poor synchronisation.[25]

The very naivety of these reactions draws attention to a problem which is not so much repressed as transparent. The millions of non-English-speaking contemporary spectators of *Dallas* know that Sue Ellen does not speak their language, but they do not care very much. In a similar situation, the spectators of 1930 would have perceived an incongruity. It is as if, at its beginning, sound film having just offered a new sense of completeness to the spectator in reconciling body and voice, then immediately upset it by the lack of credibility of dubbing or the dislocation of sound and image in subtitles. MLVs tried to remedy this by the extreme solution of dubbing the body of the actor—until the new norm of dubbed films (or marginally subtitled films) finally managed to incorporate all these changes and disturbances, thus making MLVs redundant. The linguistic problems, if they underline some of the factors relating to the role of sound in the constitution of the spectator as subject, do not, however, modify them fundamentally. Reasons other than economic for the failure of MLVs are to be found elsewhere—in the field of cultural specificity, as well as in casting and narrative patterns.

V

In the aesthetic history of European cinema—I will concentrate on French cinema, but I believe my conclusions to be applicable to other

European national cinemas—MLVs belong to the despised category of "commercial" cinema of the early 1930s. The notion that it is possible to make several versions of the same film, like a piece of clothing in different colours, was and still is abhorrent to the critic, historian or *auteur*. All commentators on MLVs, whether politically to the right or to the left, were unanimous in their condemnation. "On the seven stages," said Ilya Ehrenburg, "work is going on day and night. There are shifts for directors, concierges, caterers,"[26] while Charles de Rochefort remembered that "from 8 am to 7 pm, a Serbian version; from 8 pm to 7 am, a Romanian version . . .".[27] Nino Frank added, "They shoot while they eat, shoot while they sleep, shoot while they wash, shoot while they talk."[28] One critic from the ultra-right journal *Action française* declared: "We are fed up with these counterfeiters who should be punishable by law, with this cheat which consists of putting the name of a famous *auteur* on some miserable 'ersatz' by a third-rate director."[29]

The important point here is that the criticism of MLVs always went hand in hand with a phobia of the cinema in its industrial as opposed to artistic dimension. Directors of MLVs or "remakes" were no more flattering. René Clair, who shot *Break the News* in Britain (the English-language version of *Le Mort en fuite*, directed by André Berthomieu), declared "it ought to be burned . . . It was based on an idea which had been used already for another film; and that kills all inspiration."[30] As Clair's opinion exemplifies, the main objection to MLVs from European "art" directors was their standardising attitude to film-making, a conception of cinema tainted by its lack of concern for originality and creativity. On the other hand, the necessity of showing films in the language of their country of exhibition confronted Hollywood with the ethnic, linguistic and cultural diversity of its audience. Suddenly studios were aware that Latin American audiences did not appreciate films in Castillian accents, that British accents provoked mirth in the Midwest, and that in the Midlands Yankee voices seemed equally funny. Hollywood was also alerted to a large ethnic range on its home territory.[31]

Such cultural diversity ran counter to the need to rationalise production costs, making MLVs an exemplary meeting point of the economic and the cultural. The irreducible nature of cultural difference even affected the attempt to standardise shooting schedules. It became the practice early on to divide shooting time into as many arbitrary units as there were different languages, since the more logical break-down, by scene, proved impossible (for a simple bilingual version, one team worked days, the other nights; in the case of three languages, each team worked for eight hours, etc.). It was found that the same scene required widely different screening times according to the country it was destined for.[32]

Not only did cultural difference upset the rationalisation of the shooting process; it could also undermine success based largely on technical superiority. *The Unholy Night*, an MGM prestige production, from a novel by Ben Hecht and directed by Jacques Feyder in Hollywood, scored very disappointingly at the box-office when it came out in its French version in Paris. *The Parisian*, on the other hand, a formulaic filmed play about the return of the illegitimate son of the hero (Adolphe Menjou) at the age of 20, produced by Pathé-Natan and directed by Jean de Limur, was a triumph. Clearly the major element in box-office appeal was not the production values, but the audience's familiarity with certain narrative patterns, as this contemporary commentary made clear: "Story would be simply impossible in Hollywood . . . Mere glance at the idea furnishes ample proof that the Americans are disqualified by temperament from picking themes for this market. Such a story wouldn't get a second glance in California. Here it is accepted quite placidly."[33] What is brought out here is the crucial importance of intertextual familiarity with genres and narrative patterns in the source material—in this case the boulevard play and its archetypical plot revolving around illegitimacy and adultery—for audience appeal and identification. It could be objected that this analysis disregards the importance of the director. The example of *L'Equipage* shows the auteurist factor to be minimal in this case.

Though shot with a time gap, *L'Equipage* (Pathé-Natan) and *The Woman I Love* (RKO) are typical MLVs in that they share the same source material (a novel by Joseph Kessel), the same director (Anatole Litvak), and the same music (Arthur Honneger) and some scenes were re-used wholesale—a staple technique of MLVs where crowd and street scenes were generally presented in long shot and used as a basis for all versions. Despite being virtually the same film, *L'Equipage* was much more successful with audiences in France than *The Woman I Love* in the USA. This difference is hard to impute to the actors, since Miriam Hopkins was at least as considerable an actress as Annabella, and Paul Muni (who had just received an Academy Award) was as good as Charles Vanel. Contemporary reviews of both films show that the American version does not "work" as well as the French one. Two reasons can be found: the credibility of the plot and the question of morals.

Changes to the film show that an attempt was made to adapt the story to fit American censorship and moral codes. The French version begins on a platform at the Gare de l'Est in Paris in 1918: the hero, Herbillon (Jean-Pierre Aumont), is going to the front, saying his farewell to both his family and a young woman, Denise (Annabella). The couple exchange vows of eternal love. The young man is going to join the other member of his air crew, who is, unknown to all characters, none other than Denise's husband (Charles Vanel). The American version adds a long scene prior to the station platform adieux which aims to anchor the film in the myth of Paris for a North American audience (the couple meet at an operetta called *Love in Paris*). More importantly, it shows Denise as seduced by Herbillon against her will. Later on, when Herbillon confronts her with the "horror" of her adultery (for he has come to like and respect her husband), reference is made to the beginning of the film and she reminds him that he initially pursued her. In the French version Denise is left to take full responsibility—and guilt—for her desire for Herbillon. Despite this effort at adaptation, however, the character played by Hopkins was considered by several contemporary critics as "unsympathetic". The relative failure of the American version is easier to understand if we consider the narrative, and the fact that a considerable number of French films in the 1930s privileged the symbolic or real father–daughter axis to the detriment of other Oedipal relationships (see most films with Raimu, Jules Berry, Victor Francen, Harry Baur and, indeed, Charles Vanel). The relationships between Annabella and Charles Vanel in *L'Equipage*, and the fact that the lover of her own age loses out to the older man, was perfectly acceptable to the French audience of 1935, but less so to North Americans accustomed to different models, among them the victory of the young pretender.[34] Equally, the accent that the French version puts on male bonding, also culturally typical, runs against the stronger drive in contemporary Hollywood films toward the romantic heterosexual couple.

The contrast between acceptance in one culture and rejection in another is characteristic of American-produced MLVs. When contemporary reviews in the country of exhibition can be traced, they constantly show such discrepancies. *Une Femme a menti*, a Paramount production which triumphed in Paris, outraged Italian audiences (under the title *Perché No!*). The Hungarian version of *The Doctor's Secret* was a resounding flop domestically, despite—but also because of—the fact that its crew and cast included great Central European names. The production was cheap; the same decors were used for the eight versions of the film, totalling $49,000 (whereas the contemporary French and Spanish language versions of Olympia cost $100,000 each). The same costumes were used in all versions, and the Hungarian public were apparently shocked to see their national star Gizi Bajor so poorly dressed. The reception of the Polish version of The Doctor's Secret in Poland is equally telling: there, the fact that the version had been filmed by a Polish director of repute (Ryszard Ordynski) provoked negative reactions on account of the perceived discrepancy between the status of that director and the mediocrity of the film.[35]

Besides, Hollywood's vision of a country rarely coincided with the idea that country had of itself. Hence the hostile reactions in European countries to films based on North American texts. As Variety put it: "We have tried to understand the Spanish psychology, given them pictures about things of which they know more than we do and have naturally laid ourselves open to ridicule."[36] Not surprisingly, closer cultural understanding between European countries promoted better reception of European-produced MLVs like Le Tunnel and The Threepenny Opera.

VI

Actors in MLVs are another locus of conflict between cultural and economic factors, as well as a focal point for the contradiction inherent in the tendency towards both standardisation and differentiation. In principle, the advantage of MLVs was that they allowed the possibility of using local stars, but this turned out also to be their drawback. One of the major reasons for the success of Hollywood films with non-American audiences was the attraction of stars who had become international. Conversely, one of the main obstacles to the export of European films to the USA was their actors' relative lack of celebrity. MLVs underlined and reinforced this situation. As Film Weekly remarked: "No longer will British actors be able to increase their following by appearing in foreign cinemas; no longer shall we see German and French artists on our screens. If multi-lingual talkies succeed, as I think they are bound to, stars, instead of being inter-national, will be purely local."[37]

Against this potential obstacle, Hollywood had recourse to polyglot stars: Adolphe Menjou, Maurice Chevalier, Brigitte Helm, Greta Garbo. But here again, interesting contradictions emerged. The foreign accent, for example, had to be diegetically integrated. That being so, it had to be light enough to be acceptable, but strong enough to be picturesque (allegedly Chevalier was forbidden by Paramount to take English lessons). But for the majority of those who could act in only one language, other problems surfaced.

Beyond their impact in the film itself, the commodity value of actors was greatly curtailed by MLVs. For instance, foreign actors posted in Hollywood were encouraged to limit their press statements to the press of their country of origin, as their publicity potential in the USA was nil. Too Americanised for their compatriots, but condemned to remain foreigners in the USA, they were relegated to a sort of media 'no man's land' which uncannily reflects the fate of the MLVs themselves. On the whole, the film industry of their own country was not too happy about their presence on American territory, and in some cases went as far as taking sanctions against them (concurrently, the French actors' union tried to stop its members accepting dubbing work). But, more importantly, it became evident that too much publicity for actors working in MLVs, in Europe as in the United States, inevitably attracted attention to the 'production-line' aspect of these films, and provoked possibly detrimental comparisons—for example, if stars in another version were of higher international status. This goes some way towards accounting for the striking lack of publicity given MLVs at the time.

More work needs to be done on the part played by actors in the inflection given to the different versions of a same film. Ideal candidates for comparison are obviously those where the only variable is the actor, as in Pabst's *Threepenny Opera*. The tremendous success of the French version in France, for instance, can be attributed in part to the deliberate effort by the actors to provide easier access to a "foreign" text. Albert Préjean made no mystery of having tried to turn Mackie into a sympathetic character to fulfil his French audience's expectations. However, it is difficult to judge the success of such strategies at a historical distance. Retrospectively, Jean Gabin in Kurt Bernhardt's *Le Tunnel* (1933) brings to his character the existential weight incorporated in his "myth" of the 1930s, particularly compared to Richard Dix, his equivalent in the British-made version (*The Tunnel*, directed by Maurice Elvey). Where Gabin is intense, Dix is neutral. The question is whether the value we attribute to Gabin, which derives from the accumulation of all his other parts, was perceptible in 1933.

Actors in MLVs, then, were in a contradictory situation. If they were famous, they invested the film with particular traits for their audience; for instance, Jessie Matthews in *First a Girl* takes the film in the direction of her "clean and cheerful" persona, the opposite of the highly ambiguous rendering of the same character by Renate Muller in the German version, *Viktor und Viktoria.* In a way, the ideal actor in MLVs was an unknown, someone who could be easily moulded (which is what MGM tried to do), but the films then suffered in both impact and publicity value.

René Jeanne and Charles Ford, among others, attributed the failure of MLVs to the fact that most of them were adaptations of plays.[38] However, as the success of films such as *The Parisian* shows, the failure of most MLVs came not from their excess of "theatricality" but rather from their insufficient relationship with generic and narrative patterns of French theatre with which the contemporary audience was familiar. A similar study of other national contexts would almost certainly reveal similarities.

In conclusion, I would venture that the main usefulness of MLVs for film history and for the 1930s in particular may be to point towards a better understanding of what a national "popular" cinema is. MLVs illustrate the importance of the linguistic factor in a definition of a national cinema, and their failure, beyond economic factors, cannot be separated from other cultural considerations, particularly at a time of audience hypersensitivity, given the novelty of dialogue. MLVs also show in an exemplary fashion that a national cinema is defined principally by its degree of intertextuality with the culture of its country, and in particular with its dominant narrative patterns. Playing on all the possible variations (director, technicians, actors, studio and location), MLVs kept only one immutable parameter: the story.

Notes

1. Charles Ford, "Paramount at Joinville," *Films in Review*, vol. 12, no. 9, November 1961, p. 542.
2. This archaeological work has been facilitated by changes in attitudes to film history as well as by the greater availability of prints. Some of this work is represented in this book by the essays of Andrew Higson, Joseph Garncarz and Martine Danan.
3. Raymond Chirat, *Catalogue des films français de long metrage, films sonores de fiction, 1929–1939* (Brussels: Cinématheque Royale de Belgique, 1975).

4. Except in very rare cases where some art cinemas experimented with showing several versions of the same film (but then always *auteur* films)—for instance, the Studio des Ursulines in Paris programmed French and German versions.

5. Nino Frank, *Petit cinéma sentimental* (Paris: La Nouvelle Edition, 1950).

6. C.J. North and N.D. Golden, "Meeting Sound Film Competition Abroad," *Journal of the Society of Motion Picture Engineers*, vol. 15, December 1930, p. 750.

7. North and Golden, "Meeting Sound Film Competition Abroad," p. 752.

8. For example, in Poland, where audiences rebelled (12 June 1929) against German subtitles, and in France (9 December 1929), where seats were torn out at a screening of *Les Innocents de Paris* in Nice.

9. *Variety*, 6 November 1929.

10. On Franco-Italian versions, see one of the few articles on the subject by Rémy Pithon, "Présences françaises dans le cinéma italian pendant les dernières années du régime mussolinien (1935–1943)," *Risorgimento*, vol. 2, no. 3, 1981, pp. 181–95.

11. *Variety*, 12 February 1930.

12. *Variety*, 14 January 1931.

13. *Variety*, 9 April 1930.

14. *Variety*, 14 January 1931.

15. Frank, *Petit cinéma sentimental*; Henri Jeanson, "Cinq semaines à la Paramount, choses vécues," *Le Crapouillot*, numéro spécial, November 1932; Ilya Ehrenburg, *Usine de Rêves* (Paris: Gallimard, 1936); Charles de Rochefort, *Le Film de mes souvenirs* (Paris: Société Parisienne d'Edition, 1943). Marcel Pagnol, quoted in "Une aventure de la parole, entretien avec Marcel Pagnol par Jean-André Fieschi, Gérard Guégan et Jacques Rivette," *Cahiers du cinéma*, vol. 173, December 1965, pp. 24–36.

16. *Variety*, 14 January 1931.

17. *Variety*, 21 January 1931.

18. Dudley Andrew, "Sound in France: The Origins of a Native School," *Yale French Studies*, vol. 60, 1980, pp. 94–114; Douglas Gomery, "Economic Struggle and Hollywood Imperialism: Europe Converts to Sound," *Yale French Studies*, vol. 60, 1980, pp. 90–3.

19. *La Cinématographie française*, 23 September 1938.

20. David Bordwell, Janet Staiger and Kristin Thompson, *The Classical Hollywood Cinema* (London: Routledge and Kegan Paul, 1985).

21. Théophile Pathé, "Doublage des films étrangers," *Le Cinéma* (Paris: Corréa Editeur, 1942), pp. 135–41. Rick Altman notes a similar concern expressed by American sound engineers at the coming of sound, in "Sound Space," in Rick Altman, ed., *Sound Theory, Sound Practice* (New York/London: Routledge, 1992), pp. 46–64.

22. North and Golden, "Meeting Sound Film Competition Abroad", p. 757.

23. *Film Weekly*, 30 September 1929.
24. *Variety*, 18 June 1930.
25. *Variety*, 6 November 1929.
26. Ehrenburg, *Usine de Rêves*, p. 117.
27. De Rochefort, *Le Film de mes souvenirs*, p. 212.
28. Frank, *Petit cinéma sentimental*, p. 66.
29. *L'Action française*, 24 October 1930.
39. René Clair, interviewed by John Gillet, *Focus on Film*, vol. 12, Winter 1972, p. 41.
31. *Variety*, 7 May 1930.
32. As *Variety*, 7 May 1930, put it, "The French thought they'd top it by having all companies and making scene by scene, only to find what might merit expansion and building-up for French edification did not go for another audience." As the example of *L'Equipage/The Woman I Love* below suggests, this scene by scene discrepancy is another characteristic of MLVs.
33. *Variety*, 7 May 1930.
34. See Martha Wolfenstein and Nathan Leites, *Movies, a Psychological Study* (Glencoe, IL: Free Press, 1950), and Ginette Vincendeau, "Daddy's Girls, Oedipal Narratives in French Cinema of the 1930s," *Iris*, vol. 5, no. 1, January 1989, pp. 70–81.
35. Marek Halberda, "Polskie film made of Paramount," *Kino* (Poland), May 1983, pp. 22–5.
36. *Variety*, 7 January 1931.
37. *Film Weekly*, 25 November 1929.
38. René Jeanne and Charles Ford, *Histoire encyclopédique du cinéma, vol. iv: Le cinéma parlant (1929–1945)* (Paris: SEDE, 1958).

10

Hollywood's Hegemonic Strategies
Overcoming French Nationalism with the Advent of Sound

Martine Danan

Hollywood's secure dominant position in the international film market prior to the advent of sound was suddenly jeopardised by the fragmentation of foreign markets caused by the cultural and affective impact of newly introduced film dialogue. The nationalistic feelings aroused by sound films proved to be a much more formidable challenge to Hollywood's international hegemony than the projected union of the main European film industries in the late 1920s. It soon appeared that especially in France, a country with a strong nationalistic heritage and an important film culture, Hollywood had to contend with fierce resistance from a majority of spectators who demanded that movies be produced in their native language.

Confronted with the technical and cultural difficulties of finding a satisfactory method for exporting American sound films to France, the American film industry was at first deeply divided over the very future of its international business, as I will demonstrate in the first part of this chapter. Studio executives' assessment of Hollywood's ability to respond to this new challenge in 1928 and early 1929, when they were preparing to export their first sound films to France, ranged from an overly pessimistic sense of doom to an "imperialistic" attitude that Hollywood would somehow continue to impose its will over the French market, and other world markets, as a result of its sheer power and superior know-how. Moreover, the protectionist policies developed by the French state after its sudden involvement in cinema affairs in 1928 increased instability and created further cause for worry among American film industrialists, who ended up boycotting the French market from April to September 1929.[1] In addition to this difficult political situation, there were many unknown factors concerning the potentialities of the French market and the nature of the public's reactions to sound in general, and to English-language films in particular.

As a consequence of all these uncertainties, especially in 1929, the majors embarked upon a flurry of contradictory, initially simplistic, and generally unsuccessful plans, including rudimentary dubbing, subtitling and adaptations with intertitles, which I will describe in the second part of this essay. The unexpected hostility of the French public to all these crudely translated English-language films and enthusiasm for the first domestic sound films produced in France initially made Hollywood's struggle for the reconquest of its international hegemony even more chaotic. The failure of the large-scale multiple-language strategy in 1930 was an additional blow to the American film industry, as I will demonstrate in the third section of this essay. In the end, however, this series of failures ultimately forced Hollywood to devise more culturally sensitive strategies. Sensitivity to French culture led to the production of French "original" features towards the end of 1930, and, most important, the implementation in 1931 of technically improved dubbed versions. This form of dubbing, which was facilitated by the emergence of a standardised international film style, has remained the norm for American popular films in France ever since. Thus, the story of Hollywood's failures and victories during the first three years of sound-film export to France is the story of its remarkable technical, economic and artistic adjustments, all for the sake of retaining its hegemony over world markets.

Foreign Reconquest or Retreat?

Even before it had made any attempts at exporting its first sound films, Hollywood feared what would happen to its international film market. In November 1928 *Variety* published a particularly alarmist article entitled "US Leaving Foreign Tongue Markets to Locals and Indies; Sound Eliminates Much Export." The author of the article predicted the "end of the dominance of American produced pictures in foreign fields" with the advance of talking pictures, since he believed that there would be no satisfactory means of producing quality sound movies for both the domestic and the European markets. In his opinion, the excessive production cost of foreign-language films for specific markets would force American majors to export only to the other English-speaking countries, while "independent producers [would be] making the cheaper grade of silent pictures."[2]

Yet, only a few days later, the triumphant Parisian release of the first picture with synchronised sound effects—Van Dyke's *White Shadows on the South Seas* (*Ombres blanches*)—temporarily restored Hollywood's faith in its international power of attraction: the film gave American observers every indication that "sound and dialog pictures [would] enjoy ever greater patronage here than the former silent films."[3] The opening of Warner Bros' *The Jazz Singer*, hailed as the first true "talker," was impatiently awaited by Parisian crowds in January 1929. Its success seemed to allay any immediate fears Hollywood might still have had concerning its French market. But in spite of the French public's eagerness to see and hear Hollywood productions, the cumbersome use of titles projected on a second screen for the single dialogue scene of the movie could only serve as a transitory solution to the language problem.[4]

Anticipating the difficulties that could eventually arise with foreign exhibition, some Hollywood producers sought other ways of minimising the translation problem at little cost. The use of dubbing—already employed for the postsynchronisation of silent films—was seriously contemplated by January 1929 when a "recently perfected" device appeared to facilitate the synchronisation of dialogue and images. A new American company, the Sonoratone Corporation, was created primarily for the purpose of producing films for the French and German markets with this invention. Warner Bros was also preparing at that time "to use the device for invading the foreign markets," in particular France, Italy, Germany and Spain.[5] Synchronisation, however, was apparently not as effective as these entrepreneurs believed it to be, and these earliest dubbing experiments remained short-lived.

With no perfect translation method in sight, some producers tried instead to encourage narrative styles that would facilitate the export of Hollywood products. For example, United Artists resorted to a chorus-like narration for *The Iron Mask*, directed by Allan Dwan, with Douglas Fairbanks in the role of D'Artagnan. The film was released in February 1929 with short spoken parts "in the form of minute and a half appendages as prologs to the first and second halves," and when the hero finally die[d] at the end, "an unseen voice then repeat[ed] one of Fairbanks messages."[6] These brief verbal passages artificially inserted into the plot were a deliberate strategy "to solve the present problem of showing pictures in foreign countries" since, it was believed, "[t]he speech of the invisible chorus could readily be rendered in any language."[7] Needless to say, such an awkward solution did not satisfy audiences, and the talking sequences were later removed altogether from the movie.[8] In the latter part of 1929, extravagant musicals with limited dialogue were more successful in achieving a film style suited to the international market.[9]

Foreseeing the shortcomings of all these approaches (and anticipating the strategy that became commonplace in 1931), Warner Bros and Paramount had also started experimenting with foreign-language shorts for specific markets by the end of 1928. As with the transition to sound within the United States, these films could serve as market tests before launching into a full-scale innovative strategy for the international market.[10] In mid-November 1928 Warner Bros had completed its first sound film in a foreign tongue (*Zwei und Fierzigste Strasse*), which was to play in the German colonies in the United States.[11] The following year, Warners made fifteen additional foreign shorts (mainly musicals in German), but it also started producing some foreign-language features and was already thinking of erecting European studios for production in languages other than English. Paramount, the only other studio "indulging in this foreign stuff," chose a different approach for most of the twenty foreign-language shorts which it had produced by the beginning of October 1929: using its News Laboratory in Long Island, the studio recorded Spanish-language speeches by foreign consuls or dignitaries who were invited to address their countrymen in their own tongue; these filmed speeches were then sent for distribution in the speakers' native countries.[12]

Instead of producing expensive language-specific films with uncertain returns, a number of studios were hoping that they could make movies which, with only partial modifications, could equally respond to the foreign audiences' desire to hear their own languages. As early as February 1929, First National announced it was planning to produce "the first international talker" with English, French, Italian or German songs by the star, Irene Bordoni, to be incorporated into the film according to the countries in which it was going to be exhibited.[13] But the April 1929 Paris and Berlin premiéres of Warner Bros' shorts, with either French or German versions of English songs interpreted by Isa Kremer, were purportedly the "first European showings of talking films in languages other than English."[14] Other experiments were attempted in the form of films in which multiple languages were used concomitantly. In May 1929 MGM completed its first three-reeler "featurette" with two of its actresses speaking Spanish lines and two others (Marion Davies and Norma Shearer) speaking French, while a month later Paramount completed its four-language feature, with Maurice Chevalier in the French-speaking role.[15]

Although such partial multiple-language productions were the precursors of the actual multilinguals (i.e. the simultaneous filming in several languages of internationally suitable films with foreign teams of actors) which became Hollywood's main strategy a year later, in early 1929 the studio managers' vision of what the future would hold was far from clear. As all the contradictory approaches that flourished within a few months indicate, Hollywood executives swayed between overconfidence in their ability to find a solution, given their industry's unsurpassed strength, and unusual misgivings about their position, not only because of technical limitations but also because of the unpredictability and unknown worth of international markets at the time. Unsure of which direction to take, Hollywood kept experimenting with ways to keep its hold on the non-Anglophone markets while preparing to retreat in case of total failure. Even George Canty, the well-informed Motion Picture Trade Commissioner to Europe, expressed "slight uneasiness" about the American studios' ability to maintain their dominant position abroad in his report to the Department of Commerce on the export situation for the beginning of 1929, although he believed they would be able to do so "from the quality standpoint at least," especially for sound films.[16] In a more ambivalent statement from May 1929, Louis Mayer at MGM felt that the popularity of American films was so great that it would transform English into a universal language (a belief that may have been prophetic, after all). Yet fearing that this transformation might not occur quickly enough, Mayer also considered selling detailed scripts to foreign producers who would then be in charge of translating and filming them in their own countries.[17] Similarly, Jesse Lasky (in charge of Paramount studios) hesitated between selling the rights to American talking pictures and reproducing American features abroad, in which case a "print would be sent from America to the producer who would engage a cast to do exactly the same as the American cast, only in their native language."[18]

Growing Opposition to Makeshift Strategies

These long-term plans, however, did not solve the most immediate problems, especially in France, where the public proved to be clearly intolerant of foreign languages. As early as March 1929, a *New York Times* critic warned American studios with the following statement: "[N]o audience will prefer a talking film if it cannot understand the words. English-speaking pictures will hardly be acceptable to the majority of French movie fans."[19] Indeed, when a few months later French theatres exhibited English-language subtitled films in which denser dialogue supplemented songs, the audience started reacting with hostility. At a June showing of American shorts at an exclusive Parisian theatre, the public was so irritated that "after a dozen words had been spoken the crowds whistled and booed until the picture was withdrawn." This dissatisfaction was not an isolated case: "Without exception every time an American talker has been flashed on the screen in Paris it has got the razz and what a razz!"[20]

Even with technically improved superimposed subtitles, English-language films occasionally caused actual riots: when *Fox Movietone Follies of 1929* opened at the Moulin Rouge in December 1929, the Montmartre spectators, who were a "rather hard-boiled clientele," were so furious that they had been deceived into seeing an English-language film (as the theatre manager had omitted any reference to language in his advertisements) that the "mild disturbances" on the first day turned into violent riots the next two days. On the second night, the police had to clear the 1,500-person audience, "which called for refunds and made a show of anti-American feeling against the English dialogue of the picture." The third demonstration was reportedly the worst, "with the mob tearing up carpets and seats and demolishing everything breakable about the place."[21]

Such negative reactions had prompted American distributors to make "special foreign versions": sound films transformed into silent or partially silent films (with only songs and background noises remaining) with added intertitles. These archaic-looking adaptations were not even satisfactory as silent films because the titles sometimes occupied the screen for longer than the actual footage. Paramount's release of *Love Parade* (*Parade d'Amour*), with Maurice Chevalier, was surrounded by enormous publicity, backed by the first national radio campaign, but it still failed to satisfy French spectators, who were tired of another "slashed out" "hybrid synchronous version" with English dialogue cut out and replaced by titles in French.[22] Silencing the spoken word was clearly an antiquated response to the technological revolution which had taken place with the advent of sound, and with the greater availability of French-language films, the public was becoming increasingly intolerant of these mechanical-sounding adaptations, which destroyed confidence in talking films.[23]

With the urgent need to explore alternatives to subtitling and adaptations, the American majors turned again to dubbing in October 1929, although good dubbing still remained very difficult to achieve because limitations in sound technology made it impossible to mix sound and synchronise non-direct dialogue. For example, dubbing was crudely used for Universal's *Broadway* and *Show Boat*, but these early results were so poor, according to a contemporary's account, that several pictures "were all but laughed off the screen."[24] By the end of 1929, Paramount's general manager declared that dubbing had failed to prove a satisfactory method; United Artists (in charge of RKO distribution) also soon renounced dubbing after conducting a "market test" with film critics invited to the special screening of a dubbed version of *Rio Rita*.[25] Fox, MGM and Columbia however, continued to experiment with various forms of dubbing in early 1930. While Columbia embarked upon dubbing in France to ensure authenticity of accent, MGM had one of its very popular Laurel and Hardy shorts, *The Night Owl*, dubbed into "freak French," which made "no pretense to be real French" and was modeled after a "clowned Spanish version" in "trick pigeon [*sic*] Spanish."[26] Fox also tried a dubbed version of *Manuela*, in which the actors doing the French dubbing used a "strongly flavored Spanish accent."[27] But by April 1930 most foreign film managers finally agreed that dubbing was unsuccessful and "out for all time."[28]

Thus, in early 1930, adaptations, subtitled and dubbed versions were received with growing resentment. Paradoxically, silent and sound-synchronised films remained for a while better accepted, in part because only eighty theatres were wired at the beginning of 1930, but these films would soon become completely outdated because of the public's marked preference for sound films.[29] At the end of March of that year, *Variety* published one of its most alarmist articles, whose title "U.S. May Lose Europe," in huge letters, was underscored by the subheading "May Grow Worse." The author of the article warned that American companies would be unable to withstand the competition from French-made talking pictures if more suitable solutions to the language problem were not found quickly.[30] And indeed, Hollywood had serious reasons to worry about the French film industry, whose pictures were attracting impassioned crowds.

Birth of a National Popular Cinema

The unexpected success of the first all-French sound film, *Les Trois Masques*, released at the end of October 1929, appeared as a sudden threat to American films because enthusiasm for the native tongue seemed to supersede any other criteria. In spite of its mediocrity (noted by most contemporary film critics as well as historians), the use of French and the choice of the Corsican setting for this production gave rise to such patriotic reactions that "the supremacy of American pictures in this territory" seemed to have received "a serious blow."[31]

Even more worrisome but also enticing for Hollywood may have been the record- breaking business of *La Route est belle* in January 1930. After a month in Marseilles, where it first opened, the movie had grossed 1.2 million francs or $12,000 a week, a phenomenal sum considering that average returns for American silent films were 1 million francs for the entire French territory. These incredible profits suggested to *Variety* that "dialog [was] widening the French film market tremendously," attracting a much larger popular public than silent films, as long as the films were in French.[32] *La Route est belle* and several other French movies made in 1930 and 1931 brought in five to six times the cost of their production.[33] As a result of the success of these films, overall box-office receipts for January 1930 compared to January 1929 increased by 40 per cent in Paris and 80 per cent in the rest of France.[34] The faster rate of theatre wiring in July 1930, after the Paris agreement over sound patents, turned France into an even more economically promising market than had originally been anticipated.[35]

The nationalistic sentiments aroused by the growing number of French-language films made Hollywood's task of regaining this now prized territory still more challenging. Citing *La Route est belle* as one of their examples, C.J. North and N.D. Golden, in charge of the Motion Picture Division at the Bureau of Foreign and Domestic Commerce, stressed that the appeal of such French talking pictures drew on the public's sentimental pleasure at "seeing its own actors and actresses speaking its own language in familiar surroundings"—all the more so as the 100 per cent French origin of *La Route est belle* was heavily stressed in advertising.[36] Like the "extraordinary smash of *Mon gosse de père*" (*The Parisian*), made by Pathé-Natan, this confirmed the difficulty of competing with local production in the choice of subject matter and style of narration. According to *Variety*, Hollywood would have been "disqualified by temperament" (and by the Hays Code, adopted in 1930) from telling this "racy" story about an illegitimate son reappearing at the age of 20.[37] But perhaps what the mainstream public longed for the most was a national hero with whom it could identify, like "Bouboule" in Pathé-Natan's *Le Roi des resquilleurs* (*King of the Gate Crashers*), released in late 1930. The movie featured the well-known Georges Milton in the role of the *resquilleur*, the slang-speaking street singer who rejects conformism and authority, a modernised, grumbling, yet good-natured Parisian maverick described as "screamingly funny" by a *Variety* journalist.[38] As another *Variety* article noted, the success of *Le Roi des resquilleurs*, clearly made in France by a French team for the French public, was indissoluble from its very "Frenchness": "local treatment [of *Le Roi*] is undoubtedly one of the big assets, as entirely precluding any idea in the audience's mind of a foreign-made [picture] adapted for French consumption."[39]

To most Americans, reacting from the perspective of a secure dominant culture and industrial power, this patriotism and fuss over the national identity of a product seemed quite odd; in the words of a *Variety* reviewer, it was "[s]ome kind of European quirk, that patriotism in entertainment selection."[40] Yet, this "quirk" clearly mattered, especially since the French government, suddenly aware of the impact cinema had on the popular audience, was also determined to protect the nation from excessive foreign influences. As the historian Carlton Hayes aptly warned at the time, the strong wave of patriotic feelings, which were bound to be cultivated by the state in order to strengthen national identity, made it imperative for American producers to make sufficient concessions to placate the French public if they hoped to secure a share of the business. As both Hayes and industry analysts pointed out, the majors would have to "be increasingly careful to respect French susceptibilities and to make the pictures which they exploit in France more and more French."[41]

Hollywood's future in France clearly lay with an approach which would restore the importance of the native language and maybe its culture. By the end of 1929 the multiple-language strategy, which some studios had considered implementing for several months, finally appeared as the last hope to overcome French resistance to the American "talkie" at a relatively reasonable cost.

Multilinguals, or Fake Originals

MGM initiated the most ambitious plan for multiple-language versions in mid-November 1929, when it announced a $2 million programme that involved importing actors to Hollywood for the shooting of French, German and Spanish versions.[42] By February 1930, most big producers were planning to produce films in the four main languages, by setting up troupes of leading foreign actors and artists in Hollywood.[43] Only Paramount decided on foreign-made multiple versions, and the company inaugurated a European production centre in Joinville near Paris in April 1930.[44] The Joinville studios, nicknamed "Babel-sur-Seine," were endowed with an original budget of $10 million for sixty films a year in six languages and became a "gigantic film factory" turning out "mass-produced Paramount canned goods," as many historians have vividly shown.[45] Paramount believed that the easier availability of international artists in cosmopolitan Paris would permit a more efficient and economical means of reproducing original English versions while adapting to local needs. MGM executives, on the other hand, persisted in their Hollywood-based foreign strategy, claiming that their versions would benefit from Hollywood's technical superiority and production value. They were firmly convinced that "the aura of a Hollywood production len[t] a picture a definite box-office value for the foreign market."[46]

Even the fact that polyglot actors may have had a foreign accent did not seem a serious handicap to MGM, which often hired actors who were able to play the same part in several languages, in spite of their imperfect accents. Arthur Loew, Vice-President of Loew's Inc., actually believed that famous American stars acting in a foreign language would gain increased prestige with foreign spectators. "Dialog shortcomings will be totally discounted when a previously accepted American star is shown making a dialectic effort to parley-vous [sic] in the lingo of that particular country," he naively professed.[47] MGM felt that a poor French accent and bad grammar were no hindrance to foreign success, especially in the case of comedies.[48] Improper French may indeed have reinforced the slapstick and burlesque character of comedies which were based on physical gags, incongruous behaviour, or loss of dignity, as when Laurel and Hardy were dubbed in French speaking with a strong English accent. However, by the middle of 1930, the French public's resentment toward foreign accents grew significantly. Thus, studio officials had to acknowledge that, except for comedies, all other types of films made for the European market had to feature only native artists from each country.[49]

Because of the greater emphasis on authenticity of accent and the difficulty of importing every single actor, Paramount's choice of Europe as a production centre appeared to many observers as a wiser move. In fact, *Variety* announced in a feature article entitled "Move Foreigns to Europe" that Paramount had outguessed all the other studios with its European strategy, and all the majors allegedly embraced the new "Europe or bust" slogan.[50] In spite of these claims, MGM executives retained their belief both in the greater efficiency of Hollywood production and in the contribution that Hollywood's "aura" made to the box-office value of multiple-language versions in the foreign market, and they refused to abandon their practice of producing foreign versions in Hollywood.[51] The battle between MGM and Paramount, or between standardised American production practices on the one hand, and a more decentralised approach on the other, was in fact far from settled: The "[i]ntentions of US producers as to studio work here or in Hollywood seem[ed] to change daily" and continued to fluctuate throughout 1930 and early 1931.[52]

RKO tried to conciliate both approaches, opting for "partial" multi-linguals shot with the experimental Dunning process, which the company made public in August 1930. This process consisted of photographing actors and the foreground scene through a coloured transparent positive already made of the background scene, providing a composite negative of the actors in a pre-selected environment. This approach made it be possible to shoot backgrounds in Hollywood before inserting close-up scenes with foreign actors filmed abroad. The process had the potential to save two-thirds of production costs compared to regular multiple-language versions. *Beau Ideal* was the first picture to be shot with the Dunning process, while an English-language production was simultaneously prepared: the negative of the Dunning copy was to be sent to France where French actors would be dubbed in and the sound added. However, this technique was not as satisfactory as had been hoped, and it proved to be short-lived.[53]

Regardless of the type of multiple-language version, by the end of 1930 there was little doubt that in France, more than in any other European country, the public was increasingly intolerant of foreign accents and "all imports camouflaged for local consumption." Consequently, it was becoming imperative for American producers to "consider foreign versions as so many distinct productions, instead of so many different foreign versions of the same film."[54] In the light of this situation, towards the beginning of 1931, the French-based Paramount company adopted the principle of thoroughly concealing the foreign source of its French versions by omitting the foreign origin of an adaptation or by occasionally "Frenchifying" an American director's name. (Robert Wyler, for example, became Robert Villers.[55]) This strategy was praised in *Variety*'s review of *Dans une île perdue,* the original title of which, *Dangerous Paradise,* was "tactfully omitted" in order "to allow the more gullible spectators to believe that this [was] a French original."[56] In spite of these token changes, most Joinville productions in the first year of operation failed because Paramount insisted on "merely putting French dialog in American stories, situations, humor and wisecracks."[57] By mid-1931, in a last-ditch effort to meet the French public's expectations and save the multiple-language strategy, the company started hiring French writers, directors and actors such as Yves Mirande, Marcel Pagnol, Sacha Guitry and Saint-Granier, who were to incorporate more "French content" and especially French humor into "localized versions of Paramount's American-made films."[58]

While Paramount was making a final attempt at localisation through its 1931 multilinguals, most other studios had already abandoned them. Even MGM had closed its foreign units in April 1931, and the production of multiple-language versions by American companies completely ceased in Hollywood as well as in France in 1932.[59] Their disappearance did not come as a surprise to most contemporary observers, who had foreseen their impending downfall by the beginning of 1931. Mass-produced multilinguals (including the 100 features filmed in fourteen different languages in Joinville within one year) were of noticeably poor quality and lacked the prestige of American production values and, above all, stars. The European actors who played in them often had an established live theatre career, but their reputation as movie stars did not stand up to that of Hollywood actors, whose star image in the United States and abroad was carefully cultivated by large-scale publicity campaigns.[60] "Loss of the pulling power of stars is the chief sore spot of the multis," a *Variety* journalist admitted, while a European critic noted that "Hollywood with . . . its alien performers had lost its distinction, its glamour, its personality," in short, had ceased to *be* Hollywood.[61] In a sense, multiple-language versions suffered from being too standardised and, at the same time, not standardised enough.[62] They were not standardised enough economically, since foreign versions cost between $60,000 and $125,000 on the average (with MGM spending the most—between $85,000 to $125,000), whereas average French releases were expected to bring in only $20,000 to $40,000.[63] But they were also too mass-produced to benefit from the glamour of Hollywood productions, or to address the cultural specificities of the French public.

By early 1931 it had become clear that multiple-language versions were unlikely to meet with sufficient enthusiasm abroad, and that returns were negligible in comparison with the expenditure. Some American companies, quick to adapt, started reverting once again to cheaper exports, such as silent and sound-synchronised features suitable for international distribution.[64] More prophetic American trade authorities, however, warned that future access to the European market would depend on the production of a new type of international pictures with much more action and limited self-explanatory dialogue.[65] But even this limited dialogue could be problematic if a satisfactory form of translation was not found, and, until then, a few producers cautiously turned instead to a neglected solution to the foreign issue, namely the making of foreign-language originals intended for a single language market.

Adapting to Cultural Specificity

The idea of producing market-specific movies was actually not entirely new. As previously mentioned, Warners and Paramount had produced a number of experimental shorts by 1929, primarily in German and Spanish. In early 1930 Paramount also released in Paris the first of its French experimental shorts, made in France under the supervision of Bob Kane (Paramount's general production chief in Europe) at a cost of $4,000 each.[66] Although these shorts made strictly for the French market were initially not expected to bring in large returns, they were in fact "piling up grosses" by April 1930.[67] It was not until resentment against foreign versions grew towards the end of 1930, however, that Paramount really attempted to produce "true" French features. In order to make "more thoroughly French" films, the company decided to solicit French stories by opening a literary competition to be judged by a jury of French writers. It was hoped that these well-known jury members would also spark favourable publicity for the films produced by Paramount, and vouch for the fact that these were based on authentic French originals. By distributing films based on local stories instead of simply adapting English-language scenarios, the studio became the industry's trend-setter for the 1931 season and the following years.[68] According to *Variety*, Paramount managed to produce films "as indisputably French as French-fried potatoes,"[69] making a number of films strictly for the French public without any expectations that these films would interest an American audience. A *Variety* review written in 1933 upon the New York release of *Mistigri* (directed by Harry Lachman), for example, praised Paramount's achievement as a successful French company: "It's the first screen explanation in New York of why Paramount in Paris has come to be an important film company. Because they seem to have finally, and completely, over there, gotten to understand the French mind and are making pictures for it, rather than worrying about American markets or opinions."[70]

But perhaps the independent Adolphe Osso, who had resigned as Chief of Staff for the Paramount branch office in Paris to establish his own production company (Osso), was the first non-native most successfully producing French "originals."[71] He purposely departed from American-style films and attempted to adapt to the tastes of the French public, since the French audience wanted movies that looked and sounded French. To achieve this goal, he reproduced already successful French formulas, as he did in January 1931 with *Arthur*. Its appeal with French audiences lay in a type of narrative and subject matter that American audiences would object to since, according to a condescending *Variety* critic, the movie was no more than a series of silly and risqué French clichés, with "all the regular French items—a none too logical story, lots of double crossing between wives and husbands, several songs with practically no music, lots of legs and just enough nudes to add that French post-card tang."[72] In a more serious tone, Philippe Soupault also noted how in *Un Soir de rafle* Osso deliberately imitated "all the old formulas" inspired by *Sous les toits de Paris*, *Le Roi des resquilleurs* and a considerable number of other productions."[73]

The success of these all-French formulas confirmed that the public's clear preference was for French-dialogue films made in France. But according to the 1931 report by the American Trade Commissioner in Paris, there was still one newly viable, although less desirable, alternative: "well-made dubbed versions."[74]

Dubbing: Naturalising Americanness

While Hollywood was still pursuing a policy of producing films for specialised language markets (as it continued to do throughout the 1930s), some studios began reconsidering the possibility of using dubbing for superproductions with international potential, in spite of its technical limitations. A dubbed picture was up to six times less expensive than the average French version or French film, and well below the cost of most American original productions. Dubbing also enabled a studio "to cash in the already b.o. power of the former English-speaking silent stars."[75] But when Paramount and MGM decided to try dubbing again in August 1930, this strategy was far from being accepted as the industry standard.[76] In spite of definite progress, dubbing remained a time-consuming and difficult process, taking at least eight weeks (as opposed to fourteen days for a version), and its quality was still questionable.[77]

It was not until late 1930 that the invention of the sound Moviola greatly facilitated the synchronisation of sound and image, and only in March 1931, as the result of further technical progress, did Hollywood seriously resort to dubbing again.[78] *Derelict*, a Hollywood-made Paramount production dubbed in Joinville and released in France as *Désemparé*, was touted at its Paris première in April 1931 as the first successfully concealed dubbing job. Even French critics praised the technical achievements and the perfect illusion created by the French dubbed version of *Derelict*, noting that it was very difficult for a spectator to distinguish the dubbed version from an original French-speaking film.[79] Such a skilful dubbing job, which "open[ed] considerable possibilities for French releases of American or other foreign productions lending themselves to dubbing,"[80] may have convinced American producers of the necessity of shooting most films with future synchronisation in mind.

Indeed, concerns based on the French audience's rejections of the first attempts at synchronisation guided the careful pre-planning and implementation of the American dubbing strategy in France until dubbing became the norm for popular American film imports by 1932. Close-ups, in particular, were most likely to present problems in synchronisation because lip movement was clearly visible, and careful planning and even reshooting of close-ups seemed necessary to perfect the illusion and create a satisfactory sense of realism. In the early dubbing experiments of 1930, for example, it was even suggested that actors lipsynch their foreign dialogue in order to facilitate the dubbing process in close-ups, while long and medium shots could be directly "tricked."[81] A number of other techniques were supposedly considered in 1931 to conceal the movement of actors' mouths in close-ups. One of these techniques consisted of having intimate scenes reshot in multiple languages with different casts of actors for each language version, while dubbing was restricted to long shots and panoramic views.[82] But altering actual film style was easier and cheaper, and directors were encouraged to favour long shots and forgo full face close-ups of actors.[83] When close-ups could not be avoided and dubbed voices failed to match the actors' lip movement, the insertion of special shots made dubbing more convincing. For instance, the actor who was speaking would be shown sideways or with his or her back facing the audience. Or if no suitable shot could be found in the pre-made stock, a view of the listener or even another object could be substituted.[84]

Not only the avoidance of close-ups but also the limited use of dialogue facilitated the dubbing process as well as the acceptance of dubbed versions by foreign publics. Film executives noted that films heavily dependent on dialogue tended to be less successful abroad.[85] Dubbing was therefore particularly suitable for "original action pictures" and visually oriented superproductions, according to the recommendations of the Progress Committee of the Motion Picture Industry at the end of 1931.[86] North and Golden reached the same conclusion a few months later, when they stressed the importance of applying dubbing "to films in which action predominates."[87] Paramount, for example, reserved dubbing for "foreign spectacular product," while its Joinville studio continued to produce cheaper French films to compete with local production on its own terms.[88] Thus, the search for a solution to the language problem may also have played an essential role in shaping the Hollywood style up to this day.

Although there continued to be technical difficulties with dubbing at the beginning of 1932, North and Golden insisted that dubbing was the only viable solution for the European situation because it had become a dependable, low-cost solution "that [would] bring a fair return on its investment."[89] By May 1932, the Progress Report noted a marked growth in the use of dubbing, to the point where it was almost entirely replacing separate versions, because of the "more precise methods of matching speech with the picture."[90] By mid-1932, dubbing facilities had been set up in France by all the major studios, except MGM, which had invested considerable amounts of money in dubbing plants in Hollywood.[91] By embracing dubbing technology, the United States had positioned itself to flood the world with a cheap supply of "quality" films. Demand for high-budget dubbed films increased quickly, with the number of dubbed films distributed in France rising from 25 in 1931 to 60 in 1932 and 142 in 1933.[92]

It is, however, questionable whether the higher-quality dubbing job actually deluded spectators into believing that they were watching an authentic French production. The fact that the tricks used to permit better synchronisation were not very sophisticated makes it doubtful that the public would have been deceived very long: "Dubbing, done by Jacob Karol in the Joinville studios, is exceedingly good, but even the non-pros notice that the same trick has been used for 'Shanghai Express,'" a journalist noted.[93] Above all, the success of some distinctly American films featuring well-publicized stars or based on typical American formulas (such as the noticeably exotic Westerns and the American gangster stories) suggests that spectators were fully aware of the foreign origin of many movies.

Dubbing, therefore, might represent a symbolic, make-believe artifice to conceal the alien rather than create a true mask. It was a compromise on both sides. American executives were willing to pay a tribute to the importance of "French culture," shaped by centuries of nationalistic policies, as long as their dubbing effort was financially reasonable. French spectators did prefer domestic films, but they still wanted to see the most prestigious American superproductions and stars as long as they could be reappropriated through language—the most powerful symbol of national identity. Mass audiences may have been less concerned with the bourgeois ideology of realism and the "truth of the individual"[94] than with the pleasure of being able to identify with the fantasy world of glamorous stars. Apparently able to suspend their disbelief, spectators allowed themselves to experience the emotional impact of cinema as they listened to famous American stars ostensibly utter familiar French sounds and phrases. According to contemporary surveys conducted among the mainstream public, the majority had become favourably disposed towards dubbing as long as synchronisation was done "neatly."[95] Only film critics and artists denounced the "commercial fraud" and artistic "heresy" of dubbing, this "pitiful cinema ersatz."[96] Thus, dubbing proved to be a viable solution for exporting lavish Hollywood productions to France, and has remained the norm for commercial American films for over sixty years.

Hollywood's Ultimate Success Story—But at a Price

In spite of its unsurpassed economic, technological and political power at the time of the first sound films, Hollywood would not have succeeded in maintaining its hegemony over the French market had it not learned to make reasonable concessions to foreign spectators. At first, the introduction of sound gave rise to a great sense of uncertainty among American studio executives as to the future of their film exports. The failure of a number of initial strategies soon intensified the feeling of disarray in Hollywood. American film producers appeared ill-prepared to adapt to the unpredicted resistance of the French public, which was particularly hostile to hearing the English language in its movie theatres. The multiplicity of approaches and experiments employed to overcome the public's resistance to American sound films undermined the internal cohesion of an industry whose strength relied largely on standardisation and co-ordination of efforts. It took over three years of sustained experimentation, supported by motion picture engineers, trade associations and government agencies, for Hollywood to find a satisfactory solution to the language problem exacerbated by the French public. By resorting to well-conceived, technically improved dubbed versions toward the second half of 1931, Hollywood was finally able to appease the cultural sensitivity of French nationals at a relatively low cost. With dubbing, which thus became the norm for mass cultural productions exhibited in France, film producers were able to address the French audience in a way that gave some importance to the native culture through the symbolic use of the French language, while retaining the most economical mode of production possible. The widespread acceptance of dubbing may also have had a lasting influence on the Classical Hollywood style, since action-oriented superproductions featuring internationally recognisable stars were easiest to dub and most successful abroad. Hollywood's hegemonic power, therefore, resided in its ability to rectify mistakes quickly and to make limited concessions to foreign tastes, while protecting its own economic interests. Learning out of necessity to internationalise its film style and adapt its most expensive products for the French market, the American film industry achieved a delicate balance between national and international interests, thus winning an important victory in its bid to re-establish its hegemonic position over world cinema.

Notes

1. United States Department of Commerce, Bureau of Foreign and Domestic Commerce, *The European Motion Picture Industry in 1929*, Trade Information Bulletin, no. 694, 1930, pp. 16–17; Nathan D. Golden, "Sound

Motion Pictures in Europe," *Journal of the Society of Motion Picture Engineers*, vol. 14, no. 1, January 1930, p. 17.

2. "US Leaving Foreign Tongue Markets to Locals and Indies; Sound Eliminates Much Export," *Variety*, 21 November 1928, pp. 4, 16.

3. "Paris Chatter," *Variety*, 28 November 1928, p. 2.

4. "'Talkies' in France," *New York Times*, 4 March 1929, p. 24.

5. Clifford Howard, "Hollywood Notes," *Close-Up*, vol. 4, January 1929, p. 78.

6. Sid, "The Iron Mask," *Variety Film Reviews 1926–1929* (New York: Garland, 1983), 27 February 1929.

7. Clifford Howard, "Hollywood Notes," *Close-Up*, vol. 4, March 1929, p. 99.

8. Alan G. Fetrow, *Sound Films, 1927–1939: A United States Filmography* (Jefferson, NC: McFarland, 1992), p. 315.

9. Kristin Thompson, *Exporting Entertainment: America in the World Market, 1907–1934* (London: British Film Institute, 1985), p. 159.

10. Douglas Gomery, "Towards an Economic History of the Cinema: The Coming of Sound to Hollywood," in Teresa de Lauretis and Stephen Heath, eds, *The Cinematic Apparatus* (New York: St Martin's Press, 1980), p. 39.

11. "Foreign Tongue Talker," *Variety*, 14 November 1928, p. 1.

12. "Foreign Tongue Features and Shorts Getting More Attention," *Variety*, 2 October 1929, p. 5.

13. "International Talker with Songs in Four Languages," *Variety*, 6 February 1929, p. 6.

14. 'W.B.'s Foreign Shorts Due Abroad in April," *Variety*, 20 March 1929, p. 7.

15. "M.G.'s Foreign Talker," *Variety*, 22 May 1929, p. 2; "Special Talker," *Variety*, 12 June 1929, p. 2.

16. "Silent Versions of U.S. Talkers Apt to Aid Foreign Films Abroad, States Comprehensive Report," *Variety*, 8 May 1929, p. 2.

17. Clifford Howard, "Hollywood Notes," *Close-Up*, vol. 4, April 1929, pp. 93–4.

18. "Lasky Certain Europe Sold on Talkers," *Variety*, 15 May 1929, p. 6.

19. "'Talkies' in France," p. 24.

20. "French Razzes English Shorts," *Variety*, 12 June 1929, p. 2.

21. "Blame Moulin Rouge Row on Plotters," *Variety*, 11 December 1929, p. 5; see also René Jeanne, "La France et le film parlant," *Revue des deux mondes*, 1 June 1931, p. 533; Francis Courtade, *Les Malédictions du cinéma français: une histoire du cinéma français parlant (1928–1978)* (Paris: Editions Alain Moreau, 1978), p. 62.

22. "Broadcasts Smash Hit All Over France," *Variety*, 19 March 1930, p. 4;

"Americans Must Produce Abroad to Hold Foreign Market, Claimed," *Variety*, 16 April 1930, p. 6.

23. United States Department of Commerce, *European Motion Picture Industry in 1930*, pp. 8, 9.

24. Chapin Hall, "Stars Are Dimmed," *New York Times*, 22 March 1931, sec. 8. p. 5.

25. Thompson, *Exporting Entertainment*, p. 160; "View French 'Rio Rita,'" *Variety*, 5 February 1930, p. 5; "No Dubbing for 'Rita,' 'Evangeline,' 'Trespasser,'" *Variety*, 5 March 1930, p. 4.

26. "Paris For Dubbing in French New Practice," *Variety*, 29 January 1930, p. 4; "Garbo's 'Kiss' May Set Foreign System," *Variety*, 5 March 1930, p. 5. The French version was entitled *Blotto* and the Spanish one *Ladrones*.

27. "Fox's 'Manuela' in Paris; Songs Recorded There," *Variety*, 19 March 1930, p. 7.

28. "Europe Off 'Dubbed' Film: Native Dialog by Natives only," *Variety*, 9 April 1930, p. 7.

29. "Silent Versions of U.S. Talkers," p. 2; "France Is Facing Film Crises Thru Scarcity of Pictures; Native Firms Doing Best to Cash in on 'Break'," *Variety*, 12 February 1930, p. 4; "French Puzzle Talker Debate," *Variety*, 15 January 1930, p. 4.

30. "U.S. May Lose Europe," *Variety*, 26 March 1930, p. 11.

31. "First Dialog Feature Seen as Blow to American Trade," *Variety*, 6 November 1929, p. 5; Jean Lenauer, "French Talkies," *Close-Up*, vol. 6, no. 2, March 1930, p. 238.

32. "French Bookers Watch Opening Crop of Native Talkers as Guide; 'La Route's' $12,000 W'kly Amazes," *Variety*, 22 January 1930, p. 5. For a theoretical discussion of the link between sound films, realism and mass culture, see Fredric Jameson, "The Existence of Italy," *Signatures of the Visible* (New York: Routledge, 1990), pp. 174–5; Walter Benjamin, "The Work of Art in the Age of Mechanical Reproductibility," *Illuminations*, trans. Harry Zohn (New York, Schocken Books, 1969), p. 244.

33. Richard Abel, *French Cinema: The First Wave, 1915–1929* (Princeton: Princeton University Press, 1984), p. 65.

34. "Sound Jumps Receipts 40 to 80% in France," *Variety*, 5 March 1930, p. 7.

35. Thompson, *Exporting Entertainment*, p. 161.

36. "French Bookers," p. 7; C.J. North and N.D. Golden, "Meeting Sound Film Competition Abroad," *Journal of the Society of Motion Picture Engineers*, vol. 15, no. 6, December 1930, p. 753.

37. "Menjou's Foreign Smash," *Variety*, 7 May 1930, p. 7.

38. Philippe Soupault, "'Le Roi des resquilleurs' avec Milton, and "Milton, le nouveau 'roi de Paris,'" in *Philippe Soupault, Ecrits de cinéma 1918–1931*, ed. Odette and Alain Virmaux (Paris: Plon, 1979), pp. 188–93;

"French-Made Big Hit: Film Comedy With Songs," *Variety*, 26 November 1930, p. 7. Bouboule's popularity was such that the character reappeared in a whole series of films until the Second World War II (including in the early 1930s "La Bande à Bouboule," "Le Roi du cirage," "Bouboule 1er, Roi nègre").

39. Maxi, "Le Roi des Resquilleurs," *Variety Film Reviews, 1930–1933* (New York: Garland, 1983), 17 December 1930.

40. Maxi, "Le Roi."

41. Carlton J.H. Hayes, *A Nation of Patriots* (New York: Columbia University Press, 1930), p. 195; for further details over the state's attitude to film imports and the national identity issue, see also Martine Danan, "From Nationalism to Globalization: France's Challenges to Hollywood's Hegemony" (Doctoral Dissertation, Michigan Technological University, 1994), ch. 3.

42. Thompson, *Exporting Entertainment*, p. 160.

43. "Warners Decide on Foreign Versions; Last to Give in," *Variety*, 12 February 1930, p. 4.

44. "Par. Heads Deciding in Europe where Foreign Tongue Fims will be made—Over There or Coast," *Variety*, 30 April 1930, p. 7; Colin Crisp, *The Classic French Cinema, 1930–1960* (Bloomington: Indiana University Press, 1993), p. 175.

45. Georges Sadoul, *French Film* (Falcon: 1953; New York: Arno Press, 1972), p. 57. See also Nino Frank, *Petit cinéma* sentimental (Paris: La Nouvelle Edition, 1950); Ginette Vincendeau, "Hollywood Babel," *Screen*, vol. 29, no. 2, spring 1988, pp. 30–1, reprinted as Chapter 9 in this volume.

46. "Metro Finds Foreigners Work Best in Hollywood Despite Temperament," *Variety*, 17 September 1930, p. 6.

47. "Arthur Loew Not Sold on Making Foreign Dialog Talkers Abroad," *Variety*, 23 April 1930, p. 6.

48. "Metro's 58 Foreigns; Signing More Player," *Variety*, 27 August 1930, p. 6.

49. Ibid., p. 6.

50. "Move Foreigns to Europe," *Variety*, 2 July 1930, pp. 7, 76.

51. "Metro Finds Foreigners Work Best in Hollywood Despite Temperament," *Variety*, 17 September 1930, p. 6.

52. "Europe or Coast?" *Variety*, 1 October 1930, p. 7.

53. Carroll H. Dunning, "Dunning Process and Process Backgrounds," *Journal of the Society of Motion Picture Engineers*, vol. 17, no. 5, November 1931, pp. 743, 747; "All 'Beau' Locations on Dunning Process for French Dubbing," *Variety*, 24 September 1930, p. 6; Nataša Ďurovičová, "Translating America: The Hollywood Multilinguals 1929–1933," in Rick Altman, ed., *Sound Theory, Sound Practice* (New York: Routledge, 1992), pp. 147–8.

54. *The European Motion Picture Industry Report for 1930*, p. 23; "French Disdain for Foreign Versions Becoming Stronger Than Any Quota," Variety, 10 December 1930, p. 6.

55. "Une étoile disparaît" [A Star Vanishes], *Variety Film Reviews, 1930–1933*, 6 September 1932.

56. "Dans une êle perdue," *Variety Film Reviews, 1930–1933*, 18 February 1931.

57. John Campbell, "Paris Notes," *New York Times*, 6 December 1931, sec. 8, p. 6.

58. Ibid., p. 6.

59. Thompson, *Exporting Entertainment*, p. 162; *The European Motion Picture Industry in 1932*, Trade Information Bulletin, no. 815, 1933, p. 15.

60. Yvan Noé, *L'Épicerie des rêves* (Paris: Baudinière, 1934), p. 174.

61. "US May Drop Versions: All Silents, But Spanish," *Variety*, 7 January 1931, p. 7; Clifford Howard, "Hollywood Review," *Close-Up*, vol. 8, no. 2, June 1931, pp. 113–14.

62. Ginette Vincendeau, "Les films en versions multiples," in Christian Belaygue, ed, *Le Passage du muet au parlant* (Toulouse: Editions Milan, 1988), p. 34; also in vincendeau, "Hollywood Babel.'

63. "Sad Outlook on Foreigns," *Variety*, 15 October 1930, p. 7; "All- French Picture Cleans Up: Native Film Far Over Jolson Top," *Variety*, 15 January 1930, p. 4.

64. *European Motion Picture Industry in 1930*, pp. 8–9; "US May Drop Versions: All Silents, But Spanish," *Variety*, 7 January 1931, p. 7.

65. "New World Talker Type: More Action and Clarity of Plot," *Variety*, 26 November 1930, p. 54.

66. "Kane's French Shorts Start With Poor Break," *Variety*, 29 January 1930, p. 4.

67. "Par. Heads Deciding in Europe Where Foreign Tongue Films Will be Made–Over Here or Coast," *Variety*, 30 April 1930, p. 7.

68. "Paramount Reorganizing Europe for Distribution-Production," *Variety*, 8 October 1930, p. 7; "Paris Prize Contest for French Stories," *Variety*, 31 December 1930, p. 8; "Original Stories for Foreign Markets look Like General American Production Policy," *Variety*, 10 December 1930, p. 6.

69. Maxi, "Il est charmant," *Variety Film Reviews, 1930–1933*, 15 March 1932.

70. Kauf, "Mistigri," *Variety Film Reviews, 1930–1933*, 17 January, 1933.

71. "Osso resigns as Paris Head," *Variety*, 28 May 1930, p. 7.

72. "Arthur," *Variety Film Reviews, 1930–1933*, 9 June 1931.

73. Soupault, "*Un soir de rafle*, de Carmine Gallone," in *Ecrits de cinéma 1918–1931*, p. 274.

74. United States Department of Commerce, *The Motion Picture Industry in Continental Europe in 1931*, Trade Information Bulletin, no. 797, 1932, p. 30.

75. "Dubbing Tough Routine, but Cheaper" *Variety*, 3 September 1930, p. 6.
76. "Dubbing's Comeback on Coast; Sound Men Assure Results as Desired," *Variety*, 6 August 1930, p. 4.
77. North and Golden, "Meeting Sound Film Competition Abroad," pp. 757–8.
78. Barry Salt, "Film Style and Technology in the Thirties: Sound," in Elizabeth Weis and John Belton, eds, *Film Sound: Theory and Practice* (New York, Columbia University Press, 1985), pp. 39, 40, 43; Hall, "Stars Are Dimmed," p. 5.
79. Roger Icart, *La Révolution du parlant vue par la presse française* (Perpignan: Institut Jean Vigo, 1988), p. 118; Maxi, "Désemparé," *Variety Film Reviews, 1930–1933*, 29 April 1931.
80. Maxi, "Désemparé."
81. "Dubbing's Comeback," p. 4.
82. Pangloss, "Toujours le dubbing," *Comœdia*, 13 November 1931.
83. George Stuart, "Encore le dubbing," *Soir*, 11 June 1931; "L'Union des artistes déclare la guerre à la synchronisation," *Paris Nouvelles*, 10 May 1931.
84. " 'Shanghai' Redubbed OK for French Approval," *Variety*, 2 August 1932, p. 7; "L'homme que j'ai tué," *Variety Film Reviews, 1930–1933*, 8 November 1932. See also Noé, *L'Epicerie des rêves*, pp. 172–3.
85. Richard Maltby and Ruth Vasey, "The International Language Problem: European Reactions to Hollywood's Conversion to Sound," in David W. Ellwood and Rob Kroes, eds., *Hollywood in Europe: Experiences of a Cultural Hegemony* (Amsterdam: VU University Press, 1994), pp. 78, 87.
86. "Progress in the Motion Picture Industry: Report of the Progress Committee," *Journal of the Society of Motion Picture Engineers*, vol. 17, no. 6, December 1931, pp. 907, 919.
87. C.J. North and N.D. Golden, "The European Film Market—Then and Now," *Journal of the Society of Motion Picture Engineers*, vol. 18, no. 4, April 1932, p. 449.
88. Maxi, "Miche," *Variety Film REviews, 1930–1933*, 31 May 1932.
89. North and Golden, "The European Film Market," pp. 442 449.
90. "Progress in the Motion Picture Industry: Report of the Progress Committee," *Journal of the Society of Motion Picture Engineers*, vol. 19, no. 2, August 1932, pp. 117, 118, 131.
91. "French Quota Not Drastic," *Variety*, 2 August 1932, pp. 13, 44.
92. *Motion Picture Industry in 1931*, p. 34; *The 1935–36 International Motion Picture Almanac* (New York: Quigley, 1935), p. 1075.
93. Maxi, "L'homme que j'ai tué," *Variety Film Reviews, 1930–1933*, 8 November 1932.
94. Mary Ann Doane's phrase in her article on early sound films: "Ideology

and the Practice of Sound Editing," in Weis and Belton, eds, *Film Sound: Theory and Practice*, p. 59.

95. Paul Delisle, "Dubbing ou version originale sous-titrée?," *Avant- Scène*, 31 March, 7 April and 21 April 1934.

96. René Manevy, "Notre opinion: le doublage," *Ciné-Miroir*, 22 January 1932; Jean Fayard, *Candide*, 19 May 1932; Henri Duvernois, "Doublage," *Annales*, 17 February 1933.

11

Made in Germany

Multiple-Language Versions and the Early German Sound Cinema

Joseph Garncarz

"Films make one of the very best exports you can ever have," claimed a German commentator of the early 1930s.[1] Many of the films on offer in Europe in the 1920s and 1930s certainly had a strong international appeal, but the international potential of cinema was constantly restricted by linguistic and cultural barriers. For films to be understood by the linguistically and culturally diverse audiences of Europe, they had to be translated by one means or another. Even translated films could only succeed abroad if they were compatible with the cinematic cultural traditions of the country to which they were exported.

The problem of translation was brought to a head by the conversion to sound. This essay is about one response to this problem: the production of multiple-language versions (MLVs). The first MLVs were made in 1929, the year sound was first introduced on a commercial scale in Europe. Films were shot not only in the language of their country of production, but also in one or more foreign languages—in Europe usually simultaneously, in the USA with a short time-gap. Over the last ten years MLVs have emerged from the footnotes of film history to become a research subject in their own right.[2] Two views dominate this research. Firstly, the multiple-language version is perceived solely as a strategy for solving the problem of the international comprehensibility of films posed by the introduction of sound. Secondly, there is a consensus that the strategy of making MLVs was a complete failure: "aesthetically these films were 'terrible' and financially they turned out to be a disaster."[3]

These basic positions stand in need of some revision. Firstly, the production of MLVs solved the problem of comprehensibility in the new situation of the talkies, and at the same time provided a new answer to the long-standing problem of how to market films successfully in a Europe marked by so many cultural differences. Secondly, for a number of years the multiple-language version performed the two functions of translation and cultural adaptation better than any other strategy, such as the dubbing of foreign films. Thus, contrary to the claims of most writers, I would argue that for several years following the introduction of sound the multiple-language version was the optimal strategy for enabling a film made in one country to become both understandable and popular in countries with other linguistic and cultural traditions. Most research has so far concentrated on European versions of American films. In an effort to generate a new understanding of MLVs, I want to shift the focus and concentrate on MLVs produced in Germany and intended for export to other European countries.

Too often, work on Film Europe begins from Hollywood's point of view. In *Exporting Entertainment*, for instance, Kristin Thompson makes her case for the international hegemony of Hollywood by looking at American export statistics.[4] If we look not at what Hollywood exported, but instead at what European audiences paid to see, we may generate a very different picture. Box-office ratings of films and stars, which measure the public's actual consumption of the product, suggest that during the years of the Weimar Republic Germany had a strong and successful national film culture, in which Film America played a much smaller role than has hitherto been supposed.[5] I want to apply this argument to the production and circulation of MLVs in Europe in the early sound period, to suggest that the audience for each language version rated the stars in that version more highly than those of Film America, and thus revise the prevailing understanding of MLVs as dismal failures.

The success or failure of MLVs must be accounted for on a more substantial basis than whether or not they were cast with top American stars, since it may well have been the case that the actors in each language version were major stars in their own language markets, even if they are not recognised by present-day historians.[6] Nor is there much value in the argument that export versions were aesthetically less polished than the "original" version made in the language of the country of production, since aesthetically inferior films have often become box-office hits. To explain the commercial importance of the MLVs in the early sound period, we must examine what alternative strategies were then available for solving the marketing problems that arose from the diversity of languages and cultures in Europe. The gradual decline in the importance of MLVs as the 1930s progressed should not automatically be construed as an indication of their overall failure. We ought rather to examine whether other strategies might more effectively have solved these problems at the time, and if not, why not.

Sound Films and the German Market

The German film industry exported its films to its European neighbours for several reasons. As in all other European countries, the domestic audience in Germany was too small to support expensive prestige productions.[7] Like every other European film industry, the German film industry also had to face the problem of competition from foreign companies in its own market. Finally, there were specifically German problems.[8] The *Vergnügungssteuer* (entertainment tax) imposed on cinemas meant that the capital flow back into film production was very small, while the availability of too many films resulted in cut-throat competition between distributors for cinema bookings, further reducing the profit margins of German films.[9]

The settlement of the sound patent dispute between European and American companies and the demand for sound films on the part of the German cinema-going public both enabled and necessitated a rapid switch from silent to sound films in 1929–30.[10] Sound films accounted for only 4.4 per cent of total German production in 1929 but increased dramatically to 69.2 per cent in 1930 and 98.6 per cent in 1931.[11]

Whereas in 1929 sound films were still barely significant in terms of total turnover, after 1930 it was the silent films that no longer played a part in the business. Correspondingly, in 1930 the proportion of German cinemas equipped with sound rose from 4 per cent to 36 per cent; for those showing films daily, the figure rose from 10 per cent to 90 per cent.[12]

Sound threatened to become an obstacle to exports and hence to the very existence of the national film industry. But if the export market was constrained in 1930–31, the number of German sound films available in the German market went up by a greater proportion than foreign sound films (see Table 11.1 and Figure 11.1). The relatively strong foreign market presence (but not popularity) of silent films on the German market was thus replaced by the strong market presence of German sound films, which were extremely popular.[13]

Table 11.1

	German/ Austrian silent	German/ Austrian sound	Foreign- language silent	Foreign- language sound
1925	232		272	
1926	208		261	
1927	261		238	
1928	243		249	
1929	193	7	155	26
1930	75	79	78	24
1931	9	140	49	64

Source: Alexander Jason, *Handbuch der Filmwirtschaft* (Berlin: Verlag für Presse, Wirßchaft un politik, 1930–3); and Karl Wolffsohn, *Jahrbuch der Filmindustrie* (Berlin: Verlag der "Lichtbildbühne", 1925–32).

Figure 11.1

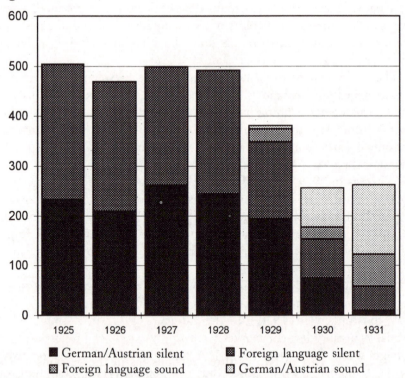

The table and figure above show sound and silent film supply in Germany between 1925 and 1931.

In fact, despite concerns about the export market in the early sound period, German films were not only successful in the domestic market. Exports, too, were soon once again buoyant, and not just for the German film industry. "Paradoxical as it may sound," wrote Erich Pommer in 1932,

> the international talking film is an accomplished fact. During the first year of the new medium neither the experts nor the public believed this to be possible. It was thought that the inter-nationalness of silence could not be adequately replaced by the national limitation of language. The spoken word appeared to have become an insurmountable barrier. It was considered that the end of the international film had arrived and, at the same time, the end of the film as the incomparable medium of culture and propaganda that it had been.[14]

How had film-makers overcome this "insurmountable barrier"? How had films once more become exportable in markets now dominated by "the national limitation of language"? In the years between the intro-duction of sound to Europe in 1929 and Pommer's pronouncements in 1932, it was not dubbing or subtitling which enabled the maintenance of film as an export commodity, but the innovative strategy of producing and distributing MLVs.

Multiple-Language Versions

The central characteristic of the MLV is that the actors in each version themselves speak the language of the country to which the version is being exported. Unlike the dubbing of a foreign film, the unity of the actor's voice and body is preserved: the audience hears the voice of the actor whom they see speaking. In the vast majority of cases, most of the actors used in the "original" version were replaced by a new set of actors speaking the appropriate language for the foreign-language versions. In the French version of *Die Drei von der Tankstelle* (1930), the "three from the filling station" were played not by Willy Fritsch, Oskar Karlweis and Heinz Rühmann, but by Henri Garat, René Lefèvre and Jacques Maury. Sometimes a multilingual actress like Lilian Harvey would act her part in two or three versions (as in the versions of *Die Drei von der Tankstelle* and *Der Kongreß tanzt*, 1931), but the English version of *Der blaue Engel* (1930) was an exceptional instance of all the roles being played by the same actors as in the "original" German version. The fact that the German actors only spoke very poor English was explained by changing the story: in the English version the pupils of Professor Rath (Emil Jannings) had to speak English all the time because they were supposedly learning the language.

Germany began making MLVs in 1929. Production peaked in 1931 and then inexorably declined. "In the first sound film period [1929–31] 66 films (i.e. 22 per cent of the total output of 251 feature-length sound films) were also shot in . . . different languages. 50 of them were shot with one other version, 14 with two and 2 with three different versions."[15] This gave a total of 84 foreign language versions for the 66 films from which language versions were made. As a company geared to exporting, Ufa made many more versions than the average (in 1931 the Neubabelsberg and Tempelhof studios made 12 MLVs out of a total of 24 films).[16]

MLVs chiefly served France and Great Britain, the "most important markets on the European Continent" apart from Germany, because these countries had been quickest to convert from silent to sound films.[17] From 1929 to 1931 only French and English versions were made in any quantity, with over 90 per cent of all versions made in these two languages. French was clearly the more important, accounting for two-thirds of the versions, while only a quarter were made in English.[18] Of the 66 films from which versions were made only 11 were *not* made in French. In the early sound era, therefore, hardly any German sound films destined for export were not made in a French version as well.

Why were there more versions in French than in any other language? The French market had become increasingly important for German film production since the mid-1920s. In 1924 the number of German films screened in France was 20; in 1926 it rose to 33, in 1928 to 122, and in 1930 it was 111.[19] Exports to the French market cannot on their own account for the large number of French language versions, since the market was in itself not that large. The strongest export territory for the German film industry was traditionally southern Central Europe. In the 1920s, apart from Austria, where there was no language problem, German films were most frequently exported to Czechoslovakia and Hungary. Surprisingly, the French language versions made by the German industry were also made for these markets. According to a Tobis circular in May 1930, "there are so many French versions because, thanks to this labelling, German films can more easily conquer the markets of the countries of Central Europe and the Balkans which are mostly allies of France."[20] Given Germany's negative image and France's positive one in Eastern Europe in the years after the First World War, it was easier to sell early German sound films there if they were available as French versions. "The very fact of *hearing* the much-resented German . . . caused havoc to the point of street demonstrations and physical destruction of the interiors of several movie theatres in Prague in the fall of 1930."[21]

The success of MLVs in solving the problem of the international comprehensibility of sound films is indicated by the fact that Germany's balance of trade for film showed a profit in 1930 and 1931 for the first time since accounts had begun to be published in 1924–5.[22] The sales of feature-length German sound films abroad earned more than foreign sound films earned on the German market, whereas German silents abroad were increasingly earning less than foreign silents were earning in Germany.

Alternative Strategies for Solving the Language Problem

In the early sound film period MLVs were *the* means of making a film comprehensible to a different language audience. Alternative strategies for solving the problem of the international comprehensibility of sound films such as dubbing and subtitling were either untenable or could not be put into effect immediately. Of the 88 foreign films shown as new releases in Berlin in 1930 and 1931, 17 (20 per cent) were shown "with German titles or with the background story in German," while 71 (80 per cent) were shown in German-language versions. Only some eight of these German-language versions were "language-doubled" (i.e. dubbed) in Germany.[23] Even if we allow that a similar number were dubbed abroad for the German market, this still suggests that about 80 per cent of the foreign sound films shown in German-language versions during the early sound film years were MLVs.[24]

No foreign film seems to have been shown in its unadapted original version in Berlin during 1930–1. Screening an original version would presuppose both linguistic competence and acceptance of the other language on the part of the audience. German was understood but not accepted in many countries such as Czechoslovakia and Hungary, while in others it was no more than an incomprehensible foreign language. In May 1930, a survey circulated among the exhibitors' trade associations in a number of European countries revealed that, generally speaking, foreign language films went down badly with their audiences.[25]

Another way of dealing with the new problem of comprehensibility was the polyglot film, in which actors from different countries each spoke their own language. *Hallo Hallo—hier spricht Berlin!* (1931–2)—or *Allô? Berlin? Ici Paris!*—tells of a Berlin telephone operator and a Parisian telephonist who fall in love. Speaking one another's language badly, they are forced to make themselves understood in both languages at the same time. This device meant that the film came out at the time without subtitles, but the process could only be used when the plot allowed each actor to use their mother tongue.[26] What is more, they could only be understood in those countries where the languages spoken in the film were familiar.

If there are obvious reasons for the low number of polyglot films of this type, why were more films not subtitled or dubbed in the early sound years? Why did either subtitling or dubbing not prevail over the production of MLVs straight away? In the case of subtitles, audiences of the period were not receptive to the idea of reading subtitles at the same time as they were trying to follow the pictures.[27] "The help of titles can only make the situation worse for a time," wrote Andor Kraszna-Krausz in 1931, "in that they seriously distract from the intrinsic means of expression of the sound film, clumsily underline the absence of any possibility of immediate understanding, and are too taxing for cinemagoers, winding them up and making them tired and irritable."[28] Another crucial reason for the rejection of subtitled foreign-language films was that such films audibly retained the language of the original, clearly marking the film as foreign. In 1931 René Lehmann argued from the point of view of the French that

> the audience of the popular houses only want to hear films speaking French and they are quite right too. For the foreign-speaking film to find a few specialist cinemas in Paris and thus a select audience is all well and good, but the vast cinemagoing public of Paris, the provinces and the colonies, will not tolerate having its eardrums assaulted by the sounds of an incomprehensible language.[29]

Unlike sub-titling, dubbing eliminates the foreignness of the original language by replacing it with the local one. It was not the case, as some have suggested, that the production of MLVs in the early sound period was necessary because dubbing was not technically possible.[30] As Hans-Michael Bock makes clear, films had in fact been dubbed as early as 1929:

Gustav Ucicky's sound film-operetta *Der unsterbliche Lump* and Kurt Bernhardt's Prussian ballad *Die letzte Kompagnie*, both billed as "A sound film by Joe May—Ufa production", were made in 1929/30.[31] Dubbed versions of both films were also produced for abroad. [Joe May] worked on these using a technical process that had been invented by the engineer Ludwig Czerny and which May himself (also a patent-holder) had been involved in developing.[32]

The dubbing process quite quickly became technically acceptable. A French journalist, for instance, reported that "the cinemagoers who have seen *Désamparé* have been able to see for themselves that the dubbing is well done and that it is extremely difficult to distinguish it from an original version where the actor is speaking his own language." Even though there may have been some complaints about "a certain metallic resonance in the sound," the verdict on the technical standards of dubbing was still mainly positive: "all in all the process helps to give the perfect illusion."[33] This perfect illusion was particularly successful in films produced as optical versions, which guaranteed lip-synchronisation. The production of optical versions involved the actor speaking the foreign text out loud, without having to understand what the words meant or perfectly mastering the pronunciation; the print would then be dubbed by a native speaker. Dubbing was also a much less costly method than MLV production for solving the problem of language transfer. A version in another language added two-thirds of the production costs of the original version to the cost of the film, because the actors in the language version had to be paid as well as the actors in the original version.[34] With dubbing, even if there was an extra expense for the dubbing itself, both the 'double payment' of the stars and the additional costs for the crew and use of the studio were eliminated.

Despite being both technically feasible and cheaper than MLV production, dubbing did not catch on straight away. The May 1930 trade survey came to the conclusion that "dubbed films were unsuccessful or impossible [for the mass audience]."[35] This was due to the fact that contemporary audiences could not bring themselves to identify the voice of one person with the body of another in the creation of a new "synthetic person." "It was strange, almost shocking, to hear a familiar [German] voice coming from a totally unfamiliar [American] body," wrote Claire Rommer in November 1931:

> My colleague's voice had wandered away from him—had disappeared into a stranger—from whose mouth it now runs on incessantly—DESPITE his tongue not uttering those words—despite his lips never framing them! A strange homunculus-like being has been summoned into existence by a conjuring trick.[36]

Siegfried Kracauer, writing in 1930, was equally unimpressed:

> If sound films are to retain the internationalness of silent film you must either move the emphasis from the dialogue back to the pictures, or onto the sounds as well, or shoot every film in all the main languages right from the outset. The attempt to pass off Americans as German-speakers is an absurdity.[37]

Evidence suggests that contemporary cinema-goers were quick to spot when foreign films were dubbed: for the German cinema audience simply hearing foreign actors speak German without an accent was proof that the film was dubbed. The more impossible it was for the speaker and actor to be one and the same, the greater the rejection: "You really have to watch out!" said the French fan magazine *Pour Vous* in March 1931. "We are hard put to understand how an African from Chad can be speaking in French, or how a Frenchman can express in his language the humour and jargon of a Mexican adventurer."[38]

Things were gradually changing, however. In November 1931 a special supplement of the technical journal *Filmtechnik-Filmkunst* promoted dubbing as an acceptable method for making a film comprehensible to a different-language audience:

> We have . . . given space in this supplement to a number of articles aimed at briefly outlining the problem [of dubbing], clarifying the ideas and showing what is possible. This time only the initial, superficial, vague obstacles need to be cleared out of the way and basically what it comes down to is: it works. You can translate sound films as well.[39]

In France, too, a growing number of voices considered dubbing to be an acceptable means of translation by 1931: "it is interesting to note that after having been subjected to a lively, almost general offensive, dubbing is now finding its supporters."[40] According to a 1933 observer of the scene, the German audience had also come to accept dubbing:

audiences have become used to German conversation dubbed to American lip movements. The critics do not even mention it in their reviews unless it happens to be particularly ineffective, which is seldom the case today. Despite the campaign against dubbing, which filled the German press when the first dubbed pictures appeared here, there is no doubt that it has come to stay and that the average public accepts it without worrying about who owns the voice that comes out of the loudspeaker.[41]

If we attribute the rejection of dubbing to audience perceptions that the voices and bodies did not belong to one another, then we must see the acceptance of dubbing as a cultural learning process, in which viewers closed their minds to the knowledge that the person apparently speaking the words and the person who has actually spoken them are not the same.[42] This learning process made it possible for the film industry to use the cheaper translation process as the standard practice after 1933.

The original reluctance to accept hearing a foreign star speaking in the voice of someone using the local language was not the only reason why the MLV strategy established itself in the early days of sound film. MLVs continued to be made after dubbed versions had long been accepted by German and French audiences: in 1936, for instance, there was a French version of the German comedy *Glückskinder*. Indeed, MLVs were still being made, albeit in ever smaller numbers, as late as the 1950s. The 1955 remake of *Die Drei von der Tankstelle/Le Chemin du Paradis*, for example, was shot in a German and a French version, like the 1930 film.[43]

Why were MLVs still being made when a cheaper, widely accepted process of speech transfer was available? The choice of how to make a film comprehensible for audiences who spoke another language depended not on the level of the capital invested but on profitability. Even when dubbed foreign films had long been accepted, producing an MLV could still be profitable given an appropriately sized sales territory and degree of demand. "If the potential return in a language territory is greater than the production costs of an original version, then the production of another language version is entirely justified," wrote Eugen Kürschner in 1931:

If the potential return is lower than the production costs of an original version but higher than those of an optical version [when the actor pronounces the foreign text and it is dubbed by a native speaker], then the only acceptable financial course is the production of the latter version. The acoustic version [i.e. the dubbed version as we know it today] will always be the medium for inter-nationalness where translation into a foreign language in the relevant language territory cannot offer profitability by the first two methods.[44]

I would argue that the reason why MLVs still had any chance at all of showing a profit at a time when dubbing had come to be accepted was that they not only responded to people's linguistic diversity, but were also a new response to the problem of cultural diversity as well.

The Problem of Europe's Cultural Diversity

Contrary to what has often previously been supposed, the German cinema-going public's favourite films and stars in the Weimar period were those in their own national tradition. American films only came second in terms of box-office success, while films from other European countries usually trailed in third place.[45] Surveys in *Film-Kurier* on the success of films with the public suggest that from 1925 to 1930 67.5 per cent of audiences were going to German films. According to these surveys, Hollywood films accounted for only 19.4 per cent of German cinema-going, while 13.2 per cent of all tickets sold at the box-office were for films by fellow Europeans.[46]

Analysis of the most successful films of the period according to their national origin reveals some quite clear patterns in favour of German films and traditions. The popular German films set standards in that they drew on and served specific national cultural traditions. These traditions provided the most successful genres of the period: war films (e.g. *Unsere Emden*, 1926; *In Treue stark*, 1926); musicals (e.g. *An der schönen blauen Donau*, 1926; *Die Försterchristl*, 1926); and mountain films (e.g. *Der Kampf ums Matterhorn*, 1928; *Die weiße Hölle vom Piz Palü*, 1929). Foreign productions were successful when they chimed with the cultural traditions that were dear to German audiences. The most successful foreign films with the Weimar public were set in Europe, had biblical themes (e.g. *Ben Hur*, 1926), featured European actors (e.g. *Love*, [1928]), and used accepted standard plots revolving around an unhappy ending, as in, for example, *The White Sister* (1925).

According to Colin Crisp, French audiences also preferred their own national films:

attendance figures at the screening of French films, whenever they have been measured, have proved significantly higher than at screenings of films of other nationalities dubbed into French. At the Renaitour enquiry in 1937 the American delegates produced figures which demonstrated this preference conclusively: in 1936, of the 75 most popular films in France the top six were French; only 15 of the 75 were American, against 56 French. . . . Sadoul quotes an estimate of 70% of the share of receipts going to French rather than dubbed films in 1935.[47]

If this pattern, whereby audiences preferred films from their own country, was typical not only of Germany and France but also of other European countries in the 1920s and 1930s, an export-geared film industry had to adapt its own products to serve the national cultural traditions of the target country. In the 1920s European and American film companies employed different strategies to increase the success of their films abroad. American companies used creative talents imported from Europe like Emil Jannings in *The Last Command* (1928) in order to improve their own market opportunities with European audiences.[48] European co-productions such as *Michel Strogoff* (1925–6) and *Überflüssige Menschen* (1926) were packaged to be successful in both the countries involved in the co-production. The remainder of Europe's national film output was selectively marketed so that only those films not particularly rooted in the culture of the producing country were exported.

The strategy of varying films for different target countries had already existed in the 1920s, and the differentiated silent film versions became the model for the MLVs. Between 1914 and 1928 it was customary to assemble different versions of films using either takes shot sequentially with a single camera or else takes shot simultaneously by several cameras.[49] This strategy was necessary for the international marketing of a film, because several negatives were needed to strike a large number of prints, and duplicate negatives could not be produced without loss of quality until the second half of the 1920s (1926 in the USA, 1928 in Europe).[50] The technical requirement to produce several non-identical negatives for the international market provided an opportunity to differentiate the product culturally, although the nature and number of the variations was limited by the need for production efficiency. Stories could be varied by changing the way a few scenes were directed only if this was simple to achieve. The European versions of *Love* and

The Gold Rush (1925), for example, both had unhappy endings, while the Hollywood versions were more optimistic. In *Love*, Greta Garbo's love affair ends in suicide in the European version, while in the Hollywood version it has a happy ending. The European version of *The Gold Rush* shows Charlie's love of Georgia (Georgia Hale) to be an illusion, while in the American version the love story is finally, against all odds, crowned with success.[51]

The Language Version: forms of cultural adaptation

As with silent film versions, the extent of an MLV's adaptation to the cultural environment of the target country was limited by the demands of production efficiency. Talking of his first experience with a bilingual picture, and of making the German and English versions simultaneously, Alfred Hitchcock told François Truffaut:

> Before the shooting [of *Murder*, 1930], when I went to Berlin to talk over the script [of *Mary*, the German version], they proposed many changes that I turned down. As it happens, I was wrong. I refused them because I was satisfied with the English version. Besides, we didn't want to shoot two versions that would be too different from each other, for reasons of economy.[52]

The story told in the "original" version was regularly altered in the MLV if it was concerned with questions of nationality and the adaptation could be done by simple means. According to Ernst Hugo Correll (Ufa's head of production), Serge de Poligny, the French editor of *Gold*, who had already directed several French versions for Ufa in Zeisler's production unit,

> pointed out in a pretty forceful memo that if its success in France was not to be jeopardised, a French version could only be made if Ziemsen was French and thus the whole plot, set in Germany in the film, was set in France, so that it would therefore have to become a film which moved between France and England.[53]

As a rule the nationality of the characters and location of the plot was adapted for the target country. *Gloria* (1931), for instance, was set in Germany in the German version and in Paris in the French version; similarly, *Ihre Majestät die Liebe* (1930–1) was set in Berlin and Paris. Only if the historic setting or the national image brooked no alteration would the plot location stay the same, as with the French version of *Der Kongreß tanzt*, which, like the German version, is set in the Austrian world of operetta at the time of the Congress of Vienna.

In terms of direction and cinematography, most language versions hardly differ at all from their originals. "Serge de Poligny told Raymond Borde, Director of the Toulouse Cinémathèque, that he was always left a certain amount of scope within a take and only the start and finish had to coincide with the original."[54] So far as set, costume, the spatial positioning of the characters, length of take and editing are concerned, as a rule hardly any marked difference is discernible.[55] There is also very often no significant variation in respect of casting. The jovial little man embodied by Heinz Rühmann in *Die Drei von der Tankstelle* has his counterpart in Jacques Maury's character in the French version. The three elderly gentlemen admirers of Käthe von Nagy in *Ihre Majestät die Liebe* and of Annabella in the French version are cast true to type in each case. Versions in which roles are interpreted significantly differently appear to be the exception: whereas in *F.P.1 antwortet nicht* Hans Albers plays a "daredevil," in the English version, *The Secrets of F.P.1*, Conrad Veidt plays a "gentleman."[56]

MLVs were a new response to Europe's cultural diversity. During the silent era it was not usual to cast actors from the target country in export versions. It has previously been supposed that, since Hollywood had a hegemonic position in the international market, then versions of American films cast with European stars were less successful because "their 'name value' turned out to be considerably smaller than that of the American stars with their enormous studio-designed 'build-up' (in *Variety*'s parlance)."[57] In fact, in most cases precisely the opposite was the case: because of the audience's preference for actors from their own country, the casting of a language version with actors from that country could increase the film's chance of popularity in that country. A French journalist reported in 1931 that:

> It was in fact fairly unusual to entrust untried screenwriters and actors with the job of writing and interpreting French versions. The Americans had quite soon come to realise their mistake. They called on the help of our better actors, Yves Mirande, Jacques Deval, and our best loved artistes. And the results were very noticeable.[58]

If one judges the nationality of the stars not by where they were born but by the national-cultural context in which they first became stars, all the top stars during the period of the Weimar Republic were German, judging by the evidence we have from the film magazine listings for 1923–6 (see Figure 11.2). Lya Mara, for instance, was born in Riga, Latvia, but only made films in Germany during the Weimar period.[59] The most popular American star by far was the child actor Jackie Coogan (in the 1923–6 success ratings for male stars he reached eleventh place with 2.8 per cent of the votes). Coogan probably owed his success to the fact that although the public demand was there, the Germans had a taboo about building up child stars. In general, however, these statistics suggest it was German stars that were popular with German audiences, not American stars.

Figure 11.2.   Weimar Film Stars Top Ten 1923–1926

Top ten female stars	*Top ten male stars*
1. Henny Porten	1. Harry Piel
2. Claire Rommer	2. Otto Gebühr
3. Lil Dagover	3. Harry Liedtke
4. Lya Mara	4. Conrad Veidt
5. Lya de Putti	5. Charles Willi Kayser
6. Lee Parry	6. Willi Fritsch
7. Lilian Harvey	7. Alphons Fryland
8. Mady Christians	8. Ernst Hofman
9. Xenia Desni	9. Paul Richter
10. Dary Holm	10. Emil Jannings

Calculated on the basis of annual ratings in: *Neue Illustrierte Filmwoche*, Berlin, no. 23, 1924; *Deutsche Filmwoche*, Berlin, no. 19, 1925; no. 19, 1926; no. 11, 1927.

I have yet to locate statistics for France which measure the popularity of the stars of the 1920s and 1930s according to their national origin. It is evident, however, from contemporary popularity contests in the fan magazine *Pour Vous* that the main competition was between French and American stars, since stars of other nationalities often simply failed to get nominated.[60] German actors were therefore presumably less popular with French audiences than French and American stars.

In the light of these national preferences, it obviously made sense for German films to be cast with German stars and for the French versions of top-ranking German films to employ popular French actors. As Erich Pommer put it when commenting on *Der Kongreß tanzt*, "Apart from the fortunate Lilian Harvey whose linguistic gift and popularity present a basis of universal understanding, popular stars of various nationalities were employed in [the French/British version of] this film in order to arouse public interest equally in all countries."[61]

Lilian Harvey, who had been in films since 1924, shot up in Germany's popularity stakes in the 1920s to become its number one star (in 1924 she was not nominated, in 1925 she was third and in 1926 she came top). The same applies to Willy Fritsch, who had been making films since 1921 (not mentioned in 1923, twelfth in 1924, first in 1925, fourth in 1926). Because of their popularity—and their "chemistry"—it seemed a good idea to put the two stars in films together (*Die keusche Susanne*, 1926; *Ihr dunkler Punkt*, 1928). Together, they had runaway successes with *Liebeswalzer* (tenth place in 1929–30), *Die Drei von der Tankstelle* (1st place 1930–31) and *Der Kongreß tanzt* (first place 1931–2).

The French versions of *Die Drei von der Tankstelle* and *Der Kongreß tanzt* star Lilian Harvey alongside Henri Garat in the part that Willy Fritsch played in the "original" German version. Garat was already popular as Mistinguett's partner in the Parisian music hall at the Casino de Paris and Moulin Rouge, and as a Saturday matinée idol. As Francis Courtade notes of the casting of Garat in French language versions, "it was certainly a clever move on the part of the German producers: they had chosen a French actor idolized by the masses . . . so that the French-speaking audience would be a pushover."[62] In a competition in the fan magazine *Pour Vous* in October and November 1931 readers had to choose their favourite stars from a total of 160 actors and actresses, French and foreign, who had appeared on French screens during the year.[63] They were asked to choose "the most photogenic star whose moving image was the happiest, the most statuesque, the most pleasant to look at."[64] Henri Garat was voted "the most photogenic French male star" and Lilian Harvey "the most photogenic foreign female star."[65] According to these polls, Harvey and Garat were thus the most popular film couple in France in the early 1930s.

The strategy of casting actors who were successful in the target countries while leaving the film's other parameters more or less the same could only be successful if the film's subject matter was susceptible to an international interpretation. According to Erich Pommer, "right from the inception of a film it is endeavoured to take into account all the factors that make for success. The subject matter of the film is the main consideration. The idea itself must be capable of being understood all over the world. In the scenario it is absolutely necessary to take into account those great human emotions that are the same in all countries."[66] As a result, no foreign-language versions were made of popular German films that revolved around German traditions little understood abroad. Thus there are no foreign-language versions of films like the military comedies *Reserve hat Ruh* 1931 and *Der Schrecken der Garnison* 1931.[67] The success of this strategy of selecting international subject matter and differentiating the language versions nationally by casting stars of the target country is suggested by the following report from 1932:

> UFA-ACE and Pathé-Natan have brilliantly demonstrated that Franco-German co-production can bring nothing but success. So far no single UFA-ACE film has been a flop; on the contrary these films have been among the top films of both the previous and the present season [1930–1 and 1931–2].[68]

More Effective Cultural Adaptation Strategies

As the problem of the comprehensibility of foreign films was increasingly solved by dubbing, the strategy of making MLVs simply as a form of cultural adaptation was not sufficiently effective, because they often cost more than they could earn.[69] There were two other means by which films could be tailored culturally to suit foreign markets, and these strategies gradually became more attractive than the MLV route. Both strategies allowed films to be cast with the top stars of target countries. But they also allowed the parameters of the narrative to be culturally differentiated, something which had been largely avoided with MLVs on the grounds of production costs. This greater cultural differentiation was also possible because, unlike the MLVs, creative control was now entirely placed in the hands of the nationals of the country for whom the films were being made.

The first strategy was to sell not a film but the rights to remake that film elsewhere in Europe. According to *Film-Kurier* in 1931, "experts are . . . of the opinion that this, rather than 'versions' productions, is the way the international film business . . . will go."[70] Whereas with MLVs the film shot in the original language provided the model that the foreign-language version would be based on, in a remake the new version no longer had to adhere to the details of the original. Stories could be altered to fit the film better to another cultural milieu. Such was the case with *First a Girl* (1935), the British remake of the German comedy *Viktor und Viktoria* (1935), in which the lower-class Berlin variety hall was replaced by the more middle-class British music hall. With remakes, not only was it possible to cast a country's own stars, like Jessie Matthews in *First a Girl*, without having to pay for them to go abroad, but the entire film was controlled by the producers and creative talents who were specialists in their own culture and better placed to adapt the subject matter.

The second strategy, which offered optimal cultural adaptation to whatever the other country might be, and which had already been adopted by Hollywood in the 1920s, had nothing to do with making variations, versions or remakes of a film. This means of attempting to make a film more successful in a key export market involved either producing "foreign" films at home or using domestic capital to produce films in the target country itself. Even if in this case final control remained in the hands of the foreign financier, the creative process was still controlled by nationals of the country for whom the film was destined. From 1933 to 1939 Alliance Cinématographique Européenne (ACE), a subsidiary of Ufa, produced French films for the French public in Ufa's Babelsberg studios. Continental Film Société à Responsabilité Limitée, another Ufa subsidiary, resorted to this strategy during the Occupation, and after 1940 produced films in France geared to the preferences of the French audience, using French film-makers but remaining under German management. Although from an economic point of view Continental may have been seen in France as an attempt by the Nazis to colonise the French film industry, from a cultural perspective its films were considered "as representative of the indomitable French spirit."[71] Continental's strategy was a success: over 50 per cent of the biggest hits with the French public during the occupation period came from Continental, despite the fact that from 1940 to 1945 it only made about 14 per cent of all the films shot in France.[72]

Few of these strategies for making films that might be successful in more than one European market are any longer of significance. Arguably, this is a result of the integration of popular film cultures in Europe from the 1970s onward. Whereas in the 1950s hardly any film was equally popular in both France and Germany, in the 1980s the number of hits that they shared shot up dramatically. Never before have so many people seen the same films throughout Europe as they do today. The films which are successes on a European scale today are nearly all American-produced. As the tastes of Europe's national audiences have grown closer together, the strategies for adapting films to different national European cultures have become increasingly unnecessary. The phenomenon of the MLV has thus vanished from the cinemas as irrevocably as the remake of European films across national frontiers or the production of foreign films by domestic companies in Europe.

If we include the American film market in the equation, the integration of popular film culture appears to be a one-way street. European audiences are used to American films, but the preferences of American audiences are largely unaffected by European film. That is why there are no remakes of American films in Europe but there are remakes of European films for the American market. If European films are not made in English, remakes are necessary not only because of the cultural difference between the USA and Europe but also because the American public will not accept dubbed versions of foreign films.

Conclusions

The model developed here of how the problems of a film's comprehensibility and its success were solved across linguistic and cultural frontiers under changing technological and cultural conditions shows us the phenomenon of the MLV in a new light. In 1929 and for a few years thereafter, the production of a film in several language versions was no quirky blip in film history but, in Germany at least, the most effective way to make a film both understandable and popular for an audience who spoke another language. Firstly, it solved the new problem of language transfer posed by the coming of sound in a better way than any other process. The MLV did not give rise to the problem of the "synthetic" person which was broadly the reason for the initial rejection of dubbing. The actors did the talking themselves so that bodies and voices retained their coherent identity. Secondly, by casting popular stars from the target country in each language version, the chances of the film's success were improved because as a rule actors from elsewhere were less popular than those of the target country. This is only discernible as a successful strategy if one revises the idea that Hollywood films enjoyed universal popularity in Europe and empirically substantiates the relative success of different film stars in the various European markets.

The phenomenon of the MLV, which for a few years in the early sound film era was the best solution to the problems of Europe's linguistic and cultural diversity, rapidly lost its importance in the mid-1930s because better strategies for solving both sets of problems became available. Through a cultural learning process dubbing came to be broadly accepted by European audiences, so that this cheaper process could be employed to make a film understandable in export markets. If its subject matter made a film appear likely to be a particular success in other countries, then the film would be remade with the creative talents of the target country in order to obtain a product that was adapted to suit the cultural preferences of the target audience. Although dubbing has retained its significance in Europe, the strategies of cultural adaptation have lost their importance, since they only made sense in a Europe marked by cultural differences and divergent cinematic tastes.

Translated by Brenda Ferris.

Notes

1. Alexander Jason, *Handbuch der Filmwirtschaft* (Berlin: Verlag für Presse, Wirßchaft un Politik, 1930–3, vol. 3, p. 44.

2. Ginette Vincendeau, "Hollywood Babel," *Screen*, vol. 29, no. 2, Spring 1988, pp. 24–39, reprinted in this volume; Nataša Ďurovičová, "Translating America: The Hollywood Multilinguals 1929–1933," in Rick Altman, ed., *Sound Theory, Sound Practice* (New York: Routledge, 1992), pp. 138–52; Michaela Krützen, "Esperanto für den Tonfilm," in Michael Schaudig, ed., *Positionen deutscher Filmgeschichte* (Munich, 1996), pp. 119–54.

3. Vincendeau, "Hollywood Babel," p. 25, reproduced here on p. 189.

4. Kristin Thompson, *Exporting Entertainment: America in the World Market, 1907–1934* (London: British Film Institute, 1985).

5. Joseph Garncarz, "Hollywood in Germany: The Role of American Films in Germany, 1925–1990," in David W. Ellwood and Rob Kroes, eds, *Hollywood in Europe: Experiences of a Cultural Hegemony* (Amsterdam: VU University Press, 1994), pp. 94–135; Joseph Garncarz, "Populäres Kino in Deutschland. Internationalisierung einer Filmkultur" (Post-doctoral thesis, University of Cologne 1996).

6. On the question of why film historians today know few top stars from the Weimar Republic, see Joseph Garncarz, "Warum kennen Filmhistoriker viele Weimarer Topstars nicht mehr? Überlegungen am Beispiel Claire Rommer," in *Montage/av: Zeitschrift für Theorie & Geschichte audiovisueller Kommunikation*, vol. 6, no. 2, 1997, pp. 64–92.

7. This explains why *Metropolis* was one of the German film industry's biggest financial flops, and seriously threatened Ufa's existence, although it was the fourth most successful film out of about 500 first-release films in Germany in 1927–8.

8. See Thomas Elsaesser, "Kunst und Krise. Die Ufa in den 20er Jahren," in Hans-Michael Bock and Michael Töteberg, eds, *Das Ufa-Buch* (Frankfurt/M: Zweitausendeins, 1992), pp. 96–105.

9. In the early sound era 15 per cent of cinema receipts were taken as tax. That amounted to an annual revenue of 40 million Reichsmark. Jason, *Handbuch*, vol. 2, p. 39.

10. Harald Jossé, *Die Entstehung des Tonfilms* (Freiburg, Munich: Verlag Karl Alber, 1984).

11. Jason, *Handbuch*, vol. 3, p. 21.

12. Jason, *Handbuch*, vol. 2, p. 27.

13. This trend actually stemmed from the introduction of sound and not the 1930 quota law which limited the number of foreign films on the German market. Although Germany's 1930 quota of foreign films was ninety, Berlin, which had an above average number of cinemas equipped for sound, only screened sixty-four sound films, clearly demonstrating that the entire quota was not taken up.

14. Erich Pommer, "The International Talking Film," in Frank Arnau, ed., *Universal Filmlexikon* (Berlin: Universal Filmlexikon G.m.b.h., London General Press, 1932), p. 14; reproduced here as Document 17.

15. Jason, *Handbuch*, vol. 3, p. 24.

16. Karl Wolffsohn, *Jahrbuch der Filmindustrie* (Berlin: Verlag der "Lichtbild-bühne", 1923–33), vol. 5, p. 305.

17. Jason, *Handbuch*, vol. 2, p. 26.

18. Three films were made in Italian versions, while there was only one language version made in each of Polish, Hungarian, Rumanian, Czech and Spanish.

19. P.A. Harlé, "En face de l'Allemagne," *La Cinématographie française*, no. 652, 2 May 1931.

20. "La politique du cinéma allemand," *La Cinématographie française*, no. 647, 28 March 1931.

21. Ďurovičová, "Translating America," p. 264 n. 25.

22. Jason, *Handbuch*, vol. 3, p. 45; Wolffsohn, *Jahrbuch*, vol. 5 (1933), p. 338.

23. Wolffsohn, *Jahrbuch*, vol. 5, p. 259.

24. The proportion of German films dubbed in Germany for export was at least as great as this. Wolffsohn, *Jahrbuch*, vol. 5, p. 259.

25. "Antworten auf 10 Fragen über die Tonfilmlage Europas," *Film-Kurier*, 31 March 1930.

26. The subtitles in some modern versions were added later.

27. Some talkies in the early sound period had intertitles instead of subtitles.

This process led to a reduction of the moving image and was used to make it possible to show sound films in silent cinemas that had yet to be converted to sound.

28. Andor Kraszna-Krausz, "Warum synchronisieren," *Filmtechnik-Filmkunst*, 28 November 1931, p. 1.
29. René Lehmann, "A propos du 'dubbing'," *Pour Vous*, no. 133, 4 June 1931.
30. Wilhelm E. Labisch, "Gleich und doch verschieden: 'Versionen'. Wie zu Beginn der Tonfilmzeit fremdsprachige Fassungen hergestellt wurden," *FILM-Korrespondenz*, no. 1, 18 January 1974, pp. 25–7.
31. There was at the time an English and a French version of this film. I have only been able to consult an incomplete archive print of the German film and the dubbed English version.
32. Hans-Michael Bock, "Ein Instinkt- und Zahlenmensch. Joe May als Produzent und Regisseur in Deutschland," in H-M. Bock and Claudia Lenssen, eds, *Joe May: Regisseur und Produzent* (Munich: Edition Text + Kritik, 1996), p. 148.
33. *Pour Vous*, no. 129, 7 May 1931.
34. Krüzen, "Esperanto," p. 149.
35. "Antworten auf 10 Fragen über die Tonfilmlage Europas," *Film-Kurier*, 31 May 1930. Yugoslavia and the Netherlands were the only countries where there seems to have been acceptance.
36. Claire Rommer, "Stimmenwanderung," *Die Filmwoche*, no. 48, 30 November 1932.
37. Siegfried Kracauer, "Im Westen nichts Neues," *Frankfurter Zeitung*, 6 December 1930; quoted in Kracauer, *Von Caligari zu Hitler: Eine psychologische Studie des deutschen Films* (Frankfurt/M: Suhrkamp, 1984), p. 459.
38. "La question des langues," *Pour Vous*, no. 121, 12 March 1931.
39. Kraszna-Krausz, "Warum synchronisieren," p. 3.
40. Lehmann, "A propos du 'dubbing'"; L.M., "Il faut mettre au point la question du 'Dubbing,'" *Pour Vous*, no. 129, 7 May 1931.
41. C. Hooper Trask, "On Berlin's Screens," *New York Times*, 5 February 1933, p. 4, quoted in Thompson, *Exporting Entertainment*, p. 163.
42. Even though the change from a general rejection of dubbing to acceptance may not have been solely due to improvements in dubbing technology, technical advances such as the separation of sound and picture which took place in 1933 certainly did play a part in the rapid spread of this process. Michael Volber, "Mit dem Ton kam die Synchronisation," *Film-Echo*, no. 8, 24 February 1996, pp. 64–6.
43. Ulrich J. Klaus, *Deutsche Tonfilme: Filmlexikon der abendfüllenden deutschen und deutschsprachigen Tonfilme nach ihren deutschen Uraufführungen, vol. 1, 1929–30* (Berlin: Ulrich J. Klaus-Verlag, 1988), p. 52.
44. Eugen Kürschner, "Folgerungen für die Produktion," *Filmtechnik-Filmkunst*, 28 November 1931, p. 9.

45. See Garncarz, "Hollywood in Germany," pp. 102–9.
46. *Film-Kurier*, no. 129, 2 June 1930, p. 2 (the percentages were rounded up). The market share of foreign European films was greater than that of American films for the first time in 1929–30. It is not quite clear whether this was attributable to the production of versions that were better tailored to the market.
47. Colin Crisp, *The Classic French Cinema* (Bloomington: Indiana University Press, 1997), p. 12. The statistics for the 1950s and 1960s show that French films were much more popular with the French public than American films and that these, in their turn, were more popular than those from other European countries. Data from Michael Thiermeyer, *Internationalisierung von Film und Filmwirtschaft* (Cologne, Weimar, Vienna: Böhlau, 1994), p. 320.
48. Joseph Garncarz and Ginette Vincendeau, "Emigration and European Cinema," in Ginette Vincendeau, ed., *Encyclopaedia of European Cinema* (London: Cassell, 1995), pp. 127–9.
49. Jean Mitry, "Le problème des versions originales," *Image et son*, vol. 369, February 1982, pp. 122–5; A.V. Barsy, "Der 'zweite' Operateur," *Die Kinotechnik*, vol. 7, no. 15, 1925, pp. 368–9.
50. Barry Salt, *Film Style and Technology: History and Analysis* (London: Starword, 1983), p. 222.
51. Joseph Garncarz, *Filmfassungen. Eine Theorie signifkanter Filmvariation* (Frankfurt/M: Peter Lang, 1992), pp. 58–65.
52. François Truffaut, *Hitchcock* (London: Panther, 1969), p. 83.
53. Ufa Protocol, 2 October 1933.
54. Francis Courtade, "Die deutsch-französischen Koproduktionen," in Heike Hurst und Heiner Gassen, eds, *Kameradschaft—Querelle. Kino zwischen Deutschland und Frankreich* (Munich: Institut Français de Munich/CICIM, 1991), p. 170.
55. The most noticeable differences between "original" and language version in this respect seem to be in American rather than European films, or so it would appear from, for example, a comparison of the American and German versions of *Anna Christie*.
56. The English version is different from the German one in terms of the plot as well. It cuts out elements that do not directly advance the plot and is almost thirty-seven minutes shorter. Since I am only acquainted with the British re-release version entitled *The Secrets of F.P.1*, it is not impossible that these changes were first made in 1938.
57. Ďurovičová, "Translating America," p. 152.
58. "La question des langues," *Pour Vous*, no. 121, 12 Mach 1931.
59. Cf. the article on Lya Mara in Hans-Michael Bock, ed., *CineGraph. Lexikon zum deutsch-sprachigen Film* (Munich: Edition Text + Kritik, 1984), loose-leaf collection, 5th issue.

60. "Notre jeu des sourires," *Pour Vous*, no. 77, 8 May 1930; no. 78, 15 May 1930; no. 79, 22 May 1930; no. 82, 12 June 1930; no. 89, 31 July 1930; no. 91, 14 August 1930. Since the choice was between only twenty stars, they all had to appear in the two Top Ten lists. These success ratings are therefore not a means of measuring the popularity of the stars in terms of their national origin.

61. Pommer, "International Talking Film," p. 15.

62. Courtade, "Deutsche-französischen Koproduction," p. 169. There is a brief biography of Garat in *Pour Vous*, no. 161, 17 December 1931; see also the biographical article by Ginette Vincendeau in Vincendeau, ed., *Encyclopaedia of European Cinema*, p. 168.

63. *Pour Vous*, no. 153, 22 October 1931; no. 154, 29 October 1931; no. 155, 5 November 1931; no 156, 12 November 1931.

64. *Pour Vous*, no. 151, 8 October 1931.

65. *Pour Vous*, no. 161, 17 December 1931.

66. Pommer, "International Talking Film," p. 13.

67. Compare the German films successful in Germany with the list of films of which MLVs were made: see Garncarz, "Hollywood in Germany," pp. 122–4. A list of the versions can be found in Jason, *Handbuch*, vol. 3, pp. 131–3.

68. "France and Germany," *La Cinématographie française*, no. 699, 25 March 1932. *Die Drei von der Tankstelle* and *Der Kongreß tanzt* were not co-productions in the usual sense. Both films were produced by Ufa, and the French versions were distributed by L'Alliance Cinématographique Européenne (ACE).

69. See the comparison of the French film *L'equipage* with the American MLV *The Woman I Love* in Vincendeau, "Hollywood Babel," pp. 35–7, reproduced here on pp. 199–200.

70. "Foreign version of successful film. *Die Privatsekretärin* will speak English. Sale of all rights to England," *Film-Kurier*, 2 April 1931. The leading role of the private secretary is also played by Renate Müller in the English remake. The French trade press also singled out the sale of the right to remake a film as a new marketing method.

71. Evelyn Ehrlich, *Cinema of Paradox. French Filmmaking Under the German Occupation* (New York: Columbia University Press, 1985), p. 55; George Sturm, "UFrAnce 1940–1944. Kollaboration und Filmproduktion in Frankreich," in Bock and Töteberg, eds, *Das Ufa-Buch*, pp. 408–14.

72. Ehrlich, *Cinema of Paradox*, p. 47 and Appendix A. The Continental films were also in distribution in Germany up to 1944–5 but were not a great success.

12

Polyglot Films for an International Market
E.A. Dupont, the British Film Industry, and the Idea of a European Cinema, 1926–1930

Andrew Higson

Amid the pervasive internationalism in the latter half of the 1920s, the successful film director was one whose work could transgress national boundaries. The German director E.A. Dupont was one such figure. He had a formidable international reputation, working variously with Ufa in Germany, Universal in Hollywood, and British International Pictures (BIP) in England. As Dupont himself put it while working in Hollywood,

> artistically speaking, I am not a continental European; rather, I try to produce pictures according to international taste. Europe has a lot to learn from America, and America could learn some things from Europe. It is not impossible to unite both of the film industry's endeavours, namely to succeed not only with audiences and critics, but also at the box-office.[1]

This sense of cultural exchange, literally embodied in Dupont's journeys between Berlin, Hollywood and London, is in many ways indicative of the relations between Film Europe and Film America. The vagaries of his career and his professed artistic internationalism thus exemplify much that is at stake in the tension between American market hegemony and European resistance.

Although the focus of this chapter is in part a single director, my concern is not with traditional questions of authorship. Dupont provides the starting point for a much broader investigation of the economic conditions which made it possible for him to have the sort of career he enjoyed, as a marketable commodity in a global system of exchange in the latter part of the 1920s. By charting Dupont's career in Britain between 1926 and 1930, and the context in which it took shape, I will attempt to elucidate some more far-reaching issues concerning the construction of both a national cinema in an international market-place, and a pan-national European cinema that might be strong enough to resist Hollywood's international market hegemony.

Dupont had been directing genre films and latterly quality productions in Germany since the late 1910s, but he only gained prominence outside German-speaking territories in 1925 with *Variété*. This spectacularly stylish film set in the world of the circus and the variety show was a huge critical and box-office success in both Europe and the USA, and is still his best-known film. After gaining such an international profile, it was almost inevitable that Dupont would be attracted to Hollywood, but it was less predictable that after one failure with Universal, a director of his stature and at the height of his career should move in late 1926 to the impoverished and low-profile British film industry, and stay there for four years.

Dupont's presence in Britain was, however, symptomatic both of developments in the British film industry and of the attempts in the late 1920s to establish a pan-European cinema capable of competing with Hollywood on its own terms. British production had sunk almost into oblivion in the middle years of the decade, but 1927 was a crucial year in its recovery, witnessing the emergence of Gaumont-British and BIP, two major vertically integrated combines which were well-enough capitalised to embark on extensive production programmes. The Cinematograph Act of that year ushered in a new era of state intervention in the film industry in the form of quotas determining the level of foreign imports into the British film market. This economic protectionism boosted the confidence of the production sector of the industry and attracted unprecedented levels of external investment. The most enterprising companies of the period were now run by dynamic businessmen along established capitalist lines for achieving market control. They sought not simply to re-vitalise the domestic scene but to establish British films in the international market-place, with the potential for far higher profits. The major obstacle, as in other European national cinemas, was the strength of the American export drive. One means of overcoming this obstacle was to participate in the Film Europe project, by setting up co-production and reciprocal distribution deals with other European companies.

A figure of Dupont's standing was able to find a niche in a newly aspirational British film industry looking towards both Europe and the USA. Indeed, Dupont was central to BIP's policy of producing big budget, high-profile international films, and his reputation was a key factor in their ability to address world markets. With the introduction of sound, the international film took on a new form: the different language versions of the multiple-language film, which for a short time appeared to be the answer to the problem of producing talking films for the world market. With his links to both the British and German film industries, Dupont was again central to BIP's efforts to become the leading international producer of such films. For a brief moment at the turn of the new decade, with the establishment of the Tobis-Klangfilm cartel and the policy of multiple-language production, leading figures within the European film industry entertained high hopes that the introduction of sound would be the springboard from which Europe might capture the world film market from the American majors.

Dupont and the "British Hollywood"

Dupont came to England in December 1926 to work at the new British National Studios at Elstree, having severed his ties with Universal in July 1926.[2] British National was no ordinary venture. Despite its name, it was in fact a well-capitalised international initiative developed by a leading American entrepreneur, J.D. Williams, and it was no doubt such credentials that attracted Dupont. Williams had already made his mark on both the Australian and the American film industries. After starting out as a travelling showman in USA and Canada, in 1911 he set up what subsequently became the largest cinema chain in Australia, as well as a major distribution network. In 1917, back in the USA, he co-founded the First National Exhibitors' Circuit and developed it into a production/exhibition combine and one of the most powerful film companies in the country. After leaving First National over policy differences, he moved into the British film industry with his much-publicised plans to establish a "British Hollywood" at Elstree and, in the long run, to rationalise the then highly fragmented British film industry. In order to secure sufficient funds, Williams had brought in another American, I.W. Schlesinger, who owned the most important South African film combine, Africa Film Trust.[3] Although it was soon absorbed by BIP, British National was thus a major initiative not just within the British film industry, but within the international film industry as well.

Despite the eclipse of British National, Williams and Schlesinger continued to play enterprising roles behind the scenes of the British film industry, through other ventures designed either to establish British cinema as a force to be reckoned with on the world stage, or to develop a pan-European film industry. Williams was behind World-Wide, an international distribution organisation specialising in importing European films to the American market, with close links to BIP. He was also a keen supporter of multiple-language productions in the sound period. Schlesinger was on the board of BIP, and later became a significant protagonist in the sound patent wars through Associated Sound Film Industries, the British end of the Tobis-Klangfilm cartel.[4]

The Elstree studio complex—"the biggest studios yet known on this side of the Atlantic"—was a controversial venture because the plans emerged just at the moment that certain British industrialists and film-makers were optimistically proposing that a "national studio" be established.[5] For an American to be stealing their thunder was almost too much, and Williams had to make strenuous efforts to convince the trade that this was not another bid by Hollywood to take over production in this country. In particular, he did this by publicising the project in terms of its British credentials. These included his plans to attract British directors and stars now in Hollywood back to their country of birth.[6] In the end, the trade would seem to have been won over, one commentator describing the building of the Elstree complex as "the most important event our studio world has encountered in its history."[7]

Through his first signing, the up-and-coming Herbert Wilcox, Williams acquired a controlling interest in Wilcox's film *Nell Gwynn*. This lavish film starring Dorothy Gish was a sign of things to come. It was a great success when premièred in New York, where Williams himself touted it as "the finest picture made in England, and one of the best ever made anywhere." He also managed to secure American distribution for the film through Famous Players, a rare achievement for a British film at that time.[8] Wilcox himself later recalled that it was "a riotous success throughout the world."[9]

Williams's stated policy was to make quality pictures rather than genre films, adhering to the highest technical standards and drawing on the English dramatic tradition. The aim, in other words, was to make films which could compete with the best that Hollywood could offer, on the assumption that these were the only films likely to win a place in the lucrative American market. Williams justified these ambitious plans by claiming, not without reason, that many of the most successful American pictures already had some sort of European connection, in terms of personnel or the source of the story.[10] It was in this context that he hired Wilcox, Dupont, and another up-and-coming young director, Alfred Hitchcock, as well as the internationally renowned British cameraman Charles Rosher, who had made his name in Hollywood.[11] Signing "the famous producer" Dupont to British National was something of a coup for this new venture: the trade press called it "an important event in British film history."[12] There were few British directors with his experience, stylistic flair and sense of production values, and few who could claim a success on the scale of *Variété* (released in Britain as *Vaudeville*), still considered in 1928 "one of the greatest attractions shown in this country."[13] Dupont embodied the best of the international market, carrying with him the qualities of both German cinema and Hollywood, which for many commentators inside and outside the trade represented the most advanced film styles of the day.[14]

Dupont's job at British National was described rather grandiosely as Director-General of Production, and it was announced that his first film would be *Moulin Rouge*, which was to be completed before his contract expired in April 1927. Dupont's first task, however, was to work on the studio's debut film, *Madame Pompadour*, which was already in production with Wilcox directing. Various reports in the trade press give different roles to Dupont, but whatever the precise details, Dupont and Wilcox worked together on the film.[15] It was very much an international production: the stars were an American, Dorothy Gish, and a Latin-American, Antonio Moreno; the cameraman was American, the costume designer was French, and the whole project was supervised by a German (Dupont). As *Kinematograph Weekly* noted, "even the subject [is] a German comic opera version of French history. Let us accept this internationalism in the true spirit of Locarno, however, recognising the value of the ingredients of what should certainly be a magnificent production."[16] Further, the film was scheduled to be distributed internationally by Famous Players, who also put up some of the finance for the film.[17]

The Rise of British International Pictures

Williams's personal ambitions for British National were thrown into turmoil when the other members of his board ousted him amidst allegations of profligacy in his international production deals. John Maxwell, the head of one of the leading British distributors, Wardour

Films, was brought in to manage the company.[18] Maxwell's plans proved very similar to Williams's: to establish a major British combine with international aspirations. To this end, he registered British International Pictures, which took over British National (including the Hitchcock contract) in April 1927, and merged it with his existing interests.[19]

In the same week, it was announced that Dupont had parted amicably with British National and was part of a new Anglo-German initiative, Carr-Gloria-Dupont Productions. Their policy was also to make relatively high-budget international films, involving a collaboration between the British interests who controlled the company, and the German production company Gloria, with whom Dupont had been associated previously. Such arrangements were typical of pan-European co-production deals in the Film Europe period. Once again, it was suggested that the first film to be made would be *Moulin Rouge*, which Dupont had been unable to shoot at British National. It was also announced that the German cameraman Werner Brandes and his fellow countryman, the designer Alfred Junge, were to work with Dupont on the film. The company claimed that their scheduled films were assured of distribution in the United States and Europe.[20] It is surely not without significance that BIP's take-over of British National and the formation of the Carr-Gloria-Dupont company—two supreme indications of business confidence—took place only some three weeks after the Quota Bill was introduced into Parliament.[21]

Carr-Gloria-Dupont can be seen as a bid by Dupont to regain control over his career and to promote his identity as a director. In nearly two years since the production of *Variété*, he had directed only one film, *Love Me and the World is Mine* for Universal, and had been reduced to assisting another less experienced director on *Madame Pompadour*. The independence of the Carr-Gloria-Dupont venture seemed to put him back in the driving seat, but he was still thwarted in his efforts to get *Moulin Rouge* off the ground. In July 1927 there were rumours of a break-up of the company, and in August Dupont signed a new contract with BIP—yet again to make *Moulin Rouge*, as well as other titles yet to be decided.[22] *Moulin Rouge* was to be a European co-production, with one of the largest German companies, Emelka, and what was left of the Carr-Gloria-Dupont group contributing £35,000, of what was reportedly an £80,000 budget, an enormous sum in those days.[23] Without a doubt, this was a major project for the British film industry and was billed at the time as the most ambitious and lavish production ever made by a British firm.[24] Even before shooting started, the world distribution rights were sold "at record prices, such is the name and fame of Dupont after his achievement in *Variety*."[25] The film was eventually trade shown in March 1928. The historian Herbert G. Luft suggests that Dupont signed a long-term multi-million dollar contract with BIP that same year, with the intention that the films be co-produced with the German companies Emelka and Südfilm.[26] In fact, Dupont's next film for BIP, *Piccadilly* (1928), was co-funded by Gloria-Dupont-Emelka, suggesting that the original Carr-Gloria-Dupont initiative had been renegotiated, and was working under the BIP umbrella.[27]

Both *Moulin Rouge* and *Piccadilly* were British films with international aspirations reflecting those of BIP and most of the other players in the pan-European film movement. As the programme booklet produced for the premiere of *Moulin Rouge* put it,

> the eyes of the world are on Dupont, and his big effort to make for British International a film which will go to every country and show what a British film producing organisation can do when it attempts to be really international and masses the artistic resources of Europe to make one picture. . . . This is veritably an international film.[28]

Moulin Rouge featured the Russian star of several German films, Olga Tschechowa; a well-known French actor, Jean Bradin; and Eve Gray, an Australian. *Piccadilly* had two American stars in Gilda Gray and Anna May Wong, as well as the British star Jameson Thomas. The three Germans, Dupont, Brandes and Junge, dominated the production teams of both films. The internationalism of the films was not simply a question of personnel but was embodied too in the spectacular scale and the self-conscious exoticism of the films.

Dupont also attempted to establish a consistent authorial image by reproducing the showbusiness milieu and the racy romantic intrigues of *Variété*. *Moulin Rouge* was set in the famous Paris music-hall. A young man, André, engaged to Margaret, falls in love with his fiancée's mother, Parysia, a beautiful dancer in the Moulin Rouge stage-show. *Piccadilly* was set in a smart London night-club done out in a style so fashionably modernist that reviewers thought it more continental than English.[29] Its plot again linked romance to sexual transgression: a danseuse is losing her appeal with the customers after her dancing partner goes to America; the proprietor, who is also her lover, brings in a new attraction, an exotic

Chinese dancer, Shosho (Anna May Wong), who has been working as a scullery maid at the night-club. When the proprietor becomes romantically involved with her, the film explores a fascination with both working-class and ethnically other settings, linking sexual transgression to the transgression of class and ethnic boundaries.

The spectacular cosmopolitanism of these films impressed yet worried contemporary British reviewers. Their ambivalence took the form of three sets of overlapping concerns. Firstly, there was the issue of what constituted "good film-making." Dupont and his collaborators were lavishly praised for the technical perfection, the look of the films and the pictorial effects. *Moulin Rouge*, for instance, was "sumptuously mounted, exquisitely photographed," "the most glittering thing that has come out of an English studio."[30] At the same time, "if the technique is remarkable . . . plot value is negligible."[31] The film-makers were criticised for failing to make the visual attractions work for the storylines: spectacle was inadequately integrated into the narratives, and according to prevailing stylistic conventions, plot values were improperly attended to. Reviewers felt *Moulin Rouge* a thin story, unnecessarily dragged out with scenes of Paris and the night-club revue which might have been "interesting in a news pictorial, but tediously pad out a wholly inadequate plot."[32] One reviewer even suggested that the slowness with which the story unfolds meant it would be of little interest to British audiences.[33]

The second set of concerns exhibited by British reviewers were primarily moral. Reviewers objected to the "unpleasant" continental taste of *Moulin Rouge*, especially its "persistent continental sex element."[34] The film foregrounded images of desire and eroticism in a way that seemed more "continental" than British, and altogether too exotic, too risqué. It was a story of *amour fou*, a melodrama of unbridled passion and sexual transgression, in which desire and the erotic were handled both literally and metaphorically. Some reviewers complained that it was "at base a leg show," a chance to display semi-clothed female bodies as a legitimate part of the stage-show.[35] More metaphorically, the city of Paris and the dancer Parysia embody desire. In a series of touristic, picture-postcard shots of Paris and its night-life, the conventional delights of this "city of temptation," as one intertitle puts it, are laid out as a series of attractions for the spectator. The Moulin Rouge and its star performer Parysia represent this temptation through the image of the female body and the intense exchange of gazes between admirer and image.

The third set of concerns expressed by British reviewers about Dupont's films revolved around the matter of national cinema. Several writers questioned whether films so intransigently international and "euphemistically British," could really be of any relevance to the development of a properly British cinema.[36] *Moulin Rouge* was an "international hotchpotch": "one would not suspect it had any connection with this country," complained one reviewer, while another thought it "just about as unEnglish as a film could be."[37] The distinction between the needs of British audiences and those of other European audiences was clear: while "*Moulin Rouge* should please Continental audiences who like this kind of erotic nonsense," it was "the most un-British film ever made in Britain"; as such, it was implied, it would have little appeal for domestic audiences.[38] In statements such as these, the problems of the international film become all too clear.

Not only did *Moulin Rouge* not seem British, but it also did not adhere to the widely recognised standards of the Hollywood film. It lacked the swift, efficient narrative drive of contemporary American cinema and was much more concerned with atmosphere and character psychology. For the most part organised around looks rather than action, and image rather than plot, the film lingers over each moment, intensifying the psychological depths of character subjectivity and the surface gloss of the image, especially when the female body is on display. Subjectivity is handled through heavy symbolism, superimpositions, dissolves and parallel editing. These devices can, of course, be found in Hollywood films, but not quite to the extent they occur here. When André kisses Margaret, the image of her mother is superimposed over her face ("André, you've never kissed me like this before"). Later, André lies unconscious while Margaret's life is in danger because she is driving a defective vehicle; superimposed over his image is a shot of a clock and a pendulum ticking away the moments of his fiancée's life.

In the frankness with which it dealt with desire, *Moulin Rouge* was not British but (continental) European. In terms of its visual style and psychological intensity it was not American but European. It was thus a part of the Film Europe project not simply in terms of its production set-up but also through its look, its sensibility and its formal composition. The European setting—significantly one that is both geographically specific and culturally general—is important too. This is Paris, not France; but it is quite knowingly the stereotypical Paris of the emergent global village, representing exoticism, sensuality and passion, rather than a real geographical space.

The same ambivalence of space in *Piccadilly* upset some contemporary critics. Again, the setting was specific—Piccadilly, in the West End of London, with some additional scenes in Limehouse—but its representation was nebulous, and British critics again thought it too continental. The rootedness of place had become the rootlessness of the international film, in which authenticity had been replaced by the impressive allure of the exotic image. The technical achievements of the film, its spectacular finish, the artistry of the camerawork, the quality of acting from the international cast, were all much admired. The plot, however, was seen as too risqué by British critics, despite the fact that the script was by the established English novelist Arnold Bennett.

As in *Moulin Rouge*, the film plays on cultural exoticism, especially on the ethnic otherness of Anna May Wong's character, confirming that the multiculturalism of the international film was always contained by the discourses of colonialism, and the celebration of white, Western values.[39] The fascination of the narrative lies in the extent to which it explores the underworld of kitchens, Chinatown, and the East End, and dabbles in extending its cultural repertoire. But the threat of the colonial other is removed by the murder of Shosho, erasing the transgressions of class and race that the main body of the film has entertained.

Like *Moulin Rouge*, *Piccadilly* plays on the atmosphere of cultural exoticism, the details and splendour of costume and decor, and visual style at the expense of narrative energy or economy. The narrative moves fairly slowly, piling love triangle upon love triangle as numerous character touches and cameo performances retard the flow of the story. Several narratively redundant sequences serve primarily to display the female body as eroticised object of the gaze. The film draws on the prevailing American model, but its self-conscious style, constantly moving camera and aesthetic of display all suggest a European quality film. In this combination of American and European standards, one can see clearly the extent to which the film was designed for the international market-place.

Dupont's BIP Talkies

At Elstree, all the Englishmen speak broken German and all the Germans speak broken English. An international hodge-podge language is emerging; one feels momentarily that a mutual understanding between peoples is possible through film. (Did we ever

actually shoot at each other, you Elstree boys?) . . . Not only have
the films made at Elstree reached the whole world; the whole world
now seems to come to Elstree.[40]

The conversion to synchronised sound forced the internationalists in
the film industry on to a new footing. Motion pictures could no longer
be understood so carelessly as the outpourings of an international
language; they were now, precisely, "talkies," and they talked in many
different languages. Speech seemed potentially to limit the international
circulation of films to circulation within language-specific markets, and
at the same time to limit pan-European co-operation as well as
American penetration of European markets. BIP's internationalist ambitions, like those of so many other companies, were inevitably troubled
by the gradual conversion to sound. A series of temporary measures was
adopted during the transitional period. Both *Moulin Rouge* and *Piccadilly*
were subsequently re-released with synchronised music tracks, for
instance. As BIP changed over to full sound production, however, they
pioneered the practice of multiple-language production.

Dupont made three talkies for them during this period: *Atlantic*
(1929), *Two Worlds* (1930) and *Cape Forlorn* (1930).[41] These were all
made as multiple-language productions, with Dupont directing German
and French versions as well as the English versions, except for the
French version of *Atlantic*, which Jean Kemm directed in 1930, using
various scenes from the Dupont version. *Atlantic*, BIP's first venture into
multiple-language production, and possibly the first multiple-language
film screened anywhere in the world, was co-produced with Emelka,
with the French firm Etablissements Jacques Haik coming in later to
co-produce the French version at Elstree.[42] According to the German
correspondent of *The Bioscope*, the announcement that the film was to
be made in two languages "was nothing short of sensational here."[43]
Dupont developed *Two Worlds* (*Zwei Welten/Les Deux Mondes*) independently for another German company, Greenbaum Films, itself
part of the Emelka group, with BIP coming in later. The French version
was co-produced by the new Vandal and Delac Consortium.[44] The three
language versions of *Cape Forlorn* (*Menschen im Kafig/Le Cap Perdu*)
were co-produced by BIP and Emelka.[45]

Dupont's BIP films were distributed in most overseas markets by J.D.
Williams's World-Wide Pictures.[46] Box-office figures for this period
are notoriously difficult to obtain, but contemporary reports suggest that
Piccadilly was "a notable success" in the USA.[47] Both the English and

German versions of *Atlantic* were critically acclaimed by trade and press alike: *Film Weekly*, for instance, called it "a complete justification of talking pictures."[48] Both versions were also reported to be very popular with audiences in their respective "home" markets and in most other markets where they were shown—although not, significantly, in the all-important American market.[49]

Internationalism and Market Control

British National Pictures; Carr-Gloria-Dupont Productions; British International Pictures; World-Wide Pictures: the pretensions of these company names are in many ways symptomatic of the intense capitalisation, modernisation and rationalisation of the British film industry in the late 1920s and early 1930s. The Carr-Gloria-Dupont enterprise, for instance, was heralded in Britain and Germany as a major departure for international film production,[50] and is typical of the many agreements made between British and German film companies in these years. Likewise, the shift in terminology from British National to British International is vital—not so much in terms of the differences between the two companies, but in so far as it indicates something of the new confidence of the British production industry in 1927, and the global aspirations of at least some of the key players. BIP's John Maxwell argued explicitly that it was necessary to produce films for export to generate greater revenue. To do this the distribution side of the business had to gain access to a significant proportion of the world market.[51] Hence the links between BIP and the grandiosely named World-Wide Pictures, which was set up ostensibly to secure a place in the North American market for quality European films.

Access to and control of markets is obviously a vital aspect of any expanding capitalist enterprise. Horizontal and vertical integration in the home market was a way of controlling that market, while success there could be used to underwrite further efforts in export markets. The policies of British companies such as BIP are part of the internationalisation of the film industry as a whole in this period, and the Dupont contracts simply an indication of that process. The trade papers of the period record the global to-ings and fro-ings of film industry executives and the multinational deals which they made. European stars and directors changed places or visited the United States. Anyone with any ambition went to Hollywood—inevitably the main terminus for all these journeys and exchanges—for experience.[52] Rather than being unique, Dupont's contracts with British National and BIP are thus characteristic of the period.

British companies staged their bid for access to world markets on three fronts: the continental European market, the American market, and the rest of the world, which effectively meant the British Empire market. The two single most important markets outside Britain were the United States and Germany. Contemporary trade papers detail many Anglo-German deals in this period, including Gaumont-British's reciprocal distribution deal with Ufa in 1927, and BIP's acquisition of a controlling interest in the German renter, Südfilm, which also had links with Emelka.[53] A contemporary report described this as "one of the biggest Anglo-German deals since the war."[54] BIP were also involved in several other production, distribution and investment contracts, including the various co-production deals for the Dupont films.

The attraction of Germany was that it was an advanced production centre with a large well-organised market, "the most valuable of the European continental markets."[55] Südfilm provided BIP with a distributor under their control in the German market, and also gave their own films direct access to the market, since Südfilm had the right, under the German kontingent regulations, to import fourteen films per year.[56] Südfilm was thus acquired as part of the general policy of building up outlets for BIP films in Europe—they also, for instance, set up a deal with the Austrian company Sascha in 1928, and Stefano Pittaluga's Italian company in 1929.[57] It was announced later that Südfilm would also act as a producer for BIP, because of a shortage of studio space in Britain, making eight of BIP's twenty films for the year in German studios, four of them under the direction of another German, Richard Eichberg.[58] These films would be distributed in Central Europe by Südfilm. Eichberg was already well-known in Britain for his earlier success with *Crazy Mazie* (*Die Tolle Lola*, 1927) and other Lilian Harvey pictures.[59] His BIP films were to include three Anna May Wong vehicles, *Song* (1928), *City Butterfly* (1929) and *The Flame of Love* (1930).[60]

Film Europe

For BIP, these deals were just one aspect of a much broader internationalist policy, and the links with the American film industry, especially through J.D. Williams, were probably as strong as those with Germany. But the Anglo-German deals should also be seen in the context of Film Europe, and the efforts to establish a sort of pan-European cartel which might compete more equitably with the American film industry. As other contributors to this volume have demonstrated, some of the stronger German film companies had been involved in pan-European ventures since 1924. Britain, however, played only a marginal role in such ventures before the revival of the domestic production scene in 1926–7.[61] By 1928, the British trade press was awash with reports of European deals involving British companies. These deals were designed precisely to resist American domination and to increase the market share of European companies:

> the fight with America can only be started if the European countries co-operate among themselves. . . . The national field on our Continent is too small for any single country . . . We can only achieve what we want to achieve, if sales to neighbouring countries are secured on the basis of reciprocity under all conditions.[62]

BIP's executives were among those who felt that pan-European cartelisation could secure a continental market large enough to generate the sort of revenue that would be necessary to compete with the major Hollywood studios in the international market-place. Dupont's Anglo-German films were designed with precisely these ambitions in mind.

For a vertically integrated company like BIP, internationalism was a policy to be exploited at the level of both distribution agreements and production plans. BIP were caught in an ideological bind, however. Their own success as a company on the international scene owed a great deal to the general climate prevailing in the British film industry, which had been revitalised by the protectionist regulations introduced in 1927. But those regulations were only able to be carried through Parliament by the strength of the nationalist rhetoric surrounding the Bill. The trade discourse of the period was marked by two sets of terms which were if not entirely synonymous, then at least closely related. One set of terms concerned the opposition between national and international; the other opposed tradition and modernity. A national cinema was assumed to be one that reflects indigenous cultural traditions. A company strong in the international market-place, however, was assumed to be modern, forward-looking, with a strong industrial base, operating the latest production and marketing techniques, including international co-productions, international distribution and reciprocal trade agreements with foreign markets. Producing films for such markets had little to do with reproducing indigenous traditions; hence the criticisms of *Moulin Rouge* and *Piccadilly*. Yet at the same time, a company such as BIP was obliged to address itself to its primary market, and in particular secure its place in that market in ideological terms.

The Transition to Sound

BIP's internationalism and the Film Europe idea moved into a slightly different arena with the transition to sound. One important development was the formation of the Tobis-Klangfilm-Kuechenmeister cartel, the other was a new type of multiple-language film production aimed at the international market. Tobis-Klangfilm brought together interests in the radio, phonograph, electrical and film industries, and was the most powerful version of the Film Europe idea yet to emerge. With production bases in several countries, it was decidedly a European multi-national company, with the majority shareholding held by the Dutch-registered Kuechenmeister group.[63] In mid-1929 the *New York Times* reported that "the new alliance is regarded . . . as establishing a united European front against the American talkie interests."[64] It was to continue to hold this position for some years, although it was never in fact a major force in the British film industry, where American sound-film interests were more firmly entrenched.

It is debatable in this context whether BIP should be seen as a pawn or a key player in the international sound-film economy. Well-made and marketable films and highly reputed directors do not on their own constitute sufficient exchange value given the highly competitive nature of production. BIP's integration of production, distribution and exhibition interests in the British market made it attractive to overseas film companies because of the access it offered to the largest and best-organised market outside the USA. In other words, BIP was attractive because of its scope for potential exploitation; hence the various reciprocal distribution deals with European companies.

BIP did, however, respond quickly and dynamically to the coming of the talkies, converting its studios and adopting a sound-film production schedule as fast as anyone (the first British sound film is usually held to be their Hitchcock project, *Blackmail*, 1929).[65] They were not alone, since the British film industry was second only to the United States in moving rapidly to a sound cinema.[66] This was very much due to the fact that Britain was such an important export market for the American film industry that American companies had given every encouragement to British exhibitors to wire for sound.[67] In this context, it is not surprising that BIP looked to both the USA and to Europe in converting to the new conditions of sound cinema, going for American RCA equipment, but pioneering the production of multiple-language films for the European market.[68]

This twin strategy and more generally the extensive presence of American companies in Britain meant that Britain's commitment to the Film Europe idea was always going to be ambivalent. As one commentator noted at the time, "co-operation with the English film industry had always been the basis for the international film business of the Germans [but] the goals toward which the German and English were striving conflicted, since the English film industry is under strong American influence."[69] In fact, as Thomas Saunders demonstrates, German companies were equally ambivalent in their attitude towards Hollywood and the American film market.[70] Indeed, it is probably fair to say that every company large enough to make an appreciable difference in the formation of pan-European ventures was at the same time looking for an American distributor to provide access to the North American market. Links with American companies were important for the new vertically integrated majors in Britain, since showing American films in the domestic market and gaining access for British films in the American market were both considered vital sources of income. BIP's bid to maintain a reasonable share of world markets was therefore calculated not on the basis of becoming attached to an exclusively European cartel, but on the production of multiple-language films and the continuing development of overseas distribution arms. Their strategy of producing several different language versions of each sound film was a logical extension of their existing internationalist production policy.

J.D. Williams made the case for multiple-language production as a means of maintaining a stake in a world market now made up of a series of relatively small "language markets" in June 1929. He proposed setting up another huge twenty-stage studio complex near London, with the intention of making London the world centre for multiple-language talkie production—that is, production for markets beyond the English-speaking world. His central argument concerned the professed cost-effectiveness of the strategy: "The first essential is a studio of such magnitude as to enable it to meet the talking picture needs of the individual continental countries at an outlay far below what it would cost each country to make its talkies at home, and at the same time enable British talkies to be made at a similarly reduced cost." Williams proposed using two or three stages per production, leaving sets standing. Production would start on the English version, with continental co-producers present; when the necessary shooting on each set was completed, the next language unit would move in with their own star cast, so that in the end each stage would have a different language unit on it. Williams argued that overall costs per picture would be reduced, since the different language productions would share story costs, the hiring of a "master director," set-building, costumes, and the shooting of "long shots, atmospheric and crowd shots and other material, all of which is later available for use in Continental versions made in the studio." He claimed that costs per picture would be reduced by 30–40 per cent, making it economically feasible for European producers to make sound films for their own language market, which up till then had been seen as prohibitively costly.[71] Although his plans for a new studio complex came to nothing, Williams's argument was typical of how multiple-language production was justified at the time. Not everyone in the industry was so enthusiastic about multiple-language production, however. P.L. Mannock, one of the more trenchant British trade journalists, for instance, noted that, in the face of the competition offered by Hollywood,

> a sort of pan-European production is being aimed at in self-defence. But the very introduction of speech into films is a barrier. America has voluntarily abandoned to a large extent a vital ingredient of films—their internationality. This would be a big chance for Europe if silent films were being feasibly supported by finance—but they are not. Consequently Anglo-Continental talkies—almost a contradiction in terms—are being planned.[72]

Mannock was, in effect, proposing that the British film industry should exploit the contemporary instability in filmic standardisation, but that it should do so not by trying to establish a new standard via multiple-language production, but by adhering to the old standards of the silent film, with all its potential for international distribution. Such views could not last long in the trade. Even so, it was this same lack of standardisation in sound-film production for the international market by American companies in 1929 which enabled European producers like BIP to get a head start over Hollywood in the assembly-line methods of multiple-language production.[73] Indeed, there was much talk at the time of the possibility of London or Berlin becoming the world centre for multiple-language production, displacing Hollywood and New York.[74] In the end, of course, the American majors took the lead with Paramount's Joinville studio near Paris, although *Kinematograph Weekly* could still claim in 1930 that "British films lead the world in the development of the tri-lingual picture."[75]

As Ginette Vincendeau points out, the multiple-language film was as much a product of European resistance to American domination as it was of Hollywood's efforts to maintain their hegemony at the moment of the transition to sound.[76] There is, indeed, evidence of some anxiety on the part of the American trade as European producers entered the field of sound-film production. As one report noted, there was considerable demand from audiences for films in their own languages. At the time, the American film industry was experiencing severe technical difficulties in meeting such demand in an economically viable manner. Given the perceived quality and box-office success of early sound films made in Germany, France and Britain (*Atlantic* is one of the films cited in this respect), the report foresaw "considerably greater competition for American films in those countries than at any time previously."[77]

In so far as multiple-language production is a product of European resistance to American hegemony, it is yet another version of the Film Europe idea. BIP's multiple-language schedules depended on close collaboration with co-producers in the German and French industry. Even during the silent period, the international film had had to be modified for different markets, most obviously by translating intertitles into the appropriate language. Multiple-language production saw an intensification of this process, since the modification was carried out much more extensively at the production rather than the distribution or exhibition stage. After the conversion to sound, however, internationalism could no longer be established in a single shooting schedule, but was dispersed across the several casts, sound tracks and image tracks of the multiple-language film. Hence the English, German and French versions of *Atlantic*, *Two Worlds* and *Cape Forlorn*, each of them retaining the storyline and certain spectacular visual material from the "original," in so far as one exists, but each with unique dialogue scenes and casts of star quality in their own market.

Internationalism is written into the films in other ways too. *Atlantic* is set entirely in the high society world of an ocean liner which sinks after hitting an iceberg. Impressive modernist sets and—in the English version, at least—a mingling of American and British characters make for a certain cosmopolitanism. *Two Worlds* sets a melodramatic romance in the context of national and ethnic rivalries between Austrians, Jews and Russians. *Cape Forlorn* is topped and tailed with exotic scenes of Hawaiian night-life, although most of the film is set in a remote lighthouse off the coast of New Zealand. The stylistic bravura that had brought Dupont to the notice of critics in Europe and America was again strongly to the fore with striking and often spectacular camerawork and an experimental use of sound full of aural attractions. It is particularly interesting to note how Dupont was able to retain his characteristically fluid mobile camera even in these early sound films.

Into the 1930s

As a strategy for maintaining a place in the world talkie markets, multiple-language production was short-lived, in existence in a major way for perhaps two years at the most. Rachael Low suggests that the last BIP multilingual was F.W. Kraemer's *Dreyfus*, the English version of which was trade shown in April 1931.[78] Certainly, by this stage, BIP's major multiple-language producers, Dupont, Kraemer and Richard Eichberg, were no longer with BIP. Why did the multilingual practice die out, and why was there no longer a place for Dupont at BIP? Partly it was to do with the expense of sound film production, and especially of multiple-language production. Partly it was to do with the perfecting of dubbing as an alternative means of producing different language versions of sound films. Partly it was to do with America's hold on world film markets, and the relative sizes of the domestic markets of the British and American film industries. And partly it was to do with the international economic depression.

In the end, clearly, the policy was not cost-effective. The logistics of organising the necessary co-production resources and apparatus were huge. The economies of scale envisaged for multiple-language production were not enough to make it feasible to "translate" in so costly a way a film intended solely for a limited language market. Each language version required its own cast, with its own stars tailored to the particular market, while experience proved that scripts needed to be re-worked for each version.[79] International co-productions were also not always available for quota registration; the English-language version of *Two Worlds*, for instance, was not registered as a British film.[80] Nor could it have helped his own case that Dupont had a reputation for profligacy, which would not have gone down well in such a cost-conscious environment.[81]

On a broader scale, the introduction of sound, the problem of addressing foreign-language markets and the difficulties in Europe with the Tobis-Klangfilm group only increased the desire of the American majors to exploit the British market. In the case of BIP's cinemas this was made all the easier since they had already adopted RCA equipment.[82] The Hollywood studios had also pulled out of multiple-language production by late 1931, having realised that foreign-language versions could not generate a profit, and turned instead to dubbing, which was now technically sophisticated enough for general use.[83]

As Ginette Vincendeau points out, however, the rejection of multiple-language production methods cannot be explained entirely in economic terms. The method had always to balance cultural requirements against industrial standardisation. Multiple-language versions proved expensive because each version had to be culturally distinct if it was to appeal to the audiences in the language-market at which it was aimed. In the end, the economics of multiple-language production ensured that the films could never be distinctive enough, while their cultural requirements meant that they were by no means as standardised as the financiers would have liked.[84] The multiple-language film thus failed to resolve the perennial tension between a national cinema defined in terms of cultural distinctiveness and indigenous tradition, and an international cinema whose standards were established by Hollywood and imposed world-wide. From this point of view, *Atlantic*'s ocean liner, sailing through waters that lie beyond national boundaries, or the anonymity of the lighthouse in *Cape Forlorn*, are the perfect settings for the multiple-language film. And, of course, it is in large part the spoken language of these films which establishes national identity.

BIP could not afford the production values of *Atlantic* on a permanent basis. In an effort to cope with the financial demands of sound production, and with the fact that they had been unable to break effectively into the international market dominated by the American distributors, they moved gradually to a more modestly budgeted production policy. Increasingly, they concentrated on films designed to exploit sound within the domestic market (especially the "inexportable" genres of low-budget comic and musical films derived from the music-hall tradition). In this way, they hoped to use to its fullest potential the major national cinema circuit which they now owned. This effectively signalled the end of Dupont's British career, although he must have seen the writing on the wall since he had already begun negotiating his exit from Britain, and his re-entry into the German film industry.[85] The scaling down of BIP's production policy can be seen already in *Cape Forlorn*: the setting for all but a few minutes is the very basic and distinctly unglamorous lighthouse, and except in a handful of brief scenes there are only five characters in the film.

BIP, rather more modestly renamed Associated British Picture Corporation (ABPC) in 1932, remained one of the two major British combines.[86] Tobis-Klangfilm remained a powerful force on the European sound-film scene. And multiple-language films continued to be made on a small scale.[87] Of course, this was by no means the end of British cinema's internationalism. While BIP/ABPC concentrated on the domestic market, other companies looked increasingly towards the USA. Gaumont-British, the other vertically integrated major, effectively took over Maxwell's policy of high-budget productions aimed at the export market, and particularly the American market. They were also involved in various European co-productions as well as making English-language versions of several German films, a modified version of multiple-language production.[88]

Perhaps the most prominent international success for a British film came in 1933 in the form of *The Private Life of Henry VIII*, made by the Hungarian Alexander Korda: here was a new internationalism to equal Dupont's years in the British film industry, one which again had its roots in both Europe and the USA. It is perhaps not without significance that Korda had himself directed multilinguals at Paramount's Joinville studios for a time. Nor should it be overlooked that Korda was just one of many European émigrés working in the British film industry in the mid-1930s. The rise of Nazism and the relative strength of the British film industry in these years were clearly major motivations for this transnational movement of film-workers. Just as important, however, was the fact that the circumstances of Film Europe in the late 1920s had clearly paved the way for such cosmopolitan developments.[89]

Notes

This chapter substantially expands upon a paper commissioned for the 4th Internationaler Filmhistorischer Kongress, Hamburg, 21–24 November 1991, and subsequently published as "Film-Europa: Dupont und die britische Filmindustrie," in Jurgen Bretschneider, ed., *Ewald Andre Dupont: Autor und Regisseur* (Munich: Edition Text + Kritik, 1992), pp. 89–100. My thanks to

CineGraph, the organisers of the conference, for the facilities they made available, to Karel Dibbets, Ginette Vincendeau and Thomas Elsaesser for sharing ideas and materials during the preparation of the original paper, and to Peter Krämer and Nick Riddle for help with translations.

1. Quoted in *Der Film*, 7 March 1926, p. 24 (translated by Peter Krämer and Nick Riddle).
2. *Film Kurier*, 3 August 1926, p. 1, reported that he had dissolved his contract with Universal and was planning to set up an independent company to be financed by the American magnate Dohenny, father of Gloria Swanson's manager, with the first film to be *Moulin Rouge*, to star Swanson. See also *The Bioscope*, 23 December 1926, pp. 25 and 27; 20 January 1927, p. 54. Possibly Dupont went to Germany after leaving Universal; certainly he was in Germany later in the year (see *The Bioscope*, 23 December 1926, p. 25). J.D. Williams, head of British National, was also in Germany in July 1926, on a fact-finding mission to enable him to plan the building of the Elstree Studios (*The Bioscope*, 8 July 1926, p. 33).
3. See Terry Ramsaye, *A Million and One Nights* (New York: Simon and Schuster, 1986; first published 1926), pp. 679ff.; Herbert Wilcox, *Twenty-five Thousand Sunsets* (London: Bodley Head, 1967), pp. 67ff.; Kristin Thompson, *Exporting Entertainment: America in the World Film Market, 1907–1934* (London: British Film Institute, 1985), pp. 43 and 46; Benjamin Hampton, *History of the American Film Industry* (New York: Dover, 1970; first published as *A History of the Movies* in 1931), pp. 176ff. and 278; *Kinematograph Weekly*, 5 November 1925, p. 31; 17 December 1925, p. 30; 7 January 1926, Supplement, p. xviii; 22 April 1926, p. 56.
4. On Williams and World-Wide, see *Kinematograph Weekly*, 24 May 1928, p. 42b; 23 August 1928, pp. 28 and 29; 8 November 1928, p. 35; 15 November 1928, p. 32; 10 January 1929, p. 50. On Schlesinger, see Thompson, *Exporting Entertainment*, pp. 152–3; Rachael Low, *Film-making in 1930s Britain: The History of the British Film, 1929–1939* (London: George Allen and Unwin, 1985), pp. 75 and 183; and *Kinematograph Weekly*, 7 November 1929, p. 22; 14 November 1929, p. 23.
5. Supplement to *Kinematograph Weekly*, 7 January 1926, p. xviii.
6. *Kinematograph Weekly*, 5 November 1925, p. 31, and pp. 27ff.; 12 November 1925, pp. 55 and 58; 17 December 1925, p. 30; 7 January 1926, p. 69.
7. P.L. Mannock, *Kinematograph Weekly*, 22 April 1926, p. 56.
8. 17 December 1925, p. 30; 7 January 1926, p. 69; 28 January 1926, p. 48; 11 February 1926, pp. 43 and 44; 25 February 1926, p. 54; the quotation is from *Kinematograph Weekly*, 4 February 1926, p. 60.
9. Wilcox, *Twenty-five Thousand Sunsets*, p. 68.

10. See J.D. Williams, "Two keys to the American market," *Kinematograph Weekly*, 7 January 1926, pp. 55–6 (reproduced here as Document 14).

11. *Kinematograph Weekly*, 13 January 1927, p. 51; *The Bioscope*, 27 May 1926, p. 38; 15 July 1926, p. 13.

12. *Kinematograph Weekly*, 18 August 1927, p. 27; *The Bioscope*, 23 December 1926, p. 27.

13. *The Bioscope*, 22 March 1928, p. 53; *Kinematograph Weekly* earlier reported "the success of *Vaudeville*" (4 March 1926, p. 53). In 1926 Iris Barry had cited Dupont as one of only thirteen film directors likely to be known to the general public in Britain; see *Let's Go To The Movies* (New York: Payson and Clarke, 1926; reprint edition: New York: Arno Press, 1972), p. 222.

14. See, for example, the comments of Lionel Collier in *The Picturegoer*, vol. 16, no. 93, September 1928, p. 23: "If our producers . . . would study German technique . . . and American studio efficiency methods, they would make quicker strides still towards achieving what we all desire, a strong British production output.'

15. *The Bioscope*, 23 December 1926, p. 27; 30 December 1926, p. 9; 13 January 1927, p. 51 (which also noted that he had been offered the impressive salary of £12,000—though not the £42,000 suggested by the lay press).

16. *Kinematograph Weekly*, 23 December 1927, p. 15.

17. *Kinematograph Weekly*, 15 March 1928, p. 38.

18. *The Bioscope*, 13 January 1927, p. 46; Linda Wood, ed., *British Films, 1927–1939* (London: BFI Library Services, 1986), p. 7.

19. *The Bioscope*, 14 April 1927, p. 23; *Kinematograph Weekly*, 14 April 1927, p. 27.

20. Press release, April 1927 (held on "E.A. Dupont" microfiche at British Film Institute Library, London); *The Bioscope*, 14 April 1927, p. 21; *Kinematograph Weekly*, 14 April 1927, p. 34.

21. The Bill had its first reading in Parliament on 10 March 1927; the founding of Carr-Gloria-Dupont was announced in the trade press on 14 April 1927; the same issues of the trade papers reported the take-over of British National by BIP; Gaumont-British, the other emerging combine, was registered as a company on 24 March 1927.

22. *The Bioscope*, 14 July 1927, p. 22; *Kinematograph Weekly*, 18 August 1927, p. 27; *The Bioscope*, 15 March 1928, p. 42.

23. *Kinematograph Weekly*, 17 November 1927, p. 50; Herbert G. Luft, "E.A. Dupont," *Films in Review*, vol. 28, no. 6, June 1977, pp. 348–9 and 356; quotation from Joe Grossman, "Red Letter Days," in Leslie Banks *et al.*, *The Elstree Story* (London: Clarke and Cocheran, *c.* 1948), p. 86.

24. *The Bioscope*, 22 March 1928, p. 53.

25. *Kinematograph Weekly*, 18 August 1927, p. 34.

26. Luft, "E.A. Dupont," p. 348. I have been unable to verify the details of this report, but production credits on his next four films and various reports in the British trade press confirm the general tenor of Luft's claim, if not the financial magnitude of the contract.

27. See Luft, "E.A. Dupont," pp. 348 and 356.

28. Programme booklet produced for the première at the Tivoli Theatre, 1928, held at the British Film Institute Library, London.

29. See *The Bioscope*, 6 February 1929, p. 27: "It must be admitted that the Piccadilly of the screen bears a somewhat foreign appearance." *Kinematograph Weekly*, 7 February 1929, pp. 56–7: "The atmosphere created at the nightclub and Limehouse are spectacularly fine, but he has gained a continental rather than a typical London effect."

30. *Daily Mail*, 23 March 1928, p. 8; *Daily News and Westminster Gazette*, 23 March 1928, p. 7.

31. *Kinematograph Weekly*, 29 March 1928, p. 49.

32. *Daily Mail*, 23 March 1928, p. 8; see similar comments in *Kinematograph Weekly*, 29 March 1928, p. 49.

33. *Sunday Graphic*, 25 March 1928, p. 13.

34. *Daily Telegraph*, 23 March 1928, p. 8 (see also *Kinematograph Weekly*, 29 March 1928, p. 48: "some distinctly unpleasant scenes"); *Daily Sketch*, 26 March 1928, p. 21.

35. *Kinematograph Weekly*, 29 March 1928, p. 49

36. *Kinematograph Weekly*, 29 March 1928, p. 49.

37. *Daily Sketch*, 26 March 1928, p. 21; *Daily Telegraph*, 23 March 1928, p. 8; *The Picturegoer*, vol. 16, no. 93, September 1928, p. 23.

38. *Daily Express*, 23 March 1928, p. 11. For similar comments on *Piccadilly*, see the reviews collected on microfiche at the BFI Library. In addition, see *Kinematograph Weekly*, 7 February 1929, pp. 56–7; *The Bioscope*, 6 February 1929, p. 37; *Close-Up*, vol. v, no. 1, July 1929, pp. 45–7; and Marjorie Collier, "That Chinese Girl," *The Picturegoer*, May 1930, p. 26.

39. See Tim Bergfelder's chapter in this volume.

40. Karl Ritter, "Die deutschen Filme in Elstree," *Film Kurier*, 7 June 1930 (translation by Peter Krämer and Nick Riddle).

41. It was also announced that Dupont was to direct another circus film called *Tambourine* (*The Bioscope*, 24 May 1928, p. 32) and another film called *Punch and Judy* (*The Bioscope*, 10 April 1929, p. 25), although evidently neither project came to fruition.

42. See Luft, "E.A. Dupont," pp. 348–356; and *The Bioscope*, 26 February 1930, p. 24; 25 June 1930, p. 14. *Kinematograph Weekly* reported that Dupont "will take all his scenes with the English players and then repeat the same action with the German players on the same set. This will be the first time that such a thing has been done" (13 June 1929, p. 27). See also *The Bioscope*, 12 June 1929, p. 26; 17 July 1929, p. 24; *Film Weekly*,

25 November 1929, p. 4; Clarence Winchester, ed., *The World Film Encyclopaedia* (London: The Amalgamated Press, 1933), p. 351; Rachael Low, *The History of the British Film, 1918–1929* (London: George Allen and Unwin, 1971), p. 92; Ginette Vincendeau, "Hollywood Babel," *Screen*, vol. 29, no. 2, Spring 1988, p. 28, reproduced as Chapter 9 in this volume. The Hollywood studios did not move into multiple-language production until November 1929 (see Thompson, *Exporting Entertainment*, p. 160, and Douglas Gomery, "Economic struggle and Hollywood Imperialism: Europe Converts to Sound," *Yale French Studies*, no. 60, 1980, p. 83).

43. *The Bioscope*, 19 June 1929, p. 12.

44. *The Bioscope*, 17 April 1929; 26 February 1929; 8 January 1930, p. 23; 12 February 1930, p. 23; 19 February 1930, p. 23; 26 February 1930, p. 26 ('mainly a Greenbaum (Berlin) production'); see also Dr Alfred Bauer, *Deutscher Spielfilm Almanach 1929–1950* (Munich: Filmladen Christoph Winterberg, 1976), p. 47.

45. Luft, "E.A. Dupont," pp. 350 and 356.

46. *Kinematograph Weekly*, 24 May 1928, p. 42b; 23 August 1928, pp. 28 and 29; 15 November 1928, p. 32; 8 November 1928, p. 35; 10 January 1929, p. 50.

47. *Kinematograph Weekly*, 25 April 1929, p. 21; it had earlier been reported that the Secretary of the American National Board of Review had called *Piccadilly* "the finest picture yet imported from England and one of the finest pictures to reach this country" (quoted in *Kinematograph Weekly*, 17 April 1929, p. 14). Swedish press commentary on *Moulin Rouge* also makes interesting reading: "so far Europe's best film" (*Aftonbladet*); "*Moulin Rouge* is something more than a film; one would like to say it is a battle-call, a declaration of war against the American film" (*Folkets Dagblad Politiken*); "one of the most remarkable films ever shown" (*Stockholm Dagblad*); all quoted in *The Bioscope*, 24 May 1928, p. 23.

48. *Film Weekly*, 25 November 1929, p. 4.

49. *Kinematograph Weekly*, 21 November 1929, p. 24; 2 January 1930, p. 65 (on success in Denmark); 9 January 1930, p. 32; 6 February 1930, p. 32; 6 March 1930, p. 33; 14 August 1930, p. 36; *The Bioscope*, 20 November 1929, p. 29; 30 October 1929, p. 23; 11 December 1929; 1 January 1930, pp. 59 and 88; 8 January 1930, p. 26; 19 February 1930, p. 33; 25 June 1930, p. 14; 10 September 1930, p. 22. C.A. Oakley, however, claims that *Atlantic* "was not outstandingly successful in this country, the dialogue in particular being found stilted" (*Where We Came In*, London: George Allen and Unwin, 1964, p. 110). According to Luft, "E.A. Dupont," "*Cape Forlorn* was too morbid for the taste of the international public, except the Germans" (p. 350).

50. *The Bioscope*, 14 April 1927, p. 21; *Kinematograph Weekly*, 21 July 1927, p. 29.

51. *Kinematograph Weekly*, 29 March 1928, p. 29.
52. In early 1929 it was reported that Dupont's *The Berg*, later re-named *Atlantic*, was to be one of two BIP units going to the USA to make sound films, though the proposal evidently came to nothing (*Kinematograph Weekly*, 25 April 1929, p. 21).
52. *The Bioscope*, 15 December 1927, p. 21.
54. *Kinematograph Weekly*, 9 February 1928, p. 41. See also 29 March 1928, p. 40. Herr Goldsmid bought back BIP's majority holding in Sudfilm in late 1929, "but the company will continue to be the 'pivot of British films' in Germany." (*The Bioscope*, 23 December 1929, p. 24) and will continue to release BIP films, including *Atlantic* (*The Bioscope*, 23 December 1929, p. 27).
55. Colonel Bromhead of Gaumont-British, *Bioscope British Film Number*, 18 June 1927, p. 33; see also John Maxwell, quoted in *Kinematograph Weekly*, 29 March 1928, p. 29.
56. *Kinematograph Weekly*, 9 February 1928, p. 41.
57. *The Bioscope*, 1 March 1928, p. 22; *Kinematograph Weekly*, 28 March 1929, p. 33. At least one film was made under the Sascha agreement: *Bright Eyes* (1929), directed by Geza von Bolvary, starring Betty Balfour.
58. *The Bioscope*, 23 February 1928, p. 31.
59. *The Bioscope*, 23 February 1928, p. 31.
60. See the chapter by Tim Bergfelder in this volume.
61. See *Kinematograph Weekly*, 8 July 1926, p. 34; 21 July 1927, p. 29; *The Bioscope*, 5 August 1926, p. 19.
62. *Kinematigraph Weekly*, 21 July 1927, p. 29.
63. See Bruno Kieswetter, "The European Sound-picture Industry," *Electronics*, September 1930, pp. 282–4; Thompson, *Exporting Entertainment*; Staiger and Gomery, "The History of World Cinema"; Gomery, "Economic Struggle and Hollywood Imperialism"; Gomery, "Tri-Ergon, Tobis and the Coming of Sound", *Cinema Journal*, vol. 16, no. 1, 1976; Robert Murphy, "The Coming of Sound to Britain," *Historical Journal of Film, Radio and Television*, vol. 4, no. 2, 1984; and Karel Dibbets, "L'Europe, Le Son, La Tobis," *Le Passage du Muet au Parlant. Panorama Mondial de la Production Cinématographique (1925–1935)* (Toulouse: Cinémathèque de Toulouse/Editions Milan, 1988). See also pp. 15–16 above.
64. *New York Times*, 2 July 1929, p. 9.
65. *Kinematograph Weekly*, 28 March 1929, p. 25; 25 April 1929, p. 21; 13 June 1929, p. 21; *The Bioscope*, 10 April 1929, p. 25; 12 June 1929, p. 26.
66. See C.J. North and N.D. Golden, "Meeting Sound Film Competition Abroad," *Journal of the Society of Motion Picture Engineers*, no. 15, September 1930, pp. 750–2.
67. In 1926 C.J. North estimated that "American distributors get at least thirty-five per cent of their revenues from the entire foreign field by way

of the United Kingdom," while "about thirty per cent of the gross revenues to motion picture companies from all sources is obtained from their overseas trade" ("Our foreign trade in motion pictures," *Annals of the American Academy of Political and Social Sciences*, part 128, November 1926, pp. 102 and 101).

68. Kristin Thompson suggests that First International Sound Pictures, which was licensed by Tobis-Klangfilm, was a producing wing of BIP (*Exporting Entertainment*, pp. 152–3), but she may be confusing British *Instructional* Films or British *Talking* Pictures with British *International* Pictures. British Instructional merged with Pro-Patria and First International Sound Pictures in 1929 (*Kinematograph Weekly*, 9 May 1929, p. 32; 16 May 1929, p. 33); the Tobis-Klangfilm-Kuechenmeister interests were subsequently represented in Britain by Associated Sound Film Industries, in which British Talking Pictures had a 45 per cent interest (see *Kinematograph Weekly*, 7 November 1929, p. 22; 14 November 1929, p. 23; Low, *Film-making in 1930s Britain*, pp. 75 and 183; Kieswetter, "The European Sound-picture Industry", pp. 283–4; Murphy, "The Coming of Sound," pp. 148–9).

69. Kieswetter, "The European Sound-picture Industry," p. 283.

70. See his chapter in this volume.

71. "Now is the time!," *Kinematograph Weekly*, 20 June 1929, p. 23; see also *The Bioscope*, 11 September 1929, p. 22. Williams was still talking about a large-scale multiple-language studio, now inevitably known as World Studio Centre Ltd, some six months later (see *The Bioscope*, 1 January 1930, p. 71; 8 January 1930, p. 20), and in February of the same year it was announced that Maurice Elvey, one of the country's leading directors, had joined forces with Williams (*The Bioscope*, 5 March 1930, p. 19). Williams was never short of plans. Earlier in 1929, *The Bioscope* reported that trade leaders had been discussing his plans for a British Motion Picture Academy, offering training and artistic and technological promotion (17 April 1929, pp. 22–3).

72. *Kinematograph Weekly*, 2 May 1929, p. 20.

73. Vincendeau, "Hollywood Babel," pp. 29–30.

74. See Hansard, 22 July 1930, vol. 241, cols 1949–50; *Kinematigraph Weekly*, 30 May 1929, p. 17; 20 June 1929, p. 23; *The Bioscope*, 1 January 1930, p. 70; 5 March 1930, p. 19. On the other hand, in Germany, there was an equivalent expectation that "Germany will be the future center of production in Europe" (Ludwig Klitsch of Ufa, quoted in *Lichtbildbühne*, 29 July 1930, itself translated and quoted in Bruce Murray, *Film and the German Left in the Weimar Republic*, Austin: University of Texas Press, 1990, p. 151).

75. See Gomery, "Economic Struggle and Hollywood Imperialism," pp. 83–4; Vincendeau, "Hollywood Babel"; Dudley Andrew, "Sound in France: The

Origins of a Native School," *Yale French Studies*, no. 60, 1980, pp. 98–103; and Thompson, *Exporting Entertainment*, pp. 160ff. Quotation from *Kinematograph Weekly*, 7 August 1930, p. 21.

76. Vincendeau "Hollywood Babel," p. 28.
77. North and Golden, "Meeting Sound Film Competition Abroad"; the quotation is on p. 750; the reference to *Atlantic* is on p. 755.
78. Low, *Film-making in 1930s Britain*, p. 93.
79. See, for example, "European Co-operation," *Kinematograph Weekly*, 14 August 1930, p. 49; see also Joseph Garncarz's chapter in this volume.
80. See Low, *Film-making in 1930s Britain*, p. 403.
81. See, for example, the comments of Joe Grossman, former studio manager at Elstree concerning Dupont's early British films, "Red Letter Days," pp. 87–8.
82. Gomery, "Economic Struggle and Hollywood Imperialism," pp. 82–3.
83. Ibid., p. 84; see also Appendix C in Rudy Behlmer, *Inside Warner Bros (1931–1951)* (New York: Simon and Schuster, 1985), pp. 341–3.
84. See Vincendeau, "Hollywood Babel," p. 29.
85. There were reports in the German trade press in 1930 that Dupont was to be appointed Head of Production at the Emelka studios. One paper, *Der Film*, argued vociferously against appointing an artistic director in financial control at a time of such economic difficulty (22 February 1930, p. 1), and perhaps because of this politicking the appointment never materialised (see also *The Bioscope*, 26 February 1930, p. 24; 19 March 1930, p. 28; and *CineGraph*, Lieferung 17, "E.A. Dupont," B2). It had already been reported that *Cape Forlorn* "will be E.A. Dupont's final BIP subject" (*Kinematograph Weekly*, 1 May 1930, p. 31).
86. *Kinematograph Weekly*, 28 September 1933, p. 16.
87. Vincendeau, "Hollywood Babel," p. 29; also Garncarz in this volume.
88. See Andrew Higson, "'A Film League of Nations': Gainsborough, Gaumont-British and 'Film Europe'," in Pam Cook, ed., *Gainsborough Pictures* (London: Cassell, 1997), pp. 60–79.
89. On developments in Britain in the mid-1930s, see Andrew Higson, *Waving The Flag: Constructing a National Cinema in Britain* (Oxford: Clarendon Press, 1995), ch. 4; and Higson, "Way West: Deutsche Emigranten und die britische Filmindustrie," in Jörg Schöning, ed., *London Calling: Deutsche im britischen Film der dreissiger Jahre* (Munich: Edition Text + Kritik, 1993), pp. 42–54.

13

Negotiating Exoticism
Hollywood, Film Europe and the Cultural Reception of Anna May Wong

Tim Bergfelder

As a historical case study for the problems facing integrated European film initiatives, the developments of the "Film Europe" project of the 1920s and 1930s provide a number of poignant lessons. Torn between intense competition with Hollywood, rapid changes in international production methods and technology, and self-defensive national interests, the initial enthusiasm for creating a pan-European cinema turned ultimately to inertia. To focus exclusively on the overall economic failure of this endeavour is, however, to deny the Film Europe project both its internal coherence and its cultural legacy. Many recent critical evaluations of the period have been written from the vantage point of a vested interest in a particular national cinema. The conclusions such accounts reach are not neccessarily wrong, but they tend to adopt a rather selective perspective. Thus, a scholar commenting on Hollywood's global aspirations would obviously emphasise America's overall market and cultural dominance in Europe.[1] Such an approach, however, ignores the fact that, despite an American stronghold in European distribution, not all Hollywood films achieved the same degree of popularity in different countries.[2] This approach tends to underestimate the sometimes considerable level of resistance to the cultural impact of "Americanism" and the perceived "invasion" by Hollywood, not to mention the more specific and localised objections against particular kinds of representations, genres and stars.

Some historians of French, German or British cinema, on the other hand, view the internationalism of this period as a culturally insignificant or at best transient phase after which a "self-contained" national cinema

would reconstitute itself.[3] These arguments reinforce rather homogenis-
ing and narrow concepts of national cinema and national identity. They
also replicate the same cultural defence mechanisms and protective
strategies which hampered the objectives of Film Europe in the first
place. It is perhaps not surprising that the main issues surrounding Film
Europe (cultural hybridity versus national authenticity; transnational
film production versus national film cultures) are being revisited in the
late 1990s with renewed urgency. In a period witnessing the contradictory drives of media globalisation, multiculturalism and the violent
re-emergence of nationalism, the developments of Film Europe assume
a particular significance.

My intention here is not to dispute either the influence of Hollywood
on the developments of Film Europe (though it was not a monolithic
one), or the vital importance of nationally specific discourses. If we want
to understand the Film Europe project in its own right, however, and
to make productive use of its history for today's concerns, we require a
critical perspective which acknowledges the dialogic and transnational
nature of this endeavour. My chapter will concentrate primarily on the
relationship between the German and British film industries and their
respective cultural contexts. I will look at the ways in which the Film
Europe project attempted to negotiate these national contexts and the
impact of Hollywood with its objective of fostering "international" stars
and films. I will focus in particular on the brief European career of the
Chinese-American actress Anna May Wong between 1928 and 1934.

In a recent article on the industrial developments between Europe
and Hollywood in the 1920s and 1930s, Thomas Elsaesser invoked
the emblematic images of the "traveller" and the "voyage."[4] These
two tropes are highly appropriate for many narrative trajectories and
protagonists of Film Europe's international productions. Instead of
circumscribing geo-political entities and centred national identities,
these narratives frequently focus on the margins, boundaries and
junction points of Europe. Locations may include train stations (*Rome
Express*, 1932), ports (*Song*, 1928), aeroplanes (*FP1*, 1932), nightclubs
(*Piccadilly*, 1928), or exotic islands (*Rapa-Nui*, 1927). These places are
more or less self-contained, and clearly separated from a homeland or
national community that might be implied but which is always absent.
These spaces are inhabited by outsiders, people of indeterminate
national identities, who have either just arrived at these extra-territorial
locations or are about to depart from them. Many of these narratives
include lengthy transnational journeys.

The films' spatial fluidity is also frequently accompanied by temporal indeterminacy. A good example of this is the genre of the "film operetta" which, in its associations with the Austro-Hungarian empire, invokes multicultural connotations as well as a nostalgic vision of the European past (see, for example, *Congress Dances*, 1931). What appears to be a lack of historical and geographical specificity in this context could, however, be interpreted as a distinctive marketing strategy. The nostalgia for a continental European cultural heritage provided a potential selling angle both within Europe and for the American market. The box-office success of Ernst Lubitsch's *Old Heidelberg* (1927) and similar productions had proven that there was a viable market for this kind of refashioned Old-European folklore in the United States.[5] The motif of transnational mobility and the idea of the multicultural melting pot also attempted to emulate the international appeal of the Hollywood product. After all, quite similar narrative and stylistic strategies of blurring geographical and cultural specificities had helped to make Hollywood films adaptable in global markets.

The theme of "uprootedness" evident in these international films finds its corrolary in the circumstances of their production. During the 1920s and 1930s, a wide spectrum of film-makers were involved in transnational and transatlantic traffic, ranging from technical personnel to directors, producers and stars. The American industry, in particular, benefited from the widespread mobility of this period and actively encouraged it with its "trophy hunts," as Fritz Lang famously called the practice of Hollywood agents and producers travelling to Europe to sign up promising talent.[6] These transfers were not always as successful or as permanent as the celebrated cases of Greta Garbo or Marlene Dietrich, and there are a number of actors who resumed their European careers after a brief interlude in Hollywood (for example, Lilian Harvey and Emil Jannings).

To focus on the irresistible lure of the American industry for Europeans is in any case to ignore the considerable transnational traffic that went on within Europe during this period. For actors and actresses, such movements were arguably more risky than for those production artists for whom cultural specificities and language barriers were less crucial.[7] In fact, very few truly "European" stars emerged even during the brief heyday of Film Europe. Lilian Harvey may be considered such an exception. British by birth, she became one of the most successful stars of early German sound cinema.[8] Ideally suited for German and British language versions, her Anglo-German accent also appealed to

French audiences, who found her flawed French diction a particularly charming asset.[9] However, most of the other German or French stars who attempted to conquer other national audiences had to compete not only with the indigenous stars of these countries, but also with the star appeal of the imported Hollywood product. A few stars managed to cross over into other cultural contexts, sometimes accompanied by a significant change in their star persona and status, as can be seen in the case of the British careers of Conrad Veidt, Elisabeth Bergner, or Anton Walbrook.[10]

In the same way that Hollywood tried to sign up Europeans, European film industries attempted to attract Americans to the other side of the Atlantic. From the 1910s onwards, the German film industry had tried with varying success to build imported American actors such as Fern Andra, Betty Ammann and Louise Brooks into stars. In the late 1920s and early 1930s, the British film industry similarly attempted to capitalise on the importation of Dorothy Gish, Gilda Gray and Esther Ralston.[11]

The Chinese-American actress Anna May Wong is one of the most intriguing examples in this category of transatlantic stars. Wong's brief stardom in European films (mainly Anglo-German co-productions) between 1928 and 1934 illustrates some of the most pertinent issues in the relationship between Film Europe and Hollywood during this period. It bears witness to the struggle for economic and cultural hegemony over European markets, which was fought not only in studios and executive boardrooms, but also in the contemporary film press. It exemplifies the translations and transfers of cultural products and discourses between European countries, and the conflicting urges within various national film cultures both to counter and to imitate the industrial practices and conventions set up by Hollywood. In the following pages I shall look at the ways in which Wong's European career fitted into the overall production strategies and cultural parameters of the Film Europe project. I shall also analyse how her star persona was adapted and reconstructed for European audiences, negotiating the concepts of Hollywood stardom and Americanness with notions of the "exotic other" and the Oriental woman. One of the most intriguing aspects of this analysis is the difference in the ways in which German and British commentators appropriated that star persona, articulating it differently according to the prevailing discourses of each specific culture.

Before discussing Wong's European films in more detail, I will outline briefly her earlier career in Hollywood and some of the discourses that differentiated this period from what was to follow. Born in 1905 (according to other sources, 1907) in the Chinatown district of Los Angeles, where her family had been living for three generations, Wong entered films as an extra in 1919.[12] Her first starring role came in 1922 in the first ever Technicolor feature production *Toll of the Sea*, an adaptation of the Madame Butterfly story relocated from Japan to China. Despite the film's success, she was once more assigned by a succession of different studios to minor supporting roles in a variety of genres. Of these films, the only one that can be seen as having had a significant impact on her career was the Douglas Fairbanks production *The Thief of Baghdad* (1924), in which she played a Mongolian slave girl. Though definitely marked as an exotic other in her various roles, Wong nevertheless appeared in a variety of different ethnic guises, for example as an Eskimo in *The Alaskan* (1924) and as the native American princess "Tiger Lily" in *Peter Pan* (1924).

The ethnic eclecticism evident in Wong's early roles fitted perfectly with Hollywood's appropriation of exoticism in the 1920s and 1930s. Mark Winokur has argued persuasively that Hollywood's representation of ethnicity in this period was heavily influenced by the Art Deco movement through the mediation of contemporary fashion styles and advertising aesthetics:

> By stylizing the accoutrements of ethnicity, Deco allowed its audience to maintain a safe distance from it. While using the patina of exoticism to sell everything, Deco aestheticized colonialism. Ethnic motifs became floating signifiers because they were streamlined in such a way that their original frames of reference disappeared . . . Stylization replaced the social realities of the present with the past.[13]

According to Winokur, this process of stylisation reached its perverse if logical climax by the end of the 1920s, when Hollywood's representation of the ethnic other displaced "real" ethnicity altogether, replacing ethnic actors with white performers portraying exotic characters. In the context of Hollywood exoticism and the consumption value associated with it, Wong had to remain a repressed presence for, as Winokur suggests,

> Anna May Wong's version of Art Deco does not work because she

is authentically Asian; history begins to creep back into her character with an unacceptable realism, a history that would, by the 1920s, include the Chinese Immigration Exclusion Act, the ill treatment of Chinese in the United States, the special exclusion of Chinese women, and the subsequent picture bride and prostitute phenomena.[14]

It is clear from this quotation and from the social contexts it invokes that Hollywood negotiated its version of exoticism within the historically specific cultural climate of American nativism. In other words, cinematic exoticism cannot be seen as a universal and immutable ideological practice. Neither can it be exclusively determined by textual factors such as *mise-en-scène* or narrative trajectories, or even by industrial strategies. Rather, it is a constantly renegotiated and shifting discourse, dependent to a large degree on the specific frameworks of reference available at the level of reception. Hollywood's aesthetic of stylising the exotic into a global consumer product was taken up in Film Europe's narratives, which sold decentred identities to different national audiences. The appeal of Wong's star image within the context of Film Europe was that it had the potential to combine the attractions of pure exoticism with American modernity, thereby circumventing the problems of national specificity which faced many indigenous European stars. In this respect, Wong's trajectory paralleled that of her black contemporary Josephine Baker, who became a niche star in French cinema after her cabaret successes in Paris and Berlin.[15] As in the American context, however, nationally specific social discourses and repercussions, which were extraneous to the films themselves, complicated the perception of Wong's star image.

Anna May Wong arrived in Berlin in the spring of 1928, under contract to the producer-director Richard Eichberg. The reasons and circumstances of her move are open to speculation, although her Hollywood career was stagnant enough for her to consider other options. It is possible, though again not verifiable, that Wong's contact with the German film industry was initiated through her connection with the German expatriate director Paul Leni, for whom she worked in Hollywood on the Universal detective thriller *The Chinese Parrot* (1927).

Eichberg's signing of Wong can be seen as part of a wider strategy in his designs for pan-European productions. Frequently described as one of the "most American of German directors," Eichberg had made his name since the 1910s as the producer and director of action-orientated, fast-paced, spectacular and often exoticist genre films.[16] Working on the periphery of the major companies (producing independently, but with the financial support of larger firms such as Emelka and Südfilm), he was also renowned in the industry for establishing new stars (his discoveries included Ellen Richter, Lee Parry, Lilian Harvey and the operetta singer Martha Eggerth). By the time Wong arrived in Berlin, Eichberg had found production partners in London and agreed on a deal with British International Pictures (BIP) to film a series of sound productions in Elstree. In return, BIP would co-produce silent films made by Eichberg in German studios. Apart from her potentially transnational appeal as a Hollywood star and as an exotic, the signing of Wong had another practical advantage, in that her linguistic ability enabled her to be cast not only in English, but also in German language versions.

The first film to be made under these arrangements was the silent feature *Song* (a.k.a. *Schmutziges Geld*), shot at the UFA studios in Neubabelsberg, starring Wong and the German actor Heinrich George, and released in the summer of 1928. The film set the narrative pattern for most of Wong's subsequent appearances in European productions, making her the personification of female as well as racial suffering in narratives that almost always end in her death. The prototype and model for these narratives, intertwining colonialism and sexual conquest, is the Madame Butterfly story, widely circulated at the time in various literary, stage and film versions.[17] In *Song*, Anna May Wong plays the eponymous heroine, "a human piece of driftwood" (according to an intertitle) who falls in love with a rough cabaret artist and professional knife-thrower who abuses and exploits her devotion. When he is temporarily blinded, Song cares for him in disguise, wearing the perfume and fur coat the man associates with the woman he once loved. By the time he finds out the truth and finally repents, Song has been fatally wounded in a sword dance performance in a night-club.

The film was clearly intended to be a showcase for Wong's star qualities; the cinematography emphasises her face in expressive close-ups, and the show numbers both display her dancing talent and provide opportunities to present her androgynous physique in a number of revealing costumes. Her great acting moments in conveying joy and tearful resignation are always played out in complete isolation. In relation to the narrative trajectory of her character, this kind of *mise-en-scène* could be seen to construct a separate space for her performance, establishing her as an outsider not only in the story, but also in visual terms. Consequently Wong's otherness remains contained, her exoticism rendered "safe." The extraterritorial location in which the narrative is set, and which conforms to the archetypal spaces of the international film I referred to earlier, adds a further distancing device.

Song not only established a stylistic and narrative formula for Wong's European films. It also set a pattern for their critical reception in the German and British press which was symptomatic of different national attitudes towards the Film Europe project in general. On the whole, German reviews conveyed a sense of much greater support and enthusiasm for the international ambitions of the European film, provided that the German industry played a central role in these endeavours. This support for internationalism, however, remained decidedly Eurocentric and drew its line at the Hollywood product. Particularly in more specialised publications such as *Film-Kurier*, the threat of American dominance translated frequently into pejorative comments on the formulaic nature of American films, and occasionally even on the Anglo-Saxon "character" (which would, significantly, include the British). Thus, attempts by European film-makers to imitate Hollywood conventions were viewed at least with reservation, if not suspicion. Eichberg's style of direction and production was often scrutinised in this respect.

If we look at the press reception of *Song* and similar films in Britain, on the other hand, we find that the the project of integrating European film industries and styles hardly featured at all. Particularly in publications aimed at exhibitors and at a mass (rather than cinephile) audience, a continental European influence on British cinema was seen as far more alien and even menacing than any Hollywood production could be. A too manifest continental style carried with it connotations of being too high-brow or too theatrical for general audience appeal. Thus, while Richard Eichberg was admonished by his German critics for following American models too closely, the British press had exactly the opposite complaint. In contrast with the position of the German press, the threat that the American film industry posed was perceived by British critics to be predominantly economic rather than cultural. Consequently, the adoption of Hollywood conventions (in other words, competing with Hollywood on its own terms), alongside a pragmatic use of continental technology and know-how, was seen as a valid production strategy.[18] The long-term prospect envisaged with this strategy was less an integrated European film culture than an economically fortified national British cinema.

Despite these fundamental differences in principle, the British and German press reception of Wong's films did converge in one respect. In both countries, reviewers could agree on the appeal of Wong herself. It was her star image which helped to alleviate the problems of narrative and style the films might cause in different national contexts. At least in this respect, the signing of Wong was a success for the international European film, although it proved a shortlived one.

For German reviewers, *Song*'s melodramatic narrative was seen as having a universal appeal, and its production and Wong's performance were perceived as great contributions to Germany's international film aspirations. The film publication *Lichtbildbühne* proclaimed: "This German film will, in its success, announce the glory of Anna May Wong throughout the world as one of the greatest film artists."[19] The evening newspaper *8-Uhr-Abendblatt* was more possessive: "Anna May Wong is ours now, and we won't let her go again."[20] All of the reviews saw Wong's performance as the centrepiece of the film. Noting the international influences on this co-production, Ernst Jäger wrote in the *Film-Kurier*: "All the collaborators agreed on the proceedings, all differences disappeared, since the film's only intention is to serve the woman in front of the camera."[21]

The British press reception of *Song* (released in September 1928 as *Show Life*, and in the US as *Wasted Love*) equally centred on Wong's performance, praising it as a "masterpiece of subtlety."[22] For *Kinematograph Weekly*, it was a major point of appeal that this was "Anna May Wong's first starring vehicle," though with regard to the narrative it predicted that "it is a picture to attract high-class rather than popular audiences."[23]

By the time *Song/Show Life* was released in Britain, Wong was working in Elstree on the BIP production *Piccadilly*. Like *Song*, this film betrays its international aspirations. Directed by the German E.A. Dupont, who had scored an international success in 1925 with *Variété/Variety*, it starred two American actresses (Wong and Gilda Gray), and drew on the technical expertise of the German production artists Werner Brandes (cinematography) and Alfred Junge (art direction).[24] The script, by the bestselling British author Arnold Bennett, centred on the love intrigues behind the scenes of a fashionable London night-club. Wong plays the scullery-maid Shosho who eventually becomes the new dancing star at the club, replacing the former headline act (Gray) in the affections of the audience as well as the night-club owner. In the end, Shosho is shot dead by a jealous Chinese friend.

The Bioscope saw the fact that the film was a British production as an important selling angle.[25] Not all reviews were so enthusiastic about such a cosmopolitan endeavour being labelled "British." The journal *Close-Up* set the tone for a critical attitude in Britain towards co-productions and multinational film teams, a tone which would grow considerably in the coming years:

> This is the perfect British film. That means to say it was made by a German, with a German cameraman; its leading lady is an American of Polish extraction and its second lady an American of Chinese extraction; the leading man is English and the second man Chinese; the art direction is by a foreigner and the story is by Arnold Bennett, who must have had the toothache or an Income Tax paper at the time . . . There must be something wrong somewhere.[26]

After *Piccadilly*, Wong returned to Berlin and Eichberg to appear in her last silent film, *Großstadtschmetterling* (a.k.a. *Asphaltschmetterling*, a.k.a. *Die Fremde*, 1929). Like their previous collaboration, *Großstadtschmetterling* was a tailor-made star vehicle for Wong and a full-blown melodrama, this time set among the demi-monde of artists and gamblers in Nice. Wong, dressed in the latest Parisian fashions, starred as a show-girl who falls in love with a struggling artist, becomes his model and steals money for him, only to renounce her love in the end when she realises that he has found another woman. The film was again co-produced by BIP, and featured the French actor Gaston Jacquet as the principal villain.

Overall, *Großstadtschmetterling* was well-received in Germany and Britain (where it was released as *Pavement Butterfly*), and the highest praise was given to Wong's performance. The *Film-Kurier*, however, noticed an unhealthy foreign influence on the film's narrative and style, which it identified as "the Anglo-American icing on this cinematic cake, which covers the story of the poorly treated Chinese girl in saccharine." The same review also registered some exasperation with the way in which all recent Wong films seemed to dispense with her character in the course of the narrative: "The Eichberg team did not dare to let a happy white man share the same bed as the undressed body of a Mongolian woman. The erotic hypocrisy of this German Anna May Wong film could have originated in an English boarding school for girls."[27]

It is very likely that the film's perceived chasteness had more to do with the producers' desire not to get into trouble with the British Board of Film Censors (BBFC) or to jeopardise the movie's British release. Narratives of miscegenation were seen by the BBFC as highly problematic if not taboo, particularly in view of possible distribution in the colonies of the British Empire. As Ruth Vasey has pointed out, British censorship provisions regarding mixed-race relationships were largely concerned to maintain prestige in their colonial possessions.[28] All of Wong's European films, irrespective of whether they were shot in Berlin or London, adhere to a large extent to these British sensibilities. In those cases where miscegenation occurs, the repercussions for Wong's screen characters are drastic and seemingly inevitable —all of these films end in her death. In *Großstadtschmetterling*, where her relationship with a white man is not consummated, she survives.

When *Großstadtschmetterling* was released in Britain later the same year as *Pavement Butterfly*, the transition to sound in the British film industry was almost complete. Trade papers such as *The Bioscope* had by this time already established separate categories and columns for silent features, thereby signalling their phasing out. Eichberg's relationship with BIP thus entered a new stage, the production of big-budget international sound features, to be shot at Elstree simultaneously in three different language versions (English, German, French). The French co-production partner in this plan was Etablissements Jacques Haik. The first film to be made under these agreements was the Anna May Wong star vehicle *The Flame of Love* (1930, released in France as *Hai-Tang/L'Amour maitre des choses*, and in Germany as *Hai-Tang/Der Weg zur Schande*). The plot resembled those of Eichberg's previous films with Wong: as the member of a dance troupe touring Tsarist Russia, she suffers from her unrequited love for a dashing officer. To save her brother from execution, she sleeps with a villainous arch-duke; unable to live with this shame, she commits suicide shortly afterwards.

The production of the film was a difficult and costly experience. The tight planning necessary for multiple-language film-making proved to be especially problematic for Eichberg, a director who was renowned for his practice of improvising on the set.[29] Though completely in charge of the German version, he was given co-directors for the English and French versions (Walter Summers and Jean Kemm). There were also variations in the casting of the male lead (John Longden and Franz Lederer) and other supporting roles. Wong, however, played the lead and spoke her lines in all three versions.

Despite all efforts, the film was a resounding flop, and the French partner Etablissements Jacques Haik cancelled future involvements with Eichberg.[30] The British press reception of *The Flame of Love* was decidedly lukewarm. Wong was still seen as a major asset, and her "drawing power" and "very effective performance" were highlighted among some positive comments regarding the use of sound technology; but the film as a whole left no great impression: "This story . . . can hardly be said to rouse the emotions, as all the characters belong to the stage rather than to real life."[31]

The German press was equally disappointed with the film, though for different reasons. Despite positive comments on the German diction Wong had acquired for the role, her unique performance style was seen as incompatible with the new medium of sound. *Lichtbildbühne* noted: "Anna May Wong's incredibly subtle and expressive art, enhanced by her exotic appeal, was one of the greatest treasures of the silent film. With deepest regret one cannot help noticing that a lot of this appeal has been lost with the introduction of dialogue."[32] The critic Ernst Jäger came to a similar conclusion: "Anna May Wong was a silent miracle. Her intellectual diction merely adds curious novelty." The same review also included some bitingly ironic remarks about what the critic perceived as the film's British cultural influence:

> It is interesting to see how well the producer Eichberg has understood the English mentality: eroticism without sex-appeal, exoticism without miscegenation; instead, tender melodies are played on the piano in a homely setting. Hai-Tang's lover is her brotherly friend, he watches her dancing, alluringly undressed, but apart from that—nothing happens between them. This is truly English.[33]

What becomes apparent in these different national reactions is that the British press was clearly more eager to embrace the new possibilities of the sound film. This required a move towards new narratives and a greater degree of screen realism—in short, a greater synchronisation with Hollywood's current sound productions. *Flame of Love*, however, was seen to resemble too much the melodramatic histrionics of silent and continental European cinema. The German press had precisely the opposite concern, and was far more reluctant to accept a technology which was seen to debase an essentially visual medium, a cherished narrative style, and the "true" qualities of silent screen acting. Since this had a detrimental effect on the perception of Wong's star image in Germany, one of the few common denominators between the German and the British reception of her international films disappeared. In its place, national differences resurfaced more strongly than ever.

The critical and box-office failure of *Hai-Tang/The Flame of Love* effectively ended Wong's career in pan-European and multiple-language productions. Eichberg announced in 1930 his future plans for collaborations with BIP, which included another star vehicle for her.[34] This project never materialised, though Eichberg continued his European co-production ventures well into the 1930s, before emigrating to the United States in 1938.[35] Wong remained in the public eye with various stage performances in Britain as well as on the Continent, but with no immediate film offers from either Germany or Britain, she returned to America in 1931.[36]

Hollywood did not perceive her as star material, and she was immediately assigned to minor roles, mostly in B-pictures. A notable exception was her supporting part as Marlene Dietrich's Asian confidante in Josef von Sternberg's *Shanghai Express* (1932), a prime example of Hollywood's own version of the "international" film. The international casts of Film Europe were replicated in *Shanghai Express*, with European actors who had become Hollywood studio properties (the German Marlene Dietrich and the British Clive Brook). But instead of Wong, the "real" ethnic other, it was Dietrich who became the locus of exoticism. As Mark Winokur has argued, "Hollywood was particularly interested in the use of white women as exotics. Their particular ethnic designation is almost irrelevant in their films, or at least very subordinate to the quality of "exotica."[37]

Wong returned to Britain in 1933, but the three films she made here in the next two years can only be seen as a postscript to her earlier European career. The first of these, *Tiger Bay* (1934), was a low-budget production directed by J. Elder Willis for Wyndham Films. Neither the story nor Wong's performance had a great impact on critics or box-office results. Wong's next British feature, *Java Head* (1934), directed by J. Walter Ruben for First Division, was notable insofar as its narrative reversed the thematic priorities of Wong's earlier "international" efforts. In its focus on a colonial merchant dynasty in nineteenth-century Bristol, and in its realistic period detail, the film was more a heritage melodrama than an exploration in cultural hybridity. Recentred from the borderlines to the issues of home, family, tradition and Britain, it reduced Wong's character (the Manchu wife of one of the sons) to a colonial trophy.

Java Head represented a quite different production and narrative strategy from the one adopted in the earlier pan-European films. Instead of blurring national distinctions, it consciously projected and propagated an image of (British) nationhood. As Ruth Vasey has pointed out, British producers became "more interested in the ready-made English-speaking market of the British Empire than in the problematic European arena."[38] Selling national narratives abroad thus became a strategy that was to be followed throughout the 1930s, most prominently in Alexander Korda's imperial epics.

Wong's final appearance in British films was in the Gainsborough production *Chu Chin Chow* (1934), an adaptation of Oscar Asche's long-running stage musical version of the Arabian Nights story "Ali Baba and the 40 Thieves." In its truly bizarre kaleidoscope of ethnic signifiers, blurred national identities and cultural registers, *Chu Chin Chow* was something of an epilogue to the internationalist style of Film Europe. It featured the Hollywood actress Wong as a treacherous slave girl next to beturbaned English music-hall comedians, operetta stars, and a German theatre and film actor (Fritz Kortner) in black face-paint. The fake-Oriental sets were built by the German-Hungarian art director Ernö Metzner and the dance sequences were staged by the choreographer of the London Festival Ballet, Anton Dolin.

The circumstances for such a production had, however, changed dramatically from the days of Eichberg's and BIP's collaborations. Kortner and Metzner, both Jewish, were effectively exiles from Hitler's Germany rather than professional travellers by choice. European film industries were in the process of reorganising themselves around notions of "national identity" rather than Film Europe, while Hollywood continued to assert its influence. The take-over of the German film industry by the Nazi state provides the most drastic and extreme example of this reorientation. By this time British cinema had rediscovered the appeal of Britain's imperial glory. It had also found a solidly national icon in the dowdy, working-class Northerner Gracie Fields.[39] Remnants of exotic glamour, on the other hand, were incorporated into the "home-grown" star image of Jessie Matthews which did not require ethnic otherness.[40] Moreover, this use of exoticism conformed broadly to the ethnic exclusiveness adopted by Hollywood. With such a shift towards addressing a defined national community and selectively targeted cultural markets, the hybrid extravaganza of *Chu Chin Chow* had passed its sell-by date. Wong subsequently returned again to the United States, her career by now in sharp decline. By the early 1940s she worked for "poverty row" studios such as Republic and PRC, and except for three minor film appearances and a shortlived TV series in the 1950s, she had effectively retired from film-making by the late 1940s. Still only in her fifties, Wong died in 1961.

In concentrating on the economic contexts and critical reception of Anna May Wong's films, I have tried to show how her involvement in European cinema originated and functioned within the overall framework of inter-European industrial co-operation and competition with Hollywood. A more exclusively textually-focused analysis of her films might, perhaps, centre much more on the sado-masochistic gender dynamic underpinning all these narratives of abuse, victimisation and self-sacrifice. It might identify the visual and narrative strategies the films employ to isolate and ultimately to exorcise the disturbing racial and sexual "other." The problem with this approach is that it tends to homogenise the cultural diversity of reading strategies and preferences which are surely crucial in understanding the trajectory of Film Europe. Any study which prioritises a film's supposedly immanent meaning ultimately displaces historical spectators and their cultural context in favour of the relationship between an "ideal" spectator and a relatively stable filmic text. While such a critical strategy may have genuinely progressive aims, it inevitably assumes the problematic notion of fixed identities and a fairly schematic interaction between films and audiences.

Equally problematic would be a critical discourse which transfers all agency solely to specific production strategies and industrial contexts. To argue that the developments of Film Europe are reducible to purely economic considerations implies that one can separate an industry from the complex social structures and cultural discourses in which it operates. Such an interpretation, however, would have to deal with the considerable paradox that Wong's films, however textually organised towards the exclusion of the "other," were simultaneously made with the intention of promoting the same "other" as a star. As I have shown, the critical response to this objective was contradictory. If we want to determine the cultural impact of the Film Europe project in general and Anna May Wong in particular, and if we want to know how concepts such as "hybridity" or "pan-nationalism" were perceived at the time, we need to consider more than production contexts and the films themselves. In shifting attention from production to reception, a multitude of different "texts" and meanings emerge, mediating historically determined positions, aesthetic conventions and expectations, social and other public discourses, and marketing strategies.

In the following pages, I shall look at some of the different meanings that emerge when British and German commentators take hold of and interpret Anna May Wong's star persona. These differences can be accounted for in terms of the culturally specific frameworks of reference which inform these receptions. What will become clear is that the international film, designed to cross national boundaries within the Film Europe network, is not a static text, loaded with determinate, immanent meanings, but a complex and hybrid text, capable of being taken up in different ways within each specific cultural context. Anna May Wong's star persona becomes a key signifier within this context of cross-cultural reception.

Perhaps not surprisingly, the contemporary European reviews of Wong's films rarely touch upon the narratives' ideology of racial representation. The comments by Ernst Jäger in the *Film-Kurier* quoted above are notable exceptions, though they are primarily directed at highlighting perceived sexual attitudes in Britain and Germany. Instead, the most common framework of reference is provided by the conventions and expectations of the silent melodrama, as ubiquitous descriptions such as "touching," "moving" and "emotional" attest. Most of the appraisals of Wong's performance focus on her acting technique, highlighting her body language, her movements and gestures, and how these elements convey particular emotions. In other words, Wong is constructed in the reviews of her films as the archetypal "tragedienne" of silent cinema, seen in the tradition of (and frequently compared with) stars such as Lillian Gish or Asta Nielsen.

The emphasis on a seemingly universal "art" of acting can be seen as a critical strategy for disavowing cultural difference. Within the economic framework of the Film Europe project, this strategy was crucial in making any star image exportable to a wide range of different countries. That German and British reviewers associated Wong predominantly with her acting seems to imply that this strategy worked, at least up to the point of the introduction of sound when different expectations of screen acting emerged in both countries. However, such a discourse had to be reconciled with Wong's quite visible ethnic otherness. Articles and publicity material on Wong approached this issue quite differently in Germany and Britain, but what emerged in both countries was a projection of contemporary, culturally specific conceptions of identity and exoticism onto Wong's perceived star persona.

Since the late nineteenth century, exoticised concepts of China were explicitly used in public discourses in Britain to justify Anglo-American colonial and imperial interests, and later to strengthen the ideology of the "yellow peril" in the face of Chinese immigration. The way in which Wong's ethnicity was perceived in Britain was largely dependent on these extra-textual discourses, and how they were negotiated with the image Wong projected on screen. In Germany, the link with China and the Far East was far less tangible: Germany had lost all of its colonies at the end of the First World War, and Asia had never been a significant factor in its imperialist endeavours. For Wolfgang Reif, the exoticist discourses on Asia in Germany in the 1910s and 1920s had highly conflicting and divergent ideological agendas.[41] On one hand, exoticist projections could be used as a critique of Western industrialisation and modernisation. On the other hand, exotic motifs formed an integral part of modern leisure and consumption—in the marketing of tourism, fashion and design.[42]

It is worth noting that none of Wong's European films rooted her in a distinctly Chinese or even Asian setting, or gave her roles a past or family background. In most cases they carefully avoided assigning her screen characters a definite "Chinese" identity. Even in those films where she is identified as Chinese, this identity is frequently offset by adding "Western" characteristics to her image, such as her eclectic fashion style, or her "shimmy" dance in *Piccadilly*. In contrast, Wong's off-screen persona and her ethnicity were discussed in Germany in more or less essentialist terms. Though there are occasional comments on her career in Hollywood, she is not generally referred to as an American citizen, or even as a Chinese-American, but as resolutely Chinese. However, the way in which this perceived ethnicity is portrayed through constant references to and comparisons with Chinese art, crafts and literature, effectively turns Wong into an artefact herself, a figurine in the style of Western chinoiseries. An interesting as well as representative example of this can be found in the art director Ali Hubert's portrait of her, published in 1930:

> She personifies the spirit of the great Li-Tai-Pe, and brings to life for us the tales of 1001 nights . . . On her tender and youthful body, expressing every movement with the indescribable grace of the Oriental woman, towers her head which, although completely Mongolian, is beautiful by European standards. Her eyes, for a Chinese unusually large, deep and dark like a Tibetan mountain lake, gaze with enormous expressiveness. Her well-shaped, slightly

voluptuous lips form a striking contrast to the melancholy darkness of her eyes. Her hands are of outstanding beauty, slim and perfectly formed. Only a Van Eyck or a Holbein could capture her on canvas . . . Externally, she appears American: smart, confident, and chicly dressed. But inside, she is purely Chinese, wearing long hair, and believing in reincarnation, convinced that in her next life she will swing as a humming-bird on the branches of a pepper-tree.[43]

One could say a great deal about the fetishising tendency of this portrayal, and its almost literal "mapping" of Anna May Wong's body. What is equally interesting, however, is the eclecticism of its ethnic and national descriptions (Oriental, Mongolian, Tibetan, etc.) and its cultural references (Arabian Nights, Chinese poetry and nature drawings, classical Western painting). Though ostensibly intended to authenticate Wong's Chinese identity and to render her Americanness as merely superficial, the portrait actually refers back to a much more diffuse concept of projective exoticism.[44]

The persona that comes across in the British press portraits and articles on Wong during her years in Europe is quite different, and allows for a more complex, though no less ambivalent, consideration of ethnic issues. Most importantly, Wong's Americanness becomes a much more central aspect of her identity. Almost all British portraits make lengthy references to Wong's roots, upbringing and early career in Los Angeles. In a *Picturegoer* portrait, programmatically titled "East meets West in Anna May Wong," the author, Marjory Collier, goes to great lengths to define the actress as a contemporary Western female film type, the "flapper," and stresses her "American timbre." The article reverses the "external–internal" distinction set up by Hubert, claiming that, "exteriorly, Anna May Wong is Chinese. But her mental outlook is almost entirely Western."[45] Written ostensibly for a female readership (the article was published in a column entitled "Screen Types—As A Woman Sees Them"), Collier correlates contemporary ethnic and gender discourses. She argues that the sexual freedom Wong projects both in her films and in her off-screen persona is incompatible with the repressed social status of women in Chinese society.

Having established the otherness of the perceived "pure" Oriental woman, the article then sets up Wong as an intermediary: "Hybridism is inherent in all her screen performances, and for all her distinctive face and features one hesitates to pronounce her as representative of a type." Collier juxtaposes a number of quite different sets of reference:

the acceptable Asia of the chinoiserie ("gardens, mountain scenery, Sung vases and K'ang Hsi plum blossom jars"), the unemancipated state of Chinese women, and Wong's hybrid identity. It is, however, precisely the link between Wong's "hybridism" and her American identity which allows Collier to celebrate the actress as a modern and progressive female icon which defies stereotyping. Wong's Americanness distances her from the more "threatening" manifestations of hybridity and miscegenation, resulting from breakdowns in colonial segregation or from Chinese immigration (in the contemporary British crime novels of Edgar Wallace and Sax Rohmer, for example, mixed-race Chinese were marked as particularly villainous). In its clear separation of value-different conditions and contexts for hybridity, this reading strategy might explain why progressive attitudes towards Wong herself could be accommodated to the discourses of the "yellow peril."

There are several other British star portraits of Wong during this period which adopt a seemingly "progressive" attitude, as long as issues of repression and prejudice can be located elsewhere. In an interview article in *Film Weekly* Wong complains about the stereotypical representation of Chinese characters in Hollywood: "I was so tired of the parts I had to play . . . Why is it that the screen Chinese is nearly always the villain of the piece? And so crude a villain—murderous, treacherous, a snake in the grass."[46] She then continues to express her gratitude to British producers, who have offered her roles that were "real, not film, Chinese." The article as a whole leaves an ambivalent impression. Its title, "I Protest," strengthens Wong's plea for more complex representations, although it is debatable whether her European film roles actually achieved this. In any case, the piece is accompanied by a photograph of Wong that can be seen to undermine the text's apparent intentions: she is portrayed as staring menacingly sideways, and clutching a dagger in her hands, thus visually conforming to the Hollywood stereotype of the "Dragon Lady" the article sets out to critique.

For the historian of the 1920s and 1930s, the transnational trajectory of Wong's career provides an exemplary case study of the economic and cultural limitations and possibilities of the Film Europe project. As exotic other and as an American, Wong provided a solution to the problem of finding a star image which would be acceptable to a wide range of different national markets. It is evident from these examples that the marketing and mediation of Anna May Wong's star persona in Europe did not add up to a coherent or unified image. The fact that her image was bound up in contradictions and conflicting cultural perceptions was not an obstacle, however, but part of the success of the image. In other words, Wong's public persona (blending her on- and off-screen image) functioned to some extent as a free signifier which could be imbued with various meanings. The casting of Wong was thus one of the strategies which enabled her films to be relatively successful in different European markets, which was one of the central aims of the Film Europe initiative.

From the beginning Wong's European producers and directors aimed at rendering her exotic identity indeterminate and therefore widely consumable. At the same time, Wong's image was taken up within and adapted to specific Orientalist and social discourses in different countries. Wong's German reception showed a particular resistance to accepting the American dimension of her persona, and interpreted her instead within an essentialist framework of Asian ethnicity. The British press, on the other hand, was more perceptive of her status as a "cultural hybrid," but dissociated this notion from any social significance within a British context. Indeed, wider socio-political considerations, and especially those of British colonial prestige and immigration, imposed a constraint on the kinds of narratives that were permissible for Wong. A way out of this minefield of ethnic discourses was to concentrate on Wong's performance style as an example of a universal art of acting. Yet again, an Anglo-German consensus of what constituted screen presence and acting quality was only in evidence up to the advent of sound, after which national expectations began to differ sharply. To a large extent, it was this development in audience preferences, coinciding with the economic implications of the conversion to sound, that ended Wong's transnational appeal.

For a time, however, Anna May Wong's roles in various pan-European co-productions demonstrated one of the ways in which the international film could succeed. Contrary to those who see the international film as a bland or standardised product with no national-cultural roots, the focus on reception indicates the extent to which such texts could be taken up meaningfully within different national-cultural contexts. Anna May Wong's star persona articulated the complex hybridity which rendered those texts more or less acceptable in the different markets that made up the pan-national distribution networks central to the Film Europe project. Wong thus expressed an identity capable of appealing successfully across cultural and national boundaries.

To consider Anna May Wong's European career a success for Film

Europe, if only a temporary one, still requires some qualification. German and British critics frequently referred to enthusiastic audience feedback and to a firm base of Wong admirers. Yet, compared to the top Hollywood and national stars of the time, and despite the hyperbole in the contemporary press, Wong never became a major box-office attraction. Her role as a cultural rather than a purely economic emblem for Film Europe is, however, significant. If we want to assign any cultural importance or legacy to the Film Europe project, and if we want to avoid national parochialism, we need to reassess the multiple interactions between films, secondary discourses, and audiences. In such a process, the perception or negotiation of identity and "otherness" becomes crucial. As my case study suggests, particular film cultures are constructed through culturally diverse interpretive strategies at the level of reception. Some of these strategies may conform to what we perceive as dominant representations or social discourses (the expression of an imagined national consensus, ideology, or unity) but they may also reveal interesting sidelines, diversions and productive contradictions. This approach might help to widen the scope of what any national cinema could encompass—in terms of transnational narratives and stars, or cross-cultural influences. One of the most important lessons of the Film Europe project might be that such "interferences" form an integral part of any film culture. In concentrating on this aspect, we might arrive at a more inclusive view of film history, and become less dependent on static hegemonic oppositions.

Notes

Thanks to Peer Moritz, Hans-Michael Bock, and Deniz Göktürk for their help and inspiration.

1. The standard text for this approach is Kristin Thompson, *Exporting Entertainment: America in the World Film Market, 1907–1934* (London: British Film Institute , 1985).
2. See, for example, Joseph Garncarz, "Hollywood in Germany. The Role of the American Film in Germany," in David W. Ellwood and Rob Kroes, eds, *Hollywood in Europe: Experiences of a Cultural Hegemony* (Amsterdam: VU University Press, 1994), pp. 94–135.
3. See, for example, Ginette Vincendeau, "Hollywood Babel," in *Screen*, vol. 29, no. 2, pp. 24–39 (reprinted in this volume); for a German pespective see Uta Berg-Ganschow, "Deutsch, Englisch, Französisch," in Wolfgang

Jacobsen, ed., *Babelsberg. Ein Filmstudio* (Berlin: Argon, 1992), pp. 169–174. See also Andrew Higson, *Waving The Flag: Constructing a National Cinema in Britain* (Oxford: Clarendon Press, 1995).

4. Thomas Elsaesser, "Heavy Traffic: Perspektive Hollywood: Emigranten oder Vagabunden," in Jörg Schöning, ed., *London Calling: Deutsche im britischen Film der dreißiger Jahre* (Munich: Edition Text + Kritik, 1993), pp. 21–41.

5. See my "Surface and Distraction. Style and Genre at Gainsborough in the late 1920s and 1930s," in Pam Cook, ed., *Gainsborough Pictures* (London: Cassell, 1997), pp. 31–46.

6. Elsaesser, "Heavy Traffic," p. 23.

7. See my "The Production Designer and the Gesamtkunstwerk," in Andrew Higson, ed., *Dissolving Views: Key Writings on British Cinema* (London: Cassell, 1996), pp. 20–37.

8. See Christiane Habich, *Lilian Harvey* (Berlin: Haude und Spener, 1990). See also Katja Uhlenbrok, "Verdoppelte Stars. Pendants in deutschen und französischen Versionen," in Sibylle M. Sturm and Arthur Wohlgemuth, eds, *Hallo? Berlin? Ici Paris!: Deutsch-französische Filmbeziehungen 1918– 1939* (Munich: Edition Text + Kritik, 1996), pp. 155–68.

9. Uhlenbrok, "Verdoppelte Stars," p. 157.

10. On Veidt, see Sue Harper, "Thinking Forward and Up. The British Films of Conrad Veidt," in Jeffrey Richards, ed., *The Forgotten Thirties* (London: Tauris, 1998).

11. See Andrew Higson, "Way West. Deutsche Emigranten und die britische Filmindustrie," in Schöning, ed., *London Calling*, p. 47.

12. For more biographical information on Wong, see Philip Leibfred, "Anna May Wong," in *Films in Review*, vol. 38, no. 3, March 1987, pp. 146–53; and his "Anna May Wong's Silent Film Career," in *Silent Film Monthly*, vol. 3, no. 2, February 1995, pp. 1–2.

13. Mark Winokur, *American Laughter: Immigrants, Ethnicity and 1930s Hollywood Film Comedy* (Basingstoke: Macmillan, 1996), p. 202.

14. Ibid., p. 212.

15. Nancy Nenno, "Femininity, The Primitive, and Modern Urban Space: Josephine Baker in Berlin," in Katharina von Ankum, ed., *Women in the Metropolis. Gender and Modernity in Weimar Culture* (Berkeley: University of California Press, 1997), pp. 145–62.

16. See Corinna Müller, "Richard Eichberg," in Hans-Michael Bock, ed., *Cinegraph. Lexikon zum deutschsprachigen Film* (Munich: Edition Text + Kritik, 1985), pp. D1–6.

17. See Gina Marchetti, *Romance and the "Yellow Peril." Race, Sex, and Discursive Strategies in Hollywood Fiction* (Berkeley: University of California Press, 1993), pp. 78–89.

18. See my "The Production Designer and the Gesamthunstwerk."

19. *Lichtbildbühne*, 25 August 1928.
21. *Film-Kurier*, 21 August 1928.
22. *The Bioscope*, 19 September 1928.
23. *Kinematograph Weekly*, 20 September 1928.
24. Andrew Higson, "Film Europa: Dupont und die britische Filmindustrie," in Jürgen Bretschneider, ed., *Ewald André Dupont. Autor und Regisseur* (Munich: Edition Text + Kritik, 1992), p. 46. See also his chapter in this volume.
25. *The Bioscope*, 6 February 1929.
26. *Close-Up*, vol. 5, no. 1, July 1929.
27. *Film-Kurier*, 11 April 1929.
28. Ruth Vasey, *The World According To Hollywood, 1918–1939* (Exeter: University of Exeter Press, 1997), p. 148.
29. *Filmjournal*, February 1980, p. 22.
30. *Filmjournal*, February 1980, p. 22.
31. *The Bioscope*, 12 March 1930.
32. *Lichtbildbühne*, 28 February 1930.
33. *Film-Kurier*, 27 February 1930.
34. *Film-Kurier*, 1 February 1930.
35. Müller, "Richard Eichberg."
36. See Leibfred, "Anna May Wong," p. 2.
37. Winokur, *American Laughter*, p. 209.
38. Vasey, *The World According To Hollywood*, p. 91.
39. See Higson, *Waving The Flag*, pp. 142–62.
40. See my "Surface and Distraction."
41. Wolfgang Reif, *Zivilisationsflucht und literarische Wunschträume. Der exotistische Roman im ersten Viertel des 20. Jahrhunderts* (Stuttgart: Metzler, 1975); see also his "Exotismus und Okkultismus," in H.A. Glaser, ed., *Deutsche Literatur: Eine Sozialgeschichte, Band 9: Weimarer Republik–Drittes Reich: Avantgardismus, Parteilichkeit, Exil* (Reinbek: Rowohlt, 1983), pp. 155–68.
42. Eckhart Schütz, "Autobiografien und Reiseliteratur," in Bernd Weyergraf, ed., *Hansers Sozialgeschichte der deutschen Literatur, Band 8; Literatur der Weimarer Republik 1918–1933* (Munich/Vienna: Carl Hanser, 1995), pp. 549–601.
43. Ali Hubert, *Hollywood. Legende und Wirklichkeit* (Leipzig: E.A. Seemann, 1930; reprinted Heidelberg: Das Wunderhorn, 1988), pp. 106–7.
44. For a similar view, see Walter Benjamin, "Gespräch mit Anna May Wong. Eine Chinoiserie aus dem alten Westen," in Tilman Rexrodt, ed., *Walter Benjamin. Gesammelte Schriften. Vol. 4, Part I* (Frankfurt: Suhrkamp, 1972), pp. 523–7.
45. *The Picturegoer*, May 1930, p. 26.
46. *Film Weekly*, 18 August 1933, p. 11.

Documents

In this section of the book, we have included a number of previously inaccessible documents, including internal trade association correspondence, trade paper editorials and articles, to illuminate our contributors' discussion of transatlantic film relations. The documents are grouped into three topics, and each group is prefaced by a short introduction.

Group 1: German Conceptions of "Film Europe"

- Document 1: "European Monroe Doctrine," *Lichtbildbühne*, no. 23, 1 March 1924 (translated by Brenda Benthien) 328

- Document 2: "Hebdo Film and the 'Monroe Doctrine,'" *Lichtbildbühne*, no. 53, 10 May 1924 (translated by Brenda Benthien) 330

- Document 3: "Europe—America," *Lichtbildbühne*, no. 71, 21 June 1924 (translated by Brenda Benthien) 331

- Document 4: Felix Henseleit, "A European Front," *Reichsfilmblatt*, no. 10, 6 March 1926, pp. 3–5 (translated by Thomas J. Saunders) 333

- Document 5: Helmuth Ortmann, "Film-Europe II," *Reichsfilmblatt*, no. 17, 24 April 1926, pp. 2–4 (translated by Thomas J. Saunders) 335

- Document 6: Felix Henseleit, "Film Europe," *Reichsfilmblatt*, no. 30, 24 July 1926, pp. 74–5 (translated by Thomas J. Saunders) 338

- Document 7: Karl Wolffsohn, "Europe for the Europeans," *Lichbildbühne*, no. 247, 16 October 1926, pp. 9–11 (translated by Thomas J. Saunders) 341

Group 2: Kontingents, Quotas and the American Response

- Document 8: Chronology of European Quota Regulations, 1921–34, from Kristin Thompson, *Exporting Entertainment: America in the World Film Market, 1907–1934* (London: British Film Institute, 1985), pp. 211–12   347

- Document 9: Oscar Solbert, Report to Will Hays, Autumn 1925   349

- Document 10: Edward G. Lowry, "Certain Factors and Considerations Affecting the European Market," Internal MPPDA memorandum, 25 October 1928   353

- Document 11: French Film Decree of May, 1928   379

- Document 12: Note from US State Department to the governments of France, Germany, Czechoslovakia, Austria, Hungary, Italy and Spain, April 1929   381

- Document 13: Lars Moen, "The International Congress: A Constructive Help–or a Futility," *Kinematograph Weekly*, vol. 148, no. 1156, 13 June 1929, p. 25   382

Group 3: European Access to the American Market and the International Film: J.D. Williams and Erich Pommer

- Document 14: J.D. Williams, "Two Keys to the American Market: Quality and Variety will Open all Doors," *Kinematograph Weekly*, 7 January 1926, pp. 55–6   387

- Document 15: J.D. Williams, Speech at the Annual Conference of the National Board of Review, 26 January 1929   390

- Document 16: Erich Pommer, "The International Picture: A Lesson on Simplicity," *Kinematograph Weekly*, 8 November 1928, p. 41   392

- Document 17: Erich Pommer, "The International Talking Film," *Universal Filmlexikon*, ed. Frank Arnau (Berlin, 1932), pp. 14–15   394

Group 1: German Conceptions
of "Film Europe"

The following texts offer representative examples of the discussion of Film Europe in the German trade papers. While scarcely models of tight argumentation, and with one exception comfortably vague in their recommendations, they have a fairly consistent rationale and share a number of features common to writing on this theme. Most salient is the pre-occupation with America. Already by the mid-1920s Germany's post-war encounter with Hollywood had acquired a narrative of its own, from anticipation to infatuation to disillusionment to recrimination. That narrative was also applied to the wider European experience of American film. And it was precisely in the assertion of common responses to Hollywood that Film Europe found its logic. Likewise conspicuous is the blend of economic and cultural interests which allegedly dictated European film collaboration. Concerns to preserve a cinematic identity distinct from America dovetailed neatly with the desire to regain market shares lost to America since the Great War. The prospect for both might be elusive, but it could hardly be dismissed as unreasonable when presented in this way, particularly given that the European exhibition circuit roughly equalled the American in size. Finally, German treatment of Film Europe did not always distinguish scrupulously between domestic issues and European ones. What was good for Germany was often assumed to be good for the continent as a whole. Although it would be an exaggeration to see in this hegemonic aspirations, and one-sided to assume that Germany was alone in embracing Film Europe for national reasons, it does accurately reflect the primacy of self-preoccupation over European consciousness.

Thomas J. Saunders

Document 1: "European Monroe Doctrine," *Lichtbildbühne*, no. 23, 1 March 1924 (translated by Brenda Benthien)

Much is being said about the relationships between America and Germany and how they are, ought to be, or might be. These opinions are not always entirely objective, nor are they always informed by a thorough familiarity with the situation. The discussion seems suspect when chauvinistic phrases weave themselves into the argument. But one thing is clear: the importation of American films into Germany increases in direct proportion to the decrease in the number of German films imported into America. To put it more precisely: instead of the three or four films that were formerly exported to the United States from Germany, not one German film is currently being accepted.

We might consider the reasons for this. It has yet to be established that the American film producers have banded together conspiratorially to prevent the import of German productions altogether. It is alleged that fear of German competition has moved them to do so. We will doubtless do more justice to the facts if we keep these rather exaggerated rumours to a minimum. No nation in the world can be pleased to see its own products forced up against a wall by imported foreign goods. But America has no need to fear this. The "German menace" is certainly overestimated more in Germany than in America itself.

The issue takes on a new aspect when one asks whether the American public's lack of interest in German film might not be the reason for its sparse distribution. There is no basis for this supposition either. German films have proven to be very successful in America. If the opportunity created by their success has not been used to open the gates to German productions, the fault lies with the Germans, not with the Americans. We have noted here on numerous occasions that it is unworthy, as well as absolutely false from a business point of view, for such a large production country as Germany to allow German–American film sales to be handled by agents who have been sent over here. If we wish to sell valuable goods which need individual treatment, such as films, we must be prepared to assume any costs for their import. Rather than taking occasional trips to the United States, German companies should have established affiliates acquainted with the marketing and sales of the product (even if only in the form of an association) long ago. A branch in New York is no more expensive nowadays than one in Hamburg. But it seems as if our industry does not wish to learn from the experiences of other industries, and that it prefers sporadic business in Berlin to systematically organised sales in an importing country. In these pages we have often discussed the serious international damage this does to the financial position and economic prestige of the German film industry. It cannot be denied that American film is beginning to make considerable headway in Germany. It must also be admitted that American film currently poses a financial threat to Germany. This is because, as we know, the structure of the American film market ensures that the producer covers his production costs and makes a suitable profit from domestic sales, so that he is in the position of setting the prices for all importing countries without needing to consider the financial well-being of his company. Today the American businessman who wants to introduce his films into Germany can allow himself to hand over his films for a pittance and use his revenue for advertising, since the only "profit" he is interested in making lies in securing market share, not in the current sales price. To repeat: the American businessman is in the fortunate position of being able to undercut every bid, since he is entering Germany with a film on which he has already covered his expenses.

We can learn from this! It is politically sound to walk into a nation which one hopes to conquer economically with the gesture of someone spreading goodwill throughout the world. There can be no dispute that we must put ourselves in the same situation as America; we must get German films into America, not for immediate financial gain, but in order to secure the market. This strategy of assuring market share must be pursued with absolutely Napoleonic energy, if German film production is to regain its former prominence. Such a strategy also represents a way of strengthening the German film industry in the world as a whole.

Now that the goal has been established, we must outline the marching route. Although Germany is once again a serious factor in the conduct of the film industry, it is nevertheless impossible for us to cover the costs of first-rate performances (not to mention securing a return on investment) through domestic sales. This is just as true for other nations that produce films. It can generally be said that with the exception of the United States, no nation in the world is able to cover its negative costs in its own country. Once and for all, this characterises the weakness of European film-producing nations by comparison to America—so long as they march separately.

Everything depends on prominent European industrial heads acknowledging that their primary weakness lies in their fragmentation—even if it is a "splendid isolation." In our opinion, the new guiding principle for European film politics must be: band together, to even out the financial weaknesses of individual markets through competition. If we can bring together the leading personalities of the influential European nations at one table, and if we can establish the general principle of regulating mutual distribution according to existing levels of production, we will enter a new era in the conduct of film commerce that includes the goal we have outlined. Let us begin by discarding all utopian ambitions—we are practising *realpolitik*—and let us declare at the outset that what is important is the basic agreement on film sales and distribution, not the details. This agreement must be sought, and it must be attained. It does not represent an innovation in business conduct, but only an extension of practices already in force in domestic commerce and in the European block!

In those nations not under American control it will be possible to cover production costs and make a profit only through European solidarity. A reasonably well-financed film will be able to break into the American market only through the same strategy; unconcerned by the need to cover production costs, we can sell the film using the same methods as the American producer in Europe. Our motto must be: create the European film, conquer the market, secure the market share—no more profit-making at any price! It is no longer the fluctuating dollar that determines the European producers' sales policies, but rather a healthy economic attitude towards the maintenance of competition, strategies for advertising, and the best and most effective launch of the product. After this initial period, true business can begin, just as, for the Americans, true business in Germany only begins once they have secured their market share.

Lichtbildbühne is immune from accusations that it is propagating nationalistic alliances because it has taken this stance since its inception, without budging an inch. We do not call for chauvinism, either in Germany, Europe or America. The European bloc of film-makers whose formation we advocate has no axe to grind with the United States. It is intended solely to allow economically weaker producers to enter the world arena armed with the same weapons as the Americans. Such a suggestion will and must seem just to the citizens of the United States, who proclaim the slogan of their democratic nation at every opportunity: everyone deserves an equal chance! There is no doubt that the American industry will come together at one table with the representatives of such a bloc, without reservations, to ensure the solidarity of the international film industry. For this is the general goal toward which all elements of the film industry strive, consciously or unconsciously. Moves in this direction can be found everywhere. The opportunity will present itself in the near future for an experienced hand to gather up the scattered threads.

Document 2: "Hebdo Film and the 'Monroe Doctrine,'" *Lichtbildbühne*, no. 53, 10 May 1924 (translated by Brenda Benthien)

In its most recent issue, *Hebdo Film* takes up our thoughts on a "European Monroe Doctrine" and concludes that its consequences would be German hegemony within a Film Europe. Our worthy French colleague hereby shows that he has not entirely understood the fundamental idea of our campaign, which we have summed up in the catch-phrase "European

Monroe Doctrine." We merely discussed European solidarity as a means of stabilising all of Europe's film industries, and how we might make use of it. There was no discussion of hegemonic intentions on the part of any country, and if indeed one nation produces quality films in greater quantity than another, it can hardly be faulted for it. In any case, this would not affect the idea behind the above-mentioned catch-phrase, which we have frequently and energetically promoted; the point is to help even the weaker among us find justice.

Document 3: "Europe—America," *Lichtbildbühne*, no. 71, 21 June 1924 (translated by Brenda Benthien)

Anyone who has been reading the European trade papers carefully in recent weeks will have reached the conclusion that the European film industry's position in relation to the American market has fundamentally changed. The call is for active film policies; we have begun to use our own resources. The tenor of all these publications is the same—we must create a situation in which Europe faces America as a competitor on equal footing.

Historically speaking, this movement began with our article entitled "European Monroe Doctrine," which an American trade paper termed "the agenda of European film activism." We have nothing to add to our earlier position.

While on his educational trip abroad, our publisher confirmed that no other problem faced by the European film industry has touched the American mentality as has that essay. The idea of a European union, which we have proposed, has not been rejected at all. The Americans are certainly sympathetic to the fact that every industrialist in the world wants to do business. Moreover, from the first we have emphasised that our idea of a European film union contains no barbs aimed at America. We have continually pointed out that the pooling of European film talent serves the sole purpose of creating normal film relations with America.

There is no doubt that the normal trade conditions sought by European film producers are currently being opposed by the Americans. The reasons for this are very simple. First, the businessman wants to restrict his market to his own product; but in addition there is a psychological element common to the perception of many American producers. They see film as a product with specific material features that allow it to be monopolised, like oil or rubber. This conception is false. If a film that electrifies the audience is made anywhere in the world today, audiences all over the world have a right to see it. If isolated industrialist power-mongers think they can keep such films from their audience forever, their hopes will one day come crashing down around their ears.

There is certainly no official boycott of Europe, but the United States is almost hermetically sealed against imports. This rejection is not at all directed toward one country in particular, but rather toward all of Europe.

This policy sets itself a very clear goal. The hope is to weaken, or even completely shut down, European film production. In this context it should be mentioned that an attempt will be made to bring European cinemas under American control, thereby ensuring American domination over production.

There is proof in numbers. In 1922, 425 European films were imported and duty-paid, but only six were actually sold. This is a striking indication of American interest in European film production.

The situation can only be changed by a resolute consensus among European film producers. We must be clear on the point that we will only be able to trade with America when we succeed in appearing as competitors on an equal footing. This is only possible if we reserve Europe for European film production, just as the Americans provide for their country from their own production. We must strive with all means possible to cover the European countries' demands for film with mutual film exchange, thus rendering the American film superfluous. Only when the Americans are forced to gain access to the European market on a basis of peaceful understanding will the American market be opened up to European films.

We can only mention psychological prerequisites briefly in this context. At the point where European film production wishes to replace American films, it must assume an internationalist point of view, making films which will not just find acclaim in their own countries. We are not in the least suggesting that the English should imitate German films or the Germans American ones. The producers must only refrain from making films that are attuned to the needs of one individual country, as with the German problem films.

One of *Lichtbildbühne*'s favourite ideas, which we have mentioned repeatedly since the end of the war, is that the leading film-makers of the world might meet at an international congress to initiate a general agreement on international film trade.

Depending on how things stand, we might need to alter the plan to do without American representation, although we believe it to be important in any case to hear the voice of American film producers at this opportunity. Communication is always preferable to conflict. Clear understanding will enable us to better expend the energy that a conflict always requires.

The agenda of this congress, which we have suggested might take place in London, must include a call for the opening of the American market to Europe. Considering the state of flux in which the European film-producing nations currently find themselves, now would seem to be the most appropriate psychological moment for the call to such a congress. The idea of an international film congress ought to be promoted by all film-makers who care about the future of our industry. There are even many sensible Americans who are greatly interested in it.

We have reached an agreement with America's leading film trade magazine, *Motion Picture News*, to promote the settling of open questions about world film at an international congress. We can already point out that world-renowned European trade journals will co-operate with us and *Motion Picture News* toward this goal (see the *Hebdo Film* article entitled "On the March!" in the current issue).

There is no question that European film production will increase when it finds a market in Europe itself. This automatically requires restricting the import of American films, which will no longer be in such demand. For Germany, this entails fixing quotas—a method which is in urgent need of revision, as we have already stated. The quota system currently permits American film imports to earn more than four million marks in revenue. We need only mention this figure to show that this condition is untenable, from the points of view of both film production and general monetary policy.

The slogan that must dominate European thinking in questions of films today is unity. The coming weeks must bring forth practical suggestions for changing current conditions to produce those which we have recommended.

It may be assumed that the European public will step forward with positive suggestions in the very near future.

Document 4: Felix Henseleit, "A European Front," *Reichsfilmblatt*, no. 10, 6 March 1926, pp. 3–5 (translated by Thomas J. Saunders)

Perceptive people know that the increasingly sharp struggle emerging against America's policy of conquest is not only an economic battle; it is first and foremost a cultural struggle which the old world must wage against the eroding influence of American film and which, if current indicators can be trusted, will shortly be waged in unison. We currently face the following reality, which speaks an unequivocal message: Film America, released indiscriminately in our theatres, has produced the opposite of what it intended. It has not been able to promote its own interests, but rather has pulled the rug out from beneath itself. With its energetic but misguided and incautious assault on the European public, it has slowly but surely won the antipathy of European citizens. This wearing down of the American advance by the audience is actually good for our product: but it has to be remembered that run-of-the-mill American pictures—shallow, often silly, always too flighty, almost always full of (for us) false emotionalism—are the main cause of a general and undeniable flagging of interest in movie-going. The public has become sceptical about American films, a feeling which can be attributed to the army of average American films, and a feeling which naturally tends to be transferred to most of the American products which we do not want to miss because they are works of art of international rank. Yet it is usually the fate of everything valuable to be choked by unworthy, average and below average products. Thus the handful of outstanding American films, even though they earn the praise they deserve, can hardly undo the antipathy of the public toward American film.

In this point we fully subscribe to the views expressed by Director Melamerson in his programmatic statements regarding the plans of Deulig-Film in a press reception at the Adlon Hotel:

> One of the key points is to avoid total subjugation by American influence. The most important part of this struggle for existence is to create films which in Germany and the rest of the world can stand beside the achievements of the Americans. It is not a matter of the average American film; on this score everything that can be said has been said already. It is a matter of those top American pictures to which German producers owe creative inspiration, German distributors owe enrichment and German theatres owe a full box-office. We certainly do not wish to squeeze these films out of our market. But we aim to create something of comparable value for Germany and the world.

Today we can claim the capability and self-confidence to create in European cinema a cultural factor which can make good the ravages wrought by the average American film's lack of taste. Beyond all national variations, racial distinctions and differences in national character we can claim a foundation upon which European culture is based and that the different cultural streams of Europe can be united in a single current: in short, there is such a thing as European identity. This also applies to cinema: from *Postmeister* through our Ibsen film to *Mattia Pascal* one can trace the contours of European film culture. The European film, if it is to initiate a new wave, if it actually is to encompass the cultural values of the old world and check-mate the American wave in Europe, is of course only conceivable on the widest possible basis—because the individual producer lacks the resources. In this context we propose the international production partnership, a notion which has already been discussed here. That the Deulig Film company has taken up this idea is to be welcomed. The following comments on it came from Mr Melamerson:

Unfortunately such motion pictures are not only a matter of taste and competence, but also a matter of resources. By itself Germany is not in a position to make such films, and the task is therefore to broaden the German film to a European film, eventually even with Americans, though not to make an American film.

To promote the European cinema is therefore no longer a vain, half-literary hobby but is determined by vital economic and cultural interests: we have to create a European cinema in order to resurrect the interest in film which the Americans have buried. We know that it will be a difficult fight—but perhaps the future will show that we are economically stronger in ourselves than many vacillating proponents of the business cycle believe! Whatever may come, the fight against America is not against Americanism itself (which within its own borders may be bearable) but rather a fight for German cinema and its future, a struggle in other words for a worthy carrier of our culture.

Document 5: Helmuth Ortmann, "Film-Europe II," *Reichsfilmblatt*, no. 17, 24 April 1926, pp. 2–4 (translated by Thomas J. Saunders)

In a ridiculously short time span, hardly one decade, Film Europe has become a colony of Film America. The once (just several years ago!) prosperous industries of France, Italy and Scandinavia have shrunk to complete insignificance; German production, severely disabled, is kept alive artificially by a false leg (quota system) and false hopes ("we will conquer the American market"). The fault, so we are always told, lies in the generally poor economic position of Europe; the main problem allegedly the lack of capital. We (in Germany, France, Italy, Scandinavia, in Europe) do not have money to produce, thus no means to defend ourselves against the superior capital resources of the American industry, which forces its films on us.

This argument would be convincing if the Americans had bought up large numbers of European cinemas, organised large distribution networks of their own in Europe and acquired essential means of promotion (such as the trade press). In fact they have done no such thing. It is European theatre owners who play American films and pay high rental fees for them; European distributors handle American films; the European press promotes them. The Americans have not spent large sums to conquer the European market. They have not done much more financially than arrange occasional visits of their film stars to Europe. We, the ones who are financially weak, we, who lack money for our own production, have spent enormous sums for the purchase and distribution of American films, and for promotion to help make them successful. It is not true that the American industry has won the struggle with "silver bullets" or that our "poverty" made defence impossible. It is all too true that a defence was not even mounted.

Recall the situation in early 1919. The leading associations of the German film industry—producers, distributors, exhibitors—came together in a meeting with the commissioner for import and export. Was it to discuss how the German film industry could best defend itself from the expected invasion of American films after the peace treaty? No, it was to secure the release of foreign exchange, even before the peace, to purchase American films! Exhibitors and distributors pursued this in unusual harmony. Both saw American film as the main chance—and both hoped that foreign competition would force German producers to moderate prices. The commissioner—a representative of the national bank was also present —did not grant them this favour. They had to tame their impatience, though not for long. The disgrace of Versailles gave them the opportunity they wanted. The race could begin for acquisition of American films, which soon appeared across the country.

And lo and behold, success appeared to confirm the exhibitors' and distributors' actions. The press and the public approved of what they had done: these American films were wonderful: tempos, performing, directing and technical accomplishments were unheard of! No one in Germany or Europe could match them! Charlie Chaplin—only the Americans had a sense of humour and could make comedies! Jackie Coogan—only the Americans were able to produce films with children! Only they knew how to use the camera! Only they could . . . they could do everything; they could make films. We poor Europeans by contrast—well of course we had *Müde Tod, Caligari, Scherben, Fridericus, Nibelungen, Der letzte Mann, Erotikon* and other Scandinavian films; *Quo Vadis* and other Italian films; works from Abel Gance and much besides which came from Paris. All this was quite interesting, but, but (here a revealing smile), will the Americans enjoy these? They certainly will not, and thus these films are not good.

The number of unquestioning enthusiasts for American film was legion and the success of these films—doubtless for the most part very well made—became epidemic. Whoever did not succumb to the mass suggestion, whoever dared to believe in European genius, whoever considered German and European film equal to American in technique and artistry and set their importance for Europe over that of American film, whoever valued success in Europe more highly than in New York—he was blind, prejudiced, outdated, unmodern, lacking in judgement. As pitiful and pathetic as this all was, it was universal. America triumphed not with "silver bullets," not because its films were of superior quality: it triumphed because Europe abdicated! Because it lost all self-confidence and all faith in the value of its own achievement! Hence the strange confusion which ensued: the American market was to be conquered with German films even though everything produced in America was deemed superior. It was considered perfectly fine that American film occupied the American market. Let them conquer Europe, so long as we go down gloriously in hope in America. Europe did not interest us.

One day, however, the European exhibitor made the astonishing discovery that his box-office receipts from screening of the much-praised American films were steadily dropping. Already his hopes had been disappointed in many other things. European films had not become cheaper but very much more expensive as American competition forced the European producer to keep raising budgets. The producer, of course, had to keep pace with the Americans in order to stay alive. And for American film itself the theatre owners had to pay much higher rental fees than they did for German films before the American invasion. Now, in addition, the customers stayed away and receipts kept falling. Now the theatre owner found that screening of good German films of relatively modest means brought larger audiences than the American spectacles which certainly cost millions of dollars. The American film was no longer profitable.

I can spare myself the task of tracing the reasons for this phenomenon, which is revelation only for the naive. Felix Henseleit has explained it by reference to the different mentalities of the American and European population. Films made in the American style for American tastes became wearisome in Europe as soon as the appeal of the new and foreign evaporated and the clamorous promotional techniques proved a bluff. At the end of his article Henseleit suggests that German (European) exhibitors should only pay half the rental fee for American films in order to compensate for reduced income; here I do not agree with him. Films that the public does not want to see should not be screened by exhibitors even if they are free, unless the exhibitor wants to do his business lasting damage. And he would not screen them any longer, from today, if good, appealing German (European) films were in plentiful enough supply, if European production were not, thanks to the American invasion, in such desolate condition. The theatre owner has long since realised that the revivification of the European film, choked by long years of enthusiasm for America, is a matter of life and death for him. He has the task of pressing this realisation upon the distributor!

The distributor controls the liquid capital of the film industry. A significant portion of the admission price paid by the public at the box-office of the theatres comes to him in the form of rental fees. He is accountable for how he passes on this money! As long as he gives the lion's share for purchase of American films, things cannot improve. Only if the European distributor is freed from the American mirage—only then, when he recognises the task of strengthening and supporting European film production and making it really useful to the European market—only then will the hour of rescue strike for the European film industry.

Document 6: Felix Henseleit, "Film Europe," *Reichsfilmblatt*, no. 30, 24 July 1926, pp. 74–75 (translated by Thomas J. Saunders)

While Europe pays high regard to intellectual revolutions, ideological conflicts and similar things, it has watched the rise of America somewhat incredulously and helplessly, also rather condescendingly and in any case from a passive and withdrawn position.

Over there things moved forward at a gallop, people caught up in more or less significant technical and economic tasks, tirelessly worshipping the idol of setting new records.

Young, flexible, resilient, the American cleared all hurdles. We observed this gallop somewhat suspiciously but for the most part admiringly, tending to believe that it would run itself into the ground before it could become a threat to us. But this silent hope has proven illusory; for now we have to acknowledge that the rise of America was inevitable and divinely ordained. It was the assault of youth on the old Europe which is burdened by centuries of tradition. The younger generation which came from over there and to which we were initially prepared to submit because we thought we recognised fresh blood—oddly without much resistance if not perhaps without some sadness—made the mistake of all new-comers and all so-called unprejudiced youth: it quickly became arrogant. It brought nothing but itself, its very youthfulness. In America that worked perfectly. Unfamiliar with Joseph and his brothers the American could consider himself the beginning and end of things. Nevertheless America tried to assert an intellectual position and came looking for places to demonstrate it, without realising that the old world had long since moved beyond it. Europe, nurtured on the dream of rejuvenation, quickly realised that youth alone does not suffice. Having rejoiced and shouted hosanna, it now just as quickly sank into the fatalistic mood of Ash Wednesday. Yet one good thing came of this: Europe was forced to come to its senses.

This rapid transition, this up and down again, which took place in quite a short time and without great fanfare, can best be examined in the development of cinema.

Europe approached film, once it had shed its early fairground image, with literary ambitions. Franco-Italian film hegemony, which thought it could draw strength from the traditions of other art forms, was easily swept aside by America. After the war Europe became totally intoxicated with

America's filmic gifts. Most recently we have begun to realise that over there as here all that glitters is not gold.

Each side of this exchange misread the other. America flung us its films indiscriminately, and we snatched at them ravenously and indiscriminately. The consequences are now making themselves felt. Had there been a balanced cross-pollination, a complementing and mutual enrichment, the current mood of hostility, which undermines our best talent, may never have arisen.

The clash of old world and new, which was inevitable also in film as a way of finding a reasonable balance of power, could have assumed more sensible forms. Today we face a major confrontation, which under the circumstances is perhaps a given, but which will still consume much energy.

The notion of Film Europe therefore emerged from crisis. The immediate occasion was doubtless the clash with America, but we believe that it was only the occasion. Whoever now thinks that the notion of Film Europe only has roots in hostility between America and Europe (unfortunately this is still the common view!) shows that he has not rightly understood the breadth and importance of such a movement.

It would be narrow-minded and short-sighted to deduce a rationale for Film Europe from the opposition between America and Europe. To seal Europe off hermetically from American film would be pointless, meaningless and even tactically unwise. There's no point mobilising Film Europe for this purpose alone.

It is equally senseless for America to continue to shut itself off from Europe. America needs Europe, in two respects: it will not be able to completely exclude European films, even if there is not an urgent demand for these on the American market, because it will not be able to escape their influence. Furthermore America is looking for intellectual substance. Europe is providing—intensively in the last half year—the brains. As of tomorrow America will not be able to entertain the absurd, unwise and unproductive notion that it should swallow Film Europe.

By the same token Europe needs America; no longer, as several years ago, to intoxicate itself on a beverage which in the end proved to be spiked lemonade. Today we will choose according to the quality of the American product and, insofar as the balance of power permits, according to the needs of our market.

These perceptions are no longer utopian ones, either here or over there.

The idea of Film Europe is therefore not only the main rallying point of a large anti-American defensive front; it is the leitmotif of the entire range of common intellectual and economic interests which belong together in Film Europe and which can be co-ordinated without special exertion.

To speak first of the intellectual interests:

The nations of Europe are bound together, despite major external differences, by a venerable culture and older traditions. They have gone through much together. In short, they share enthusiasm for the same artistic ideals. In particulars there may be much divergence but in the central, overarching ideas there is always common ground to be found, notwithstanding historical wars of succession or any other past or future war. We can refer to the three names of Goethe, Shakespeare and Voltaire: in these names there is something which unites Europeans, which erects a bridge from nation to nation and reveals a central ingredient of European civilisation—one which is and must be foreign in essence, if not alien intellectually, to, for instance, the American, because he stands outside the European experience.

This argument can be easily applied to the realm of cinema. The European film audience wants European themes. Such an assertion is not the product of theoretical hair-splitting but an experienced fact: a German will always find a domestic picture—taken on average—more accessible than a roughly equivalent foreign one. By the same token, referring again to average work, he will find a French picture more accessible than a roughly equivalent American film; the reverse is also true. (The most recent reports to this effect from Paris about German box-office success illustrate this; and would furnish proof if proof were still required.)

None of this is about national fanaticism but confirms rather the adage that the closer to home one is the more at home one feels. We are not so rootless and alienated from our homeland that we could deny German nature and character (in the positive, untainted sense). The good German film, the good European film will strike the heart and feelings much more strongly than the average American picture-which at best manages to create interest—will ever be able to do. This is perfectly natural and not a revelation from intensive research. There is probably no debate to be conducted about it.

This alone is enough to make the coalition of Film Europe necessary —not by decree but by sentiment. Film Europe can be held together by stronger ties than a fortuitous tie of struggle and crisis, for coalitions in battle are notorious for their short duration.

What was utopian just yesterday is today beginning to become reality: the most accessible avenue forward, one which could be cleared without undue effort, was that of European production partnerships. As prelude to it we have witnessed the emergence of Franco-German co-operative production which, as its programme demonstrates, is going to play an important role in the current season and which is also the pacemaker of a movement which is more than fortuitous and embodies much more than a merely temporary phenomenon.

We now have German–Italian, German–Russian and Anglo–German production partnerships.

The idea of European co-operative production is good and is to be welcomed as a prelude to Film Europe. But it is only the beginning. In the future, be it near or far, the idea of a European syndicate must be pursued. Its creation by the exhibitors will perhaps be one of the next stages in development. The notion of syndication is one which is currently being tested in Germany. We still do not know whether or to what extent it will pass the test. If it does prove profitable it will be time to discuss how it can be exploited for building Film Europe.

The third item will be to find a platform uniting the interests of European distributors, a platform which does not yet exist. A joint European distribution arrangement would be able to work much more rationally and profitably. At present much energy and money flows away from the main body of the European film industry—the concern is for individual profit rather than to create a healthy circulation in the European film economy. There is no rationally organised European film trade. That may suffice for individual profits but it costs the European film industry as a whole dearly. European distribution partnerships or organisations could well concentrate the potential represented by over 20,000 European cinemas.

That we have so far been too lax where the notion of pooling European strength has occasionally come up probably derives from failing to recognise our real position of strength. One need only imagine: 20,000 theatres—this is the cornerstone of a European film alliance!

Document 7: Karl Wolffsohn, "Europe for the Europeans," *Lichtbildbühne*, no. 247, 16 October 1926, pp. 9–11 (translated by Thomas J. Saunders)

In our concluding remarks on the international congress in Paris we noted as a success the paving of friendly relations between France and Germany. We took the position that the European industry will perish without an understanding between France and Germany, in terms of film finances just as in other areas of the economy. There is no doubt in our minds, and we have expressed this often enough in *Lichtbildbühne*, that the economic crisis in the film business can be traced simply and singly to the fact that in relation to the potential market, we have imported too many American films. The task of an industry is to regulate as much as possible production and distribution according to the existing demand. We have the quota system as a regulator but have not known how to make it flexible enough to adjust to the needs of the market. More will be said about this topic when the quota issue *per se* comes under detailed discussion in the individual branches of the industry, especially in the associations. However, if we want to stabilise our national industry we must, respecting the nature of film, take care that our profit possibilities abroad are secured. Not Germany alone, but in the same measure all countries currently producing films, thus especially France, Italy, Sweden etc., have the same obligation. All these producing countries suffer mainly because they are dependent on their own market and lack secure avenues to realise profits abroad. Like Germany, they have to rely on the surprise hit, which no serious and forward-looking entrepreneur can or should count on in the long run.

We clearly recognised this situation already at the beginning of 1924 and published a pathbreaking article on film politics, "European Monroe Doctrine," in which we plainly and unequivocally argued that recovery of German production was only possible if not only Germany but also all of Europe came to its senses with measures, regulations and agreements which in the first instance would stabilise production in each country and make it profitable in Europe. In this article we clearly acknowledged that neither Germany, nor France, nor England nor Scandinavia alone would be in a position to assert itself as a producer unless a basis was found for co-operation. We argued very precisely at that time that such a European combination was in no way aimed at forming a bloc against America. We viewed this European bloc as advisable only because it would allow us to set the entirety of European production as equal partner over against American production on the international market.

Unfortunately neither Germany nor the other European countries drew the obvious conclusions. The article found resonance throughout the entire European trade press; but the political atmosphere was apparently not yet ripe to see the generally acknowledged core idea translated into action.

In America things were different. When the publisher of this paper made a study trip there in March 1924, directly following the appearance of the article, he had the opportunity to discuss it with key American leaders. From these discussions he gained the impression that at the time the Americans took the idea of a European bloc much more seriously than Europeans did. The European, and unfortunately also the German, industry does not recognise the strength which it possesses. Under the burden of financial and artistic concerns it does not have the chance to see itself and draw the right conclusions. But in our view it is high time, precisely following the congress in Paris, to put the European problem back on the table, especially since German policy *vis-à-vis* America has without question—it is time to say it unsparingly—been a fiasco. We saw this situation coming. We had occasion to discuss it openly with individuals and in our paper. However, we did not, unfortunately, encounter the sympathy of the leading circles of the industry: today we have to admit that we have lost the first battle with America. If we extend this metaphor, deliverance from the current situation can only come through the co-operation of European film producers. Nor should we forget that there should be included among European countries not only those currently producing but also those which sooner or later will establish their own production. We should not succumb to the illusion that film production in only possible in Germany or in France or Italy and Scandinavia. Cinema is still in its infancy and in the future we foresee that every country, even the very small ones, will seek to promote their culture, identity and economy world-wide by means of film. Just as today Rumania intends to make its own films, tomorrow Bulgaria or some other small country will not be denied its right to produce, be it in ever so small dimensions. And just as today we have newspapers in almost every small city, so each country, with the same right, will take up film as a means of contact with the rest of the world.

Viewed from this perspective, it is time to discuss the problem of France–Germany and with it the issue of a "European combination." Only such a combination can achieve the dimensions required to face a country like America with its 15,000 cinemas. Altogether Europe has an even larger number of film theatres. America, for instance, would show much less interest in negotiations with Agfa than with the powerful I.G. Farben conglomerate, which would be an equal negotiating partner and naturally more valuable and attractive. Things are essentially the same in film affairs.

If recognition for a European bloc takes hold—and to us it appears that this is happening since the Paris congress—not only the German industry, but in our opinion all film-producing countries of Europe will profit. Then we could imagine a time when America joins a Pan-European and American Film Congress in order to set a long-term production plan and contribute to its realisation. Without internationally co-ordinated production America too will one day face a situation like that in today's Europe and confront a worrisome future.

Already in 1924, after publication of our article, Lupu Pick took the step from theoretical discussion to practical recommendations. In an article published on 28 June 1924 in *Lichtbildbühne*, "Europe's Film Syndicate," he mapped out clearly his conception of European co-operation. The core of his argument ran as follows:

If the total production cost of a film is set not to exceed the figure X, the costs should be shared according to this formula:

England	22%
Germany	18%
France	16%
Italy	10%
Scandinavia	12%
Austria	12%

The remaining 10% would come from the actual country of production. From this table it is clear that almost three years ago Pick publicised an approach which in its main principles can still be supported. There might need to be some tinkering with this after detailed discussion but the core issue is still the co-ordination of European countries in film, the securing of distribution and profitability of European film, namely, those pre-requisites for making production and the recovery of the entire industry possible.

Recently Wengeroff took up this plan and tried to realise it with inadequate resources. His notions were completely utopian, in total misunderstanding and contradiction of the outline presented by ourselves and Lupu Pick in 1924. We aimed to create several groups of European film companies for the purposes of co-operation; Wengeroff dreamed that the industry of a country could be united within a single trust, in turn linked with that of another country. Back then we pointed out the fallacy in this position and we continue to see it as unfeasible. In our opinion only the possibility outlined by Pick is well suited to bring health to the European and with it the German industry.

With this means of making film production in Europe profitable, the American market will interest us only as extra income. We would be strong enough, as outlined above, that we could sit down at the negotiating table with the American trust as an equal. At the moment such negotiations are not on a healthy foundation, so that they never yield results which serve European and with them German interests.

Unfortunately the key leaders of the industry do not clearly recognise this. They hope that the recovery of the German industry will come from abroad. They hope that acquisition of foreign credit will prop the German film industry up again. In our opinion the recovery of German production and the German industry can only come from within as we remove those elements which are obstacles to growth and incorporate those which stimulate German (European) production. These, however, are issues which are not central to the main theme we wish to address and feel compelled to discuss. The American threat shrinks daily because American films have failed not only in Germany but also in all of Europe. European film is in higher demand in Europe than ever before. Should we not therefore evaluate how to take charge of this nearby and relatively secure market rather than orient ourselves to sales in America. A business built on a single customer will always, by virtue of its structure, be risky. We therefore believe that it is time to discuss openly the question of a "European Monroe Doctrine" to uphold European and German interests —without thereby saying or wanting to say to the Americans that we are looking for an economic war in film, which would doubtless be damaging to both sides.

The American problem is not yet solved, despite the close ties of individual German and American companies. In the attempt to raise central problems for clarification it has been overlooked that the vital interests of a country can never be clarified by means of compromise, just as in general compromises always have the effect of only postponing the issue. In our opinion ties with America can only, as outlined above, be resolved by means of collaboration among European production countries. Consequently, contact between the leading figures of the individual countries is more necessary now than ever. What is still lacking for attainment of this goal is clear policy and the will to serve one's own industry by supporting the industry of other European production countries. However, if we reach this goal, our ties with America will be much simpler and more secure.

Group 2: Kontingents, Quotas and the American Response

Kristin Thompson's chronology of European quota regulations provides an overview of the development of this strategy to protect domestic industries from American incursions. The two internal MPPDA memoranda outline the need for the American trade association to have a European representative, and describe what that representative—the only fire horse on duty, as Edward G. Lowry described himself—did in diplomatic negotiation with representatives of the European industries and governments. The tenor of Lowry's comments strongly supports the argument made by Jens Ulff-Møller that in these negotiations MPPDA officials were accorded a status similar to that given to representatives of the United States government. Lowry's report also contains extracts from a number of internal MPPDA documents indicating the extent to which its officers, at least, were prepared to consider self-imposed restrictions on the number of American films exports as a solution to the European problem. The final documents in this section detail the French film decree of 1928, establishing a quota, and the American response. These documents also make clear that the representatives of the American film industry could call on extensive State Department support in such negotiations. By contrast, a commentary by Lars Moen on the 1929 International Exhibitors' conference in Paris draws attention to the absence of any European organisation comparable to the MPPDA as a crucial point of weakness in the European film industry's defences.

Richard Maltby

Document 8: Chronology of European Quota Regulations, 1921–34, From Kristin Thompson, *Exporting Entertainment: America in the World Film Market, 1907–1934* **(London: British Film Institute, 1985), pp. 211–12 (Sources: Trade Information Bulletin series,** *Film Daily Year Book,* **Commerce Reports,** *Jahrbuch der Filmindustrie, Moving Picture World)*

1921:   1 Jan.—Germany institutes quota: 15% of negative footage produced in Germany in 1919 allowed in, 1921–4.

1925:   1 Jan.—Germany switches to 1:1 quota for features imported.
Italy—exhibition quota: one week in every two months, theatres must show an all-Italian programme.
Hungary—every film exchange handling twenty or more films per year must produce one Hungarian film.

1926:   Hungary—importers must sponsor one Hungarian film for every thirty imported.
3 Sept.—Austria institutes a two-year quota of 20:1. Twenty import licences granted a producer for every domestic film made (licences can be sold).

1927:   1 Jan:—Austria lowers 20:1 quota to 10:1.
1 Apr.—Britain's Quota Act: renters must handle 7.5% British films, graduating to 20% by 1935–6 season. (Begins at 5% for exhibitors).
6 May—Portugal: Each programme must include at least one 300-metre (one reel) film made domestically.
1 Oct.—Italy: Exhibition quota decrees 10% of screen time must be Italian films. (Not enforced due to lack of domestic films).
Oct.—Austrian quota adjusted to 18:1, retroactive to 1 Jan.
Nov.—New German Kontingent system for 1 Apr. 1928 to 30 June 1929 specifies number of imports based on estimated needs of market; of 260 features, ninety held in reserve and 170 given to German companies on basis of 1926 and 1927 distribution. (Approximately a 1:2 system).

1928:   1 Jan.—Austrian quota put back to 20:1.
1 Jan.—Hungary gives option: either one Hungarian film must be produced for every twenty imported or a heavy surcharge must be paid on imports.
12 Mar.—France institutes 7:1 quota with licences granted only

on basis of French film exports. (Negotiations with American industry result).

1 May—French export rule abolished, replaced with straight 7:1 quota.

24 Aug—Italy agrees to class as Italian films those of foreign countries which import Italian films.

5 Dec.—Austrian quota becomes 23:1, retroactive to 1 Jan.

13 Dec.—German quota allotment for 1 July 1929 to 30 June 1930 set up: 210 import licences to be issued.

1929:   1 Jan.—Austrian quota returns to 20:1.

1 Feb.—German Kontingent system extended till June 1931. Of 210 import licences, 160 to German distributors in proportion to the number of German films they handled in 1928–9; other 50 to companies exporting German films. (Works out to a 1:2.5 quota).

1 Apr. to 24 Sept.—American offices in France close in response to proposed 3:1 quota.

27 May—French adopt 4:1 quota, but boycott continues.

19 Sept.—France's new quota renews old 7:1 basis for licensing imports. Extended to 30 Sept. 1930 or one more year if no agreement is reached by 1 May 1930.

1930:   1 May—no agreement is reached; the French quota of 7:1 extended to 30 Sept. 1931.

July—German quota reserves two-thirds of permits for silent films (90 sound permits, 129 silent actually issued).

1 Oct.—Hungarian 20:1 quota dropped, substitutes unlimited import licences at fixed fees.

1931:   1 July—France abolishes quota for countries with no restrictions on French imports for one-year period. Negotiations begin with Germany, only country with a quota affecting France.

July—Austria lowers number of import certificates needed per film from three to one and a half, fixes price of certificates.

1 July—German quota renewed on same basis for a year. For 1931–2 season, 105 sound, 70 silent licences. (Based on number of German films distributed in previous eighteen months.)

1932:   23 Apr.—Czechoslovakia institutes quota of 240 features per year (later reduced repeatedly, finally to 120). Certificates are required, which rise steadily in price. American firms respond with boycott.

1 July—Germany restricts dubbed imports to 50% and dubbing must be done in Germany.

29 July—France bans dubbed versions not dubbed in France. Restrictions declared on the number of theatres in which original-language versions can be shown.

1933: 24 July—Only 140 dubbed films can be released in France in the year ending 30 June 1934; dubbing must still be done in France. Theatre restrictions continue.

1934: 26 June—94 dubbed films allowed into France for upcoming six months. Theatre restrictions continue.

Document 9: Oscar Solbert, Report to Will Hays, Autumn 1925 (Motion Picture Association of America Archive, 1927 Foreign Relations File)

When I say that the producers must collectively organize, I mean that some modified form of co-operative marketing or to some effect the forming of a co-operative export association to co-operate along simple lines of agreements, should be organized for trade abroad. The time has come when the film trade must be organized on the same lines as that of any other large export, like steel, copper, or textiles. Some of these industries have found certain forms of co-operative marketing to be a necessity in obtaining a more regular and sound market and therefore better profits. The details would have to be worked out to suit the situation.

Some co-operative form of marketing abroad should be organized through the MPPDA. Such a collective association is not only encouraged by our government but protected by the Webb–Pomerene Act. It would seem to me that if each company sent only its best pictures to the number that Germany, for instance, could use them, more money would be earned on them than if the total production were exported. Fewer and better pictures, at longer runs, it seems, would earn more money than a large number containing indifferent and poor ones, each picture making a short run.

Let us take Germany, for instance, and use round numbers. Let us say Germany has 3,000 theatres, which with 300 days will give 900,000 playing days. For argument's sake let us say 1,000 American films are produced. The saturation point for American pictures, let us say, is 600. It stands to reason also that no more than 600 of these pictures are good and suitable for the German market. If there was a choice, would it not be much more profitable to run 600 pictures into 900,000 playing days than to divide this number of playing days up amongst 1,000 pictures containing poor and

349

unsuitable ones? If this is correct, it would seem to me that the position holds good for each individual company. Given, for argument's sake, that Germany can take 60 percent of our film productions, why is it not possible by some means of co-operative organization in the MPPDA wherein each member pledge to send into a country as Germany, for example, only 60 percent of their production. Besides the censorship at the source, there might be another expert on censorship for advisory purposes in this organization to help pick the suitable pictures for the foreign market. It would be a simple matter to check up that no one company send in more than their allotted share. At the end of each year a reckoning could be had that would be satisfactory to all companies involved. The quota for each foreign country, plus a margin for increasing the demand, would be arrived at by our own foreign managers, and not in any way indicated by foreign governments or producers. Co-operative marketing that would fit the peculiar circumstances of the moving picture trade would increase profits for the members as well as reduce overhead in each foreign country. It is also the surest way to build a solid foundation of our foreign trade as well as to increase future demands in all markets for our moving pictures.

It is urgently recommended first of all a Foreign Department be organised as a part of the MPPDA under Mr. Will Hays. The functions of which Department should be to gather, correlate and disseminate to the producer members, timely and accurate information on all that may pertain to the moving picture trade abroad. This organization should have a central office with the MPPDA with its representatives abroad in strategic points and gathering the required information both as to physical data of the film business and film industry abroad, as well as the tendencies and actions of the foreign governments toward importation of foreign films. The home office should be in direct and constant communication with all Departments of our Federal Government that might be of aid to the moving picture trade.

A cooperative export association also should be formed, the members of which would comprise the foreign managers of the different producers, the president and several members of the MPPDA. Rules of trade and regulations in standards of business and ethics would be drawn up by the Association and subscribed to by its members. Among other things, this would include uniform contracts and methods of distribution. Here would be a great part of the strength of the Association, if this regulation amounted to a price fixing, which would be the case if a uniform method of release on a percentage basis to the exhibitors was agreed upon. These regulations would also prescribe year by year, or shorter term, the percentage of total number of pictures to be sent to different countries.

Such a cooperative association would present a solid front in any country to its government or combined producers or exhibitors. There could be an association of offices, in each big country or territory with a representative from the export association at its head. This man would be in direct communication with the home export association; he would be in charge of the intelligence available to all members of the association on the ground; and he would be the spokesman of the association in all difficulties. Such an association of officers would reduce overhead for all members and make necessary contact and communication easy under the rules of the association. The export department of each producer would continue functioning as before. The intelligence department of this association because of its functions and being detached from producers, would constitute an excellent advisory committee to help in selection of pictures for foreign trade.

A separate export association is recommended so that there can be no criticism that non-members of the Motion Picture Producers and Distributors Association are excluded from it. The president of the MPPDA would be the president of the Co-operative Export Association along with whatever part of his staff would be necessary. The offices of the MPPDA would be offices of the CEA.

A general agreement in broad terms would be drawn up stating the objects of the Co-operative Export Association. Each producer joining the association would then have to sign a separate contract with the association. This contract, of course, would be agreed upon by the producers forming the association. The foreign members and managers of the producing companies would be the members of the CEA and would constitute its Board of Directors. The export Departments of the producing companies would continue functioning as before and the competitive relations of their producing firms would not be changed.

The strength of such a export association under the Webb–Pomerene Act lies in their agreement on price fixing. This can be arrived at in the moving pictures by agreeing to the same forms and types of contracts. The second great advantage would be in deciding together and agreeing on the percentages of total productions to be exported to any country, so as not to flood the market, thus depressing prices as well as spoiling the market for American pictures.

Each foreign locality in this scheme could have its association of offices to insure cooperation and to cut down overhead. The representative agency of each producer would have his office in this association of offices. A representative of the CEA would be chairman of the committee comprising the heads of these agencies and he would act as spokesman of both the home office, or to represent the attitude of the local committee on any immediate question with the local government or the local film industry. This CEA representative would also be the intelligence officer in this locality. Specific duties would be to gather complete and detailed information of all data that would bear upon the sales and development of the market for American moving pictures. This information would be available simultaneously for the members of the association of offices. This information would also be sent to the home office of the CEA where it would be properly collated and distributed to foreign managers and also would serve as a basis for major polices of the association as laid down by the Board of Directors in council. As far as Europe is concerned, there might be three such associations of offices—one in London for the United Kingdom; one in Berlin for Germany, Scandinavia, Russia, Austria and Southeast of Europe, and one in Paris for the Latin countries and Switzerland. Representation for the rest of the world would be a matter for discussion. The importance of complete, accurate and timely information that would affect sales and the future market of moving pictures is beyond estimate. The secret of the success of the American meat packers in the foreign markets is greatly dependent upon their foreign intelligence. This is also true of the more than 50 odd large industries that have organized into export associations under the Webb–Pomerene Act. The gathering and dissemination of intelligence as to wants and fluctuations of the market in their commodities is a great source of strength.

As opposite numbers to these three men in charge of the association of offices in Europe, are three others in the home office of the CEA, whose duties are to be in direct communication with their particular territory. They would also collate and disseminate all information pertaining to their territory to the foreign managers of the producer members. These men, knowing the tastes of their territories, might also be used by those producers who wish in an advisory selectivity capacity. They would also have different duties of a technical business nature, such as finance, credits, shipping, commercial treaties, tariffs—in fact, experts on the technique of foreign trade.

The CEA would present a solid front of all the producing elements of this association to any foreign interests, whether government or industrial. It would also present united action in an application to our own government for help in foreign markets. It could in its own way appeal to all American industries for whom the moving picture is a free vehicle of advertising for their support with our own government. The CEA would be a source of unity and strength and action for any purpose that would promote foreign trade for moving pictures.

Foreign producers under government protection are forming into combines to counteract the American producers. Likewise the foreign exhibitor has the same tendencies, so that soon the day will come when they, too, will be united for the purpose of buying American pictures. Sooner or later—the sooner the better—American producers will be forced to collective co-operation to protect themselves in the business of foreign trade of moving pictures.

Document 10: Edward G. Lowry, "Certain Factors and Considerations Affecting the European Market," Internal MPPDA memorandum, 25 October 1928 (Motion Picture Association of America Archive, 1928 Foreign Relations File)

The design of this memorandum is to expose as clearly and as concisely as may be:

1. The economic, political and other post-war conditions that have led to the imposition of restrictions on the import, distribution, and exhibition of American motion pictures in some of the countries of Europe, and
2. The steps that have been taken by this Association through its representative in Europe to meet and alleviate, where possible, the governmental and trade burdens and hardships that have been laid upon its member companies.

It should be made clear at once that American motion pictures are not the only commodity on which European governments have imposed restrictions. In fact, our films were among the last of the exports from the United States against which trade barriers were erected. Motion pictures were not arbitrarily selected to be particularly discriminated against. They faced a general condition in Europe that affected the import to that Continent of a long and varied list of products and commodities. Indeed, it is a cause of speculation among persons most familiar with economic post-war conditions in Europe why American films were not among the first products to have trade barriers and restrictions placed in the way of their unhampered distribution.

Motion pictures are the most CONSPICUOUS of all the American exports. They do not lose their identity. They betray their nationality and country of origin. They are easily recognized. They are all-pervasive. They colour the minds of those who see them. They are demonstrably the greatest single factor in the Americanization of the world and as such fairly may be called the most important and significant of America's exported products.

They are such indirect and undesigned propaganda for the purveying of national ideals, mode of life, methods of thought and standards of living as no other country in the world has ever enjoyed. When Rome was mistress of the whole world she had no such method of purveying to her outlying provinces and colonies in Africa, Britain and elsewhere a knowledge of the

might, majesty and dominion of the Imperial power. The British of today
are masters of, perhaps, the last of the great political Empires. And today
throughout the British Empire 85 per cent of all the motion pictures shown
are American pictures, showing the subjects of King George not English
life, manners and modes but the institutions, habits of life and standards
of the United States. What is true of the British Empire is true of Germany,
France, Italy and all the chief European countries.

The British Government came slowly and reluctantly to the point of
passing restrictive legislation on imported films and only acted after the
Imperial Conference of November 1926 had pointed out:

"The importance and far-reaching influence of the Cinema are
now generally recognised. The Cinema is not merely a form of
entertainment but, in addition, a powerful instrument of
education in the widest sense of that term; and even where it
is not used avowedly for purposes of instruction, advertisement
or propaganda, it exercises indirectly a great influence in
shaping the ideas of the very large numbers to whom it appeals.
Its potentialities in this respect are almost unlimited.

"In Great Britain and Northern Ireland the proportion of
Empire-produced films to the total shown has recently been
only about 5 per cent., and in the Irish Free State the proportion
is probably not higher. In Australia, of the total number of
films imported in 1925, only a little over 8 per cent. were of
Empire origin, and on the basis of length of film the Empire
proportion was probably substantially less. In New Zealand in
recent years the proportion of films shown which were of
Empire origin appears to have been about 10 per cent. In
Canada the direct imports of films from Great Britain and
Northern Ireland in the year ended the 31st of March, 1925,
were only 13 per cent. of the total films imported. The
proportion of British films shown is also known to be very small
in South Africa, Newfoundland and India, and in the Colonies
and Protectorates, although statistical data are lacking.

"It is a matter of the most serious concern that the films
shown in the various parts of the Empire should be to such an
overwhelming extent the product of foreign countries, and that
the arrangements for the distribution of such Empire films as
are produced should be so far from adequate. In foreign cinema
pictures the conditions in the several parts of the Empire and
the habits of its peoples, even when represented at all, are not
always represented faithfully and at times are misrepresented.
Moreover, it is an undoubted fact that the constant showing

of foreign scenes or settings, and the absence of any corresponding showing of Empire scenes or settings, powerfully advertises (the more effectively because indirectly) foreign countries and their products.

"It is necessary to emphasize the fact that State action cannot be effective, and indeed, so far as any quota system is concerned, could not be maintained for any length of time, unless two conditions are fulfilled. The first is that there shall be a substantial output of films which not only conform to such requirements as to production within the Empire as may be prescribed in any case, but are also of real and competitive exhibition value. Whatever action may be taken by Governments will be useless unless producers show sufficient enterprise, resource and adaptability. On the other hand, it should be recognized that suitable Government action, whether legislative or administrative, may be an effective incentive and encouragement to private enterprise in its efforts to place the Empire film industry on a sound footing. The second essential condition is the development of effective distributing arrangements throughout the Empire, different parts of the Empire cooperating wherever possible."

This report of the Imperial Conference so fairly and so restrainedly sets forth the attitude not only of Britain but of the principal European countries toward imported motion pictures that it deserves the closest attention and consideration by the American industry.

In none of the European countries is there any legislation forbidding combinations in restraint of trade such as we have in the Sherman Act. The industrialists of Europe believe in restraints of trade for their personal protection and aggrandisement. Their governments support them in this view, and there is no public opinion that insists upon unhampered competition. It was natural and inevitable, therefore, when the end of the World War left the whole continent of Europe in political, economic and financial chaos, that the several countries should have set about protecting by trade barriers their local, domestic and national interests.

In the years immediately following the World War, these restrictions, trade barriers, quotas, contingents and obstacles to trade became so numerous, so harsh, so severe, so crippling to business and to the renewal of prosperity in Europe that the Europeans began to find them unbearable. The late Mr Walter Leaf, the London banker, said in 1926:

"The capacity for production exists, and is generally much larger than in pre-war times; but the products are stagnating because they are refused, or at least hampered by foreign tariffs and trade barriers. Hence unemployment, stagnation of industry, and a lamentable waste of potential human energy. The whole standard of living is lowered by the artificial restrictions on human efficiency. A European trade league would have open markets on at least the same scale as those of the United States, and would thus be able to compete in production on equal terms with that vast area of free trade intercourse. National jealousies force us here to employ in suicidal trade struggles the efforts which should be concentrated on the general advancement of human well-being."

Sir Alan Anderson, acting President of the International Chamber of Commerce, laying stress upon moral barriers, said:

"Greater importance is attached to mental barriers to trade than to physical ones. So long as national units believe:
1. that foreign trade is something to be regarded with suspicion instead of as the first necessity of their national life;
2. that they can continue to sell their products abroad without buying from abroad;
3. that the ruin of their neighbour is an element in their own prosperity instead of the reverse being the case;
4. that they can in any way impede the free flow of commerce internationally without their actions recoiling upon their own heads;
5. that particular sections of national communities are entitled to benefit at the expense of the general trade of the nation, attempts to remove the evil effects which spring form this state of mind will be unavailing.

"We must not expect that the walls of Trade Barriers will fall down suddenly at the trumpet blast of the League of Nations or the International Chamber of Commerce—but we need not on that account lose heart. Slowly but steadily and with increasing speed, men of all nations begin to realise how much they need to trade with their neighbours and how much they lose in the wealth and happiness of their people by unnecessary barriers against their neighbours' trade.

"Europe is sick of 'malaise economique,' not because her climate or her people or her material assets have failed, but because she is haunted by ghosts of the dead hatreds of war.

"A false idea has poisoned her mind and through her mind, poisoned her body.

"In war, the man across the frontier is an enemy to be killed, but in peace, the man with whom one buys and sells is a partner much more than a rival, and the prosperity of one partner helps another even if they live on opposite sides of a frontier.

"Our task is to exorcise this baneful ghost of hatred and to focus the opinion of commercial men all over the world on this fact that trade profits the buyer and seller and that our health, as traders, suffers if our neighbour is sick."

Dr. Julius Klein, Director of the Bureau of Foreign and Domestic Commerce of the United States Department of Commerce, points out:

"It cannot be denied that there has on more than one occasion been ample warrant for these trade barriers as temporary expedients to prevent the economic inundation of a given country during some momentarily distressing period. But such a situation by no means warrants the perpetuation of such obstructions to the world's commerce. There are legitimate and universally accepted uses for various controls of international traffic, such as tariff duties, import regulations, patent requirements, etc. But these are vastly different from the purely arbitrary and oftimes discriminatory destruction of legitimate and mutually desired commerce that is helpful to both consumer and producer.

"We do not have to search very far to find the original causes of most of these obnoxious trade obstructions. They are mainly an ugly brood that sprang from the blood and ashes of the World War. While that struggle was in progress, certain industries in each nation, under the spur of military necessity, waxed big, attaining proportions that proved to be merely bloated and dropsical when peace had been declared. A great surplus-producing capacity existed and, meanwhile, purchasing power had declined. Restriction of imports was an obvious measure for bolstering up an overdeveloped or uneconomic industry.

"Then, too, by the terms of the treaties, great empires were split up. Many new nations arose. Dislocation, confusion, bewilderment prevailed. A fever of nationalism burned with hectic intensity. War-time rancors showed a lamentable tendency to keep on rankling. Fears persisted. Instincts of self-preservation found vehement vent. The spirit of newly

357

acquired political independence was expressed in a desire for greater economic independence.

"At that time many of the national currencies were indulging in a dizzy, delirious dive towards the abyss. With the export advantage that this currency-depreciation gave them, some countries were pouring goods into their neighbors' markets at prices which the neighbors' industries could not possibly meet. Then too there were the depleted national treasures.

"Under such desperately perplexing conditions as these, it was not surprising, perhaps, that such cries should arise as—"Let's slap on restrictions, import or export! Save our vital interests from strangulation! Promote national self-sufficiency!"

"These feelings soon took concrete form in a vast variety of arbitrary restrictions, discriminations and hampering formalities that impeded the normal course of international business. Foreign traders found themselves tangled up in a maze of red tape and mulcted through a mass of complex exactions. They were mystified and baffled in trying to conform to the multiplicity of weird requirements.

"Gradually, however the situation took a turn for the better. The post-war neuroses began to be allayed. Emotions and apprehensions subsided a bit. A clearer, calmer view commenced to be apparent. It was coming to be realized that, in a good many ways, these arbitrary restrictions were harmful not only to the general welfare but to the interests of the very nations that had so eagerly set them up.

"The more far sighted business men and economists began to cast about for means of modifying or relaxing these arbitrary trade restrictions—or at least making a start in that direction. The big result of this movement was the World Economic Conference which was held at Geneva in May 1927. Fifty nations were represented by more than 300 delegates and experts. This conference discussed, in general, the most promising methods of bringing about healthier conditions in the economic world—but it devoted most of its attention to this specific subject of trade barriers.

"The participants were not impeded by any official instructions or similar limitations—so the discussions were frank and vigorous, covering the ground thoroughly. The conference did not have the power to take any authorized steps but it made important recommendations, clarifying the issues by cataloging specifically the types of commercial constructions that will survive.

"One very valuable concrete result of this conclave is the agreement for the virtual abolition of import and export restrictions. This was drawn up last October and November —also at Geneva—by formally accredited representatives of thirty-five governments. It has already been signed by twenty-seven countries, including the United States, with various minor reservations. It is not yet in force, but a further meeting was held in Geneva in July of this year, in the course of which the acceptability of the reservations put forward by the various countries was determined and the date and conditions for the enforcement of the convention were set.

"This agreement is of exceptional interest to the United States because these countries that are pledging themselves to do away with virtually all import and export restrictions are the customers for more than half of our American exports and the source of more than a third of our imports.

"We ought to derive substantial benefit when the agreement goes into effect, especially if the signatory nations interpret it broadly, in accordance with its pure animating spirit. Restrictions of the kind that it aims to abolish have proved immensely troublesome—gravely menacing—to some of the most important and promising branches of our export trade."

*   *   *

Commenting in a personal letter particularly on the results of the Geneva Conference as affecting American motion pictures, Mr Henry Chalmers, Chief of the Division of Foreign Tariffs of the U.S. Department of Commerce, writes:

"A complete list of all the commodities the importation of which is in any way restricted in all of the 20 odd countries of Europe has never, to my knowledge, been compiled in a comprehensive way. A list of the restrictions which the various countries put forward at the recent Geneva Conference and desired to reserve as exceptions to the convention is suggestive of the sort of restrictions that now prevail in various foreign countries.

"There is an important distinction, however, at least technically, between the restriction on the *importation* of a given commodity into a country, and the *limitation* on goods of foreign production imposed after they had been admitted into the country, at the time of exhibition or sale within the country. The quota restrictions on the exhibition of foreign films now practised by certain European countries constitute practically the only restriction of this second type. The only thing closely analogous to it is the practice of certain Central European countries of not granting licenses, or at least not as freely, for foreign cars to be used as taxis or public conveyances, as they did for cars of domestic manufacture. It was essentially because of this difference between the film quotas and the usual restrictions, which makes one a domestic matter and the other a customs restriction, that led to the ruling out of discussion of the film restrictions as not properly coming within the scope of the terms of the Geneva Convention.

"Since, strictly speaking, there are almost no restrictions in Europe or elsewhere that are exactly analogous to those imposed on motion pictures in certain of the countries of Europe, the film restrictions are rather distinctly a problem by themselves. The analogy to the ordinary import restrictions enforced at the custom house can be invoked only indirectly through the claim that a refusal to issue a license for the sale or exhibition of a product within the country amounts practically to the same thing as prohibiting its importation. However, there is the cultural argument with which you are very familiar, and in view of the seriousness with which a number of the European representatives took that argument, it will need to be very carefully examined to see how far it can be admitted as valid, or what concessions might be made to satisfy the national cultural considerations. For the distinction between the economic and cultural considerations involved in the film restrictions, I can do no better than to refer you to Mr. Wilson's address at Geneva last July."

A representative of this Association, Col. Edward G. Lowry, assisted by Dr. Paul Koretz, lawyer for the Fox interests at Vienna and engaged by us, attended the July conference at Geneva. At this conference American motion picture interests were especially menaced because of the written and expressed demands of France, Austria and other countries that the Conference formally decided that their restrictive measures on imports of foreign films were not in conflict with the Geneva Convention of November 8, 1927.

A decision in favour of their contention by this July Conference could not have been appealed and would have necessarily, therefore, firmly established on a legal basis the contingent system in Europe for years. The chance of getting such a decision from the Conference was increased by the fact that apparently all the interested European countries were working in concert under cover in opposition to American interests.

Therefore from the beginning the policy and plan of action of the Association's representative with the aid, advice and approval of Dr. Koretz, was to forestall a definite decision against the American industry by the Conference. In attaining this desired end, Mr. Hugh Wilson, American Minister to Switzerland and head of the American delegation at the Conference, rendered admirable service. The Conference did not approve by any affirmative action the restrictive measures of France and the other countries.

The Conference adhered to its decision to refuse to accept the French, the Austrian or any other request for the interpretation of the meaning of the Convention of November 8, 1927, and held strictly to its terms of reference. It made no reply to the French note of January 27, 1928, which in effect, asked the Conference to give approval to the present French regulations affecting films. Mr. Wilson in a strong speech reserved all our rights and intimated if future need should arise the United States would have recourse to diplomatic action or to arbitral award. The French failure to obtain the approval of the Conference to its regulations and Mr. Wilson's attitude formally reserving our rights leaves the way open for future discussions between the United States and French governments after the convention is ratified. Mr. Wilson's speech so clearly sets forth the whole situation that material portions of it are here set down:

> "When we drew up our Convention last autumn it was to do away with restrictive measures on *importation*—certain specified exceptions were allowed, but it was certainly the spirit—more than that, it was the intent—of the instrument to do away with all other types of formalities and regulations of a nature to restrict importation.
>
> "Now I ask you, what does importation mean?—in our minds, in the minds of business men, in the ordinary conception of the word? Does it mean, I ask you, merely the passing of a frontier or the passing of a frontier for a useful purpose? Does it mean that we Americans are free to ship wheat and cotton to the world, to enter the States freely, but still may be prevented from distributing this wheat and cotton by so-called internal regulations? Does it mean we can send typewriters, motor cars or any other form of our products freely to the world but that the other States may in their discretion decide which ones of these motor cars and which ones of these typewriters may be distributed and sold within their frontiers? Eliminate the question of public order and public morals and the cases are not only analogous but identical.
>
> "I cannot conceive that any body of men who have the welfare

of commerce at heart and who have given the labour that you, my colleagues, have given to this Convention, are willing to see it vitiated by a legalistic interpretation which makes it not worth the paper it is written on. If it should ever be decided that our Convention has to do with the mere crossing of frontiers for articles of trade, but leaves nations free to prevent the disposal of articles within their frontiers, then what, I ask you is left of this Convention?

"The word films was not mentioned through our debates in October. No nation having similar restrictions brought up this question. I wish this Conference would consider this point—it is an important one—that is, why was this question not raised in the first Conference? Gentlemen, I have made inquiry among the representatives of States having similar restrictions and I have ascertained from certain ones of these representatives that they did not raise the question because they assumed that once this Convention was put into force these restrictions must automatically be dissolved by the States or at least after six months as provided by Article 2 of this Convention. There was no question in their minds as to whether a restriction on importation meant only the crossing of the frontier or meant crossing the frontier for a useful purpose.

"The point may be brought out—and indeed it has been brought out in our conversations—that large film interests of the United States have dealt with the French Government on the basis of these regulations and have reached a satisfactory agreement, and therefore, why should the Government of the United States enter into this question?

"I should like to deal with this phase of the question now. In the first place, such film interests as have dealt with the French Government have acquiesced and not agreed to the procedure of that Government. They have acquiesced because they were faced with a condition in which they stood to lose heavily. They were confronted with a state of facts with which they had to deal and, under force majeure, they took the best they could get, in order to enable them to continue to do business temporarily. It obviously does not mean that the case of the United States Government is in any way prejudiced in dealing with the Convention, which has not yet come into effect, and in discussing what interpretation may be put upon that convention in the future.

"I mentioned earlier that this question was broader than the action of France alone, and I earnestly beg you to consider the consequences implied in the acceptance of the French thesis that their nation does not violate the Convention. Warning has already been served by certain States, which implies that they will consider the decision as to France as a precedent, and, as I endeavored to make clear before, this matter must not be considered alone but as a precedent by which any state which is embarrassed on economic grounds by importation may set up a machinery again of internal regulation by which it may act in harmony with the Convention but still against its purposes. It seems to me, gentlemen, that this is one of the most vital questions with which the Conference has been confronted because we must decide not a simple question of one exception, but a question of principle by which we establish a precedent which may serve or wreck the future operation of this Convention. I most earnestly hope that this question will be treated by all States in the broadest spirit and with the fullest comprehension of the dangers which lie in acquiescing in the French contention.

"I have already stated that I felt called on to speak today lest my silence should be construed as a acquiescence in the French plan or in other plans which may follow the French lead. I feel in all candor, compelled to reserve our rights, if in the future need should arise to have recourse to diplomatic action or to arbitral award under the Convention."

Part 2

This second part if this memorandum is concerned with the activities of the Association's representative in Europe.

It was in February, 1926, that Edward G. Lowry was chosen to go to Europe for the Association. His instructions were to study the whole European condition and report on it. He was further instructed to make contacts with and negotiate on behalf of the American industry with governments that had enacted or were about to enact legislation adversely effecting or restricting the distribution of American motion pictures. His instructions also contemplated the building up of friendly relations in quarters where enmity or hostility or prejudice existed against our films.

When Col. Lowry arrived in London in February, 1926, he found this situation:

Germany in the previous year (1925) had enacted a contingent law which provided in substance that for every picture imported into Germany a picture had to be produced in Germany. Under this law Paramount and Metro had effected an arrangement with the German Company Ufa which took care of their importations into and the distribution and exhibition of their pictures in Germany.

Hungary had passed a law which provided for compulsory production in that country (with the alternative of a heavy fine) by all importers of pictures. This Law was so severe and so impracticable in its terms that the American companies found it impossible to comply with it and soon after Col. Lowry's arrival in London they all were forced to withdraw and cease doing business in Hungary.

In England a quota bill was impending and had been for about a year. The agitation for such a restrictive measure was inspired and kept alive by the producers, certain popular newspapers of wide circulation and influence, such as the *Daily Mail* and the *Daily Express,* and by the Federation of British Industries. In the end the F.B.I. proved to be most potent and effective of all these influences.

The English situation, then, was the first objective. The agitation was at its height. Daily, articles appeared in the newspaper urging a quota on imported pictures. The F.B.I. and its associated organisations were active. Members of Parliament were being importuned. Speeches were being made to arouse sentiment and hasten action.

A relationship was quickly established with Sir Philip Cunliffe-Lister, President of the Board of Trade, a Cabinet Minister analogous to our Secretary of Commerce. One of the first fruits of this relationship, after many talks, was an agreement by Sir Philip to postpone action for a year in the hope that the British industry and the American industry could reach some basis of cooperation that would make legislation unnecessary. Therefore through the spring and summer of 1926 Col. Lowry remained almost continuously in London negotiating with a committee of the British industry. All of the factions and sections of the British industry could not reach an agreement among themselves, and the proposals for cooperation were not found acceptable in New York. At any rate, no response was returned. The action of the Imperial Conference (related above) made legislation inevitable and the present quota law was enacted after long debate in Parliament in 1927, effective January 1st, 1928.

It has not turned out to be as helpful and as easy to operate under as the British trade expected. When Col. Lowry was in London in June and July, 1928, he found the British distributors and exhibitors restless and unhappy. There was speculation among them as to whether the law, which runs for ten years, could be modified or repealed before reaching its statutory limitation.

These English negotiations were interrupted in April, 1926, by the urgency of the Hungarian situation. The American companies had withdrawn and business was at a standstill. Col. Lowry went to Budapest and began negotiations with the Hungarian Government. These negotiations were entirely successful and on April 29, 1926 Col. Lowry reported:

"The new tax of 4,500 crowns per meter based on negative lengths is not as low as I tried for but better than I expected to get. I have not heard yet the precise share the Hungarian exhibitors will pay, but if they pay the full 1,500 crowns per meter, our share will be about $72 per subject instead of $90, as under the old arrangement. The amount of the tax was a secondary consideration; the principal obstacle to be overcome was the compulsory production feature which provided that after the import of thirty pictures a picture had to be produced in Hungary or a fine of $6,000 paid in lieu of such production. Therefore, I did not talk about compulsory production at all in my negotiations. I simply assumed and took it for granted in all my conversations with the Government that that feature would be abandoned, abolished and wiped out as impracticable and not feasible. I confined myself to the amount of tax to be paid. Early in my negotiations they asked me if we would recognize the principle of compulsory production. I replied that we could recognize the principle but not the fact and by continuously assuming that under whatever new arrangement was made there would be no compulsory production feature, I did not have to argue it. . . .

"Through the intervention of other persons I got the Hungarian exhibitors interested in the outcome and finally when the conditions seemed absolutely right, I left Budapest on the afternoon of April 9th, without having reached a definite final agreement. I thought my departure would bring matters to a head and I felt that if I stayed on, the negotiations possibly would continue for another two or three weeks. This proved to be a correct assumption, for on Monday, April 12th, I received, as I had arranged for, a telephone message from our Legation at Budapest giving me the final terms of the agreement, under which the exhibitors were to share the tax. This was completely satisfactory and I wrote Walko, the Foreign Minister, a formal little note to tell him that it was acceptable.

"Aside from the satisfactory final terms of the settlement and the abolishment of the compulsory production provision of the order, I take the most satisfaction out of the good feelings left behind me. The Foreign Minister and all the Government people were friendly and the whole situation was sweet and not sour—as I found it. All our conversations and negotiations were conducted in the most amicable and friendly spirit. I think I left them assured of our good faith and good intention, and certainly they were most cordial, most friendly and delightfully agreeable in all their relations with me. I had a very definite feeling that I was leaving them as friends. It only remains for the representatives of the companies in charge of that territory to conserve and maintain these relations."

While in Budapest Col. Lowry drafted a report on the general European situation. On its receipt in New York this report was circulated among the executives of all member companies. For the sake of a complete record, and because Col. Lowry has not had occasion to change his views and opinions, the report is inserted here:

"In setting down the following tentative conclusion and outline of the whole European situation, I reflect partly my own present brief experience, but chiefly the concluded opinions of the American motion picture men I have met.

"Broadly speaking this is the condition our industry faces in Europe: virtually everywhere there is being made an effort to overcome the predominance of the American picture. These efforts spring from a variety of causes. One of them is the intense spirit of nationalism that now pervades all Europe. For patriotic and political reasons, governments of the several countries now seeking to restrict the importation of American pictures desire the establishment of a national picture industry in their own country that will serve as propaganda and that will reflect the life, the customs, and habits of its own people. This, so far as my knowledge runs, is particularly true in Hungary, in Austria and in England. I believe the same thing to be true in France.

"Another reason is pressure from the trade in the several countries. Here in Hungary and in England, where I have studied conditions at first hand, the main desire is to obtain access for their pictures to the great American market with its huge consumptive demand. That is, they not only want to have a supply of pictures for home consumption but they want to sell them abroad in our domestic market. They are all seeking, in their several ways, to find some means to force the American industry to help them in these two objects, as the price of doing business here.

"There are, of course, hundreds of minor causes operating to restrict the importation of American pictures. Pressure comes from playwrights, from actors, from labour interests, who see in the establishment of picture industries in these several countries the opportunity for employment.

"Broadly speaking again, the only people who are satisfied with present conditions and with the predominance of our pictures in these several European markets are the exhibitors and the great mass of people who attend motion picture performances. The exhibitors do not want to be restricted in showing American pictures because their customers like them above all others. The exhibitors want them because their customers like them. Their customers like them because they are better than any other pictures they can see. This is not true everywhere, I believe, but it is true in England and in Hungary. I am told that in Austria the good German picture is preferred to ours, but the American ranks second in popular favour.

"The American motion picture men with whom I have talked—and they are all primarily salesmen, are agreed only on one point: they have all told me that we have sent too many pictures to Europe and too many bad pictures. They say that in the years since the war, when we have had virtually no competition, we have flooded the market and have thrust upon exhibitors too many trashy pictures. I suspect this is true, for in government quarters and in the press and in other circles outside the motion picture industry, all the complaints have been centered against the great number of trashy American pictures. The remedy proposed by the representatives of our member companies—who speak as salesmen—is that we send fewer and better pictures.

"Even after my period of brief observation here, I am convinced that the time has definitely come for the American industry to formulate a concerted foreign policy both as to the character and the number of pictures to be sent abroad, also as to the method of their distribution. All of the American representatives I have seen tell me they have been writing for a year, or two years, or longer, to their New York offices urging that some attention be given to this rising tide of protest. They have eagerly welcomed my appearance as the sign of a new day for them when they will be relieved of the necessity of attempting to negotiate with governments, and meeting the clamour of public opinion which has been in part organized and in part a natural growth. They claim to have seen the present conditions coming about.

"At any rate we now face an actual condition. While I was

in London, occupied night and day with an acute situation, which is now happily averted, they were clamoring for me to come to Budapest where an even more acute situation existed. Here I am being urged to go as soon as possible to Austria and to France.

"As the one fire horse on duty, I shall attempt to rush to each fire as it breaks out, but that is not a satisfactory protection against the fire hazard that we face.

"In time we must have a central office here to which reports will be sent daily or weekly by representatives of all member companies operating on this Continent. We must establish a body of statistical information relating to taxes, laws, and all the conditions of doing business in the several countries. We must have a concerted, definite foreign policy. We must participate in and share this European business, or in the long run lose the better part of it. I am not thinking of today or tomorrow but of the long haul.

"The root of the whole business is that we make good pictures and pictures that will find a world market. No other country in Europe can do this at the present time, but several of them are resolved to have a try at it. Hardly any of the suggestions they made to us now are feasible, or practicable. In one way or another their present disposition is to make us pay the bill for their experiments. Efforts are in the making to inflame public sentiment to a point where it would prefer to see a bad homemade picture to a good American picture. This effort has not been successful so far, but I do not say it will not be if pressure becomes more powerful.

"Of one thing I am assured; our companies cannot make any headway or urge any satisfactory solution working separately. There must be concerted action and there must be a generous appreciation of the motives that animate people here in Europe seeking to establish small national industries of their own. There is no competition in sight that we need fear, but is it not better that we should content ourselves with 50 per cent. of the European business with no friction and with good will on both sides than that we should try to maintain 85 per cent. of the business in the face of opposition and manufactured ill will."

*　　*　　*

The situation in France required early attention and was one of the first problems taken up by Col. Lowry after his arrival in Paris in the Spring of 1926. Through his early contracts and associations with Jean Sapène the Association had a year's notice that the Decree issued February 19, 1928 was impending.

When Mr. Hays was in Paris in April, 1928 he gave me a review of the whole French situation to Ambassador Herrick which tells the story in outline. Following is Mr. Hays' review of the situation:

"In the light of our information, the present Decree and Regulations for the government of the motion picture industry in France had its origin in the winter of 1926. At that time Sapène was restive because he was not selling more of his pictures in the United Sates. He was aggressively seeking a market there. To stimulate the American industry to take an interest in his demands, he was running in *Le Matin* from time to time articles against the American industry.

"When Lowry first saw him in March or April, 1926, Sapène, after they became acquainted, said that he would not be satisfied until he was able to sell three or four of his pictures every year for distribution in the United States. Sapène and Lowry had many conversations on this subject and on the possibility and probability of selling Sapène's pictures in America. Finally these conversations came to a point where Sapène said in effect that unless the Americans would take his pictures he would cause them trouble in France.

"Finally at Lowry's request, Sapène stated in writing what he wanted. This communication was in the form of a memorandum for me and I received it in March, 1927 just about the time Lowry returned to New York. At that time Sapène was contemplating a visit to the United States and we urged him to come and made preparations to entertain him and show him our situation. However, he did not come and we heard nothing further in the matter until November of 1927 when Dr. Knecht and Nalpas came to the United States. They were endeavoring to sell Sapène's pictures and at the same time get an undertaking from some of our member companies that we would accept yearly a stated number of Sapène's pictures.

"While Nalpas and Knecht were in the United States engaged on this errand, the agitation stimulated by Sapène was begun in France for some form of contingent law. Lowry had returned to Europe at about the time Nalpas went to the United States in November, and in January he saw Herriot. At that time Herriot told him that he had appointed a Commission to study the whole subject of cinema control, that the Commission had reached no conclusions and probably would reach none for at least a month. Herriot said that he, in turn, would require another month to study the conclusions reached in consultation with his colleagues in the Cabinet who were interested in the matter. He welcomed Lowry in cordial terms and invited him to return to Paris in a month when he hoped the Commission would have reached a conclusion which could be discussed before any action was taken. In the meantime it was clearly understood that nothing would be done affecting the import of American pictures until Lowry had returned within the time specified.

"Within the month, that is to say on the morning of February nineteenth, Lowry returned to Paris and found in the morning papers the Decree of February eighteenth.

"No further effort was made to see Mr. Herriot until March tenth when Lowry had another long talk with him. No reference was made in this conversation to the promise previously given by Herriot that nothing would be done until Lowry's return. At this interview Herriot said he was opposed to a contingent and pointed out that no reference was made to a contingent in the Decree. He said that the Decree was for the protection of the French industry and was not copied after the laws that had been enacted in England, Germany and elsewhere providing for a contingent. He did not believe that a contingent was a wise or suitable method of promoting the interests of the French industry. This was on Saturday, March 10, 1923.

"On Monday, March twelfth, the Cinema Control Commission set up under the Decree passed its contingent regulations. These contingent regulations were further extended on April fourth.

"I had been fully informed by cable and by letter from Lowry of these several developments. Therefore, when I decided on March twenty-fourth to come to France to take personal charge of the negotiations, I was faced with this situation. I knew that in reality Sapène was the father of the Decree and the Regulations and that he personally controlled their execution. I knew that he furnished the motive power for the whole enterprise and I knew that he could be dealt with on a money basis, that is, that the whole condition could be remedied by purchasing his pictures. I had to choose between dealing with Sapène on this basis or dealing with the Government as the ostensible responsible authority. For the several reasons I have explained to you, I chose to deal with the Government as the more responsible and trustworthy factor in the situation. Had I dealt with Sapène directly, I have every reason to believe that I would have had to meet more stringent demands than he would have imposed one year or two years ago, and would have had to trust to him to deal with the government later and cause it to withdraw the Regulations under which we are unable to operate. While I had a nominal choice of dealing with Sapène or with the Government, actually the only course open to me was to deal with the Government."

Confirmatory of the above review of the situation is a report from Col. Lowry to Mr. Hays, dated Paris, November 30, 1926, which reads as follows:

"I took Sapène and Nalpas to lunch yesterday. We had a private room and stayed at table from 12:15 until nearly four o'clock.

"Sapène was never more frank and outspoken. He told me that he wanted peace and tranquillity, and that he would not get it until he sold three pictures every year to the United States. He was in a curious egotistical mood, and told me how powerful he was. He said that two years ago when nobody would pay any attention to him, meaning particularly the industry in the United States, he resolved to kick up such a row that they would have to notice him.

"He said that he was responsible for the agitation for the quota in England, and could bring about a quota in France and Italy if he so desired. He said, in effect, that he in his own person was the French industry, and that he was the most powerful man in France in the motion picture industry."

Another report from Col. Lowry to Mr. Hays, dated February 8, 1927, reads as follows:

"After he (Sapène) had talked on for two or three days in these vague general terms, about what must be done for French American cooperation in the industry. I asked him one day at lunch to tell me definitely and precisely what he wanted, what he was after, what he hoped and expected to get. I asked him to put it down in writing so that when I got home I would have a written memorandum in front of me when I discussed the matter with you, and with the heads of the industry. He promptly said that he would set down on paper precisely what he was hoping and expecting to get, and the next day he sent me the enclosure to this letter."

The memorandum of Mr. Sapène referred to in the preceding paragraph follows here:

February 2, 1927.

"The Société des Cinéromans was founded with the following program:

"1. To work towards the strengthening and improvement of the French picture industry.

"2. To collaborate with foreign films for the production in each country of pictures so treated as to be distributable every where.

"The idea of a Franco-American collaboration for the production of a certain number of pictures has been discussed with us on several occasions.

"The first was when Mr. Carl Laemmle, in the name of the Universal Pictures Corporation, proposed to us that we participate in the production of two big films a year, and this was accepted by us. However, when the proposed contract was drawn up, we were obliged to realize that, as matter of fact, the object thereof was the production in France of two American films under the control of Universal, with its cooperation and in accordance with its methods; such a proposition seemed to us impossible of acceptance for it would have constituted a renunciation by us of our principles and would have been the continuation of an error which we wished to combat, namely; the subordination of the original ideas of the different peoples to the directives of a single one of them.

"Later there were negotiations with Mr. Kennedy.

"He proposed to us the production of four or five pictures, the cost of which to be borne jointly and was not to exceed eighty thousand dollars per picture. The pictures were also to be executed with American cooperation and under the control of American technical personnel; we found ourselves again obliged to decline this new offer.

"Our object is, after having proved to the Americans, that, with our artists, our methods of work, our technique, our conception of the scenario and the powerful equipment at our disposition we can execute here original pictures susceptible of being shown with success in America, such as *Michael Strogoff* and *Les Miserables*, to obtain that an American company have confidence in us and reach an agreement with us for the distribution in America of two or three big pictures which would be produced annually by our Company, such American company to make the necessary effort for the launching of same in the United States, under the same conditions as our previous productions.

"We sincerely believe that, in addition to these two or three big pictures, we have in the rest of our production of fifteen or twenty pictures a year, certain works which would be very well received by the American public, if the pains were taken to present them to it.

"France has opened its doors to American production".

"Our public has had ample opportunity to appreciate American films and to create a success for those that are good".

"It seems just to us that the big American companies should make an effort to make the American public understand that there exist also in France producers of talent who, without having the same technique, the same stars, the same conception of execution, can make interesting pictures which would have the merit of bringing into the programs a greatly needed variety, if it be desired to prevent the public from tiring of always seeing the same type of production on the screen.

"From the practical point of view, an agreement would be extremely easy to reach. Two or three big pictures would be produced annually by the Société des Cinéromans from books and or scenarios approved in advance. Our Société would execute these pictures with entire freedom, but taking into account that they would also be shown in America.

"Such pictures would be accepted in advance for distribution in the United States by the American company which, at the time of delivery would pay, on account of the sums to be realized from their exploitation, a minimum amount proportional to the cost of the execution of the picture.

"The same would apply to the pictures of lesser importance and the number to be taken might be limited to 1 out of 4 of the annual production of 15 or 20 pictures.

"If the American company which dealt with the Cinéromans had no direct agency in France, or if it considered that its agency was not yielding sufficient results from the point of view of profits, Cinéromans might, according to the same principle adopted by it for America, exploit in France the films of the company with which it would contract.

"And if it be taken into account that Cinéromans has in

France a position which assures to it, *by far the largest location of all the companies here whether French or foreign*, the American company dealing with it would find in such an agreement a reciprocity which should be very profitable to it.

"The same system might be extended thereafter to Germany, where Cinéromans has already interesting contracts, and, little by little, to all the other countries *producing good pictures.*

"Such is the idea, simple and logical; the American company that will grasp it will find in it the possibilities of large profits. Such cooperation of companies, each financially solid, would allow of a sure extension of business, without risk and without necessitating the outlay of additional capital.

"Logical, sure and offering a *certainty for the future*, such an association in fact, which would at the same time leave to each company its independence, its originality and its flag, should reach, in a few years, a very considerable development."

The Decree issued at Paris February 18, 1928, the subsequent regulations of March 12, 1928, and the negotiations Mr Hays had at Paris in April–May, 1928, proved that Mr. Sapène was not idly boasting in 1926 and 1927.

The foreign representative of the Association was in the United States from March until November, 1927. When he returned to Europe he was called directly to Berlin where the German contingent law had just been abandoned by the Government as an acknowledged failure. This law had increased the quantity of German production, but had greatly lowered the standard of quality. The Ufa Company desired the abolition of the contingent, too, because it found it difficult under that law to comply with its contract with Paramount and Metro. A new set of regulations was issued by the Government governing the import of pictures. Several weeks were spent in negotiating with the competent government authorities to determine the scope, meaning and method of execution and administration of these new regulations.

Through December, January and until February, 1928, the entire time of the Association's representative was spent between Berlin and Paris in negotiation with the Berlin and Paris authorities, as the French situation was becoming increasingly threatening and critical. The negotiations in Berlin were concluded with a measure of success. On January 9, 1928 Col. Lowry reported by letter to Mr. Hays:

"Late on the afternoon of January 4th, just before I left Berlin for Paris, I was called to the Foreign Office to meet Mr. de Haas, the head of the American Section of that Office. He informed me in explicit terms that the Foreign Office and the Reichswirtschaftsministerium would favour and use their influence to make Germany a free and unrestricted market for us after June, 1929, when the present transitory and temporary regulations will expire. He said that he had talked with Dr. Landwehr, who is directly in control of our industry in the Reichswirtschaftsministerium: that Dr. Landwehr had heard with great attention and interest my arguments and explanations and had been favorably impressed by them. de Haas said he also had been converted to my way of thinking.

"He had one reservation to make, and that is a necessary one. Elections will be held in Germany probably next May, and de Haas pointed out that he could not commit the new Government, whatever it may be, to any course of action, but he assured me that, so far as the permanent officials in the Foreign Office and in the Reichswirtschaftsministerium could guide and influence the Government, it would be in favor of a free and unrestricted market.

"How this happy conclusion, which I did not hope for or expect for another six months was brought about is a long and involved story. My little speech at the farewell luncheon to the new German Ambassador was a factor. I established other relationships and found a series of right combinations that proved helpful and successful."

From London in November 1926 and from Berlin in December 1927, Col. Lowry reported on the general European situation. These reports follow:

London, November 24, 1926.

"The healthy, sound fundamental in all this European condition, England as well as the Continent, is that both the exhibitor and the theatre-goer continue to like American films. The customers are satisfied; both the customer of the producer at home (the exhibitor) and the customer of the exhibitor here who pays at the box office to see the pictures.

"Just so long as that condition lasts the American industry is standing on very solid ground.

"We should not feel satisfied and rest content with the feeling that this condition will endure forever. It will require constant effort to maintain it.

"The pictures are not solely responsible for the agitation against them. A great part of the agitation is a sort of blind protest against American dominance. The pictures bear the brunt of this protest because they are a conspicuous mark to shoot at. People are not happy here and on the continent. They envy us our freedom from external menace and threats. They don't give us full credit for our industry, enterprise, initiative, skill and ingenuity. It will be years before any of these people make real pictures—except the Germans. The French may make a few. But the whole state of mind must be changed.

"Meantime the American industry must exercise tact, consideration, patience and a sympathetic understanding while this state of mind exists in Europe. Wherever there is a quota or hampering restricting legislation aimed particularly at us, we must fight back, but fighting is a last resort between dealer and customer."

Berlin, December 28, 1927

"As I wrote you last year, I have been much impressed by the opinion of so many of our salesmen that we are sending too many pictures to Europe. Virtually all of the representatives of our member companies whose judgment seems good are agreed, I believe that fewer and better pictures would fetch just as much money as the great numbers of pictures we are now sending to this market.

"I wish that each of our companies could send a confidential circular letter to each of its chief men in Europe asking if a selected group of good pictures each year would not bring as great a return as the present system of sending virtually everything we make. I believe some of the companies do this now. In effect, impose a quota upon themselves and keep the trash at home. I believe the salesmen here would agree that conditions would be improved if all the companies did it. This would have the effect of making American pictures a standard of quality. Our good pictures are concededly so much better than European pictures that their prestige is injured by being mixed with the poor films sent along with the good ones.

"Sending such a great number of pictures abroad as we do also has the active effect of arousing the enmity and antagonism of the local domestic producers. This is particularly true at the moment in England, France, Germany and Austria. In all of these countries the local, domestic producers have been, and are, behind the agitation for contingents, quotas and other restrictive measures. He can make, as the event has proved, a very successful appeal to his government and to popular opinion. His argument in its main thesis is identical in each country. He says in substance: 'We (in Austria or France or Germany or England, as the case may be) cannot make pictures on equal terms with the Americans. Because of their great supply of capital and great resources accumulated during the war while we were fighting for our lives, they dominate our country. They can make and do make more pictures than all of us together. They recover the negative cost and a profit from their rich and huge home market. They can sell their pictures to us at any price because it is all or nearly all pure profit. If measures are not taken for our protection in our own country, soon you will see nothing but American pictures. Good pictures nowadays cost to make large sums of money. We cannot make these costly pictures unless we have access to the American market or unless our domestic competition is severely restricted.

" 'We have a right to have our own national pictures, but we can't have them unless this powerful foreigner is held in check. We want to see American pictures; they are the best, but we don't want to be choked to death with them and see nothing else. If we are to see our own national life in pictures, the American imports must be held down.'

"That argument has been potent in Germany, England, Austria and is now being made in France. It is made to me wherever I go. Of course, their argument is not made in a vacuum or with detachment but in heat and passion and with every conceivable effort to create prejudice and ill feeling against us and our product. In view of this general condition, identical in its main terms throughout the producing countries in Europe, in view of the opinion of so many of our salesmen that we could sell fewer and better pictures at the same or an increased return, in view of the agitation raised against us on the same basis in so many countries, I venture to raise a question and make a suggestion for a constructive procedure.

"Would it be in our interest to hold 50 per cent. of the European market without agitation and without restrictions, quotas, contingents, etc., rather than fight for 85 per cent. of the market against the increasing, rising, strengthening agitation against us?

"Would it be in our interest to supply only the best feature and super-feature pictures to this market leaving to the local and domestic producers to supply the ordinary run of programme pictures?

"Would it be in our interest to impose a quota upon ourselves to this end rather than have quotas and contingents, with all sorts of annoying provisions, imposed upon us?

"Would it be helpful to ask all the chief representatives of our member companies out here what they would think of the policy of fewer and better pictures, as outlined above?

"This is a rough and meager outline of what I believe to be our main problem out here now. I cannot stress too strongly my conviction that we must have a formulated plan and a foreign policy to which the whole organized industry can agree and will follow in so far as the common and general interest is affected. I do not think we can individually or otherwise successfully fight and antagonize the nationals of these foreign countries in which we are trading. As alien traders we have not the access to government or to public opinion that the native interests have. They do not have to be right to prevail.

"I do not believe for a moment in lying down and taking what is handed us without protest, and if restrictions are made too onerous and severe; if they lead to persecution, we must fight back. What I am seeking to reach is some agreement under which we can live in harmony with foreign interests with which we compete, that will allow us to share returns from all these foreign markets in proportion to the quantity and quality of our respective product. In a fight we are at an essential disadvantage in that the foreigner is on his home grounds. That makes all the difference. The umpire is kin to him every time.

"My brief experience out here has shown me clearly that we can't do anything permanent or constructive by merely applying a poultice to each pimple or boil or carbuncle as it appears on the surface. These agitations against us in the important European countries imply and are the sign of a fundamental condition. I am not a salesman or a merchant, but I can diagnose this situation and condition and raise the question in the minds of the businessmen most vitally concerned. What should be done about it? I can offer suggestions as I have done on the foregoing pages. We must have an office here where we can collect a body of data and keep in touch with our various member company representatives. One man with his office in his hat and his files in a suit case is not adequate to the situation. All this has been brought home to me by the need of my presence on one and the same day in Berlin, Paris and Vienna."

All of the foregoing is but a meager and bare outline of some of the larger activities of the Association abroad. It does not take into account the great number of chores, errands and services performed for individual member companies, and for the industry. Nor does this memorandum record the contacts established and work done in Italy, Norway, Sweden, Denmark, Spain and at Geneva in the interests of the industry. The records are accessible and available in the New York offices of the Association.

The establishment last March of an office in Paris has proved of value in strengthening the foreign work of the Association and in enlarging its service and usefulness to its member companies. This office was designed and should be continued as a service bureau. It is important now and will become increasingly important for the American producers to have always accessible and available a body of exact information about all the conditions that affect the distribution and exhibition of motion pictures in Europe.

It must be kept in mind that the observations, deductions and chronicle of actual conditions in this memorandum are based on the situation in Europe as it existed between February 1926 and July 1928.

Since the latter date a new factor has been brought into the equation. The American producers are now chiefly concerned with making talking and sound pictures. If this new product becomes the prevalent style in films the export trade will be radically and fundamentally affected. It quite well may be that after the present stock of silent pictures is exhausted our producers for a time, at least, will have comparatively few pictures to send abroad. The whole relationship between foreign customers and our domestic producers, it is conceivable will be greatly changed.

At any rate, no analysis of the foreign field as it will be one year from now and two years from now, can be made at this juncture. We must wait until the talking and sound pictures are further developed and until a thorough test can be had of the public response to these new style pictures.

Document 11: French Film Decree of May 1928 (text from Bureau of Foreign and Domestic Commerce, Trade Information Bulletin, no. 617)

Article I. The commission decides that the motion picture year for which the present regulations are established will run from October 1 to September 30 of the following year.

The following provisions are equally applicable during the period from March I to September 30, 1928.

Article II. The commission decides that all French films (provided that they are not in any way contrary to good morals or the public order) will receive the visa of the Film Control Commission required for their release in France, her colonies, or protectorates. This visa does not prejudice in any way the classification of these films in the first or second category, nor the rights they may have to protection.

Article III. Every film produced by a firm entirely French is considered a French film of the first category. The author of the scenario must be French, the technical director, the director and his assistant or assistants, and the cameramen must all be French; the interior scenes must be made exclusively in studios owned by French firms and situated on French territory. The leading roles may include foreign artists, but the proportion of these artists must not be more than 25%. In any case, and no matter how many leading roles there are, the right to one foreign artist is recognized, even if the number of leading roles is not divisible by four. On the request of a producer the commission will have the power to decide to permit in the leading roles a higher percentage of foreign artists than that provided for in the first resolution if the necessities for the production of the work require it.

Every film produced as above in which each item, including the direction, comprises at least 50% of French elements is considered as a French film of the second category.

Article IV. Each film produced in France which will be neither of the first nor of the second category can freely circulate in France, her colonies, and protectorates, but it will not be entitled to the advantages provided for by the decree.

Article V. The commission, desiring to protect solely the films which will be worthy of and honor France, declares that all the films protected must be important productions, produced with a view to a wide distribution at home as well as for exportation, and not simply to obtain the advantages of a protection.

Article VI. Taking into consideration the exceptionally large number of films (520 films) recently visaed by the Control Commission and to be released during the coming season, the commission fixes at 500 the number of foreign films which can be released in France during the period from March I, 1928, to September 30, 1929.

This number may be modified by the commission for the purpose of assuring at any time the number of films required by French exhibitors.

Article VII. Producers who give a satisfactory proof of the production of a French film of the first category will receive from the commission the authorization to release in France, her colonies or protectorates, seven foreign films.

Persons who give a satisfactory proof of the exploitation of a French film in one of the foreign countries, known as film-producing countries, will receive from the commission the authorization to release in France two foreign films. This number cannot be exceeded, whatever the number of buying countries may be. The producers can divide among various countries the number of import licenses to which they are entitled.

French films of the second category will have the right to 50% of the above advantages.

Article VIII. The measures taken for the protection of French films will not apply to short foreign films of which the total length does not exceed 600 meters, including titles.

Article IX. In order to be shown on the screens of France, her colonies and protectorates, every foreign film must, to obtain the visa of the French censor, be presented in the integral and original version in which it has been shown on the screens of its country of origin, with exactly the same titles, of which a French translation, guaranteed to be literal, will be supplied along with the film to be examined.

Article X. The commission reserves the right to refuse to issue censor cards in the future to any person, producer, distributor, or company, even an intermediary, who has produced, distributed, or done business with, in foreign countries, films which might reflect on the fair name of France.

Moreover, it has been decided that the authorization to bring in for 1928, without any formality, 40% of the number of foreign films imported in the year 1927 is changed and provides for 60% of such free visas.

And finally, the French films released since October last will be entitled, by a retroactive effect, to seven licenses instead of nine.

Document 12: Text of note from US State Department to the governments of France, Germany, Czechoslovakia, Austria, Hungary, Italy and Spain, all of which had either adopted or were contemplating adopting restrictive film regulations, April 1929 (text from *Film Daily*, 19 April 1929)

The government of the United States has for some time observed legislative and administrative developments in foreign countries as they affect the American motion picture industry, which has become one of the leading industries of the United States. There have been persistent and substantial demands for American pictures on the part of foreign exhibitors, and this has created an extensive foreign market for this American product.

The building up of this market has involved an investment of large proportions, and it is felt that this investment is jeopardized by certain governmental measures arbitrarily restricting the distribution of American films. The regulations are often so subject to arbitrary and unpredictable change that they introduce an element of commercial uncertainty and industrial instability to which American motion picture producers and distributors find it difficult or impossible to adjust themselves.

This government does not intend to question such measures as may be imposed by any country for the purpose of protecting through censorship the national traditions of public morals, but this government has adopted no restrictive regulations similar in any way to those enforced in certain foreign countries. It believes firmly that the interests of the motion picture industry in all countries are best promoted by the freest possible interchange of films based solely on the quality of the product.

The department has observed with sympathetic interest the increasing number of films which have entered the United States in recent years on a free competitive basis and that the American motion picture industry has always shown a willingness to collaborate in the most friendly way with representatives of the industry for the unrestricted importation of films.

It is, therefore, the earnest hope of the government of the United States that the governments to whom it is making representations will have appropriate steps taken to avoid the serious injury to which American motion picture producers are subject by restrictive regulations, and which it feels must eventually prove a hindrance to international development of the motion picture industry.

Document 13: Lars Moen, "The International Congress: A Constructive Help—or a Futility,"*Kinematograph Weekly*, vol. 148, no. 1156, 13 June 1929, p. 25

In the course of a chequered journalistic career it has been my duty, pleasant and otherwise, to cover an incalculable number of conventions, congresses, sessions and plain ordinary meetings—some of them national, some international—Shriners, Rotarians, physicians, dancing teachers, prestidigitators—and a great many kinema exhibitors conventions.

Sometimes I was a delegate, or the publicity director, but more often I was able to observe tranquillity from the reporters' bench.

And, looking back over my recollections of all those pompous sessions, I am unable to recall one tangible, useful result that has ever come out of them, the sole exception being scientific bodies which made no pretence of doing anything but listening to carefully prepared lectures and demonstrations, discussing them, accepting or rejecting reports and proposed standards, and quietly going home.

For the others, there seems to be no exception to the rule that the average convention delegate has no concern with anything but social functions, a bit of a wild time away from home, and attending only those business sessions which he can't decently avoid.

The little handful of men who are the exception to this rule—the politicians—are consequently able to work their will with the majority, for nowhere is crowd psychology better demonstrated than at a convention.

The second International Congress of Kinema Proprietors is now at an end. The delegates have returned home to put into practice the principles adopted—or to forget them. So let us, with the utmost impartiality possible, examine briefly the eight resolutions passed by this Congress, consider their practical usefulness, and perhaps hazard a few forecasts as to their application and consequences.

The Contingent

The first resolution favours national legislation to protect national production, always keeping in view the quantity of films needed for the kinemas of a country.

Thus perpetuating the principle of protecting films, not because they are good, but because of their nationality, which is not only uneconomic, but has thus far failed to show any praiseworthy results which could not have been obtained without it.

Restriction of imports on such a basis as to prevent the flooding of a market with too many films would be sound economically, but such films as are admitted should be on an equality with the domestic product. And that domestic product should be forced to fight for bookings on merit, not legislation. But let us leave this controversial and worn-out subject.

The Sound-Film

The demand that all sound-films and sound apparatus be interchangeable, and the protest against high prices of equipment, are both justified and praiseworthy. But it is commercial competition and the march of events that will take care of that, congresses or no congresses. . . .

Futility!

The proposal that the delegates from each country approach their producers with the demand that they produce films of better quality seems almost too futile to discuss. I doubt if there is a producer extant who would not like very much indeed to make better films—but picture "hits" have something of the erratic quality of lightning, and the desire to make great films is no assurance of being able to make them.

The demand that film length be held down is admirable. Continental films, in particular, are prone to take ten or eleven thousand feet for something which could have been told infinitely better in five thousand.

The protests against blind and block booking are equally sound, and particularly commendable is the refusal to show films breeding national hatreds—if they will do it. Although less important, the move for the standardisation of poster and photo sizes is commendable—but where is the machinery that is going to bring this about? . . .

Taxes

The demand for the repeal of special taxes needs no comment. The congress might very well have concentrated its entire attention on this problem, for its cure would relieve most of the other problems automatically.

Technical Questions

The demands for greater safety, encouragement of research, international standards for apparatus, and equipment exposition in connection with each congress, and an international bureau for the study of new appliances, are all too valuable and too sound to need commentary or support—but what is going to be *done* about it?

Legislation

The need for closer international relations in obtaining fairer legislation is evident—but such problems are not solved by passing resolutions. Where is the highly organised, well financed, fighting machine that is going to do this?

Non-Theatrical Competition

The protest against the renting of films to non-theatrical enterprises is right and just—every American exhibitors' convention within my memory has passed such a resolution, but I do not know that this has had any material effect.

The Answer

After which, being perhaps a bit open to the charge of "destructive criticism", permit me to show my good faith by pointing out what I think would accomplish what no such Congress ever can accomplish—results.

I have referred rather disparagingly to American exhibitors' conventions. *But*—some very fine things have been achieved by American exhibitor organisations. How? Not through conventions.

They have accomplished results, and profitable ones, by means of a *business office,* manned by capable and well paid executives, who were held responsible by the organisation for getting those results. That office is open the year round. Its executives do not become enthusiastic for four days during a convention, then go home and forget all about it.

If it is a matter of music tax, one of these executives, empowered to act for the entire organisation, gets together with the representative of the music publishers and composers—and because there are two men present, and not two hundred or two thousand, they accomplish something tangible and valuable.

If it is a matter of fighting adverse legislation, that office has the organisation and the contacts to fight that legislation.

And if these International Congresses are to be given any value above that of a great deal of hand-shaking and speech making, there must be such an international office, entrusted with full and absolute power to carry out the principles decided upon at that convention.

Such an office, located perhaps in Paris for geographical reasons, with branches in each European capital, could literally revolutionise, over a period of years, the kinema in Europe.

But without such practical means of putting into execution the splendid ideas conceived at such a Congress, they remain just that—"splendid ideas"—worth exactly nothing until they are executed.

Group 3: European Access to the American Market and the International Film
J.D. Williams and Erich Pommer

The arguments mounted in these documents by Williams and Pommer underline just how crucial the more enterprising European filmmakers of the period thought it was to gain access to that most lucrative of world markets, the American market. Central to their arguments is a particular conception of the type of film that should be made for these purposes: the international film, with a simple human story that has "universal" appeal, but which is still rooted in the national traditions of its producing country. The conversion to sound inevitably troubled such developments, and the final document details some of the efforts made to overcome the problem of language. Williams and Pommer are interesting figures, leading entrepreneurs of the period, with clear American connections. Williams was himself American and had been centrally involved in key developments in the 1910s and 1920s, but moved to the UK in 1926, setting up first a production company and then an international distribution company, described in Document 15. Pommer of course was one of Germany's leading producers, but he too had had a stint in Hollywood. The fact that both pieces by Pommer included here were published in English indicates the extent to which he was seen at the time as an influential spokesman for certain developments in European film-making.

Andrew Higson

Document 14: J.D. Williams (Managing Director, British National Pictures Ltd), "Two Keys to the American Market: Quality and Variety will Open all Doors," *Kinematograph Weekly*, 7 January 1926, pp. 55–56

In my opinion the most serious error made by the most strenuous advocates, in theory, of the restoration of film making in this country, has been in such theorists having regarded this matter as a national problem.

The desire to see fine films made in Britain is, I hope, very laudable, since I possess it and am now in process of putting it into practice; but it is unfortunate that this very important movement should in some way have attracted to itself the Little Englander.

I can understand the resentment of the people of this country at the flooding of British screens with American pictures, but I cannot understand any sane person letting that resentment blind him to the plain business issues at stake.

On our side we wish to create a really great film-making industry. We want to manufacture great films, but we know that one of the most important factors in film production is the size of your available market. Your expenditure must be less than your income, otherwise you are bankrupt. It stands to reason, then, that the greater income you can command, the more you can spend on making your pictures.

America is sixty per cent of the world's market. Therefore, if you rule out America you must be content with a forty per cent sale. That, to say the least of it, seems unambitious. I regard it as essential to the future of British film production that British films should be released in America.

Now look at the matter from the American angle. Suppose you are an American renter, then you will need, like renters everywhere, a supply of films in quantity, of quality and of variety.

In regard to the "quantity" requirement you will have little trouble. The American film market in sheer numbers, is overstocked. Please note that particularly, because I shall have to return to it.

In quality the American market's requirements are unfulfilled. I think it never likely to happen in any market that there will be an over abundance of high-grade pictures.

In variety the American film market is bankrupt. It does possess a few tangible assets in this direction. Most of these are of European origin.

You find, therefore, as an American renter, that you can get pictures in quantity easily enough; you find it more difficult to get pictures of quality; you find it most difficult of all to get variety.

Come back to Britain and take these points one by one frankly and honestly, because if you are to enter an over loaded market, you must find out where the load is leanest and you must try to cater for that deficiency.

If you do that you will obviously decide right away that the quantity circumstance is against you. The Americans, you will decide, have plenty of pictures of a kind, and you will automatically decide that there is no hope for you in making pictures "of a kind." I would like to make very clear that in my view no picture will ever get into America just because it is a picture. I know the Americans send rubbish over here, but that rubbish is sold here either by Americans themselves or by British people who have run after it. The Americans will not run after our rubbish; therefore, if you want to have it seen in America we must take it there ourselves, which would be for our film future the worst of bad business.

The "quality" circumstance offers some hope. There is a real opportunity for any good film in America, but in point of quality, you should remember you have to compete with film makers who, whatever they may lack, most certainly do possess technical knowledge to an extraordinary degree and who can edit films with faultless precision. That technical knowledge and editorial ability have, in my opinion, been grievously lacking in this country.

I could say a great deal more on this point, but for the moment I am aiming at constructive criticism. I shall content myself with saying that in this country at the moment there are not enough expert technical men to make more than twelve technically passable pictures a year—and by the word "technical" I wish to include everybody engaged in film making save the artistes, in respect of which England is a gold mine whose surface has not been scratched.

Let us look at the "variety" circumstance. The people of this country admittedly are tired of the sameness of American films. A large proportion of American films are cast in one mould. They are made by people with one-way minds. But if we are tired of American film scenery and drama, what of the American, to whom all this stuff is much more familiar?

The answer is that the American picturegoer is so sick of mass production product that desperate efforts are being made by film manufacturers to cure it, by importing foreign players, foreign authors, foreign directors and foreign locations. It is very nearly time to say that apart from the Wild West, the Frozen North and Flaming South, which usually yield contemptible pictures, there is no American film business at all. There is a great industry whose very foundations are laid on the artistic treasures and traditions of Britain, with all other European countries together adding but a trifling percentage.

Now that development of the so-called American film industry is due to the insistent call of the American people for variety in film entertainment. That is so obvious that I do not need to detail it at any greater length.

Surely, then, it is logical to go one step further and to reason that those chiefs of film companies who have gone to so much pains to import British art in the raw state will also import it manufactured, always provided the workmanship has that finish and beauty and solidity which characterises so much of the goods made in Britain?

I know that to be true. I am so sure of it that I am leaving for America within the next few days, and there I shall arrange for the release of all British National product and of such independent pictures as we may buy, because I am taking steps to guarantee that our films will be polished entertainment.

We must get that polish.

Then we must make our pictures reflect the very Soul of England . . .

And that brings me to a very crucial point where I would offer a word of caution to British producers.

The Soul of England is in English drama and not in English landscapes. You cannot "make" a film in the sense of giving it outstanding quality by standing outside and photographing your action in the most beautiful vales of Sussex or Devon or any other county. It is the story that is the soul of your picture. Story is the drama. Drama is the artifice. Exteriors are facts.

A few exteriors judiciously selected will lend to your tale an air of conviction. Many exteriors will make it commonplace. The commonplace murders drama. And added to that lack of imaginative settings, Britain is handicapped in her selection of stories. In this land of dramatic glories, far too many trivialities are filmed. I wish that, in both those respects, I could dare to assume completely the cloak of critic and quote illustrations of what I mean, but that is naturally impossible.

So if you will permit me a misquotation, the fault is not in the stars and stripes, but in British films. I wish it were otherwise, but it is useless to blind ourselves at this crisis to the real facts. It is up to everyone working in Britain with British capital to make pictures excellent in quality and revealing, as can only be done in this country, the Soul of England. That way, I am convinced, lies the only open door to America; and that door is wide enough for all of us.

It is a sheer myth to say there is a prejudice in the United States against British goods of any kind. In respect of pictures, as I have said, American producers are trying hard to make films as British as possible. Naturally they fail to capture the authentic spirit of England. That is not to be wondered at, and while the misrepresentation of England in American films is often to be deplored, it is more a matter for wonder that they get near to it at all.

And seeing all exhibitors already possess Rolls-Royce cars, I shall not be guilty of breaking into advertisement if I point out that British product is the envy of the world. That is beauty and finish and solidity.

Now let us have Rolls-Royce pictures.

Document 15: J.D. Williams, Speech at the Annual Conference of the National Board of Review, 26 January 1929 (Motion Picture Association of America Archive, Reel 8, 1928 World Wide Films File)

It has been said that the motion picture is the one universal voice of humanity.

If this is true—and I believe nothing truer was ever said—then Hollywood has been doing 90% of the motion picture talking and the rest of the world 90% of the listening. Now the fact is that the rest of the world is getting tired of listening to this Hollywood screen monologue.

Other nations have come to realise that films are much more than merchandise. Their governments are awakening to the realisation that motion pictures are the magic containers of human thought—that they are just as necessary to national progress as newspapers and books.

Europe's potential leaders, its business men and bankers realize the importance of motion pictures to their future welfare—they are determined to have their own screen press.

Great Britain, for instance, now realizes that the young people of her far-flung colonies should see motion pictures of British life. The empire upon which the sun never sets, whose glorious past, virile present, and portential [sic] future is so great—their Empire is too wise to long stand idly by while shadowy invaders of the screen steal away the attention and affections of its own youth. Good American pictures will always have a place on British screens. No one, least of all myself, would deny them what their merit deserves. But there must be good British pictures also, and they should be seen by Americans—and they will be.

And so they have earnestly set about making pictures based on their own life and literature.

You may be surprised to know that about seven hundred and ninety-five pictures will be made during the current year.

In the past two years, the capital invested in foreign production has increased tremendously. It is stated on good authority that seven times as much money went into production in 1928 as in 1927. And they are making better pictures every year.

Now the plan of our company, World Wide Pictures, is to select and import from pictures produced abroad those which we believe suitable for this country. We may bring over 30 or 40 the first year—it is doubtful if we will ever handle over 50 or 60 annually. We hope to provide a sort of clearing house for the best pictures from all parts of the world.

Our slogan is: "Photoplays made where the story's laid."

We are urging European producers to make their pictures out of doors, exactly on the scene called for in the scenario.

For instance: in our first list we have pictures made in London, Paris, Deauville, Vienna, Berlin, The Isle of Man, Sicily, the Russian Frontier, Egypt, Algiers, and so on.

The scenes and atmosphere are genuine.

The stories are different.

The stars and casts will supply new faces for our screen.

We feel sure that people will enjoy seeing these pictures for the variety and change they will afford.

Europe has much to give to the screen. America has just welcomed and benefited by its history, art and literature. Now that they are making good pictures over there I believe America will welcome them too.

The theatres and public of this country need all the good films they can get. Nobody has ever complained about there being too many good pictures.

The picture business in America today is going through the same evolution of centralization as other national industries. Unfortunately for the quality and variety of American films it is easier for the bankers to merge dollars and theatres than it is to merge brains and talents.

At the present time American production may be said to be operating on a ratio of 8 to 20,000 to 110,000,000. Eight major studios produce the pictures for our 20,000 theatres and 110,000,000 people. Think of it: no other medium of expression is so bound in the golden chains of modern business.

In fact, competition for control of the American industry points to even greater centralization of production. When it is realised that the eight major studios are all located in Hollywood—a closely-knit community remote from the rest of the world where the interbreeding of ideas, tastes and prejudices are inevitable—we more readily understand the complaint —so often heard—against the monotony and sameness of motion pictures.

Mr. Adolph Zukor, head of the Paramount company, said in a recent interview: "The industry will always need keen competition—not unfair competition, not unethical competition, but keen competition. I like to see strong companies in competition. I don't see where great amalgamations help the industry, where they help the companies, or where they help the public. Competition makes good pictures and good pictures provide attendance."

Now here is where imported pictures come in. They will more and more furnish the needed competition. What we need is many production centers, many producers working independently of each other. More liberty of thought for the creator. More variety of story and theme.

What would the world's literature be like if all the writers were herded into eight publishing houses and allowed to write nothing but what eight editors thought would pay best.

My associates in our new company believe that our organization will perform a genuinely helpful work both for the industry and public by organizing source of supply of pictures which will bring us new faces, different stories, the novelty of distant lands and scenes. Pictures which could not be made in America.

And we believe that our company should prove to be a practical step toward reciprocity in the world's film economies. The fact that their pictures have a chance in America will lessen the growing agitation against American films abroad.

What we propose is film conversation between nations instead of the present Hollywood monologue. We believe that it will be a good thing all round.

Document 16: Erich Pommer, "The International Picture: A Lesson on Simplicity," *Kinematograph Weekly*, 8 November 1928, p. 41

The towering importance of the American motion picture on the world's markets cannot be safely explained by the unlimited financial resources at the disposal of the American producers, who are clever enough to make the best and most rational use of them. Its main reason is the mentality of the American picture, which, notwithstanding all attacks and claims to the contrary, apparently comes nearest to the taste of international kinema audiences.

In making this statement, I do not want to pass judgement, either in regard to artistic or to technical qualities. The specific and unique element of the American film is the fact of its being absolutely uncomplicated. Being what is called "naive" it knows no problems, a fact which, especially in Europe, is continually and severely criticised.

Universal Appeal

But it is really preferable to have a picture too light rather than too heavy, because in the latter case there is a danger that the public will not understand the story. This is the worst thing that can happen with a picture, for individuals may find it difficult to understand things which they do not know from their own experiences and which are alien to the trend of their thought and ideas. This shows that one has to be particularly careful in selecting picture stories that touch on spiritual problems.

However, in the same measure as one finds subjects, motives and happenings which are of a typically local character, so may one encounter thoughts and events which will equally impress the feeling and thinking of all nations and countries. Only if a picture complies with this condition can it be properly called an "international film."

Spectacular Appeal

The international appeal of a picture has its foundation in its story. It is totally independent of the capital invested and of the splendour and luxury used in its production. The fact that in most cases the supers and monumental pictures have proved to be such international successes, does not disprove this claim.

Such productions always have a simple story of universal appeal, because it is simply impossible to use spiritual thoughts and impressions of the soul in a picture deluxe. The splendour in such production is not merely created for decoration—it is its outstanding purpose. So, quite naturally, the splendour is always in the foreground and suppresses the human element. But splendour means show, and a show is always and everywhere easy to understand.

A Plea for Sincerity

But this does not mean that the picture should be devoid of every national element. On the contrary, if the motion picture is not deeply rooted in the national soul, it loses its solid foundation and, therefore, its convincing and truthful elements.

It is absurd to strive for "international costumes or decorations", because this would rob the picture of its physiognomy and every element of life. It is not the outward makeup of a film which must be international, but its inner contents and value. It must have an international appeal to the soul, the feeling.

My two years of work in the United States have convinced me that this theory is correct, and, when I returned to Germany to produce to Ufa, it was a pleasant surprise to find that in my old friend Joe May I found a strong supporter of my plan to utilise my American experience for film production in Europe.

Sentiment

With this object in view, we have produced *Heimkehr* (*Homecoming*). By the way, I do not know whether it is just a queer incident or a whim of fate, the title of the first film I have produced for Ufa since my return from America should be "Home-coming", but I believe that this very first picture has proved that it is feasible to carry out my ideas and plans.

There are but three outstanding figures in the picture: two German soldiers and a German woman, Karl, Richard and Anna (Gustav Froehlich, Lars Hanson and Dita L'arlo). All other figures are of no importance whatever. And although every means was utilised to provide the picture with every impression necessary, *Homecoming* is not a "spectacle de luxe".

Now, if not only in Germany, but practically every civilised country, including America, a strong interest is manifested in this production, the reason will be that its story is of international appeal. In this respect nothing is altered by the fact that the characters are of German flesh and blood and that the picture is deeply rooted in the soil of Germany, for its story, that of a man who was believed dead and returns home after years of absence, only to find that in the meantime his wife has fallen deeply in love with this best friend, contains a spiritual conflict which is immediately understood by every nation of the world.

Document 17: Erich Pommer, "The International Talking Film," *Universal Filmlexikon*, ed. Frank Arnau (Berlin, 1932), pp. 14–15

Paradoxical as it may sound, the international talking film is an accomplished fact. During the first year of the new medium neither the experts nor the public believed this to be possible. It was thought that the internationalness of silence could not be adequately replaced by the national limitation of language. The spoken word appeared to have become an insurmountable barrier. It was considered that the end of the international film had arrived and, at the same time, the end of the film had arrived and, at the same time, the end of the film as the incomparable medium of culture and propaganda that it had been. The talking film could not bear capital investment on a large scale, since its profit producing possibilities were limited from the outset.

It was mainly business considerations and the desire to be first in the field that, for a considerable time, led the Americans to make their productions suitable for European countries by means of dialogue strips. However, it was soon realised that the language difficulty and the problem of internationalism could not be solved in this manner. Those films failed again and again because, apart from their technical inadequacy, it was apparently impossible to make the poor subject matter arising from the American mentality palatable to the European taste. Thus it was necessary to approach the problem from an intellectual angle. At the same time it was realised that the material alone, though it had attained the "intellectual export standard", could not operate both as the attraction and the interpreter. The great public of Berlin, Paris, London and New York were unwilling to give up, with the advent of the new era, the stars to whom they had been accustomed. Producers of all nationalities were already faced with the difficulty of training the silent stars for the talking film. They only succeeded in rare cases. It was necessary to call upon new gifts and to develop them to the standard of prominence. At first the most obvious expedient was resorted to, the theatrical past of famous stars being exploited. In America an attempt was made to render internationally marketable the magnificent voice of Al Jolson. It was thought that its emotional appeal would be understood everywhere. In Germany Emil Jannings' return from America was put to account. This star of the silent days, who had attained greatness with Reinhardt's great theatrical tradition, had learned English during the time of his American engagement. The Ufa could therefore very well risk making Emil Jannings, who would be understood on both sides of the Atlantic, their first choice for both versions of *Der blaue Engel*. And while the well-known Jolson films very quickly ceased to attract owing to their typically American themes, the novelty of the new medium having in the meantime worn off, in Germany they had found the means for the correct mixture, the more so as the limitations of the subject, in this instance the tragedy of the ageing teacher Unrat, were compensated for by the recruitment of a director of the calibre of Josef von Sternberg. As a matter of fact, they succeeded in the attempt to make this essentially German tragedy internationally understood. *Der blaue Engel* was the first German talking film to achieve international success.

In the meantime, the development of talking film production continued its irresistible onward march. The groping experiment became a permanent system. The realisation that great films could only be produced if a return on the substantial capital expended on them could be secured by the possibility of international exhibition led to the making of several versions as a matter of course. Right from the inception of a film it is endeavoured to take into account all the factors that make for success. The subject matter of the film is the main consideration. The idea itself must be capable of being understood all over the world. In the scenario it is absolutely necessary to take into account those great human emotions that are the same for all countries. Unfortunately, there is no safe recipe, for the slightest turn in the plot will frequently cause different reactions. That is why not all versions of a picture are successful. However, the basic idea is not everything. Far from it. Even the simplest fable, though it may everywhere appeal to both to the most primitive and the most differentiated emotions, will not answer; the impelling elements must be thought out exactly down to the most minute detail. The habits, customs, and usages of the various peoples are important matters that must be taken into consideration. Success may be decisively affected by current events, as well as by political changes and changes in the fashion. A picture that was yesterday received with hearty laughter by an entire nation may tomorrow evoke the deepest resentment. The popularity of the star is no safeguard against these dangers. On the contrary, they are a menace to his or her hard-won success. It has been realised that, ultimately, the chief problems of mankind always remain the same and that the only scope for variations is provided by environment and the treatment of the subject. That is why, as far as possible, novel yet nonetheless perennial plots are chosen—love and pain, humour and sentiment, art and nature, science and the primitive, in a word, all the immortal subjects of the poets of all the ages.

It was only recently that the Ufa have followed up their former international talking film successes—*Der Drei von der Tankstelle*—with another, *Congress Dances*, which is probably the greatest international film they have hitherto produced. In that film history is merged with modern melody, exciting topicality with compensating romance,—a mixture which lends Erik Charell's first screen production its peculiar charm. The subject justified the employment of unlimited capital, while the making of three versions ensured an unrestricted international market. Apart from the fortunate Lilian Harvey, whose linguistic gifts and popularity present a basis of universal understanding, popular stars of various nationalities were employed in this film, in order to arouse public interest equally in all countries. Nonetheless, to attempt to produce an international film and risk a substantial amount of capital is a daring thing to do. The risk has justified itself, however. *Congress Dances*, which was first shown in Berlin at the end of October, 1931, has been an unparalleled success throughout the world. The premieres in London, Paris and Vienna were sensational successes. At the time of writing, the New York premiere is imminent. The paradox of the international talking film has become a reality. The Esperanto of the talking screen has been discovered.

Index

Abel, Richard, 45
ABPC *see* Associated British Picture Corporation
Abrams, Hiram, 134, 139
Academy of Motion Picture Arts and Sciences, 212
ACE *see* Alliance Cinématographique Européene
actors and actresses *see* film stars
Advisory Committee on Social Questions *see* League of Nations
AEG, 14
Africa Film Trust, 276
Alaskan, The (1924), 306
Albers, Hans, 263
Algiers (1938), 215
All-Union Society for Cultural Relations with Foreign Countries (VOKS), 68
Allen's (Canada), 134
Alliance Cinématographique Européene (ACE) (Ufa subsidiary), 61, 266, 267
Allied Artists (UA subsidiary), 140, 142, 144
Allô? Berlin? Ici Paris! (1932), 210, 256
Allport, F.W., 89
American cinema: as agent of economic expansion, 11–14; appeal to working-class audiences, 49–50; co-operative marketing in Europe, 148, 349–53; competition from French sound films, 231–3, 242; cultural influence, 9, 11–14, 16–17, 32–4, 41, 50–1; decline in exports, 138; distribution in Europe, 132–56; dubbing for foreign versions *see* dubbing; economic importance of exports, 4, 9, 137, 187, 250; excessive exports, 43, 137, 187, 376–8; exports to France, 182, 187; exports to Sweden, 182; Hollywood as Utopia, 50–1; import of European films, 390–2; import of foreign personnel, 5, 9, 13, 213, 221, 234, 261, 285, 304; imposition of American mass culture, 33–7, 49–51; influence on women, 34, 35, 49–50; international market share, 86; local adaptability of silent film, 39–42; overseas distribution strategies, 138–42; relationship with France, 371–4; relationship with Germany, 61, 159, 160–1, 174, 333–7, 349–50; sound films for Europe *see* sound films *and also under individual countries*; use of European film stars, 220–2, 304–5; use of foreign subsidiaries, 142–4; use of overseas agents, 133–6; *see also entries for individual film companies*
Amkino, 69
Ammann, Betty, 305
Amour maitre des choses, L' (1930) *see Flame of Love*
An der schönen blauen Donau (1926), 260
Anderson, Sir Alan, 356
Andra, Fern, 305
Andrew, Dudley, 214
Annabella (Suzanne Charpentier), 218–19, 263
Antoinette Sagbrier (1927), 192
Arnheim, Rudolf, 104, 106
Arthur (1931), 238
Artists Associés SA, Les (LAA) (UA subsidiary), 142–4, 150
Asche, Oscar, 315
Asphaltschmetterling (1929) *see Grosstadtschmetterling*
Associated British Picture Corporation (ABPC), 294
Associated Sound Film Industries, 277
At the Villa Rose (1929), 211
Atlantic (1929), 209, 211, 284, 285; as international film, 291, 293
Aubert, Louis, 162, 163, 164 *see also* Etablissements Louis Aubert SA
Aumont, Jean-Pierre, 219

B&D *see* British and Dominions Company
Bad Blood (1936) *see First Offence*
Bailby, Léon, 192
Bajor, Gizi, 220
Baker, Josephine, 307
Barnstyn, J.C., 145
Baroud (1932), 209
Barry, Joan, 216
Batcheff, Pierre, 209
Battleship Potemkin (1926), 62, 69
Baur, Harry, 21, 219
BBFC *see* British Board of Film Censors
Beau Ideal (1930), 235
Belle Epoque (1992), 24
Belphegor (1921), 192
Ben Hur (1925), 8–9, 14, 20, 187, 260
Bennett, Arnold, 310, 311
Bergfelder, Tim, 302–24

Bergner, Elisabeth, 305
Bernard, Raymond, 62
Bernhardt, Kurt, 221
Berry, Jules, 219
Berthomieu, André, 217
Big Pond, The (1930), 209, 211
BIP see British International Pictures (BIP)
Blackmail (1929), 216, 288
blaue Engel, Der (1930), 253, 395
block-booking see exhibitors
Blumer, Herbert, 102
Bock, Hans-Michael, 256
Bonn, Moritz J., 82, 83
Borde, Raymond, 263
Bordoni, Irene, 228
Bordwell, David, 215
Boyer, Charles, 215
Bradin, Jean, 280
Brandes, Werner, 279, 280, 310
Brantlinger, Patrick, 35
Break the News (1938), 217
Breathless (1959 & 1983), 210
brennende Acker, Der (1922), 160
Brézillon, Leon, 21, 127
Briand, Aristide, 15, 78
British Board of Film Censors (BBFC), 312
British Cinematograph Act see Cinematograph
  Films Act
British and Dominions Company (B&D), 149
British Empire: cultural influence of cinema, 315,
  354–6, 390; international market share, 46, 86;
  and portrayal of China, 317–18; portrayal of
  miscegenation, 312
British International Pictures (BIP), 211, 274, 275,
  276, 278–94, 308, 314, 315: multiple-language
  production, 284, 288–93; Pathé agreement, 62;
  role in Film Europe, 286–8; see also Dupont, E.A.
British National Pictures (later BIP), 276–9, 285
British National Studios (Elstree) see British
  National Pictures; British International Pictures
Broadway (1929), 231
Broadway Melody (1929), 127
Brockliss, J. Frank, 133
Brook, Clive, 314
Brooks, Louise, 305
Buchanan, Thomas, 140
Burguet, Charles, 193

Cabinet of Dr Caligari, The (1919), 57, 336
Cameron, Alfred D., 198
Camp Volant (1932), 210
Canty, George R., 8, 98, 183, 229
Cape Forlorn (1930) (Menschen im Kafig/Le Cap
  Perdu), 284, 291–2, 293–4
Captain Rascasse (1928), 192
Carr, Richard, 21
Carr-Gloria-Dupont Productions, 279–80, 285
Casanova (1926), 24, 163, 193
Casque de Cuir, 150
CEA see Cinematograph Exhibitors' Association;
  Co-operative Export Association
Chalmers, Henry, 359–60
Chambre Syndicale Française de la

Cinématographie et des Industries qui s'y
  Rattachent, 184–5, 189–92, 194, 197-8
Chaplin, Charles, 138, 140, 262, 336
Charell, Erik, 396
Charters, W.W., 105
Chemin du Paradis, Le (1930) see Drei von der
  Tankstelle, Die
Chevalier, Maurice, 209, 221, 229, 230
Chirat, Raymond, 209
Chu Chin Chow (1934): as international film, 315
Ciné-France, 163, 167
Cinema Commission (France) see Film Control
  Commission
Cinema Commission (ICW) see International
  Council of Women's Congress on Cinema
  (Rome, 1931)
cinema owners see exhibitors
cinemas see film theatres
Cinematograph Exhibitors' Association (CEA),
  140
Cinematograph Films Act (1927), 33, 149, 192,
  275, 279, 364 see also quota system
Cinéromans see Société des Cinéromans
City Butterfly (1929), 286
Clair, René, 76, 217
Co-operative Export Association (CEA), 351-2
Coeur de Lilas (1931), 150
Colbert, Claudette, 209
Colette's Tears (1926), 192
Collier, Marjory, 319-20
Columbia Pictures, 231: distributed by United
  Artists, 147–9
Committee on Intellectual Co-operation see League
  of Nations
Conference on Import and Export Prohibitions:
  (1st, Geneva, 1927), 87, 128, 195, 359–63; (2nd,
  Geneva, 1928), 88–9, 197; and French quota
  system, 195, 197
Congress Dances (1931) see Kongress tanzt, Der
congresses and conferences: German participation,
  119, 158–9; as idea of Film Europe, 4, 5, 78,
  117–18, 127–9, 159; importance of cultural
  discourse, 128–9; report by Lars Moen, 382–5;
  see also entries for individual congresses
Consiglio, Alberto, 104
Continental Film Société! Responsabilité Limitée
  (Ufa subsidiary), 267
contingent system see quota system
Coogan, Jackie, 264, 336
Correll, Ernst Hugo, 124, 262
Costigliola, Frank, 11
Courtade, Francis, 265
Crazy Mazie (1927) (Die Tolle Lola), 286
Crisp, Colin, 260
Cunliffe-Lister, Sir Philip, 364
Czerny, Ludwig, 257

Dale, Edgar, 105
Dallas (TV serial), 216
Danan, Martine, 225–48
Dangerous Paradise (1930) (Dans une ile perdue), 236
D'Arrast, Harry, 150
Davies, Marion, 192, 229

Dawes Plan (1924), 12
de Feo, Luciano, 96, 97–101, 103, 104
de Grazia, Victoria, 11
de Limur, Jean, 208, 218
de Poligny, Serge, 262, 263
de Rochefort, Charles, 209, 217
Death Bay (1926), 62
Decameron Nights (1924), 161
Decla-Bioscop, 160, 161
Delac, Charles, 127
Derelict (1930) (*Désemparé*), 239, 257
Derufa/Derussa (Deutsche-Russische Film-Allianz),
    62, 168–9
Désemparé (1930) *see Derelict*
Deulig-Film, 163, 166–7, 334
Deutsche Werkbund, 68
Deutsches Lichtspiel Syndicat (DLS/German Film
    Syndicate), 126, 168
Deval, Jacques, 263
Dickinson, Margaret, 38
Diehl, Mrs Ambrose A., 102–3
Dietrich, Marlene, 304, 314
Disney, Walt, 149
Dix, Richard, 221
DLS *see* Deutsches Lichtspiel Syndicat
Doctor's Secret, The (1929): as MLV, 219–20
Dolin, Anton, 315
Donald, James, 51
Drei von der Tankstelle, Die (1930) (*Le chemin du
    Paradis*), 253, 259, 263, 265, 396
Dreigroschenoper, Die (1931) *see Threepenny Opera,
    The*
Dreyer, Carl, 78
Dreyfus (1931), 292
Drummond, Sir Eric, 98
dubbing, 6, 48–9, 212, 214, 227, 250, 256–9, 269,
    292, 293: audience reaction, 239, 258–9;
    dislocation to spectator, 48, 216, 257–8, 259;
    early failures by American studios, 231, 239; as
    expression of national identity, 48–9, 241;
    influence on action-spectacular genre, 48, 240,
    242; lipsynch and close-up problems, 239–40;
    optical versions, 257; production costs, 48, 239,
    240
Dunning process, 235
Dupont, E.A., 5, 6, 209, 211, 274–301, 310: at
    British National Pictures, 276, 278–9; at
    Carr-Gloria-Dupont, 279–80; direction of Anna
    May Wong, 310–11; international status, 275–6,
    278, 285–6; multiple-language productions at
    BIP, 284–5, 291–2
Ďurovičová, Natasa, 33
Duvivier, Julien, 210
Dwan, Allan, 227

Edison, Thomas, 23
Eggerth, Martha, 308
Ehrenberg, Ilya, 214, 217
Eichberg, Richard, 286, 292: direction of Anna
    May Wong, 307–14
Eisenstein, Sergei, 62
ELS *see* European Film Syndicate
Elsaesser, Thomas, 303

Elstree studios *see* British International Pictures;
    British National Pictures
Elvey, Maurice, 221
Emelka, 279, 280, 284, 286, 308
End of St Petersburg, The (1927), 62
Equipage, L' (1935), 209: as MLV, 218–19
Erotikon (1920), 336
Etablissements Jacques Haik, 284, 312, 313
Etablissements Louis Aubert SA, 184: agreement
    with Ufa, 60–1, 76; *see also* Aubert, Louis
ethnicity in film, 283, 292, 306–7, 317–20
Europe: opposition to American culture, 17–18,
    33–9; *see also entries under* Film Europe
European cinema *see* Film Europe *and also under
    individual countries*
European Convention of Film-Makers and
    Publishers (Paris, 1909), 23
European Film Congress (1929), 17
European Film Syndicate (ELS), 163, 168, 169
exhibitors: block-booking of American films, 10, 44,
    101, 103, 137, 187–8; concern at film exhibition
    taxes, 119, 185–7; French opposition to Sapène,
    185; German support for Film Europe, 166–7;
    licensing and taxation in France, 185–7, 194;
    proposal for European syndicate, 120, 126,
    158–9; reliance on American films, 36, 141–2,
    185, 196, 197, 335–8, 367, 375; *see also* film
    theatres
exoticism: influence of art deco, 306; in
    international film style, 280–3; portrayal of Asia
    and China, 317–20

Fairbanks, Douglas, 134, 136, 138, 140, 227, 306
Famous Players-Laskey (FPL), 40, 42, 133, 134,
    135, 140–1, 189, 277, 278: British Producers
    (subsidiary), 140; investment in British exhibition
    circuit, 140–1; Picture Playhouses Limited
    (subsidiary), 140
Fanamet (First National-Paramount-MGM), 148
FBI *see* Federation of British Industries (FBI)
Federal Motion Picture Commission, 98
Federal Radio Commission, 85
Federation of British Industries (FBI), 38, 364
Fédération Générale des Association de Directeurs
    de Spectacles de Province, 185
Femme a menti, Une (1930) (*Perché No!*), 219
Feyder, Jacques, 211, 218
Fields, Gracie, 315
film: influence on children, 92–3, 97–8, 100–1, 102,
    105; as public utility, 83, 84–5, 90, 95; as trade
    commodity, 82; *see also entries under* American
    cinema *and* Film Europe *and entries for
    individual countries*
film actors and actresses *see* film stars
Film America: definition of, 2; *see also entries under*
    American cinema *and under names of film
    companies*
Film Booking Office, 148
film congresses *see* congresses and conferences
Film Control Commission (France), 88, 193–6,
    379–81; censorship powers, 194
Film Europe, 56–81: bias to exhibition industry,
    141; congresses *see* congresses and conferences;

Film Europe (cont.)
cultural aspects of, 16–22, 33–9, 333–5, 340; definition of, 2–4, 127–8, 339; effect of Depression, 63–5, 72, 292; effect of sound, 44–50, 65–7, 126, 127, 144–6, 225, 288–92; exclusion from American market, 19–20; exhibitions and festivals, 68, 78; and national identity, 129, 150, 233, 287, 293, 315; as opposition to American mass culture, 33–9; as pan- European co-operation, 3–4, 14–16, 45, 59-63, 123–4, 125, 275, 279, 286–7, 338–45; proposal for MPPDA model, 3–4, 127, 128, 129, 384–5; as resistance to American cinema, 4–5, 8, 122, 124, 286–7, 291, 302, 333–5, 339, 366–8, 375–6; see also entries for individual countries
film import regulation see quota system
Film in National Life, The (1932), 32, 35
Film-Kurier (journal), 165–6
film stars: casting in MLVs, 209–22, 263–6; effect of foreign accents, 234, 235; France, 264–5; Germany, 263–6, 305; Great Britain, 305
film theatres: British resistance to American control, 140–1; as communal resource, 85; in France, 184–5, 232; licensing and taxation in France, 185–7, 194, 199; rental income for American films, 44
film theatres see also exhibitors
Film und Foto Exhibition (Stuttgart, 1929), 68
Films de France, 183
Filmwerke-Staaken, 168, 169
First Division, 314
First a Girl (1935), 222, 267
First International Cinema Exhibitors' Conference see International Cinema Exhibitors' Conference
First National, 126, 133, 228 see also Fanamet
First National Exhibitors' Circuit, 276
First Offence (1936), 209
Fitzgerald, F.Scott, 13
Flame of Love, The (1930) (Hai-Tang/L'Amour maitre des choses/Der Weg zur Schande), 286: as MLV, 312-14
Ford, Charles, 207, 222
Fordney Tariff Bill, 188
Fordney-McCumber Act (1922), 12, 87
Försterchristl, Die (1926), 260
Fotorama, 187
Fox Film Corporation, 133, 134, 212, 213, 231, 360
Fox Movietone Follies of 1929 (1929), 230
Fox, William, 137
F.P.1 (1932) (Secrets of F.P.1), 263, 303
F.P.1 antwortet nicht (1932), 263
FPL see Famous Players-Laskey (FPL)
France: amusement tax and fiscal policy, 186–7, 199; audience resistance to foreign accents, 234–5; block-booking of American films, 10, 187–8, 199; co-operation with Germany, 5, 60–2, 76–7, 159–60, 161–2, 167, 171–2, 184, 264–6, 343–4; European market share, 63, 64, 65–6, 75, 76–7; export difficulties, 61–2, 66, 75; hostility to English-language dialogue, 230, 242; imports of American films, 182, 188, 193, 196, 198; lack of government support, 182, 183, 199;

licensing and taxation of film theatres, 185–7, 194, 199; mergers, 76, 183–4; MLVs see multiple-language versions; popularity of national cinema, 6, 232-3, 260–1; preference for native language films, 6, 150, 225, 226, 230, 233, 237–8, 241; quota system, 77, 189–98, 361–3, 368–74; resistance to German cinema, 57; tariffs on imports, 188; valuation of imported films, 188–9
Francen, Victor, 219
Franco Film, 184
François-Poncet, André, 198
Frank, Nino, 210, 217
Freddi, Luigi, 105
Fremde, Die (1929) see Grosstadtschmetterling
French Film Decree (1928), 88, 128, 194–5: report by Will H.Hays, 369–71; text of, 379–81
Fridericus Rex (1922), 336
Fritsch, Willy, 253, 265
Froelich, Gustav, 393

Gabin, Jean, 215, 221
Gainsborough Pictures, 315
Gance, Abel, 188, 336
Garat, Henri, 253, 265
Garbo, Greta, 9, 221, 262, 304
Garncarz, Joseph, 249–73
Gaulin, Alphonse, 192, 195
Gaumont, Léon, 193
Gaumont-British, 275, 286, 294: Ufa agreement, 61
Gaumont-Franco-Film-Aubert (GFFA), 76, 184
General Electric (GE), 13, 14
General Line, The (1929) (Old and New), 62
Geneva covention on import and export prohibitions see Conference on Import and Export Prohibitions
Genina, Augusto, 169
George, Heinrich, 308
German Film Syndicate see Deutsches Lichtspiel Syndicat
Germany: co-operation with France, 5, 60–2, 76–7, 159–60, 161–2, 167, 171–2, 184, 343–4; co-operation with Great Britain, 61, 279, 285–8; co-operation with Italy, 62–3, 169–71; co-operation with Soviet Union, 62, 168–9; entertainment tax, 251; exhibitors and American films, 13, 335–8; import/export policy, 72–4; international co-operation, 159–60, 167–71, 328–30, 331–3; introduction of sound films, 251-3, 313; MLVs see multiple-language versions; nationalism in film, 72-3; Nazi policies, 4, 72–5; preference for national cinema, 10, 260–1, 264; primacy in European market, 57–8, 63, 64, 72, 160, 164, 170, 173, 330–1; production and export in Weimar Republic, 251–3, 254; quota system, 58, 63, 171–3, 189, 286, 363–4, 374; resistance to American film industry, 157, 159, 160–1, 163–7, 333–5; use of American film stars, 305
Gilman, Catherine Cooke, 103
Girl With a Hat Box (1927), 62
Gish, Dorothy, 277, 278, 305
Gish, Lilian, 317
Gloria see Carr-Gloria-Dupont Productions

Gloria (1931), 209, 262
Gloria-Dupont-Emelka, 280
Glückskinder (1936) (*Lucky Kids*), 259
Godsol, Frank, 8
Goebbels, Joseph, 4, 73
Gold (1934), 209, 262
Gold Rush, The (1925), 262
Golden, N.D., 210, 215, 232, 240
Goldsmith, Alfred N., 101
Goldwyn Company, 8, 137
Goldwyn, Samuel, 137
Gomery, Douglas, 214
Goskino, 69
Gray, Eve, 280
Gray, Gilda, 280, 305, 310
Grease Paint (1928), 42
Great Britain: co-operation with France, 62;
  co-operation with Germany, 61, 279, 285–8;
  English-language market, 46, 66; European
  market share, 63, 64; heritage culture in film, 66,
  389, 390; idea of national cinema, 35–6, 287;
  international market share, 86; quota system, 63,
  192, 275, 287, 292, 364; requirements for
  American market, 387–9; resistance to
  continental style, 281, 282, 309, 313; use of
  American film stars, 305; *see also* British Empire
Greenbaum Films, 284
Greenhill, Morris, 136, 138–41, 146
Griffith, D.W., 138, 140, 142
Grosstadtschmetterling (1929) (*Asphaltschmetterling/Die
  Fremde/Pavement Butterfly*), 311–12
Guback, Thomas, 132
Guitry, Sacha, 236

Hai-Tang (1930) *see Flame of Love*
Haik, Jacques *see* Etablissements Jacques Haik
Hale, Georgia, 262
Hallo Hallo-hier spricht Berlin! (1931), 256
Hanson, Lars, 393
Harlé, P.A., 215
Harvey, Lilian, 253, 265, 286, 308: language ability,
  265, 304–5, 396
Hate Ship, The (1929), 211
Hay, Will, 21
Hayes, Carlton, 233
Hays, Will H., 1, 5, 16, 38, 39, 83, 102, 159, 188,
  191, 349–50: and French Film Decree (1928),
  195–8, 369–71; *see also* Motion Pictures
  Producers and Distributors of America
Hays Code *see* Motion Pictures Producers and
  Distributors of America
Health Organisation *see* League of Nations
Hearst, William Randolph, 192
Hebdo Film (journal): on 'European Monroe
  Doctrine', 330–1
Hecht, Ben, 218
Heimkehr (1928) (*Homecoming*), 393–4
Hellwig, Albert, 100
Helm, Brigitte, 209, 221
Henseleit, Felix, 167, 173, 333–4, 337, 338–41
Herrick, Myron, 189, 196–7, 369
Herriot, Edouard, 15, 22, 59, 78, 193–6, 198,
  369–70

Herron, Maj. Frederick L., 19, 38, 42, 99, 100–3,
  183, 190, 192–4
Higson, Andrew, 1–31, 35, 117-31, 274–301
Hitchcock, Alfred, 262, 278, 279, 288
Hoagland, Warren L., 1
Hoare, Maj. Rawdon, 34, 37, 49, 50
Hodkinson, W.W., 9–11
Hoffman, Marianna, 102
Hollywood *see* American cinema
Homme Heureux, Un (1932), 150
Honneger, Arthur, 218
Hoover, Herbert, 11, 182
Hopkins, Miriam, 218–19
Howards End (1992), 24
Howells, David P., 133, 137
Hubert, Ali, 318, 319
Hudson Bill, 102
Hugenberg, Alfred, 163, 166, 171
Hull, Cordell, 91
Hull, David, 73
Hungary: quota system, 364–6

IAH *see* Internationale Arbeitershilfe
Ihr dunkler Punkt (1928), 265
Ihre Majestät die Liebe (1931), 262, 263
import of American films *see* Quota system
In Treue stark (1926), 260
Ingram, Rex, 209
Institute for Educational Cinematography *see*
  International Educational Cinematographic
  Institute (IECI)
Inter-Ocean Film Corporation (IOFC), 188–9
Intercine (IECI journal) *see* International
  Educational Cinematographic Institute
  (IECI)
International Cinema Exhibitors' Conference: (1st,
  Berlin, 1928), 117–19, 125–6, 158; proposal for
  European exhibitors' syndicate, 126; (2nd, Paris,
  1929), 17, 118, 126–7, 129, 158; cultural
  discourse of, 127; report by Lars Moen, 382–5;
  resolutions of, 127; (3rd, Brussels, 1930), 118,
  127, 128
International Committee on Intellectual
  Co-operation *see* League of Nations
International Congress of Cinematograph Managers
  (Paris, 1923), 93–4, 118–20, 158: lobby against
  film exhibition taxes, 119
International Congress of Kinema Proprietors *see*
  International Cinema Exhibitors' Conference
International Council of Women's Congress on
  Cinema (Rome, 1931), 102–4: criticism of
  American cinema, 102-3
International Educational Cinematographic Institute
  (IECI), 95–106: congresses (Rome, 1931 &
  1934), 102–4, 105; *Enciclopedia del cinema*, 104,
  106; formation, 95–6; hostility to Payne Fund
  Studies, 101–2; influence of Italian Fascism, 95,
  96, 104-5; influence of MPPDA, 98–104;
  journal of, 100–3, 106
international film: articles by Erich Pommer, 392–6;
  and exoticism, 280–3, 291–2; narrative style of,
  282; nostalgia of European culture, 18, 20, 21,
  24, 304; persona of Anna May Wong, 316–22;

international film (*cont.*)
    reliance on spectacle, 281, 292; travel motif, 274, 293, 303; as universal ambassador, 120
International Film Chamber, 4
International Institute of Intellectual Co-operation *see* League of Nations
International Labor Office (ILO) *see* League of Nations
International Motion Picture Congress (Paris, 1926), 82, 85, 86, 90, 94, 118–19, 121, 158, 167, 191: anti-American aspects, 122–4, 191–2; cultural discourse of, 123; discussion of documentary film, 123; German delegation, 121; influence of MPPDA, 94, 107, 121–2; proposal for permanent commission, 94–5, 125; resolutions of, 123, 125; sponsorship by League of Nations, 93–4, 120–5; trade discourse of, 122, 123-4
International Review of Educational Cinematography (IECI journal) *see* International Educational Cinematographic Institute (IECI)
Internationale Arbeitershilfe (IAH), 67–8, 71
Internationale Tentoonstelling op Filmgebied (The Hague, 1928), 68
intertitling *see* sound films
Intorgkino, 71
Iron Mask, The (1929), 227
Italian Commission for Censorship, 46
Italy: censorship of foreign-language sound films, 46; cinema as propaganda, 96, 104–5; co-operation with Germany, 62–3, 169–71; *see also* International Educational Cinematographic Institute

Jacquet, Gaston, 311
Jäger, Ernst, 165, 310, 313, 317
Jannings, Emil, 261, 304, 395
Java Head (1934), 314–15
Jazz Singer, The (1927), 211, 227
Jeancolas, Jean-Pierre, 10
Jeanne, René, 222
Joachim, Hans, 20
John Olsen & Company, 134
Joinville Studio, Paris *see* Paramount
Jolson, Al, 394, 395
Junge, Alfred, 279, 280, 310

Kamaradschaft (1931), 210
Kampf ums Matterhorn, Der (1928), 260
Kane, Bob, 214, 237
Karlweis, Oskar, 253
Karol, Jacob, 241
Kaufman, Reginald Wright, 103
Keller, Morton, 85
Kelly, Arthur, 144, 147
Kemm, Jean, 209, 284, 312
Kent, Sidney, 40
Kessel, Joseph, 218
keusche Susanne, Die (1926), 265
King of the Gate Crashers (1930) *see* Roi des resquilleurs, Le
Kinugasa, Teinosuke, 78
Klangfilm *see* Tobis-Klangfilm-Kuechenmeister

Klein, Julius, 357–9
Klitzsch, Ludwig, 62, 159
Klotz, Louis, 187
Knowing Men (1930), 211
Kongress tanzt, Der (1931) (*Congress Dances*), 24, 253, 263, 265, 304, 396
Korda, Alexander, 149, 294, 315
Koretz, Paul, 360, 361
Kortner, Fritz, 315
Kracauer, Siegfried, 258
Kraemer, F.W., 292
Kraszna-Krausz, Andor, 256
Kremer, Isa, 228
Kuechenmeister *see* Tobis-Klangfilm-Kuechenmeister
Kürschner, Eugen, 259

LAA *see* Artists Associés, Les (UA subsidiary)
Lachman, Harry, 238
Lady Lies, The (1929), 208
Laemmle, Carl, 372
Lang, Fritz, 160, 304
L'arlo, Dita, 393
Lasky, Jesse, 213, 229
Last Command, The (1928), 261
Laurel and Hardy films, 231, 234
Leaf, Walter, 355
League of Nations, 5-6, 78, 82–116: Advisory Committee on Social Questions, 105; Advisory Committee on the Traffic in Women and Children, 92; Child Welfare Committee, 90, 92–3, 97, 98, 105; Committee on Intellectual Co-operation, 82, 90, 93, 94, 95, 97, 99, 120–1, 124–5; Committee on Transit and Communications, 90; Economic Committee, 89, 90; Health Organisation, 91; International Institute of Intellectual Co-operation, 93, 95, 96, 120–1, 125; International Labor Office (ILO), 90, 91; moral influence of cinema, 92–3; Opium Committee, 94; Paris Conference (1926) *see* International Motion Picture Congress (Paris, 1926); proposal for commission on cinema, 94–5
Lederer, Franz, 312
Lefèvre, René, 253
Legion of Decency, 101
Lehmann, René, 256
Leni, Paul, 307
Lepage, Henry, 166
letzte Kompagnie, Die (1930), 257
letzte Mann, Der (1924), 20, 336
Lianofilm, 150
Liberty Trading Company, 134
Lichtbildbühne (journal): articles on European cinema, 328–33, 341–5; 'European Monroe Doctrine', 328-33
Liebeswalzer (1930), 265
Litvak, Anatole, 218
Lloyd Jones, Chester, 191
Locarno Pact (1925), 12
Loew, Arthur, 213, 234
Loew, Marcus, 8
Loew's Inc., 13
Longden, John, 312
Loucheur, Louis, 14

Love (1927), 260, 261–2
Love Me and the World is Mine (1928), 279
Love Parade (1929) (*Parade d'Amour*), 230
Low, Rachel, 292
Lowry, Col. Edward G., 14, 36, 183: report on European film market, 353–79
Lubitsch, Ernst, 57, 208, 304
LUCE (L'Unione Cinematografica Educativa), 96: Ufa agreement, 62, 169-71
Luchaire, Julien, 93–4, 120–1
Luft, Herbert G., 280
Lutetia, 183

Madame Dubarry (1919), 57
Madame Pompadour (192Q), 278, 279: as international film, 278
Mädchen in Uniform (1931), 74
Mademoiselle Josette Ma Femme (1932), 192
Maltby, Richard, 1–31, 32–55, 82–116
Mannock, P.L., 290
Manuela (1923), 231
Mara, Lya, 264
Marius (1931), 207–8
Mary (1930) *see Murder*
Mason, Herbert, 209
Matthews, Jessie, 222, 267, 315
Mattia Pascal, 334
Matz, Elsa, 102
Maury, Jacques, 219, 253, 263
Mauvaise Graine (1933), 209
Maxwell, John, 278–9, 285, 294
May, Joe, 257, 393
Mayer, Louis B., 8, 9, 229
Melamerson, David, 166–7, 334
Menjou, Adolphe, 209, 218, 221
Menschen im Kafig (1930) *see Cape Forlorn*
Metzner, Ernö, 315
Mezhrabpom, 68, 71
MGM (Metro-Goldwyn-Mayer), 8, 9, 61, 127, 137, 146, 148, 165, 184, 188, 193, 207, 211, 212, 213, 218, 229, 231, 234–40, 363, 374; strategy for MLV production, 234, 236; *see also* Fanamet; Parufamet
Michel Strogoff (1926) (*Der Kurier des Zaren*), 163, 167, 184, 192, 261, 372
Milliken, Carl, 98, 101, 103–4, 105
Milton, George, 233
Ministère de l'Instruction Publique et des Beaux Arts, 185–6, 193, 194
Miracle des Loups, Les (1924), 62
Mirande, Yves, 236, 263
miscegenation in film, 312, 313, 320
Misérables, Les (1925), 163, 167, 184, 192, 372
Mistigri (1933), 238
Mistinguett (Jeanne-Marie Bourgeois), 265
Mittler, Leo, 210
MLVs *see* multiple-language versions
Moen, Lars, 382–5
Mon gosse de père (1930) *see Parisian, The*
Morawsky: Erich, 1, 169
Moreno, Antonio, 278
Morley, David, 41
Mort en fuite, Le (1936), 217

Mostra cinematografica di Venezia, 96
Motion Picture Committee of the National Council of Women, 102
Motion Picture Patents Company (MPPC), 23
Motion Picture Research Council, 84
Motion Pictures Producers and Distributors of America Inc. (MPPDA), 1, 3, 6, 7, 14, 19, 38, 42, 46, 49, 82, 83, 85, 148: assistance from U.S. government, 39, 181–3; Foreign Department, 183, 190, 350, 379; formation of, 39; influence on IECI, 98–104; influence on Paris Congress (1926), 94, 121–2, 191–2; opposition to French quota system, 88–90, 128; Paris office established, 183; Production (Hays) Code (1930), 101, 123, 233; proposal for export co-operative, 189–90; report by Edward G.Lowry, 353–79; report by Oscar Solbert, 189–90, 349–53
Moulin Rouge (1928), 278, 284: as international film, 279–83
Moviola process, 239
MPPDA *see* Motion Pictures Producers and Distributors of America Inc.
Müde Tod, Der (1921), 160, 336
Muller, Renate, 222
multiple-language versions (MLVs): adaptation for target country, 49, 262–6; aesthetic value of, 207–8, 250; casting, 209, 220–2, 253–4, 263–6, 268, 292; categories of, 208–10, 253; as commercial cinema, 217, 221; and cultural difference, 6, 217–20, 250, 260-6, 269, 293; domestic production of foreign versions, 267; and dubbing, 212, 216, 250, 255, 256-9, 292, 293; Elstree Studio, 284, 288; and French cinema, 6, 207–24, 217–19; French-language market, 254–5; and German cinema, 6, 249–73; German-language market, 255; importance to European cinema, 6, 127, 253, 268; Joinville Studio (Paramount), 207–8, 210, 214, 234–41, 291, 294; lack of star publicity, 221–2, 236; as play adaptations, 222; polyglot scripts, 210, 228–9, 256; potential for profit, 259–60; production costs, 47, 213–14, 236–7, 257, 289–90, 292–3; as remakes, 209–10, 229, 266–7; sale of script rights, 214–15, 229, 266; Spanish language, 212–13; standardisation of production, 212–14, 217–18, 236, 289–90; studio location policy, 213; and subtitling, 256
Mundus, 133
Muni, Paul, 218
Murder (1930) (*Mary*), 262
Mussolini, Benito, 96, 100

Napoléon vu par Abel Gance (1927), 24, 163, 184, 188
Napper, Lawrence, 20–1
Natan, Bernard, 198, 210
National Association of German Exhibitors, 166
National Board of Review (USA), 390
Nell Gwyn (1934), 277
Nero, 213
Niebelungen, Die (1924), 19, 336

Nielsen, Asta, 317
Night Owl, The (1926), 231
North, C.J., 46, 210, 215, 232, 240
Novarro, Ramon, 212
Nowell-Smith, Geoffrey, 23
Nuit au Paradis, Une (1931), 150
Nuits de Port Said, Les (1931), 210

O'Brien, Dennis, 134, 147, 149
Occident, L' (1928), 198
Old Heidelberg (1927), 304
Old and New (1929) see General Line, The
Ombres blanches (1928) see White Shadows on the
    South Seas
Ondra, Anny, 216
One Hour With You (1932), 208
Opera de Quat' Sous, L' (1931) see Threepenny Opera,
    The
Ordynski, Ryszard, 220
Orlando (1992), 24
Ortmann, Helmuth, 335–8
Osso, Adolphe, 238
Otto, Daniel, 163
Our Daily Bread (1934), 106

Pabst, G.W., 208, 210, 221
Page of Madness (1926), 78
Pagnol, Marcel, 214, 236
Paolucci di Calbodi, Baron Giacomo, 96
Parade d'Amour (1929) see Love Parade
Paramount Famous Players-Laskey see Famous
    Players-Laskey (FPL)
Paramount on Parade (1930), 209
Paramount Pictures Corporation, 10, 13, 61, 146,
    194, 211, 213, 219, 221, 228–31, 363, 374, 391:
    foreign-language shorts, 228, 237;
    French-language features, 237–8; Joinville
    Studio, Paris, 207–8, 210, 214, 234–41, 291,
    294; see also Parufamet
Parent-Teachers' Association National Committee
    on Motion Pictures, 103
Paris Film Congress (1926) see International Motion
    Picture Congress (Paris, 1926)
Paris Sound Picture Conference (1930), 16
Parisian, The (1930) (Mon gosse de père), 208, 209,
    218, 222, 232
Parry, Lee, 308
Parufamet (Paramount-Ufa-MGM), 13, 61, 148,
    165, 170, 363, 374
Passion de Jeanne d'Arc, La (1928), 78
Pathé, Charles, 190
Pathé-Consortium, 163, 183–4, 189, 190, 198:
    British International Pictures agreement, 62
Pathé-Consortium see also Sapène, Jean
Pathé-Natan, 76, 198, 210, 218, 232, 233, 266
Pathé-Westi, 60
Pavement Butterfly (1929) see Grosstadtschmetterling
Payne Fund Studies, 84, 98, 101–2, 105; criticism
    by IECI, 101–2
Pegg, Carl, 3
Pépé le Moko (1937), 215
Perchè No! (1930) see Femme a menti, Une
Peter Pan (1924), 42, 306

Peters, Charles C., 101
Pettijohn, Charles, 192
Phoebus Films, 124
Phoenix Films, 62
Piccadilly (1928), 280–1, 283, 284, 303, 318: as
    international film, 310–11
Pick, Lupu, 343–4
Pickford, Mary, 134, 135–6, 138, 140
Picture Playhouses Limited (FPL subsidiary), 140
Pittaluga, Stefano, 169–70, 286
Pitts, Zasu, 21
Platten, J. Homer, 85
Pomaret, Charles, 14
Pommer, Erich, 18, 19–20, 60, 159–61, 253, 265,
    392–6; advocate of international cinema, 161
Postmeister, 334
Préjean, Albert, 221
Price, Waterhouse & Co., 143–4
Princesse Masha, La (1927), 193, 198
Private Life of Henry VIII, The (1933), 24, 66: as
    international film, 294
Production Code (1930) (Hays Code) see Motion
    Pictures Producers and Distributors of America
Progress Committee of the Motion Picture
    Industry, 240
Prohibitions Convention see Conference on Import
    and Export Prohibitions
Prometheus, 68
Pudovkin, Vsevolod I., 62

Quo Vadis (1912), 336
Quota Bill (1927) see Cinematograph Films Act
quota system: American production for, 10, 44–5;
    chronology of, 347–9; as defence of national
    culture, 36–9, 88–9; exemption of educational
    films, 99; France, 77, 184, 189–98, 361–3,
    368–74; Germany, 38, 63, 171–3, 189, 286,
    363–4, 374; Great Britain, 38, 63, 149–50, 192,
    275, 292, 364; Hungary, 364–6; and League of
    Nations, 87–90; proposals for European
    co-operation, 127, 172–4; U.S. State Department
    note, 381–2

Rabinowitsch, Gregor, 172
radio: as public utility, 85
Raimu (Jules Muraire), 219
Ralston, Esther, 305
Rapa-Nui (1927), 303
Rapallo, Treaty of (1922), 67
RCA (Radio Corporation of America), 11, 16, 293:
    sound system, 210
Reichmann, Max, 210
Reichsfilmblatt (journal): articles on European
    cinema, 166, 333–41
Reif, Wolfgang, 318
Reine Margot, La (1994), 24
Republic Pictures Corporation, 316
Reserve hat Ruh (1931), 266
Richter, Ellen, 308
Rio Rita (1929), 211, 231
RKO Radio Pictures Inc., 46, 211, 213, 231, 235:
    use of Dunning process, 235
Robertson-Cole, 148

Robins, Kevin, 41
Rohmer, Sax, 320
Roi des resquilleurs, Le (1930) (King of the Gate Crashers), 233, 238
Rome Express (1932), 303
Rommer, Claire, 257
Room, Abram, 62
Rosenberg, Emily, 12
Rosenthal, A., 2
Rosher, Charles, 278
Route est belle, La (1930), 232
Rouvroy, Maurice, 100
Rowland, Richard, 137
Royal Box, The (1930), 211
Ruben, J.Walter, 314
Rühmann, Heinz, 253, 263
Russia see Soviet Union

Saint-Granier, 236
Sapène, Jean, 172, 183-5, 189-94, 196-9, 368-74: memorandum on Société des Cinéromans, 372-4; monopoly on safety film, 184, 185; opposition of exhibitors, 185; policy to American cinema, 184, 192
Sascha, 286
Saunders, Thomas J., 157-80
Scandinavia-American Trading Company, 134
Scarface (1932 & 1983), 210
Schenck, Joseph, 33, 146, 150
Scherben (1921), 160, 336
Schlesinger, I.W., 276-7
Schlesinger, Philip, 51
Schmutziges Geld (1928) see Song
schönen Tage von Aranjuez, Die (1933), 209
Schpountz, Le (1938), 214
Schrecken der Garnison, Der (1931), 266
Schulberg, B.P., 33
Seabury, Samuel, 84-5
Seabury, William Marston, 6, 10-11, 14, 83-7, 90, 92, 94-5, 98, 107, 118: proposal for League of Nations commission, 94-5
Secrets of F.P.1 see F.P.1
Selznick, Lewis J., 137
Serruys, Daniel, 88-9, 195, 197
Shanghai Express (1932), 241: as international film, 314
Shearer, Norma, 229
Sherman Antitrust Act (1914), 14, 135, 190, 355
Short, William H., 84, 99, 101, 105, 107
Show Boat (1929), 231
Show Life (1928) see Song
silent film: acting tradition of, 313, 317; as international medium, 39-42, 93; intertitling practices, 40-1, 230; production of different versions, 261-2
Sjöström, Victor, 212
Sklarz, Georg, 169
Smith, Guy Crosswell, 134, 142, 146-7, 150
Smith, Harold L., 99, 183, 193, 194
Smuts, Jan, 91
Société des Cinéromans, 62, 163, 167, 172, 183, 198; Sapène memorandum, 372- 4

Society of Motion Picture Engineers, 101
Soir de rafle, Un (1931), 238
Solbert, Oscar, 189-90
Song (1928) (Schmutziges Geld/Show Life/Wasted Love), 286, 303, 308-11
Sonoratone Corporation, 227
Soriano Films, 150
sound films: audience response to foreign dialogue and accents, 43, 46-7, 230, 234, 235; auditory realism, 215; conversion costs, 44, 67, 70; dubbing see dubbing; English-language market, 49, 66, 229; French-language market, 65-6, 76, 150, 232; and German cinema, 251-3, 313; and international film, 127, 228, 253, 284, 394-6; intertitling for foreign versions, 230; and Italian cinema, 46; standardisation and patent issues, 15-16, 45, 126, 232, 251; stimulus to European production, 145; voice-over for foreign versions, 227; see also multiple-language versions (MLVs)
Soupault, Philippe, 238
Sous les toits de Paris (1930), 238
South America: Spanish-language versions, 212-13
Soviet Union, 67-71; co-operation with Germany, 62, 68, 168-9; Five-Year Plan (1927), 70-1; ideological factors, 69-70; import/export policy, 69-71; international exhbitions and festivals, 68; monopolisation, 69-71
Sovkino, 62, 69-71, 168
Soyuzkino, 71
SPIO (Spitzenorganisation der deutschen Filmwirtschaft), 159
Star is Born, A (1937, 1954, 1976), 210
stars see film stars
Stiller, Mauritz, 9
Stinnes, Hugo, 60, 162, 163, 184
Street, Sarah, 38
Stresemann, Gustav, 59, 78
subtitling, 47-8, 230: and MLVs, 256
Südfilm, 280, 286, 308
Summers, Walters, 312
Summerville, Slim, 21
Sunkissed (1930) (A Lady to Love), 212
Surcouf (1924), 192
Svenska, 61
Swann, Paul, 37
Sweden: imports of American films, 182

talking films see sound films
Terra Film, 1, 62, 169, 170
Thalberg, Irving, 8-9
theatres see film theatres
Thief of Baghdad, The (1924), 306
Thomas, Jameson, 280
Thompson, Kristin, 9, 16, 24, 56-81, 125, 133, 250, 347-9
Threepenny Opera, The, (1931) (Die Dreigroschenoper/L'Opera de Quat' Sous), 207, 208, 220, 221
Through the Back Door (1921), 135
Tiger Bay (1934), 314
Tippett, John D., 136
Titi-premier roi des gosses (1926) (Titi-King of the Kids), 192

Tobis-Klangfilm-Kuechenmeister, 15–16, 72, 76, 213, 254, 276, 277, 288, 293, 294: as dominant cartel in Europe, 15–16
Toll of the Sea (1922), 306
Tolle Lola, Die (1927) *see Crazy Mazie*
Trois Masques, Les (1929), 232
Truffaut, François, 262
Tschechowa, Olga, 280
Tunnel, Le (1933), 220, 221
Tunnel, The (1935), 221
Two Worlds (1930) (*Zwei Welten/Les Deux Mondes*), 284, 291–2

UA *see* United Artists Corporation (UA)
Überflüssige Menschen (1926), 261
Ucicky, Gustav, 257
Ufa (Universum Film-Aktiengesellschaft), 13, 18, 19, 20, 38, 57, 60–2, 72, 74, 163, 174, 254, 257, 262, 266, 267, 274, 286, 308, 363, 393, 395, 396: Gaumont-British agreement, 61; LUCE agreement, 62, 169–71; production of MLVs, 254; Ufa-Aubert agreement, 60–1, 161–2, 167; Ufa-Film (Ufi) formed, 72; *see also* Alliance Cinématographique Européenne; Continental Film Société! Responsabilité Limitée; Derufa; Parufamet
Ulff-Møller, Jens, 181–206
Unholy Night, The (1929), 211, 218
Unione Cinematografica Educativa *see* LUCE
United Artists Corporation (UA), 7, 46, 48, 132–56, 211, 213, 231; Allied Artists (subsidiary), 140, 142, 144; Les Artists Associés (LAA) Société Anonyme (subsidiary), 142–4, 150; as distributor for Columbia, 147–9; investment in French-language films, 150; policy on sound films, 144–50; rental income from overseas, 144–5; return to franchised distribution, 146–7; sale of foreign rights, 138–40; use of foreign subsidiaries, 143–4; use of overseas agents, 133–6
Universal Pictures Corporation, 42, 46, 134, 136, 192, 193, 213, 231, 274, 275, 279, 307, 372
Unsere Emden (1926), 260
unsterbliche Lump, Der (1929), 257

Van Dyke, W.S., 227
Vandal and Delac Consortium, 284
Vanel, Charles, 218–19
Variété (1925) (*Variety/Vaudeville*), 275, 278, 280, 310
Vasey, Ruth, 9, 32–55, 145, 312, 315
Vaudeville (1925) *see Variété*
Veidt, Conrad, 263, 305
Vereinigte Stahlwerke AG, 14
Victrix, Claudia, 192, 193, 198
Viktor und Viktoria (1935), 222, 267
Vincendeau, Ginette, 207–24

Visson, André, 34
VOKS *see* All-Union Society for Cultural Relations with Foreign Countries
von Nagy, Käthe, 263
von Sternberg, Josef, 314, 395
Vuillermoz, Emil, 164

Walbrook, Anton, 305
Wallace, Edgar, 320
Walsh, Mike, 132–56
Wardour Films, 278–9
Warner Brothers Pictures Inc., 46, 197, 211, 213, 227–8, 237: foreign-language shorts, 228, 337
Wasted Love (1928) *see Song*
Webb-Pomerone Act (1918), 190, 199, 349, 351, 352
Weg zur Schande, Der (1930) *see Flame of Love*
Weindling, Paul, 91
weisse Hölle vom Piz Palü, Die (1929), 260
Welch, David, 74
Wengeroff, Vladimir, 60, 162–4, 168, 184, 344
Western Electric, 16
Westi-Film Corporation, 60–1, 162–3, 166–9, 170, 184, 188, 189
White Shadows on the South Seas (1928) (*Ombres blanches*), 227
White Sister, The (1923), 260
Wilcox, Herbert, 149, 161, 277–8
Wilder, Billy, 209
Williams, J.D., 11, 276–9, 284, 286, 289–90, 387–92
Willis, J. Elder, 314
Wilson, Hugh, 88, 89, 360, 361–3
Winokur, Mark, 306, 314
Wolffsohn, Karl, 341–5: syndicated funding proposal, 167–8
Woman I Love, The (1937), 209: as MLV, 218–19
women: attraction to American culture, 34, 35, 49–50
Wong, Anna May, 5, 280, 281, 283, 286, 302–24: and E.A. Dupont, 310–11; early career, 306–7; and exoticism, 280–1, 306–7, 317–20; portrayal as Chinese, 318–20; and Richard Eichberg, 307–14; in *Song* (1928), 307–9; star persona of, 316–22
World Economic Conference (Geneva, 1927), 14, 87, 358
World-Wide Pictures, 277, 284, 285, 390–2
Wyler, Robert, 236
Wyndham Films, 314

Young, Owen D., 11

Ziehm, Arthur, 137
Zimmern, Alfred, 98
Zukor, Adolph, 10, 134, 391
Zwei und Fierzigste Strasse (1929), 228